A Nation of Immigrants

SUSAN F. MARTIN
Georgetown University

CAMBRIDGE
UNIVERSITY PRESS

CAMBRIDGE UNIVERSITY PRESS
Cambridge, New York, Melbourne, Madrid, Cape Town, Singapore,
São Paulo, Delhi, Dubai, Tokyo, Mexico City

Cambridge University Press
32 Avenue of the Americas, New York, NY 10013-2473, USA

www.cambridge.org
Information on this title: www.cambridge.org/9780521734455

First published 2011

Printed in the United States of America

A catalog record for this publication is available from the British Library.

Library of Congress Cataloging in Publication data

Martin, Susan Forbes.
A nation of immigrants / Susan F. Martin.
   p.   cm.
Includes bibliographical references and index.
ISBN 978-0-521-51799-7 (hardback) – ISBN 978-0-521-73445-5 (pbk.)
1. United States – Emigration and immigration – History.   2. Immigrants –
United States – History   I. Title.
JV6450.M366   2010
304.8′73 – dc22   2010031630

ISBN 978-0-521-51799-7 Hardback
ISBN 978-0-521-73445-5 Paperback

A Nation of Immigrants

Immigration makes America what it is and is formative for what it will become. America was settled by three different models of immigration, all of which persist to the present. The Virginia Colony largely equated immigration with the arrival of laborers, who had few rights. Massachusetts welcomed those who shared the religious views of the founders but excluded those whose beliefs challenged the prevailing orthodoxy. Pennsylvania valued pluralism, becoming the most diverse colony in religion, language, and culture. This book traces the evolution of these three competing models of immigration as they explain the historical roots of current policy debates and options. Arguing that the Pennsylvania model has best served the country, the final chapter makes recommendations for future immigration reform. Given the highly controversial nature of immigration in the United States, this book provides thoughtful, well-reasoned analysis that will be valuable to both academic and policy audiences for the ways it places today's trends and policy options into historical perspective.

Susan F. Martin holds the Donald G. Herzberg Chair in International Migration and serves as the Director of the Institute for the Study of International Migration in the School of Foreign Service at Georgetown University. Dr. Martin also directs the university's Program on Refugees and Humanitarian Emergencies. Previously, she served as the Executive Director of the U.S. Commission on Immigration Reform, established by legislation to advise Congress and the president on U.S. immigration and refugee policy. Her publications include *Refugee Women*; *The Uprooted*; *Beyond the Gateway* (ed.); *Managing Migration: The Promise of Cooperation*; *Mexico–U.S. Migration Management* (ed.); *Women, Migration and Conflict: Breaking a Deadly Cycle* (ed.); and numerous monographs and articles on immigration and refugee policy. Dr. Martin earned her MA and PhD in the history of American civilization from the University of Pennsylvania and her BA in history from Douglass College, Rutgers University. She is the immediate past president of the International Association for the Study of Forced Migration and serves on the U.S. Comptroller General's Advisory Board, the Academic Advisory Board of the International Organization for Migration, and the Board of the Advocacy Project.

Contents

Acknowledgments

I dedicate this book to Lawrence H. Fuchs, my mentor since he took me under his wing when I was an assistant professor in the American Studies Department at Brandeis University. Larry introduced me to U.S. immigration policy, first in the academy and then at the Select Commission on Immigration and Refugee Policy. He has been a role model throughout my career, demonstrating how one can move effortlessly between the university and the halls of Congress. His seminal work, *The American Kaleidoscope*, provided inspiration for this history of American immigration. I will always be indebted to him.

In researching and writing this book, I benefited from the assistance of colleagues and students. My particular thanks go to Andrew Schoenholtz and B. Lindsay Lowell, who worked with me at the U.S. Commission on Immigration Reform and at Georgetown University's Institute for the Study of International Migration. They read and critiqued chapters and generally kept me honest in the ways in which I detailed the work and recommendations of the commission. Lindsay and our colleague Mary Breeding produced valuable statistical tables on immigrant and temporary worker admissions to the United States.

I am also indebted to Patricia Weiss Fagen and Elzbieta Gozdziak, also now colleagues at Georgetown University. The reports we wrote on U.S. refugee and asylum policies when we were on the staff at the Refugee Policy Group (RPG) proved to be invaluable sources for Chapters 9 and 11. I am particularly grateful to Patricia for allowing me to use large segments of a report we coauthored on unaccompanied refugee children. A special word of thanks goes to the Digital Library at Forced Migration Online, which digitized and makes available the many unpublished reports that we produced at RPG. Philip Martin at the University of California also read sections of the book discussing the entry of migrant farm workers, helping me to navigate one of the more important aspects of U.S. immigration in the twentieth century.

A number of Georgetown students also helped me in my research. Irene Libov produced a detailed, annotated bibliography on Asian immigration. Alejandra Ezeta Bagnis, Elizabeth Chavez, and Gabrielle Soltys assisted my research on Latino immigration. Elizabeth Shlala collected information on the Italian Diaspora at the turn of the nineteenth to twentieth centuries. I thank all of them for their extremely valuable contributions to this volume.

I further benefited from the exceptional copyediting skills of Wilma and Raymond Harrison, my sister and brother-in-law. Beyond catching the inevitable typo and misplaced word and sentence, they ensured that the book made sense to the well-informed, intelligent non-expert. Their questions and comments were invaluable as I finalized the manuscript. I also thank Mary Cadette, and Lewis Bateman at Cambridge University Press, for their valuable editorial advice.

My thanks also go to the administrative staff at the Institute for the Study of International Migration – Shirley Easton and Alexander Gee. They held down the fort while I spent months away from the office trying to complete this manuscript. A special note of appreciation goes to my husband Michael, who cheerfully put up with my long absences in both mind and body as I focused single-mindedly on my research and writing.

I

Introduction

The United States is in the midst of its fourth major wave of immigration. Today's wave is the largest in absolute numbers, although not as a proportion of the total population. Unlike in previous waves, today's immigrants come from every inhabited continent and represent just about every country in the United Nations. As in previous waves, there is a profound ambivalence about immigration among the American public. Historically, Americans have seen their own immigrant forebears through rose-colored glasses while raising serious concerns about the contributions of current immigrants and the extent to which they will assimilate our values, language, and experiences.

This ambivalence has made immigration policy one of the most difficult on the U.S. political agenda. In the past three Congresses, the Senate and House of Representatives have debated immigration reform but have failed to come to consensus about the policies needed to address today's challenges. The difficulties they are experiencing are by no means new. Immigration reform has always been a difficult issue, requiring years of debate before any comprehensive changes are adopted. Although the problem is often described as a contest between pro- and anti-immigration forces, the reality is much more complex. Even among those who favor large-scale immigration, there are profound differences in views on the purposes of immigration and the contributions that immigrants bring to the country. Understanding the historical roots of American immigration, and American attitudes toward immigrants, helps to place today's policy debate into perspective and provides important insights into the reforms needed to address current problems and opportunities.

It is a truism that the United States is a nation of immigrants.[1] Certainly, the United States was settled by successive periods of immigration, from the first wave of colonization (sixteenth to eighteenth centuries), through the second (1830–1860) and third (1880–1924) waves of mass European migration,

---

[1] In one of the most quoted uses of the term, John F. Kennedy's *A Nation of Immigrants* made the case for repealing the national origins quotas.

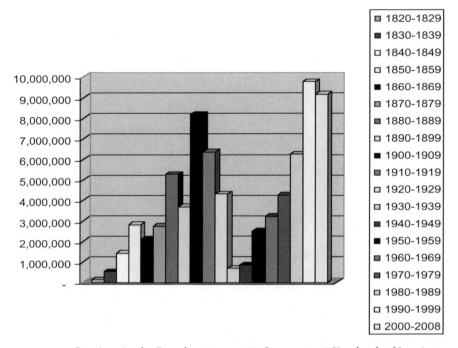

FIGURE 1.1. Immigration by Decade: 1820–2008. *Source: 2008 Yearbook of Immigration Statistics*, Department of Homeland Security.

into what is now the fifth decade of our most recent wave of migration, dominated by movements from Latin America, the Caribbean, Asia and, in smaller numbers, Africa (1965-present) (Figure 1.1).

Immigration has indeed been formative in making America what it is and what it will become. The phrase "a nation of immigrants," however, hides as much as it illuminates in lumping together all immigrants and all forms of immigration. In fact, this book argues, America has been settled from its very origins by three different models of immigration, all of which persist through the four waves described above. Lawrence Fuchs, in *The American Kaleidoscope* (1990: 8), described each model in relationship to the colony in which it most thrived:

> To oversimplify: Pennsylvania sought immigrants who would be good citizens regardless of their religious background; Massachusetts wanted as members only those who were religiously pure; and Virginia, with its increasing reliance on a plantation economy, wanted workers as cheaply as it could get them, without necessarily welcoming them to membership in the community.[2]

[2] In *Albion's Seed*, David Hackett Fischer (1991) also emphasizes differences in values and what he refers to as folkways in the settlement of Virginia, Massachusetts, and Pennsylvania. He adds a fourth folkway, represented by the settlement of the Appalachian region.

This book traces the evolution of these three models of immigration as they explain the historical roots of current policy debates and options. The focus is on 1) why each model has played an important role; 2) the contexts in which one model or another has risen in importance; 3) the impact of each on immigration and immigration policies; 4) the implications of each for the immigrants themselves; and 5) the implications of each model for the United States as a nation of immigrants. The book is organized chronologically, but separately discusses each of the models, as well as the backlash against immigration that accompanied each of the major movements. The final chapter shifts to the future, asking fundamental questions about where we as a nation are heading in our immigration and immigrant policies. Given the highly controversial nature of immigration in the United States and the heated political debate over immigration reform, my hope is that this book will provide a thoughtful, well-reasoned analysis that will be valuable to both academic and policy audiences, by placing today's trends and policy options into historical perspective.

Models of American Immigration

The first permanent English colony was founded in Virginia in 1607. Established by a trading company that was primarily interested in profits, Virginia largely equated immigration with the arrival of laborers. Indentured servants, convict laborers, and, finally, slaves were brought to the colony. Their labor was welcomed but, particularly in the case of slaves, full social membership was denied. Although the colonial leaders sought immigrants and, in the case of convict labor and slavery, compelled both convict laborers and slaves to migrate, few rights were accorded to those who came to be seen as supplying expendable and exploitable labor.

Massachusetts was also settled by a trading company, but its goals were loftier – to establish a colony for coreligionists who shared Puritan theology and values. From the establishment of the Massachusetts Bay Colony in 1630, the colony's immigration model was to welcome the true believer but to exclude and, in certain cases, to expel or even kill those whose views challenged the conventional wisdom.

William Penn was also motivated by religion in establishing the Pennsylvania colony in 1681, but he brought new ideas about religious tolerance and diversity. Although Pennsylvania was to be a haven for Quakers who faced persecution in Britain, Penn extended a welcome to other groups who wished to immigrate to the new colony. Members of religious minorities throughout Europe responded, making Pennsylvania one of the most diverse colonies in religion, language, and culture.

Fuchs (1990) asserts that the Pennsylvania ideal – that immigrants (specifically, white European settlers) would be welcomed on terms of equal rights – prevailed in the making of the new nation. The Massachusetts model "became influential in the development of a national ideology of Americanism, but it was too restrictive to form a dominant immigration and naturalization policy"

(Fuchs 1990: 8). He also argues that the Virginia ideal recurs as a model of labor migration, but, having found its most extreme form in slavery, remains suspect.

I agree with Fuchs' elaboration of these colonial models – although noting that, as archetypes, they have never existed in pure form – as well as his view that the Pennsylvania model reflects what has been best in immigration to the United States. I disagree with him, however, as to the extent that the Pennsylvania model has prevailed. Rather, I propose that each model has had salience throughout our history, with the strength of each model varying in accord with broader currents of thought and events. Each model is basically supportive of immigration, although they cast immigration as serving markedly different purposes. Each has been challenged, not only by the others, but also by more restrictive notions of nation and community. And as concerns about immigration mount, the economic, ideological, and integration arguments of the three models are used as often to justify curbs on immigration as to support continued admissions.

Here are a few examples of the ways in which the three models have played out. Exclusions based on ideological beliefs (alien and sedition acts, bars to admission of anarchists and communists), along with affirmative policies for admission of refugees from communist regimes, formed the nineteenth- and twentieth-century counterpart to the Massachusetts requirement of religious conformity. The importation of Chinese laborers to build the railroads and perform other unskilled jobs, followed by the Chinese Exclusion Act of 1882, reflected the Virginia idea of immigrants as expendable workers rather than members of the society. The *Bracero* program, under which Mexican workers were admitted on a temporary basis to fill wartime labor shortages, also followed the Virginia pattern.

The Americanization movement of the early twentieth century, conceived by proponents of immigration as a way to help immigrants achieve the promise of the Pennsylvania movement, was later "hijacked" [to use Barbara Jordan's (1995a) term in calling for a twenty-first-century Americanization movement] by restrictionists who introduced quotas on the admission of immigrants of selected national origins. It was not until the Immigration Amendments of 1965, passed during the height of the civil rights movement, that national origins quotas were eliminated. This opened immigration to new communities and set off the fourth wave of mass migration.

Today's notions and patterns of immigration may be the most complex of all. The threat of terrorism and concerns about fundamentalist Islam have led to new ideological restrictions with new theological overtones. With the end of the Cold War and the demise of Communism in most countries, U.S. refugee programs have lost their Massachusetts-style raison d'être and have still not returned to the levels of the 1980s.

At the same time, the apparently insatiable demand for labor has led to a tolerance of large-scale undocumented immigration and a proliferation of temporary worker programs, mirroring earlier periods of unfettered, Virginia-style migration. Another manifestation of the Virginia model has been a series of federal laws that have restricted the rights of immigrants (for example, to public welfare benefits and due process of law) just as their numbers have increased substantially.

Numbers and Trends in Immigration

Statistics on the number of immigrants coming to America are weak even today. Although there are reliable administrative records on the number of persons who come through legal channels, determining how many persons arrive without authorization requires sophisticated estimation techniques combined with leaps of faith in the assumptions that underlie the estimates. No records are kept today on levels of emigration – that is, the number of persons who leave the United States – although such information was collected in the past. The decennial census offers information on the stock of foreign-born persons in the United States, but immigrants are an obvious source of the census undercount, given language, cultural and legal barriers to participation in the census.

With all of these caveats about the quality of the data, it is still possible to construct a picture of the scale of immigration during the past four hundred years. Klein (2004: 58) estimates that 198,000 Europeans and African slaves came to the American colonies during the seventeenth century. Most went to the southern colonies but a high proportion was male, and death rates, at least initially, were also high. Smaller numbers migrated to New England and the mid-Atlantic colonies, but as a result of lower death rates and a more balanced male-female population, there were more opportunities for natural growth than in the south. During the eighteenth century, immigration increased. Klein estimates that 586,000 immigrants (again from both Europe and Africa) arrived between 1700 and 1775.

The first U.S. census, carried out in 1790, found a population of 3.8 million persons. The census did not ask where inhabitants had been born but did ask about national origins. The largest proportion was of English and Welsh descent, with Scottish and German descent contributing sizable proportions. In 1820, the federal government began collecting data on arriving passengers, which provides useful perspective on immigration levels. Figure 1.1 shows the number of immigrants admitted during the period from 1820 to the present. The data map the various waves of immigration.

Into the third decade of the new republic, immigration levels were modest. They began to increase in the 1830s and grew substantially in the 1840s and 1850s, only to fall during the Civil War. Immigration during this period was primarily from Britain, Ireland, Germany, and the Scandinavian countries, although Chinese and Mexican laborers also arrived.

After the Civil War, immigration began to increase again, excpt during the 1890s, when the United States suffered several major economic crises. With recovery came record levels of immigration in the first two decades of the twentieth century, with more than 1 million immigrants arriving in six of the years between 1905 and 1914. Emigrants during this period came mostly from southern and eastern Europe, and brought people who shared neither the language nor the religion of the majority Anglo-Protestant population of the United States. With the outbreak of World War I, events in Europe precluded mass emigration, reducing immigration levels from that continent. The United States recruited temporary workers from Mexico to fill the gap.

In the 1920s, immigration from Europe began to increase again, only to be permanently reduced by the imposition of numerical restrictions and national origin quotas that effectively ended the opportunity of southern and eastern Europeans to enter. As these new immigration policies went into effect, the Great Depression further suppressed immigration levels and, for the first time, levels of return migration to Europe exceeded new arrivals. Throughout the 1930s, the quota for Germany went unfilled as the U.S. State Department imposed administrative barriers to the admission of refugees from Nazi persecution, effectively precluding the resettlement in the United States of large numbers of Jews and other victims of fascism.

Low levels of permanent immigrant and refugee admissions persisted throughout the 1940s, but with U.S. entry into World War II, attention turned, as it had in World War I, to admission of temporary workers from Mexico. This program operated until 1964, employing between 4 million and 5 million Mexicans during the twenty-two-year period. Illegal immigration from Mexico also grew in those years, setting the stage for today's high levels of unauthorized entries.

With mass population displacement in Europe as a result of World War II and the Cold War, the United States reversed its refugee policies, allowing migration to increase during the 1950s and early 1960s. Congress did not agree to lift the national origins quotas, but ways were found to circumvent the restrictions for the admission of refugees and displaced persons.

More fundamental change in U.S. policies occurred with passage of the 1965 Amendments to the Immigration and Nationality Act. This legislation eliminated the national origins quotas as well as earlier restrictions on the admission of Asian immigrants. By the time of its implementation, few Europeans were able or willing to immigrate to the United States. Western Europe was importing temporary workers from southern Europe. Most of eastern Europe was behind an Iron Curtain that prevented emigration. Instead, immigrants' origins shifted to Latin America, the Caribbean, and Asia. Immigration began to increase in the 1970s but did not reach the levels of the early twentieth century, in absolute numbers, until the 1990s. As a percentage of the total population immigration is still not at nineteenth-century levels, when the overall U.S. population was much smaller. Significant levels of legal admissions have persisted into the first decade of the twenty-first century (although, at this writing, it appears that the economic recession may have reduced the numbers attempting to enter illegally).

Background to the Research

The research for this project has been almost thirty years in the making. A word about the author may be in order here. My early training was as an historian, specializing in the colonial period. My first venture into research on immigration was a series of studies for the Select Commission on Immigration and Refugee Policy (1979–1981). These studies traced issues of recurrent concern regarding immigration (language, public health, crime, and return migration), to help inform the commissioners about the issues they were addressing. This research was collected into a volume on immigration history published by the commission. In 1980, I became the research director for the commission, taking lead responsibility for the staff report that explained the reasoning behind the commission's recommendations. This role gave me insights into the formulation of policies that would form the basis of the Immigration Reform and Control Act of 1986 and the Immigration Act of 1990.

After the commission ended in 1981, I spent the next decade as policy and research director at the Refugee Policy Group, a think tank on refugee issues. During that pivotal period in refugee policy, I focused initially on the resettlement of refugees to the United States. Later, I turned my attention to asylum issues as well as to international refugee assistance issues. During this period, I had the opportunity to visit refugee camps in Southeast Asia, Central America, and Africa. I also interviewed federal, state, and local government officials, representatives of private resettlement agencies, refugees, and asylum applicants in numerous states.

In the 1990s, I served as the executive director of the next major federal body that reviewed immigration policy, the U.S. Commission on Immigration Reform (often referred to as the Jordan Commission after its chair, Barbara Jordan). During five years, the Jordan Commission held hearings and consultations in communities throughout the United States. This provided me with the opportunity to hear from experts as well as from ordinary Americans who spoke during the open microphone sessions. The commission's field visits provided further opportunities to learn about immigration in the 1990s. Whether I was accompanying the Border Patrol along the United States–Mexico border, observing refugee adjudications in Kenya, or speaking at naturalization ceremonies, these experiences gave me a unique perspective on the implementation of U.S. immigration policies. I also had the good fortune to serve as the U.S. coordinator for a binational study team with Mexico, which allowed me to visit emigrant communities in Jalisco and Oaxaca and to tour the border from the Mexican side. The dozens of congressional hearings at which I testified and the numerous personal briefings I gave to members of Congress provided me with further insights into the key issues that were on the legislative agenda. When the Jordan Commission ended in 1997, I returned to academia where I have continued to undertake research on immigration to the United States at Georgetown University. Recent projects have studied the impact of immigration on new settlement communities, efforts to address unauthorized migration at the worksite, and the admission of temporary foreign workers to the United States.

Thus, having spent much of the past 30 years intimately involved in the immigration policy process, I bring my personal experiences and perspectives to this volume. I also draw upon previously published books and articles that I have written on a range of immigration issues.[3] This volume has made extensive use of primary sources materials, including letters, diaries, journals and other personal records, contemporary newspapers, magazines and journals, public immigration records, and the papers of the Dillingham Immigration Commission (which submitted 41 volumes to Congress in 1911). I also used analyses of laws, regulations, policies, and testimony, and consulted the *Congressional Record*, court cases, and other relevant materials that lead to an informed understanding of immigration policies. I have also analyzed census and administrative data on immigration patterns and immigrant experiences. Chapters 10 and 12 draw heavily on the public and personal records of the two commissions in which I served in senior capacities (including field visit notes, public hearings, background papers, decision memos, and commissioned research) and interviews I have conducted with policy makers and implementers at federal, state, and local levels.

The book builds upon a distinguished body of recent publications on U.S. immigration history, which has been invaluable to my research.[4] I am indebted to two books in particular. Aristide R. Zolberg, *A Nation by Design: Immigration Policy in the Fashioning of America* (2006) and Daniel J. Tichenor, *Dividing Lines: The Politics of Immigration Control in America* (2002) meticulously analyzed the formulation of American immigration policy. Tichenor's analysis of the Select Commission on Immigration and Refugee Policy and Commission on Immigration Reform were particularly helpful in confirming conclusions I had reached as an insider. It was reassuring to know that an independent assessment had come to similar views about the aims of these commissions. This book has a broader scope, however, than these excellent volumes, in that it discusses the interplay between immigration policy and immigrant experiences, focusing on differences that emerge from the three models discussed herein.

---

[3] Among the more relevant articles and books, "Quaker Tribalism" (Forbes [Martin] 1982) explores the response of one Pennsylvania community to the growing diversity that stemmed from the Pennsylvania model. "The Politics of U.S. Immigration Reform" (Martin 2003) and "The Attack on Social Rights: U.S. Citizenship Devalued" (Martin 2002) explore the pressures on the Pennsylvania integration model since 1996. "A History of American Language Policy" (Forbes [Martin] and Lemos 1981) and "Language and Immigration" (Martin 2005) explores the reasons that English language acquisition has been a "hot button" immigration issue since the beginnings of the nation. "Competing for Skills: U.S. Immigration Policy Since 1990" (Martin and Lowell 2005) and "U.S. Immigration Policy: Admission of High Skilled Workers" (Martin et al. 2002) examines labor migration policies. "Beyond the Gateway: Immigrants in a Changing America" (Gozdziak and Martin 2005) assesses the impact of today's immigration on new settlement areas in the United States. "International Migration and Terrorism: Prevention, Prosecution and Protection" (Martin and Martin 2004) discusses U.S. policy responses to the events of September 11, 2001.

[4] In the years leading up to the 1965 immigration reforms, a number of important immigration histories were published that are at one and the same time predecessors and source materials for this book, including Oscar Handlin's *The Uprooted* (1952); John Higham, *Strangers in the Land* (1955); and Maldwyn Jones's *American Immigration* (1960).

A Roadmap to the Book

Chapters 2, 3, and 4 present the Virginia, Massachusetts, and Pennsylvania models, respectively. They describe the origins of the colonies, the aims of their founders, and the major migrations that took place during this first wave of immigration. These chapters highlight the push-and-pull factors that encouraged and, in the case of African slaves and English prisoners, forced movements across the Atlantic.

Immigration in the founding of the republic is discussed in Chapter 5. The chapter pays particular attention to evolving notions of membership in the American polity and how immigration fit into the process of nation building. The second major wave of immigration, which took place between 1830 and 1880, is examined in Chapter 6. The chapter focuses on the new Catholic immigration, particularly from Ireland and Germany, which was greeted with suspicion by the largely Protestant native population.

Chapters 7 and 8 focus on the third major wave of immigration, which began in the 1880s. Chapter 7 discusses the experiences of the immigrants as well as initiatives, such as the Americanization movement, to help them adjust to life in the United States. Chapter 8 discusses the movement to restrict immigration. It traces legislative actions to improve the "quality" of the immigrants to be admitted and then, in the 1920s, to impose national origins quotas.

The period from 1924 to 1965 is discussed in Chapter 9. The chapter examines the very restrictive refugee policy of the 1930s, comparing it with Cold War refugee admissions of the 1950s and early 1960s. It also discusses the reemergence of the Virginia model with the admission of Mexican temporary workers.

Chapters 10 and 11 recount the resurgence of the Pennsylvania model in the period from 1965 to 1994. Chapter 10 examines the new immigration emerging from passage of the Immigration Amendments of 1965, which eliminated the national origins quotas. The growth in immigration from Latin America and Asia are of particular focus. The chapter highlights the work of the Select Commission on Immigration and Refugee Policy and the two major pieces of legislation – the Immigration Reform and Control Act of 1986 and the Immigration Act of 1990 – that flowed from its recommendations. Chapter 11 focuses on U.S. refugee and asylum policy, discussing particularly the impact of the Refugee Act of 1980 which sought to bring U.S. policies and practices into conformity with evolving international norms and standards. The experiences of refugees from Cuba, Southeast Asia, and the former Soviet Union receive specific attention.

In Chapter 12, the immigration story is brought to the present. Unauthorized migration and post-September 11 policies are discussed as new manifestations of the Virginia and Massachusetts models, respectively. The chapter focuses particularly on the growth of undocumented migration, as well as such landmark, but ultimately ineffective, legislation as the Illegal Immigration Reform and Immigrant Responsibility Act (IIRIRA) of 1996.

Finally, Chapter 13 looks to the future, setting out my recommendations to return immigration to the United States to the Pennsylvania model. The chapter argues that America has benefited the most from immigration when we as a nation, and the immigrant newcomers, both take seriously our mutual responsibilities – what the U.S. Commission on Immigration Reform referred to as a covenant between immigrant and country. The final chapter describes four prerequisites for an immigration system that fulfills the aims of the Pennsylvania model: the curbing of illegal immigration; the revitalization of legal immigration; the reassertion of U.S. leadership on refugee and asylum policies; and a renewed commitment to the full integration of immigrants into American society.

2

"Gentlemen, Tradesmen, Serving-men, Libertines"

The title of this chapter comes from a passage in John Smith's *General History of Virginia* in which he rues the paucity of laborers among the early colonizers in Jamestown. The expense of migrating, as well as the conditions found in the colony, restricted movements to the colonies. Within a few decades, as the tobacco economy developed, Virginia had identified several sources of foreign labor. The first was indentured servants. The employer paid the migrant's passage in exchange for indented labor, which was usually for a term of from four to seven years. On release from the indenture, the worker was to be provided with tools, clothing, and land or other means of self-support, although these terms were by no means always upheld. There were prominent cases in which released servants experienced upward mobility, including landownership and political participation; but in many cases, the freed worker remained dependent on the former employer for continued employment.

The second category of "labor migrant" was composed of convicts and debtors. The governor of Virginia sought the transfer to the colony of convicts who had been condemned to death in England. Orphans were also sent to the colony, with girls particularly valuable as "breeders" because so few Virginia colonists were female. In the most celebrated case, Georgia's charter promoted the immigration of debtors and convicts who would be able to redeem themselves in the new colony while forming a barrier between the more populous British colonies and the Spanish in Florida.

The third category, and the epitome of the Virginia model, was slavery – the forced migration of Africans to the American colonies. The slave trade predated the establishment of Virginia and the large majority of slaves transported to the New World went to the Caribbean islands, Brazil, and the Spanish colonies. As early as 1670, the British had determined that active engagement in the slave trade was necessary to the growth of the colonies, leading to a royal charter for the "Company of Royall Adventurers of England trading into Africa." Later legislation broke the Royal Africa Company's monopoly and contributed to further growth in the slave trade. By the mid-eighteenth century, about

250,000 Africans had been transported to the British colonies in mainland North America. Most, but not all, went to the southern settlements.

The Founding of Virginia

On April 10, 1606, James I, King of England, granted the first Charter of Virginia to a group of "knights, gentlemen, merchants and other adventurers," later known as the Virginia Company, to establish a colony in "that part of America commonly called VIRGINIA, and other parts and Territories in America, either appertaining unto us, or which are not now actually possessed by any Christian Prince or People, situate, lying, and being all along the Sea Coasts" (First Charter of Virginia 1606). Although it was not the first attempt by the British crown to colonize the American mainland, the colony established the following year in Jamestown proved to be the first permanent English settlement in what later became the United States.

The charter recognized multiple purposes of the Virginia Company's colonization efforts. Certainly religion played a role. The colonists were to "propagate Christian Religion to such People, as yet live in Darkness and miserable Ignorance of the true Knowledge and Worship of God" (First Charter 1606). However, economic concerns were at the heart of the charter. Those granted the charter sought a financial return on their investment in colonizing the New World. The charter granted the Virginia Company all of the "Lands, Woods, Soil, Grounds, Havens, Ports, Rivers, Mines, Minerals, Marshes, Waters, Fishings, Commodities, and Hereditaments" to be found in the territory covered by the charter (First Charter 1606). The territory was to comprise two colonies, divided geographically and designated by the principal origins of the investors. The southern colony was granted to the London Company, and was to be established between "four and thirty and one and forty Degrees" latitude; the northern colony was granted to the Plymouth Company, and was to be established between "eight and thirty Degrees and five and forty Degrees of the said Latitude" (First Charter 1606). The Virginia Company was to establish a 13-person Council, operating in England, that would have the responsibility for managing the colonies. The Council would name a 13-person body, also referred to as a council, for each colony that had authority to govern, to mine for gold, silver, and copper, to mint coins, and to tax and defend the colony.

In December 1606, three ships set sail for Virginia – the *Sarah Constant*, the *Goodspeed*, and the *Discovery*, arriving in the Chesapeake Bay in April 1607 after a journey through the West Indies. After exploring the bay and making the colonists' first contacts with the indigenous population, the ships' captains settled on the James River as their point of disembarkation. Some 104 passengers disembarked in what would become the settlement of Jamestown (Bernhard 1992: 601). The sealed box they carried from England named seven men who were to form the nucleus of the council. Edward-Maria Wingfield was named president of the council, but his responsibilities were only to preside and to cast a double vote in case of a tie. The council itself had the authority to remove its president, and any member, by majority vote. The council's first such act was to remove Captain John Smith from its membership because of what they considered to be mutinous acts during the trans-Atlantic voyage (Andrews 1964: 99). Smith was restored to the council in June, however – a good move, because his leadership certainly helped the colonists survive the early months of the settlement.

These first settlers had few of the skills needed to establish a successful colony. They were knights, gentlemen, merchants, and adventurers; they knew little about farming, fishing, or foraging for food. They quickly exhausted the few supplies that had survived the long trip from England to Virginia. They had the great misfortune to arrive in Jamestown at the height of one of the worst droughts on record, which affected food supply and water quality (Stahle 1998). Dependent largely on food supplied by the Native American tribes in the area, they bickered among themselves and succumbed to disease. By the end of 1607, only 38 men survived. The arrival of a supply ship from England and Smith's tough actions as president of the council were all that brought the remaining colonists through the first winter.

In September 1608, a third supply ship arrived at Jamestown, this time bringing not only commodities needed by the colonists but also artisans and laborers. The ship also brought two women, who were the only women in the colony for about one year (Bernhard 1992: 603). The colonists began to construct buildings, plant fields, and raise livestock. According to his own journal, Smith threatened to expel any colonist who did not provide the labor needed to secure the settlement. As word got back to the Council in England, it was clear that more needed to be done if the colony was to survive and to provide a return on the investment made by members of the company.

The investors sought a new charter from the Crown, one that would provide for a more effective system of governance for the colony. In the second charter, granted in May 1609, the Virginia Company was established as a joint stock company, with a treasurer and members of the Council appointed by the Crown. Subsequently, the members, or stockholders, would elect the treasurer and Council members when there were vacancies (Second Charter 1609). The Council had authority to make laws for the colony, as long as these did not contravene the laws of England. The Council also had the authority to raise funds by selling shares in the Virginia Company and to promote settlement of the colony. The new charter expanded the territory under the control of the Virginia Company.

Perhaps the most significant change resulting from the second charter was the appointment of a governor of the new colony with wide powers over all of the colonists. Lord De la Warr (Delaware) was named the first governor. The new charter and De la Warr's appointment raised hopes for the ultimate success of the colony, leading some 800 persons to set sail for Virginia. De la Warr himself did not arrive until June 1610. In the interim, Jamestown continued to experience difficult times, with disease and hunger causing high levels of mortality. De la Warr restored some order, but he was forced to leave the colony because of serious illness. His successors, Sir Thomas Gates and Sir Thomas Dale, finally had some success in stemming the high death rates, making peace with the native population, and establishing a new settlement, Henrico, at a higher and healthier altitude than Jamestown's.

The colony still faced crisis, however, stemming from the colonists' unfitness for the work that had to be done. Although arriving boats continued to bring artisans to settle, too many colonists were described as "lascivious sonnes, masters of bad servants, and wives of ill husbands" who were unable or unwilling to work (Andrews 1964: 113, quoting Brown). The Virginia Company Council set out to correct this situation, examining more closely the background and skills of those seeking to emigrate. Gates and Dale also promulgated a series of laws to ensure discipline within the colony. Compiled into a compendium called "Laws Divine, Morall and Martiall," the new laws were published in London in 1612, part of a strategy to convince investors and would-be colonists alike that the Virginia colony was well governed and successful. Implemented with some degree of arbitrariness and harshness, though, these laws were themselves controversial.

By 1611, the colony appeared to be over the worst of the crises, having endured the "starving times." The Virginia Company sought a third charter (1611) to address some of the new challenges it was facing. Again, the company sought expanded boundaries, and again it succeeded; Bermuda was included in the Virginia Company's purview. The new charter also required regular meetings of the members of the company to oversee the work of the Council. The 1611 charter increased the power of the courts established by the company to punish offenders, including those who took "wages, apparel and other entertainment" from the Company but refused to go to the colony; those who misbehaved in the settlement; and those who returned to England and slandered the colony. Finally, the new charter allowed the Virginia Company to use lotteries to raise additional funds for the colony.

Perhaps the most important innovation in the period after the third charter was the transition from joint ownership to private ownership of land. Initially, each man in Jamestown was given three acres to farm in exchange for one month's service to the colony and a payment in corn (Andrews 1964: 124). In 1616, the Company offered 50 acres to those who subscribed £12 10s. In 1618, land was apportioned for various public purposes and grants of 50 acres were made to those who did special service to the company or would agree to settle in the colony with family and servants. In this way, grants of land became a lure to increase the number of permanent settlers. At first, the cultivation was for subsistence, with the colony exporting little to England. With the planting of tobacco, however, Virginia found its export commodity.

During this early period, the Virginia Company still suffered from a lack of colonists who intended to reside permanently in the colony. Disease remained a problem. In 1616, there were about 125 fewer colonists in Virginia than had been there in 1611 – 324 compared with 450. The numbers began to increase, albeit slowly, to a total of about 600 in 1618 (Andrews 1964: 134). The company attempted to build up the population, pledging to send 300 tenants to land in Henrico, an incorporated area that was under the company's direct control. The company also sent apprentices and servants and "young and uncorrupt maids to make wives to the inhabitants" (Andrews 1964: 134). If the women married tenants who farmed company land, the company would pay for the cost of transport. Otherwise, the husbands were to reimburse the travel costs with tobacco. Orphans, paupers, and convicts were also transported to the colony, an arrangement attractive to municipal authorities who could rid themselves of needy and criminal populations.

Yet the colony's population continued to stagnate, largely because of high death rates on board ship and in the colony. Some settlers returned to England, unwilling to remain in the colony for one reason or another. After hundreds of new settlers had been sent across the Atlantic, the population in Virginia had fallen from 1,000 in 1619 to 843 in 1620 (Andrews 1964). More troubles befell the colony in 1622 when tensions between the colonists and the native population reached new heights. A massacre followed, with almost 350 colonists killed. Outright warfare ensued, by and large won by the colonists with firearms imported from England.

The troubles affecting the colony eventually caused the downfall of the Virginia Company. The Crown established a board of inquiry to determine whether the situation could be remedied. Letters from the colonists complaining of neglect and deprivation reinforced the board's view that the company had mismanaged the colony. In fact, the company was torn apart by internal dissension and mismanagement of funds. It tried to build a profitable enterprise with too little capital and a precarious source of funding. The inquiry board recommended that the Crown issue a new charter giving itself greater authority over the dealings of the Virginia Company. After a court hearing that went against the company, its charter was vacated and the company dispersed. Virginia became a royal colony.

Populating the Colony

As in all large-scale population movements, a combination of push-and-pull factors affected migration. Economic, political, and religious changes in Britain produced emigration pressures that led to rural to urban migration within Britain as well as movements to the colonies. As discussed earlier, the Virginia Company, for its part, attempted to populate the colony with an assortment of strategies. Immigrants were lured to the colony by promises of land and wealth. When an insufficient number of people volunteered to migrate, the company encouraged municipalities to send orphans, paupers, and criminals to the colony. (The first convicts transported to the colony are believed to have come in 1617.) Not all of these early settlers chose to migrate. As early as 1618, there were reports of women who were kidnapped in England and sold in Virginia. And the first Africans arrived in Virginia in 1619; they are believed to have been brought on a Dutch ship. This section discusses the emigration pressures that prompted movement and then turns to specific forms of migration.

Emigration Pressures

Prevailing theories about the causes of migration suggest that households engage in migration to minimize economic risk, especially risk from agricultural losses in subsistence farming communities (Massey 1993). In the absence of other forms of insurance, migration to cities or to agricultural communities in other regions or countries enables families to withstand shocks from loss of crops because of weather, failures in markets caused by recessions, and loss of livelihoods caused by conflict and political instability and similar occurrences.

Societies that are attempting transformation from largely subsistence to a largely mercantile or industrial organization are particularly prone to migration pressures of this type, with new towns and cities arising to offer an alternative to the much more chancy subsistence farming. England in the sixteenth and seventeenth centuries was just such a society. Rapid population growth in combination with poor crop yields created economic dislocations for many English farmers. As Clark and Souden (1988: 30) describe in the introduction to their edited volume on migration and society in early modern England, "higher prices, declining real wages, under- and un-employment, together with rising rents and land shortages, all conspired to make poorer people leave home." Many moved locally in search of better economic opportunities; others migrated long distances to escape such severe conditions as massive famine (Clark and Souden 1988). These movements were mostly from north to south in England, but also included movements to Ireland and to the American colonies.

It was not until English population growth stalled, and even reversed in the late 1600s, that long-distance movements slowed down. As Whyte (2000: 116) posits, "a fall in the numbers of indentured servants emigrating in the later 1660s may have been related to the slackening of demographic growth within England, and the increased demand for labour in London after the Great Plague and Great Fire."

Accompanying these demographic and economic changes were reforms in the British poor laws that reduced the need for mobility and, at the same time, may have made mobility more difficult (Whyte 2000: 57–62). Medieval laws, which treated able-bodied unemployed persons as unworthy and people moving to seek work as vagrants, proved unable to counter severe economic downturns. The Poor Act of 1601 gave responsibility for providing poor relief to each township. This raised issues of residency – how long did someone have to live in a township to become eligible for relief? The 1662 "Act for the Better Reliefe of the Poore of this Kingdom" and its successor, the 1697 "Act for Supplying some Defectes in the Laws for the Relief of the Poor" established criteria for determining who was settled in a particular parish and therefore could qualify for the township's assistance (Whyte 2000). Parishes could issue settlement certificates to those who qualified by birth, land rental, tax payment, completion of an apprenticeship, or service to the township. In many cases, new townships would refuse to admit migrants without a certificate, which held the original township liable if the newcomer came upon bad times. The new laws also authorized townships to take securities from migrants to ensure that they did not become public charges.

Souden (1988: 167), examining registrations of emigrants to North America via Bristol, concludes that movements to the colonies in the seventeenth century (1654–1662, more specifically) was an extension of long-distance internal migration. Looking at the movements of indentured servants, he found that a disproportionately large number came from London. About 75 percent came from more than 20 miles away from Bristol. Significant numbers of emigrating servants had lived previously in towns or cities, although many would be working in agriculture in the colonies. Another significant number of emigrants came from marginal forest areas with poor agricultural prospects (Souden 1988 and Whyte 2000: 36 on more general patterns).

In addition to economic pressures, movements, particularly to Ireland and then the Americas, were spawned by growing British nationalism as this was manifested in the search for empire. The establishment in 1603 of the Stuart dynasty, when James VI of Scotland became James I of England, heralded a new concept of "Britain" – although it took almost a century to join the two kingdoms under a single unified crown. As was remarked by Alexander Murdoch (2004: 13) of the settlement of Ireland, but was equally true of the Americas, "For James, British plantation . . . held the key to consolidation of a British Empire that was not so much a bastion of Protestantism as of 'civilitie' and growing commercial wealth through trade." Key players in this process were the merchants and speculators who recruited emigrants to work the land so that a multitude of commodities could be shipped back to European markets. In this respect, empire and mercantilism went hand in hand to create an environment conducive to emigration. This pattern of movement is consistent with the "world systems" theory of international migration, which posits that "driven by a desire for higher profits and greater wealth, owners and managers of capitalist firms enter poor countries on the periphery of the world economy in search of land, raw materials, labor, and new consumer markets" (Massey 1993: 444–45). Initially, the movements were from England to the nearer parts of the expanding Britain – mainly toward Ireland. But, as Britain incorporated other provinces into the mainstream, emigration to the American colonies grew, and increasingly, emigrants were recruited from throughout the British Isles. In fact, by the eighteenth century, emigration from England began to decline in favor of movements from Scotland, Ireland, and Wales.

Estimates of emigration from Britain to America in the seventeenth century range from 250,000 to 500,000, a considerable proportion of an area with a total population of about 5 million. Menard's (2001: 102) best estimate is that 123,200 white persons immigrated to the Chesapeake colonies in the seventeenth century. Given the great difficulties faced by colonists, many of whom died or returned because of the hostile environment, the scale of migration during the seventeenth century is impressive. Immigration increased in the eighteenth century. Gemery (1989) estimates that there were more than 650,000 immigrants between 1700 and 1790. An estimated 216,500 English, Welsh, Scottish, and Irish people emigrated from 1700 to 1775 (Menard 2001). Only 44,000 of the eighteenth-century emigrants were from England. The reduced emigration pressures in Britain did not mean that the colonies ceased to grow, but new sources of migration were needed. For Virginia and the southern colonies, a major new source was the slave trade, as discussed later. Emigrants from continental Europe also filled some of the gap, with migrants from Germany settling throughout the colonies.

To better understand the peopling of the southern colonies, and the role of the Virginia model, we turn to a more detailed discussion of the three principal forms of emigration: indenture, deportation, and slavery.

Indentured Servants

The system of indentured servitude that populated the colony during much of the seventeenth century was established in 1620. Galenson (1984: 6) describes it in simple terms: "The cost of passage was advanced to the migrants by the Company, and the recruits in turn promised to work for stated periods; in Virginia, title to the migrants' labor during these periods was transferred to individual planters upon the planters' reimbursement of transportation costs to the Company."

Passage to the New World was expensive. Whyte (2000: 126) estimates transport across the Atlantic to cost £30–50 for a family and their possessions in the early seventeenth century. Only those with considerable fortunes could afford to pay for their own passage. For most would-be emigrants, indentured servitude proved to be a more realistic way to reach the New World. Some historians estimate that at least half of all colonists arrived as indentured servants (Campbell 1959).

An employer, or, more likely, an agent paid the passage, which would be repaid by the servant by working for a fixed number of years. The indenture system loosely followed the practices of apprenticeships and agriculture service in England (Whyte 2000). The term of indenture varied. In one sample of indentured servants leaving Bristol for the Americas, the majority committed to four years of indenture (Souden 1988: 153). Six or seven years were not uncommon terms, particularly for those who emigrated at a younger age (Whyte 2000: 127). The London registrations include the age of the indentured servants; typically, the term of service for minors was 7–10 years, depending on their age (Campbell 1959: 77). Those with skills for which the colonies had demand would likely be able to negotiate shorter indentures and more favorable terms (Souden 1988: 154). In the sample of those leaving Bristol, the largest numbers of indentured servants were yeomen (35 percent) and laborers (10 percent), but appreciable numbers were in the building trades (3.4 percent) and in the clothing (4.8 percent), leather (3.3 percent), and textile (4.5 percent) industries. Milling, metal working, stoneworking, and building trades rounded out the numbers. Less than 2 percent were characterized as professionals and gentlemen/planters (Souden 1988: 155). By contrast, indentured servants leaving from London showed the opposite occupational distribution, with more skilled workers than yeomen and husbandmen (Campbell 1958: 71). Menard (2001: 127), examining not only those who came under contract but also those who immigrated on their own and then became servants, concluded that "many, perhaps the majority, who came, both with indentures and without, lived near the margin of British society."

Menard (2001: 128–29) also emphasizes the sex and age composition of the servants who came to the Chesapeake area. During the seventeenth century, an increasing share of the migrants was younger males, under the age of 16. By the 1690s, 40 percent of the male servants were in this age group. The proportion of women increased over time, but even at the end of the century, there were two and a half times as many men as women in the Chesapeake area.

During the period studied by Souden (1988), 1654–1662, about 62 percent of the indentured servants who left Bristol went to the West Indies and the remaining 38 percent to the mainland, with the vast majority of the latter continuing on to Virginia. About 35 percent of the indentured servants accompanied masters who were sending more than 10 servants to the colonies, where, presumably, their indentures would be sold. Almost half of all masters (43.8 percent), however, had only one accompanying servant.

Reflecting the overall gender composition, about 25 percent of the indentured servants were women in the Bristol sample; there was a slightly lower proportion in the London records. Several young women from the same village often emigrated together. Some women were recruited to be house servants. Many of the women expected to marry when they arrived in the colonies. In some cases, the colonist who paid with cash or tobacco for her passage intended to marry the indentured servant when she arrived in the colony (Campbell 1959: 75).

Souden (1988: 167) points out that the indentured servants did not fit the stereotypes often heard about these migrants to the American colonies – "they were not the rogues, the whores and the vagabonds that the prevailing mythology might still lead us to believe." Instead, they were workers with low-status and low-paid occupations. As is true of most migrants, they were probably not the poorest of the poor, who would have had difficulty in reaching Bristol or other ports of emigration to arrange contracts to pay for their further transport.

Life in the colonies proved exceedingly difficult for these indentured servants, especially in the West Indies. By some estimates, mortality rates for indentured British and Irish servants working on the sugar plantations in the West Indies was higher than that of slaves (Murdoch 2004: 27). Fear of slave rebellions prompted plantation owners to continue to import indentured servants despite the high death rates. In Maryland, 40 percent of indentured servants in the 1640s did not survive their period of indenture (Whyte 2000: 128). Indentured servants to the Chesapeake area, as well as those sent to the West Indies, were "rudely thrust as isolated individuals into environments and communities that would be dramatically different from those they knew in England" (Murdoch

2004: 25). Games (1999: 89) puts it succinctly: "Servants were just another commodity, bartered freely by their masters for goods and land."

Treatment of indentured servants could be harsh. Edmund Morgan (1975) observed the perverse incentives of the system, which he believed led to the use of violence to stimulate productivity. Employers knew that workers would leave at the end of their contract and had no incentive to treat them well during the period of the contract. The workers had no wish to remain under the terms of the contract and so had few incentives to perform. Galenson (1978) points out, however, that violence was not a particularly effective way to gain greater productivity and argues that employers offered financial and other rewards to servants who performed well during the indenture.

Colonial assemblies did take action to improve the circumstances of indentured servants. Under some of these laws, servants could not be severely punished without the permission of a justice of the peace. Compensation upon completion of the indenture was established by custom, generally not by law (Andrews 1964: 209). In sixteenth-century Virginia, servants were to receive 50 acres of land, clothing, and a musket upon expiration of their term of indenture. As land filled up, though, some colonies changed to a system of cash payment. Servants in eighteenth-century North Carolina received £3 and a suit of clothes.

Although some migrants who completed their term of service then embarked on a path of upward mobility, owning land and becoming tobacco planters with their own servants (or slaves), many formerly indentured workers continued to earn wages working for others (Whyte 2000: 128). One study of 158 servants who survived servitude in Maryland in the seventeenth century found that about 50 percent eventually acquired land (Menard 2001: 40). Many of those who did not own land died or left the colony soon after completion of their indenture. Less than 15 percent of those known to have lived in Maryland for more than a decade as free men owned no land (Menard 2001).

Those who did not own or rent land could work for wages or serve as sharecroppers. Some of the wage-earners were artisans, who generally had little difficulty in selling their services. Others performed short- or long-term wage labor on plantations, often under a contract that specified the terms and length of service. These contract laborers had more rights than indentured servants and, given the labor shortages in the colonies, were often able to negotiate high wages. These contract workers received wages for their labor; the sharecroppers received a portion of the crops that they produced.

Political participation was a major difference in defining the rights of indentured servants, freeholders, tenants, sharecroppers, and wage-earners. Male indentured servants in Virginia were permitted to vote for the members of the House of Burgesses until 1655, when they were disenfranchised (Andrews 1964: 184). Freed servants were generally able to participate in civic affairs. In Menard's (2001: 42–43) sample of Maryland freeholders, the former servants served as jurors, constables and members of the militia. Some former servants even attained the rank of justice of the peace, burgess, sheriff, councilor, or officer in the militia (Menard 2001: 43). However, the franchise was generally extended only to the heads of households, limiting the access of wage-earners to the political process (Menard 2001: 51).

In Menard's (2001) sample of Maryland servants who attained freedom, the median number of years between servitude and land ownership was 7.5 years. Although custom dictated that servants should have the right to 50 acres of land, it would take time and resources to pay the surveyor's and clerk's fees for a patent, clear the land, erect housing, pay for seeds and tools, and survive until the crops could be harvested. The majority had small holdings of about 50–400 acres. Menard found 14 former servants, however, who owned at least one thousand acres at the time of their death. One of the largest landowners in Maryland was in his sample (Menard 2001: 41).

The majority of the freed servants in Menard's sample initially leased land. As leaseholders, the men were able to form their own households, with all of the rights that accrued to heads of households. They generally could pay the first year's rent with the proceeds of the first harvest in exchange for making improvements in the land (Menard 2001: 53). As Menard argues, the system proved beneficial for owner and renter alike. Leasing land gave former servants the time to create assets that could later be used to purchase land. The capacity of the leasers to accumulate assets, however, was based on the price of crops, particularly tobacco, and the price of land. When tobacco was scarce and prices were high, and land was abundant and cheap, upward mobility was a realistic goal. As the seventeenth century progressed, such opportunities diminished, both because of overproduction of tobacco and increasing scarcity of land (Menard 2001: 59–60). At the same time, opportunities began to open in other colonies, to the north and south of the Chesapeake, giving servants a greater likelihood of moving from indenture to freehold. And, in Virginia and elsewhere in the South, slaves became a more frequent source of labor, as discussed later.

Convict Labor

As early as 1611, the Virginia Company petitioned the British crown for the transport of convicts to people the colony. As described in Butler's (1896: 16) early article on convict labor in the Americas, "Governor Dale wrote from Virginia begging the king to 'banish hither all offenders condemned to die out of common goales, and likewise to continue that grant for three years unto the colonie (and thus doth the Spaniard people his Indes) it would be a readie way to furnish us with men, and not allways with the worst kind of men.'" Starting as early as 1617, a small but steady stream of convicts was transported to the colony each year. As the century progressed, convicts were also sold to brokers in the other colonies, but for much of this period, the Chesapeake Bay colonies remained the principal destination on the North American mainland (Butler 1896).

Despite the need for labor, the settlers were ambivalent about the transport of criminals. Early entreaties by leaders of the Virginia Company urged that only those of good moral character be sent to the colony. Later in the sixteenth century, Virginia passed legislation to outlaw the immigration of convicts. By then, however, the British government had found transport of convicts and debtors to be a convenient way to be rid of the costs of incarceration. The Crown generally overruled colonial sentiment, developing mechanisms to permit a smooth flow of convicts. In the Transportation Act of 1718, the British codified the practice. The act covered two types of offenses: those that were under benefit of clergy and those that were not. Benefit of clergy was afforded to lesser crimes that nevertheless could result in capital punishment. According to Kercher (2003: 530), "When a court found a person guilty of a clergyable offense, the Transportation Act of 1718 gave it the discretion to transport the prisoner to America for seven years instead of ordering a burning or flogging. A judge could also order the transportation of those found guilty of petty larceny, which was not even nominally capital." In non-clergyable offenses, capital punishment was required but the Crown could offer a pardon if the convicted person accepted transportation to the colonies.

In both cases, merchants entered into agreements with the government to transport convicts in exchange for a property interest in their labor (Kercher 2003: 530–31). Generally, migration for convicts followed patterns similar to those for migration of indentured servants. Often the same companies and brokers shipped both types of laborers (Grubb 2000: 113–14). In the eighteenth century, the British government subsidized the shipments in order to ensure they continued. The merchant who agreed to transport these criminals would receive £5 per capita plus the additional money obtained on selling the convicts' labor once they arrived in the colonies.

Grubb (2000) compared differences between indentured servants and convict laborers, finding that servants commanded a higher price than convicts. He attributed the differential to different perceptions about productivity, including a greater tendency of convicts to abscond from their contracts. Most convicts were sentenced to seven years of contract labor in the New World, a term that did not differ significantly from the terms of apprentices or of younger, unskilled indentured servants (Grubb 2000: 114). Generally, the convicts were more likely to be male and more likely to be older than members of the other groups.

The seriousness of the crimes that merited transportation varied by jurisdiction. As quoted by Ekirch (1985: 368), "At least an element of truth lay in the later observation that 'a man is banished from Scotland for a great crime, from England for a small one, and from Ireland, morally speaking for no crime at all.'" There were many reasons that convicts chose transportation over other punishments, including, for the most serious crimes, hanging or lengthy imprisonment. Even for crimes that warranted lesser punishment, transportation offered the possibility of escaping the situation that might have prompted the criminal behavior and greater opportunity to succeed economically in the New World. Conversely, transportation held great risks, particularly of dying from diseases on route or in the colonies. Moreover, convicts sometimes stayed in prison for months while awaiting transport to the colonies, and many were shackled while on board the ships.

Slavery

The "peculiar institution" of slavery ingrained itself as the principal labor recruitment mechanism several decades after the first indentured servants and the first Africans arrived in Virginia. During the early decades of the 1600s, Africans were not necessarily enslaved in Virginia. Often, they had a term of servitude that was longer than that of British servants, but still limited in time.

Menard (2001) suggests that the transition from a largely British workforce of indentured servants to a largely African slave workforce occurred in the late 1600s. Looking at probate inventories and tax lists in Virginia and Maryland, he finds that the ratio of servants to slaves shifts in the 1680s and 1690s. In the 1670s, in Maryland, there were almost four servants for each slave; by the 1690s, there were four slaves for every servant (Menard 2001: 360). Similar patterns can be found in Virginia records. He attributes the shift to a decline in the supply of servants, an increase in the price of indentured labor, and an increase in the supply of slaves. Population growth slowed in Britain, and additional colonies began to attract those who planned to migrate, lessening the pool of servants who came to the southern colonies. Direct shipment of slaves from Africa began in 1674, replacing the earlier and more costly transport via the West Indies. With the end of the Royal African Company's monopoly in 1698, he concludes, the stage was set for major increases in supply as independent traders sought to meet the demand for labor (Menard 2001: 366–67).

Although Menard (2001) explains the shift toward an African workforce, he does not explain the shift toward a slave workforce, nor the spread of slavery to other colonies. To a large extent, the motivation was economic. As Eltis (1983: 260) explains:

> The slaveowner, unlike the employer of indentured labor, could expect to receive a stream of income extending over the lifetime of the slave. If the marginal productivity of the alternative types of labor was equal, then the decision on which type of labor to use would depend first on relative transportation costs from Europe and Africa to the Americas, second on the length of the indenture relative to the life expectancy of the laborer (free and slave), and third on wage levels in America and Europe on the one hand and slave prices in Africa and America on the other. Relative wage levels would reflect the nonpecuniary factors that nonslave labor could take into account, while relative slave prices would reflect the competing uses for slaves in Africa and the Americas.

As Virginia's economy focused increasingly on one crop, tobacco, export income required a stable source of labor. In turn, the export provided a steady stream of income for the purchase of slaves. Not only did slaves continue to produce through their own lifetimes, they would also provide a continuing source of labor through natural increase. Although slaves' birth rates increased only slowly, this reasoning proved correct, with natural increase soon surpassing immigration as the source of new bonded laborers.

Economic factors alone do not explain the rise of African slavery in the United States. Racial biases certainly prevailed, in that the perceived benefits of slaveholding did not permit enslavement of Europeans. As slavery increasingly became the norm for labor recruitment in Virginia and other tobacco colonies, and then spread, particularly to the cotton-based economies, the colonies adopted laws that limited Africans' freedom and opportunity. Virginia already had laws, generally following English examples, that limited the mobility of servants and provided mechanisms for capturing, returning, and punishing runaways and those who resisted their masters. During the 1680s and 1690s, the colony codified legislation that increased penalties for such behavior when slaves were concerned:

> If any African "lift up his hand in opposition against any christian," he was to receive thirty lashes, and if he absented himself or were to "lie out" from his master's service and resist lawful apprehension, he or she could be killed. In 1691, an additional act provided for the suppression of outlying slaves: if they resisted or ran away, they could be killed and the owner paid 4000 pounds of tobacco by the government. (Nicholson 1994: 46)

Another law, passed in 1691, stipulated that no slave could be freed unless he or she had been transported out of the colony.

Virginia's economy had seen a transition from a voluntary migrant flow of indentured servants, with limited rights and opportunities, to a convict labor system that assumed there were limits to indenture, to a forced migration pattern in which the labor was valued but the worker had no rights or opportunities for advancement. Chattel slavery in its purest form becames the archetype of the Virginia model of immigration.

Relations with the Native Population

In the founding of the colonies, relations between immigrants and natives translated into relations between the largely British colonists and the indigenous Native American population. In later decades, the concept of immigrant–native relations can be broadened to include relations between newly arriving and already settled populations.

The always-uncertain relations between the Virginia colonists and the local Native American tribes deteriorated significantly in the 1620s (Washburn 1959). The Virginia Company was concerned from the start of exploration about the already resident population, warning the 1607 expedition: "you Cannot Carry Your Selves so towards them but they will Grow Discontented with Your habitation and be ready to Guide and assist any Nation that Shall Come to invade You" (quoted in Vaughan 1978). Nevertheless, some contact was necessary, for the sake of pure survival in the early years as well as to advance the prospect of converting the natives. The natives for their part viewed the colonists dubiously, concerned that they would indeed settle and encroach upon their territory. The natives' withholding of food from the colonists and strategically directed attacks in 1609–1610 almost succeeded in destroying Jamestown until the few surviving colonists were relieved by newly arriving ships with reinforcements. Low-level hostilities followed, with attacks launched by both sides, until a peace agreement was reached in 1614, largely because the colonists seized Pocahontas, the chief Powhatan's daughter, forcing him to sign a treaty. Attention turned during the next few years to conversion of the natives – to transforming those willing to adopt English manners and suppressing the rest – and to acquisition of native lands to meet the needs of a growing settler population.

The spark came in 1622 for what may have been an inevitable, violent clash between the natives, who were being pushed from their lands and despised for their culture, and the colonists, who truly believed in their own superiority and right to dominate the colony. The killing of a colonist and the shooting of the priest/warrior held responsible for the act was followed by an attack that killed almost 350 colonists, or one quarter of the total (Vaughan 1978). The English reaction was to send more arms to the colony, resulting in a brutal war whose aim was to crush the natives, killing them or driving them westward. The Crown also revoked the Virginia Company's charter, sending a royal governor to take over control of the colony.

As the colony grew, and land became scarcer, the colonists began pushing further and further west. A series of treaties forged alliances with certain Native American tribes against others, or against possible conflicts with Spanish or French colonists. Trading relationships also opened up between colonists and natives. Yet the colonists clearly had the upper hand, with imported diseases killing thousands of Native Americans and the better-armed colonists pushing the survivors off their land. By the early eighteenth century, the need for a buffer between the established settlements east of the Blue Ridge and various threats – Spanish, French, and Native American – argued for still further expansion west of the mountains. As one historian concludes:

> By the mid-eighteenth century, the rapid expansion of land-based settlement in the English colonies had sundered older ties of exchange and alliance linking natives and colonizers nearly everywhere east of the Appalachians, driving many Indians west and reducing those who remained to a scattering of politically powerless enclaves in which Indian identities were nurtured in isolation. Meanwhile, the colonizers threatened to extend this new mode of Indian relations across the Appalachians. An old world, rooted in indigenous exchange, was giving way to one in which Native Americans had no certain place. (Salisbury 1996: 458)

The immigrant–native relationship in Virginia came to characterize most of the other British colonies, where settlers pushed farther and farther westward those Indians who did not die from European diseases. This process stood in stark contrast to the Spanish colonization that took place in areas with more densely populated Indian tribes. Although many Indians in Spanish-controlled areas died from disease and conquest, the Spanish soon saw the natives as a source of labor in their sparsely settled colonies. In the sixteenth century, the Spanish established the encomienda system, described by Yeager (1995) as follows: "An encomienda was an organization in which a Spaniard received a restricted set of property rights over Indian labor from the Crown whereby the Spaniard (an encomendero) could extract tribute (payment of a portion of output) from the Indians in the form of goods, metals, money, or direct labor services." The encomienda system provided a continuing supply of labor, in this case, from the indigenous population, not indentured servants, convicts, or African slaves. That is not to say, of course, that the encomienda system was in any way superior to the British system. The Indians had no more choice in their indenture than the Africans did in their slavery. In both cases, a small number of European colonists found ways to exploit the labor of people whom they did not recognize as their equals.

Conclusion

Virginia was not the only example of the "Virginia model" within British North America. Colonists also settled the Carolinas and Georgia, generally through the immigration of a combination of large landowners, smaller freeholders, indentured servants, transported convicts, and slaves. The balance of these different groups varied from colony to colony and within colonies, but the basic contours of the Virginia model generally flourished in the other southern colonies. In South Carolina, for example, white European landowners were in the minority, and imported African slaves initially provided the majority of the labor. Georgia was established specifically for the transport of convicts.

The Virginia model of immigration presented America's first formulation of a system that would persist to the present. Foreign labor was valued and encouraged, but the majority of those admitted to the colony had limited rights. Immigration did not occur by happenstance. Rather, workers were recruited (if poor white) or forced (if convict or African) to emigrate to the New World and to labor for those who had land and capital. At first, the immigrants were bound to a specific term of service and could aspire to landownership and even wealth upon completion of their contract. With the advent of slavery, however, an increasingly large proportion of imported labor had no such opportunities. Chattel slavery, defined largely by race, superseded voluntary immigration as the most prevalent way to populate the colony. The colonists' population growth continued, but slaves became a majority in many of the southern colonies. By the late seventeenth century, Europeans in search of greater opportunity looked northward or westward for their future, as will be discussed in later chapters.

3

"A City upon a Hill"

In his "Model of Christian Charity," delivered in 1630, John Winthrop (1630) exhorted his brethren: "For we must consider that we shall be as a city upon a hill. The eyes of all people are upon us." Winthrop made clear that having entered into a covenant with God, the colonists had a responsibility to "seek out a place of cohabitation and consortship under a due form of government both civil and ecclesiastical. In such cases as this, the care of the public must oversway all private respects, by which, not only conscience, but mere civil policy, doth bind us."

The early settlers of Massachusetts were Puritans on a religious mission. Leaving an England that they believed was losing its religious soul, they sought the freedom to pursue their religious beliefs in the New World. Some were fleeing persecution in England, and they constituted what would be a defining component of American immigration – refugees who were at risk of serious harm if they remained at home. In contrast to the settlers of Virginia, these colonists were not adventurers seeking their fortune or laborers welcomed solely as workers. Rather, as Theodore Dwight Bozeman (1988: 96) describes, their migration was rooted in "flight and escape from onerous conditions in England," some economic but largely the "hanging threat of God's covenantal punishment upon an unreformed land."

Newcomers who shared the Puritan vision were welcomed into the covenant, joining a community that shared a set of religious norms and agreed to adhere to the laws and customs of the colony. Membership in the Massachusetts Bay Company, which held the colony's charter until the Crown took over in the 1660s, was based on religious qualifications. The colony grew rapidly, but membership grew more slowly. Newcomers were subject to a combination of civil and ecclesiastical laws established by the governing bodies, which were elected and composed of so-called freemen, who had been admitted into membership.

To those who did not share the beliefs of the founders, Massachusetts applied a set of exclusionary policies. For those already in the colony, there was a steep

price to be paid for dissent – the expulsion and deportation of colonists whose
views placed them outside the covenant. This chapter focuses on three well-
documented examples of such dissent: Roger Williams, Anne Hutchinson, and
members of the Society of Friends, known as Quakers. Williams is important
because Rhode Island, the colony that he established after the threat of deportation to England caused him to flee Massachusetts, introduced the notion
of the separation of church and state. Although Williams's primary interest
was in protecting religious worship from the type of state interference that he
opposed in England and Massachusetts Bay, the principle became an important precursor to later notions of a separation that protected both religion and
the state and allowed the migration of dissenters. Hutchinson drew the wrath
of the Massachusetts Bay colonists for her Antinomian religious views that
questioned the authority of the church, which she believed operated under a
covenant of works rather than a covenant of grace. After a celebrated trial that
raised as many issues of sexism as of religion, she was exiled, at first moving to
Williams's colony of Rhode Island and then to what is now New York, where
she was killed in an Indian attack. The third assault on the Massachusetts Bay
covenant came from a group of Quakers who defied a ban on their reentry
after expulsion from Massachusetts Bay and were hanged by the authorities.

The Founding of the Massachusetts Bay Colony

As was true in Virginia, the Massachusetts Bay Colony had its origins in a commercial enterprise, the Massachusetts Bay Company, which succeeded two earlier enterprises, the Council for New England and the New England Company.
The first permanent settlement in what became Massachusetts was the Plymouth Plantation – established in 1620 by the Pilgrims, a group of Separatists
from the Church of England who had first found refuge in the Netherlands
and then in the New World. Although the Pilgrims had intended to settle in
Virginia, after exploring what is now Cape Cod, they decided to remain in the
north. They established a governing system based on the Mayflower Compact,
under which 41 adults stated:

> Having undertaken for the Glory of God, and Advancement of the Christian
> Faith, and the Honour of our King and Country, a Voyage to plant the first
> Colony in the northern Parts of *Virginia*; Do by these Presents, solemnly and
> mutually, in the Presence of God and one another, covenant and combine
> ourselves together into a civil Body Politick, for our better Ordering and
> Preservation, and Furtherance of the Ends aforesaid: And by Virtue hereof
> do enact, constitute, and frame, such just and equal Laws, Ordinances, Acts,
> Constitutions, and Officers, from time to time, as shall be thought most meet
> and convenient for the general Good of the Colony; unto which we promise
> all due Submission and Obedience. (Mayflower Compact 1620)

Under the patent they had from the Virginia Company, the Pilgrims would
have been given a grant to a specific amount of land upon arrival. Recognizing

their somewhat shaky possession of the Plymouth Plantation, the residents applied in 1621 for a new patent.

By then, the Council for New England had received a royal charter to fish, trade, and establish plantations in the area north of 40 degrees latitude, and extending to 48 degrees (which is roughly the area between New York in the south and New Brunswick and Nova Scotia in the north), extending from sea to sea. The Council granted Plymouth a new patent, which remained in place until a later one, called the Old Charter, was granted in 1630. The Old Charter defined the boundaries of what now was a full-fledged colony that incorporated several townships in the Cape Cod area.

In the meantime, a new trading company was proposed by the Reverend John White of Dorchester, England, which was to have two purposes: to establish a permanent fishing colony and to serve the religious needs of the New World (Andrews 1964: 349). After several years of negotiations, the New England Company was organized in 1628 as a voluntary, unincorporated joint-stock company. With a land grant from the Council for New England, the company sent a ship to buttress a smaller settlement that had been previously established by the Dorchester members of the group, with the hope of enlarging the colony. However, a possible flaw in its land grant limited settlement. Moreover, the Council for New England had ceased to be an actively functioning entity. As a result, the stockholders decided to bypass the Council and seek a royal charter that would guarantee their right to the land. On March 4, 1629, the Massachusetts Bay Company was incorporated, in effect with control over the same territory that had earlier been granted to the Council for New England.[1]

The Massachusetts Bay Charter itself generally followed the same provisions as those assigned to the Virginia Company. In addition to setting out the mercantile purposes and governance structure for the company, the charter spelled out its religious purposes:

> whereby our said People, Inhabitants there, may be soe religiously, peaceablie, and civilly governed, as their good Life and orderlie Conversacon, maie wynn and incite the Natives of Country, to the Knowledg and Obedience of the onlie true God and Saulor of Mankinde, and the Christian Fayth, which in our Royall Intencon, and the Adventurers free Profession, is the principall Ende of this Plantacion. (Charter of Massachusetts Bay 1629)

The Massachusetts Bay Company intended to establish a colony that would restore the Church to its origins – based in Scripture and governed by those who had been saved. The first act to ensure the religious nature of the colony was to bring the Charter and, therefore, the operation of the company to Massachusetts. This immediatley distinguished the Massachusetts Bay Company from the Virginia Company, whose leadership remained in England. The

---

[1] Some members of the Council disputed the Massachusetts Bay Company's claim, leading to a series of challenges that eventually were decided in favor of the new company.

Puritan leadership feared that if the Massachusetts Bay Company stayed in England and remained open to new stock purchases, they might lose control. Moving the charter and the company to Massachusetts ensured that its leadership would remain Puritan (Andrews 1964: 390).

In Massachusetts Bay, there would be no separation between religion and the State. In his "Modell of Christian Charity," issued en route to Massachusetts, John Winthrop (1630), who was to become governor of the colony, explained:

> We are entered into covenant with Him for this work. We have taken out a commission. The Lord hath given us leave to draw our own articles. We have professed to enterprise these and those accounts, upon these and those ends. We have hereupon besought Him of favor and blessing. Now if the Lord shall please to hear us, and bring us in peace to the place we desire, then hath He ratified this covenant and sealed our commission, and will expect a strict performance of the articles contained in it; but if we shall neglect the observation of these articles which are the ends we have propounded, and, dissembling with our God, shall fall to embrace this present world and prosecute our carnal intentions, seeking great things for ourselves and our posterity, the Lord will surely break out in wrath against us, and be revenged of such a people, and make us know the price of the breach of such a covenant.

Only church members could enter into this covenant. Candidates for church membership gave a public testament to their faith, at which time they would be admitted to membership if the church members agreed with the sincerity of the testimony. The member would agree to abide by the terms of the covenant that had established the church. Each church was self-governing, with its own pastor elected and ordained by the church members. Each church also had a teacher, who was responsible for instructing members on matters of doctrine, and church elders and deacons to attend to the administration of the church.

In May 1631, the General Court determined that only church members could be freemen of the colony, thereby limiting the franchise to those men who had been judged sincere in their testament of faith. Church members were not automatically given the franchise. They had to submit to an oath that they freely acknowledge themselves to be "subject to the government." Andrews suggests that there were four categories of colonists in Massachusetts. First were the freemen, who alone could vote for governor, magistrates, and deputies. He estimated that freemen were a minority in each town and in the colony as a whole. Second were church members who did not become freemen. He estimates that number to be small as well. Third were those who were neither church members nor freemen but took an oath of fidelity to the colony and shared its aims; this was likely the largest group. Fourth were those who did not take an oath of fidelity; they were, in Andrews words, "in the colony but not of it" (Andrews 1964: 437).

Populating the Colony

The settlement of the Massachusetts Bay Colony is often called "the Great Migration." By 1642, when the Great Migration ended, about 21,000 men, women and children had migrated to New England (Cressy 1987: 63). About 13,000 came to Massachusetts during the 1630s (Crouse 1932: 4). In contrast to Virginia, most migrants to New England came as part of family groups. Anderson's (1993) analysis of 693 emigrants to Massachusetts showed that nearly nine out of ten traveled in family groups. Although men still predominated, as they did in Virginia, the ratio of men to women was much more equal in Massachusetts than in the southern colony. Anderson (1993) found that 43 percent of her sample were women. According to Cressy's (1987: 63) review of ship records, of those whose age and sex were recorded, "30 per cent were men aged eighteen and over, 21 per cent were adult women, 25 per cent were boys aged less than eighteen, and 24 per cent were young girls." The Massachusetts emigrants were younger, on average, than the English as a whole. Only 4 percent of Anderson's (1993) sample was 60+ years of age, whereas more than 8 percent of the overall English population was in this category. Given the difficulties of the journey to the New World, the relative absence of the elderly is not surprising. The heads of households were generally in their thirties, indicating that the decision to migrate was made by mature persons who brought with them their children and younger servants.

The occupational structure of the emigrants showed few yeomen (independent farmers who were freeholders); most of the 25 percent of the emigrants who worked in agriculture were husbandmen (poorer farmers) (Cressy 1987: 67). More than 50 percent of the emigrants were artisans of some type. Those working in the depressed textile industry represented 20–25 percent of the emigrants in Cressy's sample (1987: 66) and 25 percent in Anderson's (1993: 224), most of whom were tailors or weavers. About 20 percent of Cressy's (1987) sample were servants. More than half of Anderson's (1993) sample of families brought servants. Would-be migrants could find sponsors for their voyage by agreeing to be servants. Unlike in Virginia, however, such arrangements did not involve indenture for a set period of time.

As was true for Virginia, a combination of push-and-pull factors influenced the decision to emigrate to Massachusetts. As Cressy (1987: 85) explains, "Although the purpose of the colony was decidedly religious, its people were varied in their motives and characters." Certainly, economic pressures at home constituted an important reason why some chose to migrate. England suffered a series of poor harvests in the late 1620s and early 1630s, and the textile industry faced collapse and transition (Breen and Foster 1973a:203–4). The economic losses were especially acute in the southeastern part of the country, where Puritans dominated. A delegation from Braintree in the county of Essex (names that would be brought to Massachusetts with the emigrants) reported that the textile crisis affected the employment of 30,000 people. Even John Winthrop was motivated in part by economics. He was in debt and would have had to sell his land to repay it. Yet, the emigrants to Massachusetts were not, by and large, poor. Even those who came from the areas hit hardest by the textile crisis tended to be from areas that were well ahead in transitioning toward a new clothing industry that would prove to be highly profitable (Breen and Foster 1973a:203). Rather, as Anderson (1993: 36) points out, "the Great Migration uprooted relatively prosperous families with no evident economic reason to depart for the wilderness they knew awaited them."

If economics were an important but insufficient factor in the Great Migration, religion was the principal motivator. The religious motivations were themselves complex. According to Cressy (1987: 87), "the principal elements include alarm at the religious situation in England, hope for a purer religious environment across the ocean and a desire to participate in the fulfilling of the Scripture." The Great Migration was fundamentally a migration of Puritans, nonconformists who were concerned that the Church of England was straying away from a strict Protestant belief system. More interested in reforming the Church of England than in separating from it (unlike the Pilgrims), the Puritans agreed with the basic Protestant tenet that "men were saved by their faith, not by their deeds" (Miller and Johnson 1963: 9). The Puritans believed that because of Original Sin, man was prone to evil, and would overcome it only by submitting to Scripture as a testament of faith and, if God willed it, undergoing a conversion. Such conversion was possible because God had entered into a covenant with man, laying out the terms and conditions for salvation (Miller and Johnson 1963: 58). At the foundation was faith in the Bible, which, they claimed, was the supreme law and included guidance on all matters religious and secular.

The Puritans faulted the Church of England for "an attachment to man-made forms with no power to convert and hold a people" (Bozeman 1988: 77). In the Bible, they found support for a Congregationalist form of religious organization. In the Congregational model, membership in the church was limited to those who could demonstrate that they had undergone conversion and had been saved. The church members would, in turn, choose their minister. This contrasted sharply with the hierarchical Church of England, whose authorities emanated from the King and his bishops, not from the church members.

Of particular concern to the Puritans were the policies implemented by William Laud, who became Archbishop of Canterbury, the most important figure in the Church of England. Laud defended the Church of England's episcopal structures and introduced uniform rituals that the Puritans opposed. As Bozeman (1988: 103) explains, the Laudians "wished to add further ornament and to make the whole more imposing, complex, colorful and magnificent," which bore down "irreconcilably upon Puritan sensitivity."

With the support of Charles I, Laud took action to suppress the Puritans. John Winthrop, in describing his grievances, referred to "the suspension and silenceing of many . . . ministers for not conformitie in some poynts of ceremonies and refuseinge subscription [as] directed by the late canons" (quoted in Bozeman 1998: 103). Edward Johnson, who emigrated in 1630, described this "sad condition" in England as the motivating factor in migration: "When England began to decline in religion, like luke-warme Laodicea, and instead of purging out Popery, a farther compliance was sought not onely in vaine Idolatrous Ceremonies, but also in prophaning the Sabbath, . . . Christ creates a New England to muster up the first of his Forces in" (Miller and Johnson 1963: 144).

Fear of divine retribution for the excesses of the Church of England was a frequently heard reason for migrating. In 1629, a year before he sailed for Massachusetts, Winthrop wrote to his wife, "I am verily perswaded, God will bringe some heauye Affliction upon this lande, and that speedylye." He was optimistic, though, that "If the Lord seeth it wilbe good for vs, he will prouide a shelter and a hidinge place for vs and ours" (Miller and Johnson 1963: 467). Migration would not just save the emigrants from harm; establishing a Godly haven in New England would save England itself. As Edward Johnson wrote of the first colonists in his 1650 history of New England, "for Englands sake they are going from England to pray without ceasing for England, O England! Thou shalt finde New England prayers prevailing with their God for thee" (Miller and Johnson 1963: 148).

Although most of the emigrants did not face personal harm for their beliefs, a number of Puritan ministers and laymen were fleeing the threat of persecution. For example, John Cotton had resisted such ritualistic ceremonies as sacramental kneeling at Communion in his church in Boston, Lincolnshire. He organized parishioners who agreed with him in a separate covenanted group. In 1632, he was summoned before Archbishop Laud and the Court of High Commission to explain his deviance from Church doctrine. Fearing suspension from the ministry and even imprisonment, Cotton went into hiding rather than appear before the ecclesiastical court. He then determined to emigrate to Massachusetts, where he could practice his religion in conformance with his beliefs.

Those who faced persecution and those who did not face specific harm but were concerned about the state of religious affairs in England did not come easily to the decision to emigrate. Cotton explained that he made the difficult decision only after determining that God had opened a door to survival and a new ministry in Massachusetts. Thomas Shepard, countering attacks from English Puritans that the Massachusetts colonists had deserted in the fight against Laudian excesses, wrote that it would have "been far more easie unto many of us to have suffered, then to have adventured hither upon the wildernesse sorrows wee expected to have met withal; though we must confesse the Lord hath sweetned it beyond our thoughts, and utmost expectations of prudent men" (Miller and Johnson 1963: 122). Most chose to emigrate to Massachusetts only after considerable prayer and consideration. John Sill determined not to "stir till he saw the Lord leading him, and be contented to be where He will have him" (quoted in Cressy 1987: 96).

Regardless of their own religious leanings or motivations, those who migrated to Massachusetts well knew that they were coming to a colony organized around a specific religious precept. The advertisements used to recruit colonists made clear the religious nature of the Massachusetts Bay Colony. Francis Higginson, who wrote one of the earliest pamphlets about the new colony, stated "that which is our greatest comfort... is, that we have here the true Religion and holy Ordinances of Almightie God taught among us: Thankes be to God, we have plentie of Preaching, and diligent Catechizing, with strickt and carefull exercise, and good and commendable orders to bring out People into a Christian conversation with whom we have to doe withal" (quoted in Anderson 1993: 38).

Those who shared these religious principles were welcomed into the colony, where they would become full members of a community of like believers. Immigration of true believers was encouraged by the leaders of the colony as a religious duty as well as an economic benefit that would help tame the wilderness. Much of the impetus for emigration was lost, however, when the English Civil War led to Puritan ascendancy in England. Emigration plummeted after 1640, triggering an economic crisis in Massachusetts. As Gottfried (1936: 657) wrote, "cut off from the migration and trade of England, even faced with the loss of its inhabitants, the Bay found itself drained of specie and in straitened circumstances." In response, efforts were made to develop local industries and new trade routes, drawing particularly on markets in other colonies for New England's lumber, fish, and furs. By 1648, New England's economy had recovered, but immigration remained at low levels for the rest of the century. Most of the colony's growth would come from births, not new immigrants.

Relations with the Native Population

Conversion of the Indians was a clear objective of the settlers of the Plymouth and Massachusetts colonies. The Massachusetts Bay Company charter (1629) specifies "the principall Ende of this Plantacion" was to "wynn and incite the Natives of [the] Country, to the Knowledg and Obedience of the onlie true God and Savior of Mankinde, and the Christian Fayth." John Eliot is the person most associated with missionary work in Massachusetts Bay. He arrived in the colony in 1631 and was appointed as teacher in the church in Roxbury. He learned the languages of the members of the Wampanaog Confederacy but it was not until 1646 that he began to preach to them in their own language. He translated the Bible into the local Indian dialect, publishing the New Testament in 1661 and the Old Testament in 1663 (Andrews 1964: 765).[2]

The small number who became "Praying Indians" formed "Praying Towns." The impetus for conversion was as much material as it was spiritual. By the time active proselytizing began, many of the native tribes had been decimated by diseases brought by the colonists and had lost much of their land. Moving

---

[2] A highly critical assessment of Eliot's role can be found in Jennings (1971).

into a praying town gave the converts access to material resources. In turn, the colony hoped to create a buffer between the settlers and unconverted Indians. The praying Indians did not always serve this purpose; some praying towns joined Metacom, chief of the Wampanoag Confederacy (known to the colonists as King Philip), in the 1675 uprising called King Philip's War.

Massachusetts was not, of course, the first colony in what is now the United States that was intent on converting the Indians. Well before the English colonized America, the Spanish set up missions with that same purpose. According to Bolton, one of the first serious scholars of the missions, the mission had a threefold purpose: "to realize the ideal of conversion, protection, and civilization" (quoted in Bannon 1979: 305). In Florida, the missions began with the settlement of St. Augustine in 1565, although there were few signs of success (Sturtevant 1962: 61). In New Mexico in 1589, ten Franciscans established the first missions. Arnade (1960) argues that the Florida missions never succeeded because they were too bound to the military mandate of the colony. There was too little economic activity in Florida to provide the Indians with any benefits from the European colonization or from proselytizing. The British later exploited this vulnerability, using firearms and cheap goods to incite Florida's Indians to attack the Spanish missions.

Massachusetts colonists obtained land from the Indians in a number of different ways. Some was expropriated by the colonists, who argued, as did Solomon Stoddard, that "the Indians made no use of it, but for Hunting" (Miller and Johnson 1963: 457). Other land was purchased, often for "a small Price for what we bought." The low price was justified because "had it continued in their hands, it would have been of little value. It is our dwelling on it, and our Improvements, that have made it to be of Worth" (Miller and Johnson 1963: 457). Some land was transferred to the colony through agreements made with Indian leaders. For example, in 1644, five sachems (tribal leaders) turned themselves, their subjects, and their land over to the colony in exchange for its protection.

Relations between colonists and Indians began amicably but deteriorated during the course of the seventeenth century. Certainly, the Plymouth Plantation benefited from good relations with the natives, as manifest in the now-mythic Thanksgiving celebration. A 1621 treaty between the Pilgrims and the Wampanoag tribe remained in force until after the death of the tribal leader, Massasoit, in 1660. In 1662, a new treaty was negotiated with Philip, now chief of the tribe. Under the pact, Philip accepted the authority of the Crown and promised not to sell land except to buyers approved by the colony. John Eliot also stepped up efforts to convert Philip and the Wampanoags, but he failed to make much progress. Over the course of the 1660s, however, relations deteriorated between the English settlers and the Indians. Rumors spread that the Indians were planning an uprising against the colonists. By the early 1670s, the rumors turned to fact. A combination of factors appeared to cause King Philip's War, including resentment of the conversion efforts, a new treaty that gave the colony the right to approve all land sales, and the growing realization that soon the colonists would be too strong in numbers to be defied (Rantlet 1988).

Relations with the Pequot had deteriorated several decades sooner, by the mid-1630s. The Pequot were most prominent in the Connecticut Valley, which was settled by Dutch and English colonists. In 1634, after a series of killings and retaliations, the Pequot tried to negotiate a treaty with Massachusetts Bay. The colony's demand that the Pequot hand over the killers of a colonist, pay a tribute, cede Connecticut lands, trade with the English, and agree to have disputes with their enemy, the Narragansett, mediated by the English, proved to be too much for the Pequot, who rejected the treaty. Negotiations continued until 1636, when the killing of colonist John Oldham and his crew prompted the colony to launch an attack against the Pequot. In late summer 1636, the Pequot counterattacked by laying siege to Fort Saybrook. Massachusetts Bay allied itself with the Narragansett and Mohegan tribes, and the Plymouth and Connecticut colonies joined the fight after Pequot attacks against settlers increased. The war culminated in an attack by the colonists on the Peqout forces in Mystic Fort. After fierce fighting, the colonists prevailed, burning eighty structures housing about 800 Pequot. Between 600 and 700 Pequot were killed and others were enslaved, ending the Pequot as a nation.

For Europeans who knew the horrors of the Thirty Years War, the atrocities committed against the Pequot did not seem heinous. The colonists saw themselves as fighting for their very survival, thereby justifying even the worst actions. As William Bradford described it, "It was a fearful sight to see them [Pequots] thus frying in the fire and the streams of blood quenching the same, and horrible was the stink and scent thereof; but the victory seemed a sweet sacrifice, and they gave the praise thereof to God, who had wrought so wonderfully for them, thus to enclose their enemies in their hands and give them so speedy a victory over so proud and insulting an enemy" (quoted in Drake 1997: 33). The colonists fought against King Philip with the same abandon, and upon victory executed the leaders and enslaved many of the followers. When the war ended, the colony passed laws that restricted the Indians to praying towns and mandated that they carry a magistrate's certificate attesting to their fealty to the colony if they traveled outside these towns (Pulsiper 2001: 437).

Drake (1997) contends that the enslavement of the Indians served the same purpose as the banishments that were reserved for the English colonists who threatened the viability of the colony. "Indians, too, posed a threat to the towns, yet because they already lived outside the bounds of English villages, they quite simply could not be banished. Slavery, a more rigidly enforced type of banishment, therefore more closely approximated the punitive action taken against errant English men and women in the colonies" (Drake 1997: 54). At the same time, the Indians offered a new labor source to a colony that had suffered losses during the war and had not yet received significant numbers of immigrants. Although Massachusetts differed from Virginia in many important respects, the two colonies shared the need for labor and a willingness to use slavery as a solution.

Exclusion and Deportation from Massachusetts

If Massachusetts welcomed newcomers who shared the beliefs of the majority, it proved far less accommodating to those who dissented from these beliefs. The leadership did its best to discourage nonbelievers from joining the colony. The literature advertising the colony focused on its religious mission. Although some of the advertisements glossed over the difficulties that faced newcomers in terms of climate and geography, most were honest in describing what a new settler would have to overcome. Those encouraging migration made clear that would-be colonists who sought "advancement of their estates" would do well to go elsewhere, while those who "aime at the propagation of the Gospell" would be welcomed (John White, quoted in Anderson 1993: 44). As Governor Thomas Dudley wrote, "if any come hether to plant for worldly ends that canne live well at home hee comits an errour of which he will soon repent him. But if for spirituall [ends] and that noe particular obstacle hinder his removeall, he may finde here what may well content him" (quoted in Anderson 1985: 374). With the exception of servants, who might have had little or no choice, it is likely that all but the most determined would have been deterred from emigrating unless they shared the religious beliefs of the colony's founders.

To ensure greater social harmony, the colony went beyond deterrence in determining who could emigrate to Massachusetts Bay. Prospective colonists were asked to demonstrate their good moral character before they were accepted. As Breen and Foster (1973b: 12–13) wrote, "Puritan villagers excluded anyone from their midst whom they believed endangered their way of life, and unwanted strangers were frequently 'warned out' when they failed to meet the community's standards."

The colony also applied sanctions against ships that brought undesirables to the colony. The Quakers were a particular focus of such attention. Shipmasters who brought Quakers or their writings to Massachusetts were subject to fines and required to transport these undesirables out of the colony (Pestana 1983: 324). Massachusetts also enacted laws, as early as 1645, which barred the admission of persons who were likely to become a drain on public coffers. In the eighteenth century, Massachusetts passed laws that prevented "the landing of the 'poor, vicious and infirm.'" These laws "required the master of each vessel to post a bond that towns receiving any 'lame, impotent, or infirm persons, incapable of maintaining themselves' . . . would not be charged with their support" (Baseler 1998: 71). Laws excluding admission of those who would be a public charge (to use some later terminology from U.S. immigration law) were needed because townships had an obligation to provide relief to those in need. Statutes thus excluded those who might pose a burden.

Colonists were also subject to social discipline. The Congregational churches in New England practiced a form of excommunication for deviant behavior.

After the sinner had been warned and counseled, the church could and would excommunicate the sinner, banning him or her from communion, if the disapproved behavior continued. However, sin was to be expected, and even those who had experienced conversion could backslide; excommunication was neither permanent nor did it mean complete banishment from the community.[3] More serious and longer-lasting punishment was applied when the very norms of the Puritan belief system were challenged. As Breen and Foster (1973b:10) note, the Congregational model was "flexible enough to accommodate moderate differences of opinion, faith still served as a useful test for detecting and expelling extremists, thereby precluding any prolonged clash over religious fundamentals."

Three cases proved to be the test of the Massachusetts model. Each resulted in the offender's banishment and, in the case of several Quakers, execution after they reentered the colony. The first case involved Roger Williams. Williams came to Massachusetts in 1631, having received his degree from Pembroke College, Cambridge University. He was chaplain to Sir William Masham in Essex County. A year after marrying in 1629, he and his wife left Essex for Massachusetts. He served as assistant pastor in Salem and became acting head of the church after the pastor's death. He was ordained pastor of the Salem church in 1635. However, he did not become a freeman and he did not take the oath of fidelity.

Williams dissented from the Puritan leadership of Massachusetts on a number of important issues. First, he had doubts about the validity of the Charter, which were expressed in a treatise sent to John Winthrop. Williams claimed that the King of England had no title to the land and so could not grant it to anyone, arguing that the colonists should instead purchase the land from the natives. His timing in raising questions about the Charter was unfortunate, because some of the leaders of the Council for New England were then seeking recall of the Massachusetts Bay charter and appointment of a royal governor.[4] Second, he questioned the authority of civil magistrates over ecclesiastical matters. He believed that the civil authorities had responsibility for the outward state of man but not for even the most serious religious offenses, including violations of the commandments. Third, Williams was an extreme Separatist. In addition to condemning the impure practices of the Church of England, Williams believed all Massachusetts church members should separate "in mind as well as body, from all associations and connections" with the Church of England and make a public declaration of their repentance for having had communion with their parish churches in England (Andrews 1964: 473). The other churches in

---

[3] For a more detailed discussion of excommunication, see Brown (1994: 531–66).

[4] Williams bought land for his Rhode Island colony from the Native Americans, but he also sought a charter. He made one trip to England in 1643, when he obtained the first charter, and another in 1651 in an effort to confirm the charter. He returned to Rhode Island before the charter was confirmed, which did not happen until Charles II issued a royal charter in 1663.

Massachusetts disagreed and condemned the separatist leanings of Williams's Salem church.

Disagreement came to a head over a land dispute. Other churches in Massachusetts had protested the Salem church's ordination of Williams as pastor Given the protest, the general court refused the town's request for assignment of the disputed land to the township. Williams sent letters to the churches of Massachusetts accusing the magistrates of "sundry heinous offenses" and called upon the Salem church to separate itself not only from the Church of England but also from the other churches in New England. In the meantime, the township was able to obtain ownership of the land and wished to lay the controversy to rest. Williams, protesting the decision to grant the land to the township, refused to attend the church or to have religious communion with his congregation, including his wife and children. In September 1635, the general court reacted to the letters that Williams had sent out during the conflict, asking the town's freemen for satisfaction. In October, the court ordered that "Roger Williams... shall depart out of this jurisdiction with six weekes now nexte ensuing... not to return any more without license from the court" (Williams and Davis 2008).

In his history of Massachusetts, Cotton Mather sites four reasons for Williams' banishment: separatism, denial of the validity of the patent, the power of the magistrates, and the refusal to take the oath of fealty (Andrews 1964: 472). He was not banished because of the idea for which Williams was most revered by later generations – his support for liberty of conscience. It was not until he had founded Rhode Island that these views became clear. In the *Tenets of Bloody Persecution*, Williams explained his views on religious liberty: "God requires not uniformity of religion to be enacted and enforced in any civil state. Such enforced uniformity sooner or later is the greatest occasion of civil war, of the ravishing of conscience, of persecution of Christ Jesus in his servants, and of the hypocrisy and destruction of millions of souls" (Williams and Davis 2008: 87). These views led him to his equally famous views on separation of church and state: "So that magistrates, as magistrates, have no power of setting up the form of church government, electing church officers, punishing with church censures, but to see that the church does her duty herein. And on the other side, the churches as churches, have no power (though as members of the commonweal they may have power) of erecting or altering forms of civil government, electing of civil officers, inflicting civil punishments" (Williams and Davis:131–2). From Williams' point of view, this separation is needed mostly to protect religion from the state. It is only later that the principle applies equally in protecting the state from religion.

No sooner was the Williams controversy resolved than the more serious Antinomian controversy arose, with Anne Hutchinson and the Rev. John Wheelwright at its center. Hutchinson arrived in Boston in 1634 with her husband and 15 children. Followers of John Cotton, they became members of the Boston church where Cotton was teacher. Hutchinson's brother-in-law,

Wheelwright, arrived in 1636 and also became a member of the Boston church. Extending Cotton's teaching, Hutchinson and Wheelwright decried what they considered to be too great an emphasis on works instead of faith. Wheelwright is described by John Winthrop as inveighing against "such as maintain sanctification as evidence of justification . . . and calling them anti-Christs" (Miller and Johnson 1963: 132). The Massachusetts Puritans agreed that salvation came only through faith, but they also looked for signs of sanctification (that is, living in accordance with Biblical teachings) as evidence of a person's salvation (justification). Such signs were considered in determining whether to approve someone for church membership. Hutchinson and Wheelwright rejected this notion. They believed that outward manifestations of salvation meant nothing; only the presence of God within oneself counted. Moreover, they argued that those who were saved knew it by that very presence of God within them. Hutchinson went further in her trial and claimed that her actions were the result of revelation from God.

These doctrinal differences portended a serious challenge to the authority of the Puritan leadership. Hutchinson, Wheelwright, and their followers were branded "Antinomians," or persons who did not consider themselves subject to the law. If living in accordance with the law was no evidence of salvation, why should someone follow the law? This question threatened the very nature of the Puritan covenant-based community. The colony was based on compacts that defined both the secular and the sacred lives. If the individual could challenge the authority of these covenants by claiming divine revelation, order itself would be undermined. These views also challenged the authority of the ministers and magistrates, who derived their powers from the law and from their study of Scriptures, not from individual revelation. A contemporary, Edward Johnson, expressed his dismay when one of the Antinomians stated: "I had rather hear such a one that speakes from the mere motion of the spirit, without any study at all, then any of your learned Scollers, although they may be fuller of Scripture" (quoted in Miller and Johnson 1963: 15).

What made Wheelwright and Hutchinson particularly dangerous was the support they received from the newly elected governor, Harry Vane. Vane was a young man of about 24 who had only recently migrated to Massachusetts. His election in 1636 reflected continued dissatisfaction with John Winthrop, who had earlier held, and been removed from, the office of governor. Winthrop was elected deputy governor, however, possibly as a counterweight to Vane's youth. Winthrop described Vane as "a wise and godly gentleman" but also noted that Vane purported to "maintain a personal union with the Holy Ghost," which Winthrop considered a dangerous error (Miller and Johnson 1963: 129). As long as Vane was governor of Massachusetts Bay, he protected Wheelwright and Hutchinson. His term was short, however. The election in 1637 was highly contentious, necessitating a change in venue from Boston to Newtown (now Cambridge). Because Boston was the Antinomians' seat of power, the change of venue worked to Winthrop's favor; the election returned him to the governorship.

The change in secular authority allowed proceedings against Wheelwright and Hutchinson to move forward. Wheelwright had given a fiery sermon in Boston that denounced all whom he accused of walking in a covenant of works. This prompted the magistrates to put him on trial for sedition. He was convicted by a split court, but the sentence of banishment did not occur until after the election. In August 1638, a synod or assembly was called to address what was increasingly considered to be a religious and secular crisis. Twenty-five ministers and assorted magistrates met for twenty-four days. Winthrop tells us that "the erroneous opinions, which were spread in the country, were read, (being eighty in all); next the unwholesome expressions; then the scriptures abused" (Miller and Johnson 1963: 133). Some of the opinions were determined to be "blasphemous, others erroneous and all unsafe." Despite the findings of the synod, the Antinomians persisted in their views. In November, the general court convened, and on hearing that Wheelwright refused to refute his sermon or change his views, disenfranchised him and banished him from the colony.

Hutchinson was then put on trial. She was a charismatic figure who had assembled a following of her own. Not only did she have heretical views, in the eyes of the Puritan leadership, but she behaved in a manner unbecoming a woman. Winthrop reported that the court "charged her with diverse matters, as her keeping two public lectures every week in her house, whereto sixty or eighty persons did usually resort." She was also accused of "reproaching most of the ministers (viz., all except Mr. Cotton) for not preaching a covenant of free grace" and saying they were not able ministers. The court gave Hutchinson the opportunity to defend herself, which she did in the presence of 40 magistrates and most of the luminaries of Massachusetts, including Governor Winthrop and Deputy Governor Dudley and the Reverends Cotton, Eliot, and Shepard. Hutchinson held her own through a series of questions and accusations, but towards the end of the inquisition, she "vented her revelations," in Winthrop's words. Saying that her teachings came directly from revelation, Hutchinson gave the court its basis for convicting her of heresy. She too was excommunicated and banished from the colony. Hutchinson first removed herself and her family to Providence, Rhode Island, to join Roger Williams' new colony. Later, she moved to New York, where, after her husband's death, she and five of her children were killed in an Indian attack.

A third threat to the Puritan haven came from the Quakers, a radical sect in England that brought its beliefs to the colonies. The Quakers appeared to the Puritans to be an extreme form of antinomianism. They had been dubbed "Quakers" in derision of the outward manifestation of their spirituality; early adherents bore the label proudly. They believed that the Holy Spirit, the inner light, as the Quakers described it, resided in every individual. Through silent worship, the Quakers could come to know God and, they were so moved, could testify to their experience. Early Quakers often showed their relationship with God through their "shaking," as George Fox, the founder of the Society of Friends, called it. Although some Quakers gained a following as preachers of the faith, they held that there was no need for ministers to serve as intermediaries between the individual and God. As James Naylor (1653) wrote, "The new man worships a God at hand, where He dwells in His holy temple, and he knows Him by His own Word from His dwelling-place, and not by relation of others."

As did Williams and the Antinomians, the Quakers challenged both the religious and the civil norms of Massachusetts. The General Court asserted that the "doctrine of this sect of people is destructive to fundamentall trueths of religion" (Pestana 1993: 460). John Norton, who succeeded John Cotton in the Boston church, was commissioned to respond to the Quaker religious deviancy in a 1659 treatise that was largely designed to justify increasing intolerance of Quaker views. Calling the Quakers madmen, Norton wrote that "madmen acting according to their frantick passions are to be restrained with chaines, when they can not be restrained otherwise" (Miller and Johnson 1963: 11).

In addition to what the Puritans considered the Quakers' deviant religious views, Pestrano (1983: 342–48) lists a number of civil offenses committed by Quakers that threatened the Puritan way of life. Quakers were essentially egalitarian, as reflected in their speech (the use of the familiar "thee" rather than the formal "you"), in their dress (the refusal to doff their hats as a sign of respect), and in their mannerisms. They showed little respect for religious or civil authorities, and were not impressed by those the Puritans considered to be the Quakers' educational, social, or economic betters. The social origin of the early Quakers was in the lower economic class. Quakers who were servants and laborers claimed the right to preach the word of God, even to well-educated, ordained ministers. Many were women, who also spoke in public, often to other women, in the same way that had already posed a problem for Anne Hutchinson. The Quaker belief system was, in Pestrano's (1983) term, a great leveler, and in the leveling process it undermined Puritan patriarchal notions. The early Quakers who visited Massachusetts were also itinerants, traveling where their ministry took them and recognizing the authority of no township. For Puritans whose way of life was bound by convenant to church and town, such itinerancy was particularly problematic.

The Massachusetts leadership initially tried to stop Quakers from entering the colony. Increasingly, however, Quakers arrived in neighboring Rhode Island and then crossed into Massachusetts. Roger Williams took exception to the Quaker belief system,[5] but his commitment to religious liberty gave them a foothold in his colony. No supporters of religious liberty, the Massachusetts authorities took increasingly stronger steps to prevent the Quakers from spreading their beliefs or their way of life among the colony's residents. The colony tried whippings, fines, imprisonments, expulsions, and mutilations (Pestano 1983: 325), but the Quakers made a point of reentering Massachusetts to continue their preaching. Massachusetts then enacted legislation that made reentry after banishment a capital offense. Once more, banished Quakers returned to

[5] For a detailed discussion of Williams's views on the Quakers, see Lowenherz (1959: 157–65).

Massachusetts. Four of them, including a woman from Rhode Island, were hanged.

Conclusion

Williams, the Antinomians, and the Quakers threatened the Puritan orthodoxy in both civil and religious affairs. Initially welcomed to Massachusetts Bay because of their opposition to the Church of England's excesses, Williams, Hutchinson, and Wheelwright incurred the wrath of the colony's leaders for the same ideas that had made them suspect in England. By raising questions about the Charter, Williams threatened the very survival of the colony. His separatist views, grounded in his religious beliefs, also threatened the political well-being of the colony, because its enemies in England regularly accused Massachusetts of harboring opponents of the King and the official Church. By calling into question the magistrates' authority to intervene in religious matters, Williams sought to undermine the very basis of the City upon the Hill. All this, plus his refusal to take the oath of fealty, made banishment an appropriate punishment in the eyes of Massachusetts' Puritan leadership.

Similarly, the Antinomians and the Quakers posed a threat to the survival of the Puritan experiment. The City upon the Hill could only function under God's covenant if its inhabitants observed the laws set down by the higher power and as interpreted by its magistrates and ministers. Anne Hutchinson and the Quakers not only questioned the ministers' beliefs; they also laid claim to a personal relationship with God that overruled the ministers' authority. They compounded the offense by developing followings of their own, and in the case of Hutchinson and the female Quakers, by challenging the role of women in seventeenth-century life. It was clear to the Puritan leadership that if each person followed his or her personal revelation, chaos would ensue and the colony would collapse.

Banishment (what we would now call deportation) seemed an appropriate punishment to the Puritans. The leaders of Massachusetts were determined to preserve the Puritan religion and way of life, and they feared the introduction of beliefs that challenged their own. Although they welcomed immigrants who shared their views, and suffered economic loss when immigration all but ceased in the 1640s, the Puritans persistently tried to exclude nonbelievers (whether the beliefs in question were religious or civil). When these efforts failed, the Puritans banished those who challenged their norms and practices.

4

"The Seed of a Nation"

A different model of immigration developed in the middle colonies, particularly in Pennsylvania. Pennsylvania's founder, William Penn, actively sought immigrants from continental Europe to join the British Quakers, and offered them equal treatment and rights. Soon after he received the charter to the colony, Penn prophesied: "There may be room for such a Holy Experiment. For the nations want a precedent and my God will make it the seed of a nation. That an example may be set up to the nations. That we may do the thing that is truly wise and just."

Although like John Winthrop in his underscoring of the religious principles underlying the new colony, Penn differed significantly from Winthrop and the other Massachusetts leaders in his commitment to religious freedom as a defining characteristic of Pennsylvania. Penn's Charter of Privileges (1701) provided for liberty of conscience, specifying that

> no Person or Persons, inhabiting in this Province or Territories, who shall confess and acknowledge One almighty God, the Creator, Upholder and Ruler of the World; and profess him or themselves obliged to live quietly under the Civil Government, shall be in any Case molested or prejudiced, in his or their Person or Estate, because of his or their conscientious Persuasion or Practice, nor be compelled to frequent or maintain any religious Worship, Place or Ministry, contrary to his or their Mind, or to do or suffer any other Act or Thing, contrary to their religious Persuasion.[1]

Penn went beyond mere tolerance for the religious views of others. He advertised the benefits of emigration to Pennsylvania among Moravians, Mennonites, and other religious minorities. Even a town as small as Reading, Pennsylvania, had residents from six different national backgrounds (including German, French, Dutch, Scottish, Irish, and English) by the mid-eighteenth century. The

---

[1] Penn did place limits on executive and legislative branch office holders, specifying that they must "profess to believe in Jesus Christ, the Savior of the World."

religious mix included members of the Lutheran, German Reformed, Anglican, Quaker, Catholic, Mennonite, Presbyterian, and Baptist churches, and there were also a number of Jews (Becker 1982).

This chapter discusses the roots of the Pennsylvania model of immigration in Penn's Quaker beliefs and understanding of the role of government as well as in the economic and political realities of late-sixteenth-century Europe. The chapter also discusses the implications of the Pennsylvania model for social membership and the challenges that it presented, particularly in the integration of immigrants in a pluralistic society. It concludes with the reaction against German immigration, reflecting the first stated concerns about the assimilation of immigrants in a new society.

The Founding of Pennsylvania

Unlike the majority of seventeenth-century Quakers, William Penn came from upper-class roots. His father, Sir William Penn, Sr., was an admiral in the British Navy who fought under Oliver Cromwell, although he later incurred Cromwell's wrath by returning from an expedition in Jamaica without permission. He retired temporarily from the navy and moved his family to his estate in Ireland. Young William matriculated at Christ Church, Oxford University, at the age of sixteen but was expelled two years later for refusing to conform to regulations that he considered to be "empty shows and formalities that masqueraded as the religion of Christ" (quoted in Andrews 1964, vol. 2: 268). Sent to the continent by his worried father, William spent two years at the Huguenot college of Saumur in Anjou, France. On his return, he studied law at Lincoln's Inn and then went back to Ireland to run his father's estate. On the restoration of the monarchy in 1660, the elder Penn reentered the navy and resumed his position as an admiral under the Duke of York, Charles II's brother, James.

William was exposed to Quaker teachings at an early age, but became an actively practicing Friend only in the 1660s. By then, the fanaticism of the first generation of Quakers – those who had tested the Puritan order in Massachusetts with their lives – had waned, but opposition to Quakerism as heresy still prevailed. Penn was imprisoned for his beliefs despite his father's high position and close personal friendship with the Duke of York and the King.

While in prison, Penn articulated his own religious doctrines, most clearly in *No Cross, No Crown*, written in 1669 and later revised and published in a more complete version in 1682. Penn (1807: 29) defines the way to salvation as "spiritual, that is, an inward submission of the soul to the will of God as it is manifested by the light of Christ in the consciences of men; the way of taking up the cross is an entire resignation of soul to the discoveries and requirings of it." Arguing that outward worship and ceremony were not the way to God, Penn called on people to become "acquainted with God as a spirit, consider him, and worship him as such" (Penn 1807: 49).

Much of the second part of the treatise focuses on pride and the related faults of avarice and covetousness, as the source of evil, explaining why Quakers eschewed symbols of pride, such as luxurious apparel or formal patterns of speech. Curbing pride and avarice are not just religious values in Penn's mind. "The temperance I plead for is not only religiously but politically good; 'tis the interest of good government to curb and rebuke excesses; it prevents many mischiefs; luxury brings effeminacy, laziness, poverty, and misery, but temperance preserves the land" (Penn 1807: 223). Penn then presents a utopian vision of a world in which temperance prevails: "if the money which is expended in every parish in vain fashions could be collected in a public stock, there might be reparation to the broken tenants, work-houses for the able, and almshouses for the aged and impotent. Then should we have no beggars in the land, the cry of the widow and the orphan would cease, nay, the exchequer's needs, on just emergencies, might be supplied by such a bank: it would be a noble example of gravity and temperance to foreign states, and an unspeakable benefit to ourselves at home" (Penn 1807: 225).

Penn began to determine how to put his theories into practice in the New World as a series of new laws in England put the Quakers at greater risk of prosecution and persecution. The Conventicle Act of 1664 forbade groups of five or more persons to meet to worship except through the Church of England. Aimed at all nonconformist religions, it was applied particularly harshly to the Quakers, who refused to meet secretly. Charles II, and his successor James II, issued royal declarations that would have suspended enforcement of the Conventicle Act, but Parliament forced them to back down, believing that the true purpose was to support the restoration of the Catholic Church.

Penn himself was prosecuted a number of times. His most famous trial, in 1670, ended in acquittal by the jury, which the presiding judge, Sir Samuel Starling, overruled. Penn was sent to prison, but the jury brought an action of habeas corpus against the judge in the Court of Common Pleas. The judgment, rendered by the chief justice, established the fundamental principle that jury verdicts would be respected even if the judge disagreed with them. However, the prosecutions of Quakers did not abate. In fact, beginning in 1679, the penalties against the Quakers and other nonconformist churches increased, making removal to the colonies even more attractive.

Penn's interest in the Americas was long-standing. His father had been in the West Indies when he served under Cromwell. Penn also followed closely the missionary trips of fellow Friends, such as George Fox. In 1674, he became the trustee of Edward Byllinge's property, which included a share in the colony of West Jersey. (What is now New Jersey was divided into West Jersey and East Jersey until 1702.) Penn drew up the constitution of West Jersey and helped ensure that it would welcome Quakers. The constitution included liberty of conscience and placed the rights of the people above those of any proprietor or sovereign authority. It made clear that "no men, nor number of men upon earth, hath power or authority to rule over men's consciences in religious matters, therefore it is consented, agreed and ordained, that no person or persons whatsoever within the said Province, at any time or times hereafter, shall be any ways upon any pretence whatsoever, called in question, or in the least punished or hurt, either in person, estate, or privilege, for the sake of his opinion, judgment, faith or worship towards God in matters of religion" (Charter of West New Jersey 1676). Some of the ideas derived from his earlier study of English law, and others from his experiences traveling in Europe, particularly in Holland, where the Quakers were generally well treated.

Penn considered West Jersey and the other colonies that welcomed Quakers to be useful but insufficient responses to the plight of the Friends. He resolved to establish his own colony and would give full expression to his beliefs. In 1680, he petitioned Charles II for a charter to the territory that lay west of New Jersey and north of Maryland. He grounded his claim of £16,000 against the exchequer in the debt owed his father (the elder Penn had advanced money from his own funds to the navy, and there were also unpaid wages from the time of his service in the navy). Penn's timing was propitious because a policy limiting grants of new proprietorships in the colonies had not yet gone into effect. The petition was carefully reviewed by Charles's advisors, who had been advocating centralization of the existing colonies into royal ones. After some months, the decision was made to grant the proprietorship.

In March 1681, Penn's charter was issued. Having learned from experience that tensions could easily arise if proprietors were granted too much authority with respect to either the Crown or the residents of the colony, the charter invested in Penn the right to determine the form of government and the distribution of land, but he could make laws only with the advice, assent, and approbation of the freemen in assembly. Other restrictions on Penn's authority were linked to the colony's relationship to the crown. The proprietorship was required to follow certain laws of Parliament on navigation and trade, to keep an agent in London, to admit customs officers to collect duty, to send all laws enacted in the colony to the King for what was in effect a veto, and to allow a right of appeal to the King of all judgments of the provincial courts. The King agreed not to impose taxes on the colony except with the consent of the proprietor, governor, or assembly, or, in a phrase that held import only in the years just before the American Revolution, by act of Parliament. The charter also specified that if twenty people petitioned for an Anglican minister, one should be sent, thereby giving the Church of England a foothold in the Quaker colony (Charter for the Province of Pennsylvania 1681).

In 1682, Penn laid out his understanding of the role of government, establishing "the divine right of government beyond exception, and that for two ends: first, to terrify evil doers: secondly, to cherish those that do well; which gives government a life beyond corruption, and makes it as durable in the world, as good men shall be" (Penn 1682). The government itself would "consist of the Governor and freemen of the said province, in form of a provincial Council and General Assembly, by whom all laws shall lie made, officers chosen, and public affairs transacted." The 1682 *Frame of Government of Pennsylvania* specified seventy members of the provincial Council and Assembly, but in 1683, the number of Council members was reduced to eighteen, three from each county, and the number of assembly members to thirty-six. The term of office for the provincial council was a staggered one, with one-third coming up for election each year. The governor was presumed to be Penn and his successors. The governor and provincial council would propose legislation; the Assembly would determine if the legislation would be adopted. The Council and Assembly were to be elected by the freemen. Freemen held at least 50 acres of land or paid scot and lot, a form of taxation.

The *Frame of Government* granted liberty of conscience to all who professed belief in a Creator: "That all persons living in this province, who confess and acknowledge the one Almighty and eternal God, to be the Creator, Upholder and Ruler of the world; and that hold themselves obliged in conscience to live peaceably and justly in civil society, shall, in no ways, be molested or prejudiced for their religious persuasion, or practice, in matters of faith and worship, nor shall they be compelled, at any time, to frequent or maintain any religious worship, place or ministry whatever" (Penn 1682).

In the immediate aftermath of the Glorious Revolution (which ousted James II and brought his daughter Mary and her husband William of Orange to the throne), Penn lost his charter and the colony was put under royal rule. Penn's charter was restored in 1694. However, the period of royal government prompted the Assembly to resist the restriction of their powers contained in the *Frame of Government*. From the beginning, members of the Assembly had chafed at the restrictions on their right to introduce legislation. In 1688, the Assembly had obtained the right to amend legislation proposed by the Council, and in 1696 it gained the right to introduce legislation. When Penn returned to the colony in 1699, the Assembly demanded a new frame of government; this, the Charter of Privileges, was adopted in 1701. The Council was eliminated, leaving the Assembly as a unicameral legislature. The governor still held veto power, but the Assembly clearly became the most important governmental body.

Peopling the Colony

After he received the 1681 charter, Penn set out to publicize the new colony, find investors, and recruit willing emigrants. He published two tracts, "Some Account of the Province of Pennsylvania in America," and an abridged broadside, "A Brief Account of the Province of Pennsylvania." Another seven advertising pamphlets followed in the next few years. Penn circulated these widely in England, Ireland, Scotland, Wales, and Holland. Some of the tracts were translated into Dutch and German and circulated throughout the Rhineland (Dunn 1983: 323). Although his principal audience was the Quakers, his most-hoped-for colonists, Penn directed his recruitment broadly.

Penn was in financial difficulties at this time and so his first aim was to sell land in the new colony. He advertised the availability of land at two and a half shillings per acre, which was below the cost of land in England. He sold the land in large plots of 1,000 acres as well as smaller lots of 250 and 500 acres. Those who bought in the early period of investment would also receive lots in Philadelphia. To ensure a continuing income, Penn required land purchasers to pay an annual quit rent of one shilling per hundred acres. He also allowed those who could not afford to purchase land to rent it from him. The land records indicate that "about 589 persons... bought 715,000 acres of Pennsylvania land from Penn between July 1681 and March 1685" (Dunn 1983: 325). Despite this success, Penn was unable to extricate himself from debt – the cost of establishing and managing the province exceeded the revenue from land sales. The quit rents were seldom paid, so he did not have the continuing source of income that he expected. When he was unable to repay his debt to his main land agent, Penn found himself in debtor's prison and was forced to borrow more money to repay the agent's family (Dunn 1983).

Penn appointed land agents through the British Isles and in Amsterdam. Although the majority of the early land purchasers were English, Pennsylvania's population was more diverse than was true of the earlier colonies. Early Pennsylvania settlers generally came from parts of Britain that did not already have connections to colonies. For example, Scottish Quakers tended to emigrate to New Jersey, while Welsh Quakers took advantage of the opportunity to emigrate to Pennsylvania where they were able to settle in close proximity in what was called the Welsh Tract. Penn granted 30,000 acres to Quakers from six Welsh counties, later increasing the area to 50,000 acres. Most arrived in 1681 and 1682, settling in what is now called the Main Line, after the Pennsylvania Railroad that was built through the Welsh Tract in the nineteenth century. The townships of Haverford, Radner, Bala Cynwyd, and others carry the place names of towns in Wales that the immigrants had left. The Welsh Tract as a political entity was short-lived, however, as the province established county and township governments that overrode its influence.

The colony grew rapidly, mostly by immigration. In Philadelphia, birth rates were low and death rates were high until about 1720, limiting natural growth (Klepp 1989: 94). With immigration, the city grew, and the countryside grew even more rapidly. By 1690, there were an estimated 8,800 residents of southeastern Pennsylvania, of whom more than 23 percent lived in Philadelphia. By 1700, the total had grown to 21,000, of which only 11 percent lived in Philadelphia. During the 1690s, seven new townships had been established (Klepp 1989: 95).

The new province also incorporated what is now Delaware into its territory, creating what was known as the lower three counties. These counties gave Penn access to the Chesapeake Bay and therefore to the ocean. Much of the area had been settled by Dutch, Swedish, and Finnish immigrants, who now found themselves to be under the authority of the English. Penn's claim to the counties was unclear. Both the Duke of York, the brother of the King, and Lord Baltimore, the proprietor of Maryland, laid claim to it. The Duke of York argued that the Dutch had controlled the area when they were defeated in 1664, and that when the Dutch gave up their land to the English, he gained it along with the more valuable New York. Baltimore had been selling land in these counties prior to Penn's interest. Penn convinced York to lease the land to him. The deal remained controversial, however, and Delaware was established as a separate royal colony in 1703.

In the meantime, Pennsylvania needed to address the situation of the foreigners who had been living in the Delaware counties.[2] Although those who came from areas under the authority of the King of England (including Wales, Scotland, and Ireland) were clearly citizens with all the rights that entailed, the Dutch, Swedes, and Finns in Delaware were not clearly citizens, and nor would be any newcomers recruited by Penn from Holland or Germany.

The 1683 *Frame of Government* addressed that issue, setting out the rights of "aliens" in a backhanded way by describing the rights of the families of those who died before they were naturalized: "And, for the satisfaction and encouragement of all aliens, I do give and grant, that, if any alien, who is, or shall be a purchaser, or who doth, or shall, inhabit in this province or territories thereof, shall decease at any time before he can well be naturalized, his right and interest therein shall notwithstanding descend to his wife and children, or other his relations, be he testate, or intestate, according to the laws of this province or territories thereof, in such cases provided, in as free and ample manner, to all intents and purposes, as if the said alien had been naturalized" (Penn 1683). The first Assembly passed legislation to naturalize all of the non-British residents who had been living within the territory covered by the Charter (Baseler 1998: 61).

The process of naturalization was similar to that which was used in England,[3] with the exception that one could affirm allegiance if oath-taking was against one's religion – as it was with the Quakers. The applicants affirmed that they "doe Solemnly promise to keep faith and alleigiance to ye king of

---

[2] In this respect, Pennsylvania followed the same path as New York. When the English achieved victory over the Dutch in 1664 and obtained control of New Amsterdam, they inherited a population of about 1,500, not including about 375 slaves and black freemen. About 250 adult men took an oath of allegiance to the English in October 1664, representing most of the adult male population. The great majority were Dutch, but New Amsterdam had also been home to small numbers of French and Jewish colonists. Some of the original settlers remained in New York, and others emigrated back to Holland or to other colonies. In the meantime, English immigration began. The Dutch continued to outnumber the English, though, through much of the remainder of the century. In 1703, the Dutch accounted for 52 percent of the white adult male population of New York City and the English 36 percent. The French, who had accounted for only 7 percent of the population in 1664–5, and an even lower 3 percent in 1676–7, accounted for 11 percent in 1703 (Goodfriend 1992: 62). During the eighteenth century, most of the immigration was from the British Islands, with Scots, Scots-Irish, and Irish newcomers joining the English (Goodfriend 1992: 135). Unlike Pennsylvania, New York became more diverse because of British immigration and, to a lesser extent, French immigration, adding to its original Dutch settlers.

[3] Pennsylvania was not the only colony with naturalization provisions. Maryland claims to have had the first naturalization law in 1666. Pennsylvania was the first colony actively to recruit settlers from outside the British Islands, however, making its naturalization provisions much more important.

England & his heirs and Successors: fidelity and Lawfull obedience to William Penn Proprietary & Governor: of the Province of Pensiluania and its Territorys and to his heirs & Successors" (New Castle 1935). The affirmation of allegiance was made in county courts. A fee of twenty shillings could be charged, and a certificate of naturalization would be issued.

In 1700, a new naturalization law gave the governor the authority to determine "any alien, aliens, or foreigners being already settled or inhabiting within this government, or shall hereafter come to settle, plant or reside therein, having first given his or their solemn engagement or declaration to be true and faithful to the King as sovereign, and to the proprietor and governor of this province.... to be to all intents and purposes fully and completely naturalized" (Carpenter 1904). The law was overturned, however, by the crown, which held that proprietors did not have the right to naturalize foreigners (Carpenter 1904). The colonies could pass legislation setting out the rights of foreigners within their own territories, a form of denizenship (Baseler 1998). The province so acted through private acts, sometimes including a large number of applicants in one law. These laws were not common during this period, however, despite the large number of foreign residents. Between 1709 and 1773, only thirteen private bills for about 575 people were passed (Hoyt 1952: 249). In 1740, the British Parliament enacted legislation to make a uniform naturalization provision for the colonies, enabling naturalized citizens to be recognized as such in other colonies. The 1740 Act provided for naturalization of non-Catholic aliens who had resided for seven years in any colony, received the sacrament in any Protestant church, swore allegiance to the King, and professed belief in Christianity. In an especially liberal act, Jews and Quakers were exempt from some of these requirements (Baseler 1989: 62).

The recruitment of foreigners had its largest payoff in the immigration of Germans to Pennsylvania. Wockek (1989) estimates that more than 100,000 German-speaking immigrants came to North America between 1682 and 1789, with about three-quarters landing in Pennsylvania. Fogelman's estimate is somewhat lower, at 84,500. Wockek (1989: 129) describes the origins of the German-speaking immigrants: "The Palatinate, Wirttemberg, and Hesse provided a steady supply of settlers throughout the period; but as the flow of migrants increased, most Protestant areas in southwestern Germany, including the Swiss cantons of Basel, Bern, and Zurich as well as Alsace and Lorraine, and some territories in northwestern Germany contributed to the migration stream." Most Germans traveled in family units, often with others from their same village.

Quakers in Rotterdam developed a transportation system that enabled emigration from these areas at relatively low cost. What began as a slow trickle turned into large-scale migration in the 1730s. German merchants in Pennsylvania advanced credit to prospective migrants to pay for their transport. Depending on the number traveling and the amount of credit required, the immigrants would agree to a number of years of indenture. This process came to be known as the redemptioner system. As Wokeck (1989: 131) recounts, the migration system became self-sustaining: "Crucially, German settlers became willing to extend their support to strangers of their own language and general cultural background whose passage debts they redeemed in exchange for labor." The indenture itself was not as harsh as that practiced in the southern colonies, but overcrowded ships caused many to die on route. In 1738, the worst year, the death rate approached 35 percent, even higher than on slave ships.

German immigration had its ebbs and flows until the Seven Years War (1756–1763) limited transatlantic crossings. When the war ended, the pattern of migration changed, with a higher number of single immigrants and a larger proportion of indentured servants (Wokeck 1989; Fogelman 1992).

The patterns of migration are observable because foreign settlers were required to register. White males over the age of sixteen had to swear or affirm their allegiance to Pennsylvania and abjure prior allegiances. The ships upon which they arrived were required to maintain lists of their names, a practice that was common for the German immigrants who arrived in Philadelphia.

An analysis of a small set of immigrants from Baden-Durlach provides more detail about their origins. Baden-Durlach was ruled by a margrave, and most residents were in a nominal state of serfdom. Those in rural areas required the permission of the margrave before they could be released from their obligations and be able to emigrate. According to Haberlein (1993), "population growth, inheritance practices, wars, natural disasters, high taxes and mounting debts reduced a large proportion of the rural population to the status of marginal landowners." Most emigrated as part of families, and, on average, they were mature and poor. Those who emigrated in the 1730s tended to be better off economically than those who emigrated later, perhaps reflecting the growth in the indenture system for paying transport.

Migration patterns varied over the course of the first half of the eighteenth century, with events in Europe, such as the War of Austrian Succession, determining the flow of immigrants. Most settled in southeastern Pennsylvania in Lancaster or Berks counties. Those who immigrated in the 1730s tended to be landowners by the end of the 1750s. Those who immigrated in the 1750s were less likely to become landowners, again perhaps reflecting their lower status in Germany. In addition, the price of land had increased as the population rose and land availability declined.

The German colonists, along with the growing British immigration, brought religious diversity to Pennsylvania. By the time of the American Revolution, only 15.3 percent of Pennsylvania's church membership was Quaker, a smaller proportion than could be found in New Jersey, Delaware, and North Carolina (Stark and Finke 1988: 47). The largest religious group was Presbyterian (27.9 percent), reflecting the steady migration of Scotch-Irish to the colony during the eighteenth century. Members of the German Reformed Church also outnumbered the Quakers, at 17.6 percent. Lutheran (9.7 percent) and Dutch Reformed (8.6 percent) churches represented smaller but sizable populations. Anglicans,

Baptists, Mennonites, and Moravians rounded out the religious composition. Taken together, the German and Dutch denominations accounted for almost 40 percent of church membership in Pennsylvania. This distribution marked a distinct difference between Pennsylvania and Massachusetts or Virginia. In Massachusetts, more than 70 percent of church members were Congregational. In Virginia, almost the entire population was divided among Anglicans, Baptists, and Presbyterians, in that order. Pennsylvania resembled the other Middle Colonies. Only New York, with its large number of Dutch Reformed congregations, showed a sizable proportion of non-British denominations.

Religious minorities in Germany and Switzerland also emigrated. Persecution of Anabaptists was extreme during the late seventeenth and early eighteenth centuries. The Mennonites in the Palatinate were particularly affected (Wokeck 1999: 15). Although they formed only a small proportion of the population, the members of the so-called peace churches became an important part of the Pennsylvania religious landscape. In addition to the Quakers, who had adopted pacifism as a fundamental part of their belief system, Mennonites, Brethren, and Moravians believed in pacifism. Although the German-speaking groups differed among themselves and with the Quakers on other core doctrines (for example, on the role of the sacraments, particularly baptism),[4] they tended to align with each other in opposing the colony's involvement in any conflict.

Not all of the immigrants came to Pennsylvania voluntarily. The first slaves came to Pennsylvania in 1684. By 1710, as much as 27 percent of Philadelphia's population was slaves (Soderland 1989: 147). The proportion declined quickly as more European settlers came to the city, but increased again during the Seven Years War, when immigration from Europe was curtailed. Some of the slaves were brought by settlers who had originally lived in the West Indies or the southern colonies, but slave ships also brought human cargo for sale.

The Quakers were not opposed to slave ownership at this time; Quakers themselves were slaveowners. George Fox had preached that slaves should be allowed to attend religious meetings and to be educated, but he did not speak of ending slavery as an institution. Yet Quakers were seen to present a danger in southern slave colonies and statutes were enacted making it illegal for slaves to assemble. In 1693, the Philadelphia Yearly Meeting of the Society of Friends recommended that Quakers not purchase slaves, but no penalties accrued to those who did. In 1715, the Yearly Meeting advised against the slave trade. Prominent eighteenth-century Quakers took a stronger stand against slavery. John Woolman, one of the most revered member of the Society of Friends, visited slaveowners, wrote treatises against slavery, and preached about why slavery should end (Woolman 1994: 93). In the 1760s and 1770s,

---

[4] In simplified terms, the Quakers did not perform any of the sacraments, the Mennonites practiced adult baptism, and the Brethren adopted not only adult baptism but also immersion.

the Yearly Meetings in a number of colonies took further action, committing to disowning members who owned slaves. By the end of the eighteenth century, slave ownership was condemned in all Quaker meetings, including those in the southern states (Aptheker 1940).

Relations with the Native Population

Unlike the founders of Virginia and Massachusetts, William Penn did not think that conversion of the Indians was of high priority. As early as the 1640s, the Swedish Lutheran evangelist, John Campanius Holm, preached to the Indians and translated the Lutheran catechism into the Delaware Indians' language (Wallace 1956: 3). George Fox had encouraged Quakers to seek out the Indians, saying "go and discourse with some of the Heathen Kings, desiring them to gather their Council and People together, that you may declare God's Everlasting Truth, and his Everlasting Way of Life and Salvation to them, knowing that Christ is the promise of God to them, a Covenant of Light to the Gentiles" (Tolles 1963: 94–95). Fox preached to the Indians on his trip to the colonies in the 1670s. Generally, the Quakers believed that the best way to convert the Indians was by example, not proselytizing. As Wallace (1956: 4) wrote, "Quakerism never was offered to the Delaware as an organized religion, with a definite ritual and dogma, and with opportunity of organizational affiliation for Indians; very few if any Indians ever became Friends in the sense of membership in a Meeting."

Penn determined to establish good relations with the Indians as he settled the colony. As soon as he received his charter, Penn wrote a letter to the "king" of the Indians, telling them of his good fortune in receiving the land from the King of England and stating, "I desire to enjoy it with your love and consent, that we may always live together as neighbors and friends" (Tolles 1963: 95). Penn often wrote of the simplicity of the Delawares' practices in terms suggesting that they shared the same aversion to pride and avarice that he did. Tolles (1963: 96) quotes a letter from Penn to Robert Boyle, the scientist, in which he stated about the Indians, "if they have not had their passions raised to the same degree after the luxury of Europe by like enjoyments, neither have they the anxieties that follow those pleasures."

Certainly, not all of the Pennsylvania colonists shared the views of such Quaker luminaries as Penn and John Woolman, but these leaders set the tone for the Quaker–Indian relationship. In the early 1760s, when tensions were growing between the English and the Indians, Woolman (1994: 271) determined to visit a distant Indian outpost to "feel and understand their life and the spirit they live in," as he described in his journal. Woolman knew of the dangers involved, given the unsettled time, but he felt compelled to "receive some instruction from them, or they might be in any degree helped forward by my following the leadings of truth among them" (Woolman 1994: 271). During the trip, Woolman (1994: 277) indeed learned about the Indians whom he met, observing that he was led to "meditate on the manifold difficulties of these Indians who, by the permission of the Six Nations, dwell in these parts." He feared captivity by Indian warriors largely because he thought himself incapable of performing the hard work that would be expected of him, contrasting their strength with his own "tender constitution of body" (Woolman 1994: 277).

Despite this difference in attitudes about the Indians, in many respects the new colony approached the indigenous population in much the same way as earlier colonies had. Penn purchased land from the Indians and set about negotiating treaties with them. By 1683, several purchase treaties had transferred most of the land between the Maryland border and the Delaware River to Penn, who opened it for settlement. By 1718, numerous additional treaties had established Penn's control over the area between the Delaware and the Susquehanna Rivers and north to the Lehigh Valley (Munger 1993: 8–9).

Penn's successors were not averse to sharp dealing with the Delaware in the hope of gaining land. Most notorious was the Walking Purchase of 1737. By then, largely because of German and Scotch-Irish immigration into the central and western parts of Pennsylvania, the proprietors felt they needed to obtain more land and establish a governing system in the new areas. Penn's sons claimed that their father had negotiated an agreement with the Delaware in 1686 but had never laid out the territory covered. The agreement covered as much land as could be covered in a one-and-a-half-day walk westward from a specified point on the Delaware River.

This formulation was common in early land purchases. What was extraordinary is the way that the territory was covered over the day and a half. The proprietors had cleared the path and hired three walkers who set a pace beyond the expectations of the Indians who accompanied them. By the end of the designated period, they had covered twice the normal distance. Moreover, they surveyed a line northeast, rather than due east, from the endpoint of the walk, giving them still more land than the Indians had expected to relinquish. To make matters worse, when the Delaware protested, the proprietors called upon the Six Nations (Iroquois), with whom the colony had an alliance, to force the Delaware to cede the land.[5]

As in the other colonies, the Indians soon found themselves forced westward. As Wallace (1956) writes, by the 1740s, "the Delaware had lost most of their own territory, and were forced to live on the lands of their haughty uncles, the Six Nations, or on the lands of equally haughty Europeans." Unlike in the other colonies, though, outright warfare did not break out between colonists and Indians during this early period of colonization. The good relations built up between William Penn and the Delaware lasted until the outbreak of the Seven Years War, or the French and Indian War, as it was called in the Americas. Even then, the Quakers tried to maintain contact with the Indians, in 1756 forming the Friendly Association for Regaining and Preserving Peace with the Indians by Pacific Measures.

---

[5] For more information, see http://www.docheritage.state.pa.us/documents/walkingpurchase.asp.

Attitudes about "Aliens"

Pennsylvania introduced a new ethnic and religious pluralism to the American colonies. Attitudes toward a pluralistic society varied greatly. Some of the other colonial proprietors emulated Penn's recruitment on the European continent and began their own campaigns to advertise among German-speaking and other prospective migrants. As land prices in Pennsylvania increased, the other colonies advertised that their land was cheaper and more accessible. Even Massachusetts advertised in 1750 for German immigrants, guaranteeing they "will have as free an exercise of their Religion here as in any part of the British Dominions" (quoted in Baseler 1998: 58). None of these colonies had the success of Pennsylvania in attracting immigrants from continental Europe, but their efforts reflected changes in attitudes in Britain about settlement of the colonies.

By the turn of the seventeenth to eighteenth centuries, the British rulers no longer saw overpopulation of the British Isles as a problem. In fact, population growth declined in the second half of the sixteenth century, and even London was no longer seen as overly congested (possibly as a result of the Great Plague in 1665) (Baseler 1998: 37). Rather than encourage large-scale domestic emigration to the colonies, they sought foreign immigrants to people the New World. King George I, himself from Hanover, provided subsidies to encourage German and Swiss migration (Baseler 1998: 40). At the same time, some of the push factors on English migration were removed in 1688 when the Glorious Revolution ushered in a period of stability and toleration. British emigration became much less important while Scottish and Northern Irish emigration grew. Many of these immigrants, who arrived later in the colonial period, headed west into newly open territory in the foothills of the Allegheny Mountains. For a variety of reasons, then, immigration from the Continent as well as from the periphery of the British Isles was welcomed, not only in Pennsylvania but increasingly in the other colonies as well.

By no means did all of the colonists welcome the foreign (non-British) immigrants. The concerns raised about German-speaking immigrants, in particular, foreshadowed many that would be heard throughout American history about its successive waves of newcomers.

The rapid growth in German immigration prompted Governor Keith to propose the registration of foreign immigrants in 1718, a measure that was placed in law in 1727. Lieutenant Governor Patrick Gordon, informing the Assembly in 1728 that foreign immigrants would be required to sign a declaration of allegiance, explained that the order did not arise "from any Dislike to the People themselves, many of whom we know are peaceable, industrious, and well affected, but it seems principally intended to prevent an English Plantation from being turned into a Colony of Aliens" (Baseler 1998: 72). Gordon continued that the registrations were needed to ensure that that the colony was not overrun by "Irish Papists and Convicts." In 1729, the Assembly levied duties of 40 shillings on foreign immigrants coming by land or water, only to repeal the measure the following year. Instead, the Assembly enacted legislation requiring shipmasters to return all "poor and impotent" immigrants to their ports of origin or to post a bond against them becoming public charges. Fines would also be imposed on ships that imported "persons convicted on heinous crimes" (Baseler 1998: 73).

As the Germans settled and became involved in the affairs of the colony, generally supporting the Quaker faction in the Assembly, especially in questions of war and peace, they incurred the animosity of no less a figure than Benjamin Franklin. In a letter to Peter Collinson in 1752, Franklin describes the Germans who migrated to Pennsylvania as "the most ignorant Stupid Sort of their Own Nation" (Franklin and Ketcham 2003: 77). Franklin continues with a number of more specific criticisms. The first pertains to their refusal to learn the English language: "Few of their Children in the Country learn English, they import many Books from Germany, and of the Six printing Houses in the Province, two are entirely German, two half German half English, and but two entirely English; they have one German News Paper" (Franklin and Ketcham 2003: 77). Franklin is particularly concerned about the impact on the English-speaking population: "The Signs in Our Streets have Inscriptions in both Languages, and in Some places only German, they begin of late to make all their Bonds and other Legal Writings in their own Language, with (tho' I think it ought not to be) are allowed good in Our Courts, where the German Business so encreases, that there is continual need of Interpreters, and I suppose in a few Years they will be also necessary in the Assembly, to tell one half of Our Legislators what the other half say" (Franklin and Ketcham 2003: 78). Franklin concluded his analysis of the language problem, saying "In short unless the Stream of their Importation could be turn'd from this to other Colonies, ... they will soon so out Number Us, that all the advantages we have, will not in my Opinion be able to foreserve Our Language, and even Our Government will become precarious" (Franklin and Ketcham 2003: 78).

In his "Observations concerning the Increase of Mankind, Peopling of Countries, Etc.," published in 1755, Franklin continues this theme, referring to the "Palatine Boors" swarming "into our Settlement and, by herding together, establish their Language and Manners, to the Exclusion of ours?" Combining concern about language with concern about race, Franklin asks a question that is echoed by later critics of immigration: "Why should Pennsylvania, founded by the English, become a Colony of Aliens, who will shortly be so numerous as to Germanize us instead of our Anglifying them, and will never adopt our Language or Customs any more than they can acquire our Complexion" (Franklin 1755).

Much of Franklin's scorn of the Germans was political and was framed in terms of the threat they posed to the colony's security. In his letter to Collinson, he noted that the French were developing their own German area of settlement, and that the Germans in Pennsylvania could form an alliance with those German settlers against the English. His greatest concern, however, was the refusal of the Germans to join those in the colony who were preparing for what Franklin considered the inevitable next war with the French. He wrote that in the previous war, "the Germans except a very few in Proportion to their Numbers refused to engage in it, giving out one among another, and even in print, that if they were quiet, the French, should they take the Country would not molest them" (Franklin and Ketcham 2003: 78). These concerns mounted during the Seven Years War when some of the pacifist German sects joined with the Quakers to try to block new taxes for the war effort.

Like many politicians who followed him, Franklin tried to stir up animosity against the immigrants to gain political advantage. During the 1750s Franklin headed the party supported by the proprietors (who were no longer Quakers; Penn's sons converted to the Anglican Church) against the Quaker-dominated Assembly (Weaver 1957). The Germans tended not to be actively engaged in political affairs, not voting even if they were able to do so. Although many naturalized aliens voted in Pennsylvania elections, the pacifist Germans, in particular, generally did not exercise the franchise. They supported Quaker efforts to block Franklin's proposed taxes to pay for a militia and were adamantly against conscripting recruits. In 1755, the Germans turned out in record numbers to block Franklin's party from taking control of the Assembly. It was only in late 1755, when the French had taken control of western Pennsylvania and a number of colonists had lost their lives in Indian attacks, that the Quakers, still unwilling to give up their pacifist beliefs but no longer able to block military action, removed themselves from leadership of the Assembly. Franklin served as the chair of the colony's defense committee until 1757 when he went to London as the colony's agent, remaining there until 1762.

When Franklin returned, the political situation had changed markedly from the early 1750s, when he had lashed out against the German immigrants. Members of the German Reformed and Lutheran churches, the majority of the Germans in the colony, had acquitted themselves well during the war and clearly aligned themselves with the English. Even the pacifist groups had helped those who had had to flee areas under threat. By the time he returned in 1762, Franklin had turned against the proprietors and begun to advocate revocation of their charter. His earlier writings against the Germans turned out to be the undoing of his effort, however. The proponents of the Proprietary charter brought out his diatribe against the "Palatine Boors," convincing about one thousand Germans (out of a total vote of four thousand) to vote against revocation, and Franklin's proposal was narrowly defeated.

Although Franklin showed clear hostility toward the German immigrants, he also recognized that they posed some advantages for the colonies. In his letter to Collinson, he clarified his position: "I say I am not against the admission of Germans in general, for they have their Virtues, their Industry and Frugality is exemplary, they are excellent Husbandmen and contribute greatly to the Improvement of a Country" (Franklin and Ketcham 2003: 78–79). Rather, he proposed to distribute them throughout the colonies so that they would not outnumber the English in any one location. Collinson himself had proposed a series of steps that should be taken to assimilate the Germans more completely into Pennsylvania society. In addition to dispersing them, Collinson argued for encouraging their intermarriage with the English. He promoted the establishment of English-language schools in German areas, and he was willing to penalize those who did not learn English. No German should be permitted to hold even the lowest office unless he and his family spoke English. Collinson would also make German legal documents invalid, suppress German printing houses, and prohibit the importation of German books (Collinson and Armstrong 2002: 170). We will see that these types of proposals reemerge during later periods of immigration, as critics of newcomers seek ways to ease or even force their assimilation.

As was the case in later periods, there was some truth to the accusations made against the German immigrants. Many did settle in enclaves and have little contact with their English-speaking neighbors. German was spoken as a first language by multiple generations. The much-improved cross-Atlantic transportation networks of the mid-eighteenth century allowed German-speaking immigrants to maintain ties with their home countries, as these same networks allowed the English-speaking colonists to maintain communication with their families at home (Steele 1986: 260). On the security side, although there is no evidence that the Pennsylvania Germans ever intended to ally themselves with the French against the English, many did share the pacifist beliefs that blocked military preparedness in the face of what many colonists saw as a growing threat.

Conclusion

Pennsylvania is thus the locus of origin of two traditions that go hand in hand throughout U.S. history. On the one hand, it is the birthplace of a robust pluralism that celebrates the contributions of immigrants from throughout the world (or at least from the European world in the seventeenth and eighteenth centuries). William Penn not only welcomed foreign immigrants, he recruited them. By the end of the colonial period, German-speaking immigrants made up about a third of Penn's colony. The Scots-Irish Presbyterians made up another third, leaving the Quakers in the minority in their own colony.

At the same time, the very pluralism that Pennsylvania represented yielded harsh criticism of the immigrants and sometimes legitimate concerns about their ability to integrate into what was still largely an English environment. And the British and the Germans were soon to face new challenges as the colonies prepared themselves for independence. As Barbara Jordan, Chair of the U.S. Commission on Immigration Reform, said three and a half centuries later of Franklin's concerns that the German immigrants would not become anglified, "Of course, German immigrants to Pennsylvania did not become English, nor did they make Pennsylvanians into Germans. Instead, they became Americans" (Jordan 1995).

5

Immigration and the Formation of the Republic

Ambivalence about immigration was a major theme in the new republic. Although the Declaration of Independence faults King George III for curtailing immigration into the colonies, the founding fathers were not totally sanguine about the potential effects of immigration on the new nation. For example, Jefferson questioned whether immigrants would attach themselves to the democratic principles and constitutional base of the American form of government. He asked if the government might not be "more homogeneous, more peaceful, more durable" without large-scale immigration (Jefferson 1993: 212).

A primary focus of this chapter is the language spoken by immigrants. Unlike multilingual European states formed around existing and generally geographically separate language groups, the challenge of the new American republic was to incorporate a continuing flow of immigrants who spoke different tongues into a single, unified nation. The English language formed an important bond in the creation of a new identity as Americans. American English absorbed words from the languages spoken by non-English residents, changing them to reflect the American reality. Renewed immigration from non-English-speaking countries would pose a challenge, however, to the democratic principles that required "we, the people" to share a common understanding of the Declaration of Independence and the Constitution.

In this context, the chapter explores evolving notions of membership in the American polity. The Constitution authorized Congress "to establish an [sic] uniform Rule of Naturalization" (Article 1, Section 7). The first naturalization statute was passed in 1790, allowing the naturalization of "free white persons" who had been resident for two years or more. By 1795, Congress had increased the period of required residence to five years. In 1798, the requirement was raised to fourteen years as part of the reaction to conflict with France and emerging political tensions between Federalists and Republicans; it was reduced to five years in the Naturalization Act of 1802. The 1790 naturalization law and its successors required new citizens to declare their allegiance to the Constitution and to demonstrate their good moral character.

In addition to the naturalization provisions, this chapter examines the Alien Acts of 1798. Enacted in the midst of the first major threat to the security of the country, the legislation authorized the president to arrest or to deport any alien whom he deemed dangerous to the United States. It also required the captain of any vessel arriving in the United States to report the arrival of aliens on board. The Enemy Aliens Act of the same year gave the president, the power to restrain or remove alien enemy males of fourteen years and upward, with due protection of their property rights as stipulated by treaty, in the case of declared war or invasion. The debate over the Alien Acts is explained, in part, by tensions between the Massachusetts and Pennsylvania models of membership.

Finally, this chapter discusses the debate in the new republic over slavery and the slave trade. The contrast between the lofty principles of the founding fathers ("all men are created equal") and the peculiar institution of slavery is discussed with its implications for the Virginia model of immigration.

Toward the Revolution

During the French and Indian War (the colonial part of the larger Seven Years War in Europe), immigration to the colonies slowed down significantly, but with the end of the conflict in 1763, transatlantic movements resumed. The war had decisively claimed the North American colonies for the British. France ceded Canada and all its territory east of the Mississippi River to Britain, and Spain ceded Florida. With the influence of the two Catholic powers removed from North America, the Protestant mainland colonies had little to fear from outside intrusion. Yet, the war had come at high cost, and the British Parliament sought redress for the expenses incurred in protecting the colonies. A series of taxation measures followed, and each provoked greater resistance from the colonists.

At the same time, attitudes in Britain regarding emigration to the colonies shifted. As discussed in Chapter 4, some British analysts had already begun to question the population loss to England resulting from emigration to North America. During the latter part of the eighteenth century, a new concern arose – potential competition from the colonies. One of the benefits of empire was the ability to import raw materials from new suppliers and export manufactured goods to new markets. As long as the colonies remained largely agricultural, as were in the southern colonies dominated by the slave economy, Britain would benefit from the arrangement. With the growth of American cities, however, domestic manufacturing might well increase and reduce the reliance on British exports.

General Thomas Gage, the commander of the British army in North America, sounded the alarm in 1768. He recommended that the army cease allowing soldiers with trades to be discharged while still in the colonies: "Instead of clearing uncultivated Lands, which it was expected they would do, they have for the most part crowded into the Towns to work at Trades, and help to Supply the Inhabitants with Necessarys, which should be imported from the Mother

Country" (quoted in Baseler 1998: 122). Gage also thought that settlement in the western part of the colonies should be curtailed, partly to reduce tensions with the Indians that might renew conflict and partly to keep the colonists close to the transatlantic trade routes (Baseler 1998: 122). The Proclamation of 1763 had already closed the area west of the Appalachian Mountains to settlement.

To a large extent, these concerns about the colonial economy were over-blown. During the eighteenth century, better trade routes across the Atlantic were found and shipping costs were reduced,[1] allowing for growth in trade between England and the colonies. The number of ships engaged in commerce with the colonies grew substantially during the course of the eighteenth century, and innovations such as marine insurance and a commission system of trade lowered freight costs (Steele 1986: 276). Although trade slackened during the Seven Years War, it began to build again as soon as hostilities ended. The colonies continued to export tobacco, sugar, fish, and other products and to import most of their manufactured goods. Moreover, the colonies were still overwhelmingly agricultural and rural. Less than five percent of the colonists lived in towns with populations that exceeded 8,000 (Wells 1992: 100). Only 4.6 percent lived in towns of more than 2,000 in 1770 (Wells 1992: 100). In 1750, Boston was the largest city in North America, with a population of about 15,000; seven English cities were larger. London's population surpassed that of all the colonies together until 1730 (Wells 1992: 101). Ironically, it was British taxation policy, not immigration, that led to greater colonial self-sufficiency. The colonies joined in an embargo of British imports in reaction to the Stamp Act and the Townsend duties, thereby inducing more manufacturing to take place in America.

Nevertheless, for economic reasons, Britain took steps after the Seven Years War to restrict immigration to the colonies. Using its right to veto colonial legislation, the Privy Council rejected laws designed to encourage emigration from Europe. In 1767, a Georgia law that offered British Protestants free transportation was rejected; in 1771, a North Carolina law offering special inducements to Scottish immigrants was vetoed (Baseler 1998: 124). The royal governors were also instructed that they were not to approve any bills for the naturalization of aliens. Nor could they offer free land grants to new colonists (Baseler 1998: 125). As colonial resistance to the authority of the British Parliament grew in the period after the Seven Years War, the British government appeared even less willing to support large-scale immigration to what were now seen as ungrateful territories, unwilling to repay the motherland for her protection in the face of French and Indian aggression. At the same time, the Parliament preserved Britain's right to transport convicts and vetoed a number of colonies' attempts to prohibit the slave trade. The colonists saw these policies as benefiting Britain at the expense of the colonies; the slave trade supported the agricultural exports that Britain wanted while the convict transports ridded Britain of undesirables.

---

[1] For a comprehensive discussion of the transatlantic trade routes, see Steele (1986).

For their part, the colonial leaders were ambivalent about immigration and set on maintaining their prerogative to populate their lands as they saw fit. Franklin continued to argue that the high fertility rates in the colonies would serve the same purpose as rapid immigration, but other colonial figures wanted to recruit "liberty-loving" immigrants from across Europe. Thomas Paine, in *Common Sense*, argued for American independence because "Emigrants of property will not choose to come to a country whose form of government hangs but by a thread, and who is every day tottering on the brink of commotion and disturbance; and numbers of the present inhabitants would lay hold of the interval, to dispose of their effects, and quit the continent" (Paine and Larkin 2004: 72). Recognizing that "This new world hath been the asylum for the persecuted lovers of civil and religious liberty from every Part of Europe" (Paine and Larkin 2004), Paine calls on America to continue to be an "asylum for mankind" (Paine and Larkin 2004).

The Declaration of Independence summarized the colonies' concerns about British emigration and immigration policies as they affected the settlement of America: "He has endeavored to prevent the population of these states; for that purpose obstructing the laws for naturalization of foreigners; refusing to pass others to encourage their migration hither, and raising the conditions of new appropriations of lands." It is the seventh articulated abuse (out of twenty-eight), reflecting the seriousness of the charge. Colonies bent on growth from immigration and from settlement in the western territories found obstruction by the Crown and Parliament to be an important reason to seek independence.

Immigration in the New Republic

The war for independence prevented large-scale immigration into the warring states. The troops sent by the British to quell the revolt presented an opportunity, however, for the new confederation to combine its interest in a growing population with its interest in sabotaging the British military efforts. The Continental Congress made offers of free land to any soldier in the British army who deserted to the American cause. The deserters would be granted expedited naturalization and exemption from military service. The offer was directed to the British army's mercenary soldiers, largely Hessians. Atwood (2002: 194) estimates that 3,000 took up the offer.

After peace came in 1783, immigration picked up again. Estimates by Grabbe (1989) indicate that the level of immigration between 1783 and 1820 was considerable, although more modest than would occur in the nineteenth century. He estimated that a net total of 366,000 European immigrants came to the New World during this period. The number of arriving foreign passengers was higher, about 410,000, which includes those coming from the Caribbean. Many of the French immigrants, from France and the French Caribbean, came temporarily, returning to France when political conditions permitted. Grabbe's estimates are significantly higher than official census figures, which were based on estimates made in the mid-nineteenth century by William J. Brownell.

He extrapolated from actual ship arrivals in Philadelphia to calculate the estimates. Grabbe's estimates comport with those of other demographers who have reexamined population trends in the early republic.

The largest group of immigrants came from Ireland (199,000). English, Scottish and Welsh immigrants accounted for 88,000, German-speaking immigrants for 32,000, and French immigrants for 16,000. Most of the Irish immigrants came from Northern Ireland, nearly half embarking on their journey in Londonderry. The pattern of movements between 1783 and 1820 was determined by a combination of political, economic, and policy factors. During relatively peaceful periods following the Treaty of Paris (1783) and the Treaty of Amiens (1802), immigration increased. The British blockade of American seaports during the War of 1812 certainly depressed immigration, as did the fighting in Germany during the Napoleonic Wars.

On the economic front, an economic depression in the United States from 1784 to 1788 reduced immigration. In addition, a trade embargo imposed by the Jefferson administration from 1807 to 1809 decreased immigrant numbers. Although immigration rose dramatically from 1815 to 1819, when war ended in Europe and America, it dropped precipitously in 1820, when news of the Panic of 1819 reached Europe (Grabbe 1989). Factories and farms suffered economic collapse as exports declined and over-valued real estate destroyed the financial institutions of the new republic. By then, new policies had also come into effect, first in Pennsylvania and then in the country as a whole, limiting the number of passengers per ton of ship capacity. Immigration ground to a halt, not to resume in sizable numbers for a decade.

Slavery and Indenture in the New Republic

The Revolution ushered in a new era in terms of the Virginia model of labor migration. Certainly, labor was needed in the new republic. Alexander Hamilton, for example, argued the necessity of immigration to transform America from a purely agricultural to a manufacturing society capable of trading in the world economy. In his *Report on Manufactures* to Congress in 1791, Hamilton identified immigration as a benefit to both types of economic activities. "Here is perceived an important resource, not only for extending the population, and with it the useful and productive labour of the country, but likewise for the prosecution of manufactures, without deducting from the number of hands, which might otherwise be drawn to tillage; and even for the indemnification of Agriculture for such as might happen to be diverted from it" (Hamilton 1827: 22). Hamilton encouraged Congress to take advantage of the instability in Europe to promote increased immigration: "The disturbed state of Europe, inclining its citizens to emigration, the requisite workmen, will be more easily acquired, than at another time; and the effect of multiplying the opportunities of employment to those who emigrate, may be an increase of the number and extent of valuable acquisitions to the population, arts and industry of the Country. To find pleasure in the calamities of other nations, would be criminal; but to benefit ourselves, by opening an asylum to those who suffer, in consequence of them, is as justifiable as it is politic" (Hamilton 1827: 50).

The question was how immigration would take place. The first issue the founders needed to tackle was slavery. It had provided the mainstay of labor in the south for more than a hundred years. Fogelman (1992: 697) estimates that 278,000 Africans were brought to the colonies in the eighteenth century, almost matching the estimated 307,400 white arrivals.

The founding fathers were ambivalent at best about slavery. Many of the most notable champions of the new republic, including Jefferson, Washington, and Madison, were themselves slaveholders. Jefferson, notwithstanding his words about all men being created equal, wrote in *Notes on the State of Virginia* of his suspicion that "blacks, whether originally a distinct race, or made distinct by time and circumstances, are inferior to the whites in the endowments of both body and mind" (Jefferson 1993: 264). He proposed, and then withdrew, as inexpedient, legislation in Virginia for emancipation of the slaves; but he also believed that the emancipated slaves should be transported to colonies of their own and European immigrants recruited in their stead. Jefferson thought slavery inimical to the interests of the white population, leading to despotism, but he feared that emancipated slaves would rise up against the "injuries they have sustained" (Jefferson 1993: 264).

The Constitution was itself a compromise on slavery. Ending slavery was not an option, given the dependence of many states on slave labor to sustain their economies. The main debates regarding slavery involved the way in which slaves would be counted for purposes of representation in Congress and what would happen to the slave trade. For purposes tied to population size, a slave was to count as three-fifths of a person in enumeration. As for the slave trade, Article 1, Section 9 specified: "The Migration or Importation of such Persons as any of the States now existing shall think proper to admit, shall not be prohibited by the Congress prior to the Year one thousand eight hundred and eight, but a tax or duty may be imposed on such Importation, not exceeding ten dollars for each Person." The vague language – migration or importation – referred to slaves but meant that the provision also applied to other forms of migration. The provision was adopted after the southern States that most wanted to preserve the slave trade (not including Virginia, which had a surplus of slaves and wanted a monopoly to sell them farther south) agreed to join with the New England states on a commerce clause affecting navigation if the latter voted against immediate suppression of the slave trade.

Hence, under the Constitution, the institution of slavery would not be touched, but Congress had the right to end the slave trade, as it did, in 1808. During the intervening period, states could regulate importation of slaves. Most states passed legislation abolishing or deeply curtailing the slave trade, with the exception of South Carolina, which initially tried to bar the trade but reopened importation in 1803. Most of the slaves imported with the resumption of the slave trade in South Carolina were sold in the newly opening territories of the Louisiana Purchase.

When Congress debated the legislation to end the slave trade nationally, the major sticking point between North and South was what to do with Africans who were illegally traded into the country. The New England representatives wanted them set free; the southern representatives wanted them sold, with revenues going to the states or the federal government. A compromise was reached that required the confiscated ships to be turned over to state authorities. This agreement assured the northern antislavery representatives that the federal government would not become part of the slave trade and the southern pro-slavery representatives that federal officials would not turn freed Africans loose in their midst (Mason 2000).

By the time the Constitution was adopted and, even more so, by the time Congress ended the slave trade, the southern slave population was already becoming self-sustaining. Unlike in the Caribbean colonies with their high mortality rates, in the mainland colonies most growth occurred from births, not from migration. The slave trade would continue until its official end in 1808, but importation of slaves was no longer needed for the institution of slavery to maintain itself in the South. Hence, both northern opponents of slavery and southern supporters could join together in ending what all agreed was a "violation of human rights," in President Jefferson's words, without forcing a decision on the institution of slavery itself (Mason 2000: 63).

Even before the slave trade was made illegal, the Revolution ended the importation of convict labor. The colonies had long decried British efforts to dump undesirables in colonial territories, but they had had little impact on Britain's transportation policies. With the peace treaty, the British tried to resume the transport of convicts, engaging private contractors in the process. Convict transports from Ireland also resumed. American demands that the British stop the transports were to no avail, although public outrage 'yielded headaches rather than profits' for the contractors (Baseler 1998: 161). In 1788, the Continental Congress passed a resolution, recommending that the states pass laws to prevent the transportation of convicts. Several of them acted immediately, including Massachusetts, New York, and Virginia. Britain, seeing the handwriting on the wall, turned to Australia as a potential site for its convicts.

Indentured servitude, although not prohibited outright, also fell into disfavor as a mechanism through which immigrants came to the United States. Indenture had been practiced throughout the colonies. It offered a means by which even the lowliest servant could reach American shores, but it also allowed for considerable abuse, particularly when the term of indenture was very long. As we have seen, it was used liberally as a means of attracting labor to the South before slavery took hold, and it was used by German immigrants as a way to pay for expensive transatlantic crossings. The German system differed significantly from the English, however, in that indenture was used only when the immigrants (or more often their families) were unable to repay the cost of transport and only for the period needed for the repayment to take place. Although some Irish immigrants came through the traditional indenture system in the 1770s, by the time of the Revolution most were immigrating as wage laborers, paying their own expenses to come to the New World (Wokeck 1999: 214). As the voyage from Ireland was shorter than from the continent, fares were proportionately lower and more affordable.

Fogelman (1992) estimates that between 1700 and 1775 more than 103,000 indentured servants immigrated to the American colonies, an average of 1,381 each year. In the period from the Revolution until 1809, only 18,000 immigrated in this capacity, an average of 545 per year. Immigrants themselves condemned indenture, whether in the traditional or the German redemption form. They emphasized to family and friends back home that the conditions in indenture could be very harsh and that it would be difficult to gain future economic advantage after spending years in servitude. The Revolution helped curtail the flow in indentured servants by halting immigration during the war, and then shifting the patterns of trade and commerce as relations with Britain changed in its aftermath (Fogelman 1992: 64). The ideals of the Revolution further contributed to the reduction in indentured servitude. Such hierarchical systems of servitude no longer seemed appropriate, at least for white Europeans. Runaways from apprenticeships and indenture increased during the Revolution, and courts were less willing to punish or return the servants to their masters (Fogelman 1992: 63). Although the revolutionary spirit did not lead to major changes in law as related to indenture, its true importance was a shift in the understanding of the rights of the individual (at least the white European individual) that gave preference to immigration into freedom, not into servitude.

American Nationalism and Immigration

For the founders of the new republic, the role that immigration would play in forming the new nation was not all that clear.[2] Many believed that the survival of the republic required the arrival of as many immigrants as possible. The peace with Britain had given the country immense unsettled lands, and the Louisiana Purchase in 1801 only expanded the territory. James Madison gave clear voice to this perspective during the Constitutional Convention. He analyzed the importance of immigration: "America was indebted to immigration for her settlement and prosperity. That part of America which had encouraged [immigration] most had advanced most rapidly in population, agriculture and the arts" (Farrand 1911: 268). His views were seconded by James Wilson, who cited Pennsylvania "as a proof of the advantage of encouraging emigrations. It was perhaps the youngest [except Georgia settlement] on the Atlantic; yet it was at least among the foremost in population and prosperity." He remarked that "almost all the General officers of the [Pennsylvania] line of the late army were foreigners. And no complaint had ever been made against their fidelity or merit" (Farrand 1911: 269). Wilson might have mentioned that within a few

---

[2] For analysis of the varying viewpoints, see Zolberg (2006), Chapter 3, and Totten (2008).

days of its publication in English, the Declaration of Independence had been translated and published in German to give Pennsylvania's German-speaking immigrants the news of the revolution (Adams 1999).

Thomas Jefferson was less sanguine about the impact of immigration on the democratic principles of the new republic. In *Notes on the State of Virginia*, he begins his analysis of immigration by posing a question: "The present desire of America is to produce rapid population by as great importations of foreigners as possible. But is this founded in good policy? The advantage proposed is the multiplication of numbers.... But are there no inconveniences to be thrown into the scale against the advantage expected from a multiplication of number by the importation of foreigners?" (Jefferson 1993: 211). He points to the very nature of the republic that the country was trying to build: "It is for the happiness of those united in society to harmonize as much as possible in matters which they must of necessity transact together. Civil government being the sole object of forming societies, its administration must be conducted by common consent" (Jefferson 1993: 211). The American form of government, derived from natural right and natural reason, differs fundamentally from that of absolute monarchies. The problem for Jefferson is that "from such [monarchies], we are to expect the greatest number of emigrants" (Jefferson 1993: 211). Jefferson fears that the worst will happen as a result of this immigration: "They will bring with them the principles of the governments they leave, imbibed in their early youth; or, if able to throw them off, it will be in exchange for an unbounded licentiousness, passing, as is usual, from one extreme to another" (Jefferson 1993: 211).

Jefferson acknowledged that during the Revolution there had been no signs of immigrants acting in this way, but he cautions a new republic that the risk does not outweigh the benefits of more rapid population growth. If the immigrants come of their own volition, and if they are skilled craftsmen ("useful artificers" in Jefferson's language), they should be welcomed into the new republic because "they will teach us something we do not know." What Jefferson questions is the expediency of "extraordinary encouragement" of immigration.[3]

Given the potential opportunities as well as dangers of immigration, the founders sought ways to bring the foreigners into the political fold. Afraid that the United States covered too large and diverse an area to lend itself to a republican form of government, but well aware that the size of the country and its small population would promote immigration, the founders of the nation sought evidence of an underlying homogeneity that would justify their

---

[3] Although Jefferson seemed to be concerned about inadvertent passage of archaic ideas to the new republic, Elbridge Gerry of Massachusetts argued in the Constitutional Convention against immigrants serving in public office because he feared meddling by foreign powers: "Foreign powers will intermeddle in our affairs, and spare no expence to influence them. Persons having foreign attachments will be sent among us & insinuated into our councils, in order to be made instruments for their purposes" (Farrand 1911: 268).

experiment. An obvious common element (or what should be a common element) was language.

Language, in the words of John Locke (1979: 1), was "the great instrument and common tie of society." In Enlightenment thought, if men were to live together in a community, they needed to share a means of communication. It was essential that they understand each other. Words could easily be misconstrued because of the symbolic nature of language. The chance of misunderstanding increased greatly among those who spoke different languages. To the Enlightenment mind, multilingualism could not work in a properly functioning society because it would seriously endanger the common good. By recognizing the need for and supporting the dominance of one national language, the founders could ensure that the new republic would endure. As Noah Webster (1789: 20) put it, "our political harmony is therefore concerned in a uniformity of language."

Unlike multilingual European countries that formed around existing and generally geographically separate language groups, the challenge of the new American republic was to incorporate a continuing flow of immigrants who spoke different tongues into a unified nation where only one language was spoken. Such countries as Switzerland and Belgium confederated linguistically distinct territories, becoming multi-nationstates. They reduced potential friction among the different language groups by granting considerable autonomy to the smaller, incorporated units, which were able to retain their own languages. In contrast, the United States joined thirteen colonies that had a principal shared language at the time of independence, but expected to see the continuing arrival of immigrants who spoke other languages. Shared language would be the engine of the new republic.

What was less clear initially was the nature of the shared language. To many of those who had fought for independence, retaining the language of the mother country seemed antithetical to the needs of the new republic. Rumors abounded that the country would adopt a new language. Although it was never a serious possibility, it became Pennsylvania folklore that German would be adopted by the new Congress as the language of the country (Feer 1952). By some accounts, New Englanders urged that the official language be Hebrew, in recognition of Christianity's Old Testament heritage and the American identity as the chosen people (Feer 1952: 394). Thomas Jefferson and other members of the American Philosophical Society studied and wrote treatises on Native American languages, but deep-seated concerns about racial differences between the settlers and the original inhabitants precluded serious consideration of any of these tongues as the national language.[4]

---

[4] Ironically, a number of eighteenth-century scholars studied the tribal languages in hopes of finding elements that were similar to European languages in order to prove the common origins of mankind. Nevertheless, when faced with observable difference among races, ambivalence as to human equality vied with deeply held feelings about racial inferiority. See, for example, the writings of Thomas Jefferson.

Much more successful were efforts to define the English spoken in America as a language distinct from the English spoken in Britain. Noah Webster, one of the first American lexicographers, described the various reasons for an expected divergence in the two languages: "Numerous local causes, such as a new country, new associations of people, new combinations of ideas in arts and science and some intercourse with tribes wholly unknown in Europe, will introduce new words" (Webster 1789: 21). The eventual result must be "a language in North America, as different from the future language of England, as the modern Dutch, Danish and Swedish are from the German, or from one another" (Webster 1789: 22).

That the United States was already conceiving itself as a nation of immigrants had a profound influence on this view. One of the major assets of the country, and one that contributed to the vitality of American English, was the use of languages other than English. American English absorbed words from these other languages, changing them as necessary to reflect the American reality. Most of the earliest efforts to introduce language uniformity were aimed at those who already lived in the United States; and mostly, the effort was to reduce regional variations in language. Geographic mobility in the new republic helped facilitate this process, as the movement westward reduced the clustering of ethnic groups that had contributed to foreign language retention. New Englanders moved into upstate New York areas that had been dominated by the Dutch. German farmers began to move to Midwestern states to find inexpensive land to bequeath to their children. Social mobility further facilitated language uniformity – and vice versa. In America, there were few bars to upward mobility, and certainly language was not one of them – in contrast to many European countries.

The route to a shared American nationalism for both citizens and immigrants was education rather than class or geography. The early nineteenth century saw a proliferation in dictionaries and spellers. Those who produced them and encouraged language uniformity, such as Noah Webster, also promoted free universal education. Education became the engine for creating the new republic out of the sum of its disparate parts. If effective and trustworthy self-government was predicated upon the ability of a free electorate to make intelligent decisions, then universal public education was the best way to ensure the viability of the republican ideal. As Webster wrote, the success of the American experiment was contingent on "such a system of education as gives every citizen an opportunity of acquiring knowledge and fitting himself for places of trust" (quoted in Shalhope 2004: 114).

Perhaps best reflecting the role that education would play in the integration of immigrants was the chartering of Franklin College in 1787. Located in Lancaster, Pennsylvania, Franklin College was founded to educate the members of the German Lutheran and Reform churches to participate in civic affairs as well as ecclesiastical ones. Its first four faculty members, who were of German origin, would acculturate its students to life in the new United States. In one of the more ironic chapters in American educational history, the college was named for the very man who had criticized German immigrants for trying to transform an English colony into a German one. The name was meant to honor Franklin for his position in Pennsylvania politics, and he repaid the kindness with a contribution of £200 toward the new college. Franklin died three years later. Ironically, given Franklin's opinion of Germans and his deist views, his funeral was held at the German Lutheran Church in Philadelphia.

Americans sought and found in education an answer to the immigration dilemma: with proper schooling, all could share in the benefits of American society regardless of socioeconomic background or place of birth. Although many were still apprehensive about immigration, the emphasis on education as the engine of assimilation, especially into sharing the civic values of the new republic, allowed the Pennsylvania ideal of a pluralistic society to function in the new republic.

Immigration and the Security of the New Republic

If the Pennsylvania model found its voice in education and language, the Massachusetts model reappeared for a short time in response to security threats in the new republic. Two sets of policies are pertinent, those adopted regarding the return of loyalists and those adopted as part of the Alien and Sedition Acts. The reintegration of loyalists who had gone to Canada or England or hidden during the Revolution came to the fore after the Treaty of Paris was signed in 1783. Even states that were as open to immigration as Pennsylvania and New York initially drew the line at the return of those who had "aided and abetted" the enemy. Yet, many of those who had left and now wanted to return and reclaim their land had not fought for the British; they had merely fulfilled what they saw as their oath of allegiance to the Crown by not supporting the revolutionaries. Some of them still had families living in what was now the United States. Many had property or businesses, including businesses that traded with British and European merchants.

Under the Treaty of Paris (1789), which ended the war with Britain, the Confederation of United States had agreed to recommend to individual state legislatures that they "provide for the restitution of all estates, rights, and properties, which have been confiscated belonging to real British subjects; and also of the estates, rights, and properties of persons resident in districts in the possession on his Majesty's arms and who have not borne arms against the said United States." The United States also agreed not to confiscate future holdings of the loyalists. Although many states ignored these terms and held on to property to repay war debts as well as to punish the offenders, the treaty did pave the way for a set of flexible policies allowing the reintegration of those who pledged allegiance to the new republic. For most of the new states, the solution was to permit return of those who had not fought against the Revolution, but not to grant them citizenship. They could apply for naturalization but had to sign an oath of allegiance and, in some cases, were barred from holding office for at least a period of time.[5] In part, the decision to permit the return of the loyalists reflected the triumph of the mercantilist argument for a growing population. Many loyalists had skills, financial resources, or mercantile contacts needed by the new republic. In that respect, these plans had the support of those who supported a strong federal government, such as Hamilton, the leader of the Federalist Party, who saw virtue in growth.

Although Federalists were generally supportive of immigration needed to build the country, they were less sanguine about the immigration that occurred in the 1790s. Although they had been willing to support a relatively generous naturalization law at the beginning of the decade, by the end of the decade they had shifted their views. The growing radicalism of the French Revolution as well as internal dissent brought matters to a head, raising questions in Federalists' minds about the rights that were afforded to immigrants. At the same time, the new Republican Party, under the tutelage of Jefferson and Madison, saw in the Federalist reforms dangerous affronts to the liberty of all residents of the republic. In a turnaround, the two emerging political parties shifted position, with the previously suspicious Republicans becoming the champions of immigrant rights and the previously supportive Federalists moving toward ever greater restrictions. As will be seen, though, the shift is not that surprising, given the varying notions of immigration held by the two parties.

Article I, Section 8 of the U.S. Constitution gives Congress the authority to create a "uniform rule of naturalization" for the nation. Debate on what that naturalization rule should be began in the first session of Congress. As Baseler (1998) describes, three positions were taken during the debate. First were those who wanted few impediments to naturalization, to continue to encourage immigration. Second were those who wanted some period of acculturation to the republic's ideals before naturalization was permitted. Third were those who wanted to restrict naturalization. The second group generally prevailed, although they were unable to introduce the type of progressive citizenship that many of the states had adopted. The states often offered citizenship but restricted office-holding until additional years had passed. The 1790 law provided that "any alien, being a free white person, who shall have resided within the limits and under the jurisdiction of the United States for the term of two years, may be admitted to become a citizen thereof (Naturalization Act 1790)." The states retained a role in that the application was to be made at any "Common Law Court of Record, in any one of the States wherein he shall have resided for the term of one year at least (Naturalization Act 1790)." The successful applicant would have to prove to the satisfaction of the court that he was a person of good character and take the oath or affirmation prescribed by law "to support the Constitution of the United States (Naturalization Act 1790)." Children of U.S. citizens born abroad were to be considered as natural-born citizens, except if their fathers had never been resident in the United States.

---

[5] For a more detailed discussion of the treatment of loyalists, see Baseler (1998).

The law further provided that no person proscribed by any state shall be admitted a citizen, except by an act of the legislature of that state.

Although the legislation restricted the right to naturalize to free white persons, thereby removing the option for Asians and Africans, it contained no restrictions based on religion. This followed the pattern in individual state naturalization laws in the period following the start of the Revolution. With the exception of Maryland, which required that petitioners declare their belief in the Christian religion, none adopted religious tests for naturalization (although some gave preference to Protestants or Christians in the exercise of their rights). Until 1793, Vermont, for example, required state representatives to take an oath that they acknowledged the scriptures as divine inspiration and professed the Protestant religion. New Jersey specified that no Protestant "shall be denied the enjoyment of any civil right, merely on account of his religious principles" (Baseler 1998: 225).

The largely liberal concept of naturalization, with its two-year residency requirement, lasted only until 1795. In the interim, the excesses of the French Revolution appeared to have followed immigrants to the United States. The actions of French Ambassador Edmond Genêt first gave rise to concerns among the Federalists. Genêt had been commissioned to America to raise financial and political support for France, which was at war with Britain. The new republic had decided to be neutral, even though revolutionary France reminded the United States that France's help had been crucial in winning the American Revolution. President Washington and his cabinet recognized that America was too weak to take on Britain in a second war. In addition, the newly emerging parties – the Federalists and the Republicans – were split in their attitudes about the French Revolution. Neutrality postponed what would otherwise have been a more precipitous break. Genêt, ignoring Washington's decision, recruited and armed privateers to attack British ships, thereby risking American neutrality. In a direct affront to Washington, he also vowed to take his case directly to the people to overturn the government's position on neutrality. To the Federalists, as well as some Republicans, Genêt's actions, if unchecked, would bode ill for the authority of the federal government. It also raised the specter of mob rule, which was clearly developing in France. The fear, which had little support in fact, was that unruly immigrants would heed Genêt's call and lead a new mob revolution.

The Whiskey Rebellion in 1794 further implicated foreigners as risking the security of the republic. The origins of the rebellion were purely homegrown – domestic opposition to a 1791 tax on distilled spirits, designed to raise revenue to pay the debts incurred during the Revolution. Of course, opposition to taxes was a long-standing American tradition, as exemplified by the reaction in the colonies to the Stamp Tax. Although states were seen to have the need and authority to tax, the authority of the federal government was not clear cut. Hamilton had introduced the whiskey tax as a way to test this authority. From the beginning, the western settlements rose up against the tax. The federal government attempted to modify the tax to meet the concerns but none of the modifications changed public opinion. In most states, the opponents refused to pay the tax but did little else to show their displeasure. The authorities took few steps to enforce the tax.

A crisis emerged in Pennsylvania when more serious efforts were made to collect revenue from the distillers. Outright violence broke out in 1794, culminating in an armed attack on the home of John Neville, the district revenue inspector. As opposition intensified, President Washington issued a proclamation under the congressional "act to provide for calling forth the militia to execute the laws of the Union, suppress insurrections, and repel invasions," and deployed almost 14,000 militia members under his own command to suppress the rebellion. By the time they arrived, the rebellion had dissolved. Thirty-two people were arrested,[6] but all but two were later acquitted (Gould 1996: 407).

The Federalists used anti-immigrant language to build support for their actions in suppressing the rebellion, accusing immigrants of instigating it. Albert Gallatin, who played a moderating role but supported the aims of the rebels, was described as "a vagrant foreigner... who... came to this Country without a second shirt to his back" (quoted in Baseler 1998: 262). Gallatin, who was actually from a wealthy family in Switzerland, had immigrated to the United States in the 1780s. He was elected to the U.S. Senate from Pennsylvania but was forced to leave his seat because the Federalists argued successfully that only nine years had elapsed since his naturalization.

Irish immigrants bore the brunt of the accusations about their involvement in the rebellion. According to one report, Irish immigrants "have threatened to shoot every man who may not choose to oppose the old [government], in hopes to establish a new government" (quoted in Baseler 1998: 262). A more typical example was the Reverend John Corbley, a leader of the rebellion who had emigrated from Ireland as an indentured servant at the age of 14. Corbley's animosity toward the federal government stemmed as much from what he saw as its refusal to protect the West against the Indians as it did its misguided taxation polices. Corbley's own wife and two children had been killed and scalped in an Indian attack (Slaughter 1988).

As had been the case with Franklin's charges against the Pennsylvania Germans, the charges against Irish immigrants were politically motivated. The Federalists saw in Irish immigrants the backbone of the support building for the Republican Party. As Carter (1989) describes, "Both contemporary observers and modern historians agree that a continuing and major source of Republican electoral strength from the early 1790's onward was provided by the votes of the foreign-born. Among this group none were more determined or effective in their support of the Jeffersonian Republican Party than the Irish of the seaport cities of Baltimore, New York, and Philadelphia." In part, the alliance of the Irish and the Republicans was fed by their mutual suspicion and antagonism toward the British. In Pennsylvania, in particular, the Irish immigrants posed

---

[6] Other accounts put the number higher (150) and lower (20).

an electoral threat. The Pennsylvania Constitution of 1790 allowed noncitizens to vote after two years' residency and six months' payment of taxes; the Republicans made a point of getting the Irish to vote in elections and encouraging their naturalization. Since Congress was meeting in Philadelphia during this period, all Federalists, not just Pennsylvania's, were exposed to this pattern.

Although neither Genêt's activities nor the Whiskey Rebellion posed a long-lived (or even real) threat to the country, concerns about the security of the new republic led to a reevaluation of the liberal 1790 naturalization act that included both Federalists and Republicans. Although Congress was not ready to repress immigration totally, largely because of the link to economic growth and the vision of America as a sanctuary for the oppressed, the Federalists, in particular, were prepared to restrict the access of immigrants to citizenship. Samuel Dexter, a Federalist member of Congress from Massachusetts, in introducing the debate in Congress summarized the concern of his confederates, describing "the present easy access to citizenship as dangerous and insufficient to prevent improper persons from being incorporated with the American people. Longer time was absolutely necessary in which to detect persons lacking natural attachments" to the country (Franklin 1906: 49). Even James Madison, leader of the Republicans, agreed that the conflict in Europe made it necessary to revisit the terms of naturalization.

The Naturalization Act of 1795 differed from its predecessor in several respects. First, it specified that naturalization could occur only as specified by "Act of Congress." In effect, the federal naturalization process was to supersede state naturalization processes to become the only vehicle to citizenship. Second, it increased the period of time between admission and naturalization to five years. It also required applicants to declare their intent to naturalize at least three years prior to the actual naturalization. All applicants would be required to issue an oath or affirmation that they renounced "forever all allegiance and fidelity to any foreign prince, potentate, state, or sovereignty whereof such alien may at that time be a citizen or subject (Naturalization Act 1795)." At the time of naturalization, the applicants were required to show they had lived in the United States for five years and in the state in which they applied for at least one year. The applicant was also required to repeat the renunciation oath and swear allegiance to the U.S. Constitution. This could be done in either federal or state courts. The courts would determine if the residency requirement was met and if it appeared "to their satisfaction that during that time he has behaved as a man of a good moral character, attached to the principles of the Constitution of the United States, and well-disposed to the good order and happiness of the same."

In a bow to the Republicans, who were concerned about the nobles who had fled France for the United States after the French Revolution, new citizens also had to renounce any hereditary titles or orders of nobility. An attempt by opponents to link this provision to one requiring that new citizens renounce slavery, and thereby embarrass the southern Republican slaveholders who spoke of equality in supporting the renunciation of titles, was defeated. As Madison argued, the Constitution proscribed the granting of titles, but it did not proscribe slavery.

The 1795 Act grandfathered in immigrants who were already in the United States prior to its enactment, allowing them to naturalize after two years of residency. Children under the age of 21 and those born abroad to parents who were U.S. citizens obtained citizenship through their parents; in a change from the 1790 Act, though, the term "natural" was dropped before citizen. The 1795 Act continued to recognize states' limits on naturalization, adding that no one "who has been legally convicted of having joined the army of Great Britain during the late war, shall be admitted as foresaid, without the consent of the legislature of the state in which such person was proscribed."

A number of amendments failed, including proposals to take citizenship away from persons who accepted the citizenship of another country or who had expatriated themselves. Although there appeared to be support for such action, it was unclear that Congress had the right to withdraw citizenship. Madison pointed out that the Constitution had given Congress the responsibility to regulate and naturalize immigrants, not take away citizenship from those born with it.

During the next four years, the security concerns about immigration grew as the conflict in Europe and potential involvement of the United States grew. When faced with possible infringement of its neutrality, the United States rejected the advances of Genêt. When faced with possible conflict with Britain, the United States negotiated the Jay Treaty. Criticized at the time and by later historians as preferential toward the British, the treaty reaffirmed U.S.–British trade relations, required the British to recognize the boundaries of the United States established by the Treaty of Paris, provided for compensation to Americans whose goods were illegally seized by the British and for repayment of debts still owed by Americans to British merchants, and reduced tensions that might have led to outright conflict.

The French did not see the treaty in these benign terms; rather, they saw it as a testament to American violation of its supposed neutrality at best, and a clear sign of American preference for Britain at worst. Under the terms of the Jay Treaty, the United States committed to ordering French privateers out of U.S. ports and to permitting the capture of provision ships bound for French ports (Smith 1954b:39). The French retaliated by attacking U.S. ships, seizing even more than the British had done before the Jay Treaty. As the raids increased, President Washington recalled the U.S. ambassador from Paris. The French refused to recognize a newly sent U.S. ambassador, leading to a break in diplomatic relations.

When John Adams became president, he inherited the tense situation with France. He sent a delegation that included Elbridge Gerry and John Marshall, who joined Charles Pickney (who still had not been received as ambassador to France) to negotiate an agreement to stop the attacks. The French foreign minister, Talleyrand, refused to meet with the envoys, leaving the negotiations to go-betweens, later labeled X, Y, and Z. The French indicated that there would be no agreement unless the Americans provided a loan to the French government and paid a large bribe to the ministers, leading to the popular slogan,ting vow "millions for defense, but not one cent for tribute."

Papers describing the delegation's encounters with the French, in what became known as the XYZ Affair, were sent to Congress. The delegates' account united the country in opposition to France. Even the Republican supporters of the French cause were taken aback at France's apparent disregard for American sovereignty. The United States began to put itself on a war footing, preparing for what seemed to be inevitable conflict. The Marine Corps was reconstituted, the Navy received more ships, and the Army recruited more soldiers. Although no declaration of war was made, public support for military action against France was strong.

The Federalists saw in the depredations of the French proof that pure democracy, particularly if the mob is allowed to rule, will undermine the true aims of government. Calling the Federalists the heirs of John Cotton and the Massachusetts Puritans, Smith (1954b:45) describes the Federalist views on government: "The chief ends of government, according to the Federalists, were political stability and the security of society." Once again, the Federalists saw in unbridled immigration a threat to political stability and security. President Adams's nephew is quoted as saying, "The grand cause of all our present difficulties may be traced... to so many hordes of Foreigners immigrating to America... Let us no longer pray that America may become an asylum to all nations" (Baseler 1998: 270).

Even before the XYZ Affair, Congress had been considering changes in the naturalization provisions. In 1797, a Federalist proposal for a $20 tax on naturalization certificates, as a way to raise revenue, had been vigorously debated. The fault lines in attitudes about immigration are clear from the congressional debate. As Baseler (1998: 271) describes the debate, some members saw the tax as a way to ward off the immigration of those who emigrated "with a view to disturb our tranquility." One proponent had no problems with continuing immigration, but he would deny American citizenship to all but the native born. Opponents of the tax saw it as violating America's promise as an asylum for the oppressed and as both insult and injury to poor but industrious immigrants. The $20 tax and a proposal for a $10 tax were defeated, but a $5 tax was enacted.

After the XYZ Affair, a more extreme position won out in Congress. Not only was Congress prepared to pass a highly restrictive naturalization code, it was also ready to enact new laws to regulate the activities of immigrants – both friends and enemies. On May 1, 1798, the Committee for the Protection of Commerce and the Defence of the Country reported its findings, arguing that there needed to be a longer term before admission to citizenship as well as a mechanism to register all aliens and to apprehend, secure, and remove male resident aliens from countries that had declared or threatened war with the United States.

On May 2 Congress began debate on a new naturalization law. At its core was a proposal to extend the period between admission and naturalization to fourteen years; applicants could give notice of their intent five years after admission. The opposition to the fourteen-year requirement focused on two issues: whether the term was too long and whether the requirement should be applied retroactively. Although some members opposed it because they believed that even those immigrants whom the country desired would be discouraged from immigrating, others argued that it would create second-class residents who paid taxes but would be unable to participate in electoral affairs for much of their adult life. Others argued that it was unfair to those who had already expressed their intent to naturalize to make them wait the additional period.

In narrow votes in the House of Representatives and the Senate, the fourteen-year term prevailed. The Federalist concern that newcomers should be barred from citizenship until after a long exposure to American civic values, combined with increasing unease about immigration itself, created the environment for this near-tripling of the residency requirement. In a nod to the retroactivity issues raised in the debate, those who were already in the country in 1795 and those who had already declared their intent to naturalize under the 1795 Act were permitted to go ahead with naturalization under the old provisions. No alien who was a citizen, denizen, or subject of any nation with which the United States had been at war at the time of his application could be admitted to become a citizen. Also, clerks of the courts involved in naturalization were to send the federal secretary of state records of stated intent to naturalize as well as the final naturalization papers themselves. Records of intent were to include the name, age, nationality, residence, and occupation of each applicant.

The 1798 Naturalization Act also set out new regulations regarding immigration, a step that Congress had not previously taken. In the Constitution, the congressional right to regulate the "migration or importation of such persons as any of the states now existing shall think proper to admit" was deferred until 1808, but Congress was given the authority to impose a tax or duty on such importation. Conceived as a way to address the slave trade, the actual constitutional provision was much broader in granting Congress the authority to regulate immigration. Whether Congress could take such initiative in 1798 was not as clear. Many members of Congress believed that the authority to regulate immigration rested with the states. In fact, the states had been passing legislation on a range of immigration issues, including the grounds, such as criminality or pauperism, for barring immigrants, and bars in northern states on the admission of slaves.[7]

Nevertheless, Congress passed provisions in the Naturalization Act that required all white aliens to register with the closest district court or agent appointed by the president within six months of passage of the legislation. Future immigrants were to report within 48 hours of arrival. A record would be made of the name, demographics, nationality, occupation, and intended

---

[7] For a fuller discussion of state legislation, see Neuman (1993).

residence of the immigrants. They would be given a certificate of registration, which would later confirm that they had met the necessary naturalization residency requirements. Shipmasters who did not report their foreign passengers would be subject to fines, as would aliens who did not report themselves or their dependents.

Not satisfied with addressing the dangers posed by immigration purely through registration and naturalization restrictions, Congress turned next to the Alien Act of 1798, passed in June 1798, which set out the authority to deport immigrants. This Act, passed as part of a broader set of laws known as the Alien and Sedition Acts, was roundly condemned by the Republicans as a violation of the Constitution and an affront to civil liberties, but they did not have the votes to stop it. The bill was designed to expire after two years.

In a full return to the Massachusetts model, the grounds spelled out for deportation were ideological in nature, although they were couched in security terms. The bill specified that the President had the authority: "to *order* all such *aliens* as he shall judge dangerous to the peace and safety of the United States, or shall have reasonable grounds to suspect are concerned in any treasonable or secret machinations against the government thereof, to depart out of the territory of the United States within such time as shall be expressed in such order" (An Act Concerning Aliens 1798). When seen in combination with the Sedition Act passed a few weeks later, the ideological import of its provisions is better understood. The Sedition Act made it illegal to write, print, utter, or publish, or cause or procure to be written, printed, uttered, or published, or knowingly and willingly assist or aid in writing, printing, uttering or publishing any false, scandalous and malicious writing or writings against the government of the United States, the Congress or the president of the United States, with intent to defame them, bring them into contempt or disrepute, or excite the hatred of the people against them. If convicted, the person would be subject to a fine of up to two thousand dollars and by imprisonment not exceeding two years.

In attempting to implement the law, mostly unsuccessfully, the Adams administration focused its prosecutions under the Aliens Act on persons who had, they argued, also violated the Sedition Act. Two particular cases stand out. John D. Burke had fled Ireland with a sedition charge hanging over him. In the United States, he was the co-editor of the *New York Time Piece* and a leader of the United Irishmen, both known to be supporters of the Republican Party. Burke made a plea bargain to leave the country in exchange for the administration's waiving prosecution on the sedition charges. Before his deportation could be arranged, however, he went into hiding until after the Alien Act expired. William Duane was the editor of the *Aurora*, the most vocal opponent of the Federalists. Although Duane claimed to have been born in Vermont, Attorney General Pickering argued that he had left as a child, spent the Revolution outside the country, and reentered only a few years before the passage of the legislation. Pickering tried to prosecute him under both the Alien and Sedition Acts, but Duane's claim to citizenship hindered the former prosecution. In fact, no one was deported under the Alien Act before it expired, although a number of immigrants voluntarily left the country that they believed no longer wished their presence.[8]

Concerned that war with France was coming, Congress turned to the issue of what to do about enemy aliens who were on the territory of the United States. In July 1798, Congress passed An Act Respecting Enemy Aliens (Enemy Alien Act). It determined that "whenever there shall be a declared war between the United States and any foreign nation or government, or any invasion or predatory incursion shall be perpetrated, attempted, or threatened against the territory of the United States, by any foreign nation or government, and the President of the United States shall make public proclamation of the event, all natives, citizens, denizens, or subjects of the hostile nation or government, being males of the age of fourteen years and upwards, who shall be within the United States, and not actually naturalized, shall be liable to be apprehended, restrained, secured and removed, as alien enemies" (An Act Respecting Enemy Aliens 1798). The president could determine, depending on the threat posed, if the enemy alien should be relocated to another part of the country or removed altogether.

There was little controversy around the Enemy Alien Act. Congress appeared to have full authority to enact it under its war powers authority. The Act required a declaration of war and included legal protections for the alien. The law specified that a court "after a full examination and hearing on such complaint, and sufficient cause therefor appearing, shall and may order such alien or aliens to be removed out of the territory of the United States, or to give sureties of their good behaviour, or to be otherwise restrained" (An Act Respecting Alien Enemies 1798). Unlike the Alien Act, the Enemy Aliens Act had no expiration date and is still in force.

Toward a New Era

The controversial nature of the Alien and Sedition Acts forced realignment in U.S. politics. The Federalists pushed through the legislation but they were not necessarily trying to stop all immigration. Many Federalists, drawing on their Hamiltonian origins, continued to see economic and political power in population growth and wanted a continuation of immigration. Their suspicions about immigrants, however, led them to policies that restricted the rights of immigrants, generally leading them toward the Massachusetts model. Immigrants were to be welcomed but only if they were the right type of immigrants – and, preferably, would vote with the Federalist Party. For those with different values, expulsion was the appropriate response. John Adams perhaps summarized the view most cogently when he said "if we glory in making our country an asylum for virtue in distress and for innocent industry, it behooves us to be aware that under this pretext it is not made a receptacle of

---

[8] For more information on implementation of these acts, see Smith (1954, 1954b, 1954c).

malevolence and turbulence for the outcasts of the universe" (quoted in Smith 1954c: 89–90).

The Federalists would not have the last word, though, on how the new republic would address immigration issues. The Alien and Sedition Acts so mobilized opposition to the heavy-handed Federalist policies that Jefferson's Republican Party was able to establish electoral ascendancy for the next quarter century. Even so astute a politician as Alexander Hamilton failed to perceive the extent to which the attacks on immigrants and civil liberties would backfire on the Federalist Party. Although Hamilton cautioned his fellow Federalists not to move too precipitously or cruelly in enacting the new legislation, he made no effort to stop the process; he even used the provisions of the Sedition Act to his own benefit in New York by trying to shut down the opposition Republican press. In reference to the Alien Act and the Sedition Act, Hamilton wrote to Pickering, who would be responsible for implementation, "My opinion is that the mass [of aliens] ought to be obliged to leave the country" (Smith 1954a:306). Hamilton and his allies failed to see that their support of such overreaching legislation would turn the foreign-born decisively into the camp of the opposition.

For their part, the Republicans criticized the Acts for their effect on citizens as well as aliens. The strongest condemnations reflected concerns about the powers given to the federal government relative to the states and to the executive branch relative to the legislative and judicial brnaches. The opponents also emphasized the threat to individual civil liberties, particularly freedom of speech and freedom of the press. In a resolution written by James Madison and passed in December 1798, the Virginia legislature summarized the constitutional concerns regarding the Alien Act which, it said, "exercises a power no where delegated to the federal government, and which by uniting legislative and judicial powers to those of executive, subverts the general principles of free government; as well as the particular organization, and positive provisions of the federal constitution" (Virginia Resolution 1798).

The northern states generally disavowed Virginia's action. They argued that the Supreme Court, not individual states, should determine if acts of Congress are constitutional. Although they did not provide a detailed defense of the Alien Act or the Sedition Act, most appeared to see them as expedient given the unsettled times in which they were passed – with the exception of Massachusetts. Massachusetts argued that the alien acts were constitutional because they applied to "persons whose rights were not particularly contemplated in the Constitution of the United States, who are entitled only to a temporary protection, while they yield a temporary allegiance: a protection, which ought to be withdrawn whenever they become 'dangerous to the public safety,' or are found guilty of 'treasonable machinations' against the government" (Commonwealth of Massachusetts 1799).

Madison responded with a further critique of the constitutionality of the Acts. He made the case that aliens have rights under the Constitution. Although the Constitution is a compact whose parties are its citizens, and therefore

Massachusetts may be correct that aliens are not parties to the Constitution, "it will not be disputed, that as they owe on one hand, a temporary obedience, they are entitled in return, to their protection and advantage." Going further, Madison pointed out that banishment is a severe punishment for an alien because it means leaving "a country into which he has been invited, as the asylum most auspicious to his happiness; a country where he may have formed the most tender of connexions, where he may have vested his entire property, and acquired property of the real and permanent, as well as the movable and temporary kind; where he enjoys under the laws a greater share of the blessings of personal security and personal liberty than he can elsewhere hope for, and where he may have nearly completed his probationary title to citizenship" (Virginia 1799).

In the election of 1800, the Alien and Sedition Acts were fuel for political fire. The Alien Friends Act expired in June 1800 and there was no political support for its reenactment. The Sedition Act was to expire in March 1801, upon the end of Adams' term in office. The external political context had changed by the time of the election; the threat from France had diminished with Napoleon's advent to power. The arguments used by the Republicans in defense of civil liberties and limited federal power had broad appeal. The Federalist attempt to stifle the Republican press through the Sedition Act backfired as the Republicans took over the legislatures in a number of previously Federalist states, including New York, home to Alexander Hamilton. The Republicans used the assault on due process, as exemplified by the Alien Act's permitting banishments by executive power alone, to convince Americans that their own rights were in jeopardy. Immigrants who had previously been Federalists, such as Pennsylvania's Germans, came over squarely to the side of the Republicans. As Baseler (1998: 287) describes, Republicans promised to return America to a time, in their words, "when no alien law existed. Every industrious or valuable man who chose to contribute by his ingenuity or learning to your arts or manufactures, was invited to emigrate, every oppressed man was taught to believe, that here he would find an asylum from tyranny."

Although hyperbolic compared with the actual legislative changes that occurred in the new administration, these sentiments reflect a renewed commitment to the Pennsylvania model. Immigrants were once more to be welcomed – although perhaps not as generously as in 1790 – as presumptive members of the society and polity. The first step was revising the naturalization laws. Not ready to return to the very generous provisions of the 1790 Act (although Jefferson floated the idea), the Congress used the 1795 law as a model. The most important change reduced the residency requirement to the original five years adopted in 1795. The bill specified, however, that the applicant's oath would be insufficient to prove the period of residency. Rather, the registration requirement of 1798 was continued as the principal way in which applicants would prove they were eligible to be naturalized. The requirement that applicants declare their intent three years before naturalization was also restored from the 1795 law, but this provision led to later complaints by immigrants who had come to the country when the 1798 law was in effect and, therefore, could not make their intent known in a timely fashion. They argued that they would have to wait eight years before they could be naturalized. In March 1804, their concerns were taken into account, and Congress passed legislation exempting them from the requirement to declare their intent.

The naturalization provisions remained largely intact for more than one hundred years. Certainly, the full promise of the Pennsylvania model was not expressed in the 1802 legislation. It was not until 1870 that naturalization was extended to aliens of African nationality or descent; at the same time, it was explicitly denied to Asians. Only in 1952 did naturalization become truly colorblind. Nevertheless, the easing of the 1798 restrictions on naturalization paved the way for a reemergence of mass migration, though not to occur for almost three decades.

6

Building a Nation

1830–1880

Between 1820, when the federal government began to count arrivals, and 1860, almost 5 million European immigrants arrived in the United States. Although the number declined during the first years of the Civil War, it began building again by 1863. During the course of the 1860s, about 2 million immigrants came, with another 2.7 million entering in the 1870s. Never before had the country needed to absorb so large a number of newcomers in so short a time. The range of countries from which immigration took place also increased, with fewer people coming from Britain and more from Ireland, Germany, and the Scandinavian countries. In addition, under the Treaty of Guadalupe Hidalgo, the United States gained control over large areas of what had been Mexico. Although they were not, strictly speaking, immigrants because they had already been living in what became U.S. territory, under the treaty Spanish speakers found themselves under American rule. Their numbers were relatively small, however. The 1850 census, for example, counted only 13,000 Mexican nationals living in the United States.

Most of the new immigrants came as free workers, since indentured service had declined in importance as a mechanism of immigration. Concepts about the new immigrants largely followed notions as to their assimilation. Observers such as Herman Melville shared the optimism of the Pennsylvania model: "On this Western Hemisphere all tribes and people are forming into one federate whole; and there is a future which shall see the estranged children of Adam restored as to the old hearthstone in Eden" (Melville 1983: 185). That is not to say that even supporters of immigration were not concerned about the assimilation of newcomers – certainly, concerns about English language acquisition persisted. However, those who believed in the Pennsylvania model generally trusted the absorptive capacity of the republic.

At the same time, concerns about the new immigration resulted in the formation of associations such as the Order of the Star-Spangled Banner and political parties such as the Know-Nothings. Echoing the Massachusetts model's preeminent concern with ideological and theological purity, the Select Committee of the House of Representatives summarized what it saw as the dangers of immigration to long-held American values: "the number of emigrants from foreign countries into the United States is increasing with such rapidity as to jeopardize the peace and tranquility of our citizens, if not the permanency of the civil, religious, and political institutions of the United States" (U.S. Congress 1856). One Know-Nothing pamphlet assailed the annexation of Mexico because it would mean "five millions of Papists in our midst – four millions and a half being of foreign birth and four millions speaking a foreign language – all taught from infancy to hate and detest Protestantism as a crime . . . " (Brownlow 1856).

The Virginia model manifested itself in the contract labor system that brought thousands of Chinese to the United States to farm, work in the mines, build the railroads, and undertake other dirty, dangerous, and demeaning work. Between 1848 and 1882, an estimated 300,000 Chinese came to the United States. Borrowing money to pay for their transport, they followed the indentured patterns of earlier waves of migrant workers. Unlike previous patterns of indenture and more in keeping with patterns of slavery, the Chinese came to be seen as expendable workers who were to be excluded from entry and citizenship as soon as their labor was no longer needed. This chapter will explore the role that racism played in precipitating the discriminatory treatment afforded the Chinese, and later, other Asian groups.

The Advent of Mass Migration from Europe

This new era of mass migration was heralded by a measure designed to regulate immigration – the Passenger Act of 1819. Enacted in the context of the most severe economic depression yet experienced by the republic, the law federalized some of the earlier provisions, such as requiring ship captains to supply the Collector of Customs with a list of all arriving passengers at U.S. ports. The list was to indicate the sex, occupation, age, and "country to which they severally belonged." At first only Atlantic and Gulf port information was collected; Pacific ports were added after 1850. Immigration information from Hawaii, Puerto Rico, and Alaska dates only from the beginning of the twentieth century, as does the recording of information at the land borders with Canada and Mexico. The Passenger Act also regulated the number of passengers on ships and the conditions under which they would be permitted to travel, something that had previously been accomplished by state regulation, not federal.

A combination of push-and-pull factors provided the impetus for mass migration into the United States. In the aftermath of the Napoleonic Wars, Europe underwent a transformation. During this period, the last vestiges of feudalism disappeared and agrarian capitalism and industrialization took hold throughout Western Europe. Britain took the lead, building new manufacturing industries and global trade with the help of precision tools, the steam engine, clipper ships, railroads, and other new transportation innovations. British society was already highly mobile; the shift from a rural to an urban society accelerated. Continental Europe followed. By 1848 serfdom was officially banned in the Austro-Hungarian Empire and by 1860 it was banned in the Russian empire. Peasants were freed of their ties to their feudal masters and were able to make their own decisions about where to live and what to do. The ideals of the French Revolution persisted after the defeat of revolutionary France and spread throughout Europe. Notions of liberty, equality, and fraternity were taken seriously by those who also wanted the freedom to think as they chose.

Moving toward those ideals in Europe was difficult, however. Revolutions in 1830 in France and Belgium ushered in constitutional monarchies that were short-lived in France but successful in Belgium. The more widespread outbreaks of revolutionary fever in 1848 were largely suppressed or fizzled. A combination of factors precipitated the uprisings, including tensions arising over absolutist monarchical policies, rapid industrialization and urbanization, food shortages, rural poverty, and changing land-use policies. Many of the revolutionary demands focused on nationalist aspirations, especially within parts of the Hapsburg Empire, as well as on such liberal reforms as universal franchise, freedom of speech, and freedom of the press. By 1849, however, counter-revolutionary forces were strong enough to put down the nascent nationalist movements and the empire was restored.

The British had already put down the 1798 rebellion led by the Society of United Irishmen, which united Protestants and Catholics against English rule. In 1801, Ireland was brought into the United Kingdom by an act of union and placed under direct parliamentary control. Under England's earlier policy of treating Ireland as a colony, vast areas of Ireland were in the hands of absentee landlords. This contributed to the Great Famine of 1845. Although the immediate trigger for the crop damage was the potato blight, politics and economics created conditions that allowed famine. Even when an estimated 1 million people were dying from starvation or related disease, food was being shipped from Ireland to England. As Amartya Sen has said more generally about famine, "Starvation is a characteristic of some people not having enough food to eat. It is not the characteristic of there not being enough food to eat" (Sen 1982: 1). Although emigration from Ireland had been a constant for the previous century, the scale of emigration increased dramatically in response to the famine. An estimated 1 million to 1.5 million Irish left the island during the period from 1845 to 1851, large numbers of whom settled in the United States. They were fleeing not only the immediate effects of the famine but also evictions from their homes and lands when they were unable to pay the rent (Johnson 1990: 274). In fact, some landlords paid for the transport of tenants to the Americas. For example, Lord Palmerston, the British Foreign Secretary, paid for the transport of about 2,000 of his tenants to Canada, many of whom continued on to New York (Anbinder 2002). In the aftermath of the famine, emigration continued, reflecting longer-term structural reasons related to changes in the Irish economy and demography. In a shift from previous waves of Irish emigrants, the migration was island-wide and included large numbers of Catholics.

Conditions in Germany also precipitated emigration. Annual emigration from Germany, estimated to be about 1,700 in 1829, had grown to 32,700 by 1840, and reached 83,200 in 1850. In 1854, it peaked at 239,200, before decreasing back to the 80,000 emigrants per year range (quoted in Pierenkemper and Tilly 2004: 97). Economics was a prime factor. Although the potato blight was not as pervasive as in Ireland, Germany also experienced crop failures from the blight and poor wheat harvests. In some areas, where land was expected to be divided among all sons, the size of the plots of land available by the nineteenth century could no longer support even subsistence agriculture (Pierenkemper and Tilly 2004: 95). Cottage industries in other parts of Germany suffered from competition with growing industrialization in England, which was able to produce textiles and other products cheaper than could be done at home. Politics played a role, particularly in the aftermath of the 1848 revolution when thousands of disappointed liberals chose to emigrate rather than live under Prussian oppression. Religion did not play as prominent a role in the nineteenth century as it had done in earlier waves of emigration, but the enforced unification of the Lutheran and Reformed churches and tensions between Catholics and the Prussian state contributed to emigration.

Similar factors set the stage for mass emigration from Scandinavia.[1] Sweden and Norway experienced a transition in their land ownership and usage practices, as the bonders (independent farmers) sold or subdivided their land and the torpares (tenant farmers) found themselves with plots too small to support themselves (Stephenson 1926: 722). Opposition to the policies of the official state religions was a further contributing factor. Crop failures in the 1860s also stimulated emigration.

Once immigration to America began from a specific region or community, it often became self-sustaining as a result of the information sent back by previous emigrants. Immigrants in America also sent remittances that were used to pay the transport of family members. Improvements in transportation within the United States, particularly the canals and railroads, allowed immigrants to spread out through the country. But, what was of greatest interest to prospective immigrants was the economic opportunity that they would find, combined with the greater political and religious rights and social mobility of the American republic. These were the "pull" factors that influenced migration patterns in the nineteenth century.

The United States presented opportunities in both cities and rural areas. Wage rates for unskilled labor far exceeded the earnings that most immigrants could have hoped to reach in their home countries. During the 1850s, for example, wages in Ireland were 44.4 percent of U.S. wages. In Germany, the differential was not as high but wages there were still only 52.5 percent of U.S. wages. For Norway and Sweden, the gap was much larger; in these countries workers were paid 27.2 and 24.2 percent of U.S. wages, respectively (O'Rourke and Williamson 2001).

[1] Also see Lowell (1987).

Many immigrants settled in gateway urban areas, such as New York and Boston, and in new manufacturing cities, such as Lowell, Massachusetts. Often, immigrants experienced urban life for the first time in America, frequently living in ethnic ghettos. The Irish, compared with the Germans or Scandinavians, were particularly likely to settle in urban areas along the East Coast. The Irish constituted more than 80 percent of Boston's foreign-born population and 50 to 60 percent of New York's and Philadelphia's foreign-born residents (Ward 1968: 352). In these urban centers, the Irish and other immigrants found economic opportunities in construction, manufacturing, and domestic service.

For the large number of immigrants who wanted to retain an agricultural way of life, the United States was clearly a land of opportunity. Under a series of statutes, the federal government provided advantageous terms for the purchase of land in the opening territories of what was then known as the Northwest Territory, covering what are now the states of Ohio, Indiana, Illinois, Michigan, and Wisconsin, as well as the northeastern part of Minnesota. The Northwest Ordinance of 1787 specified that the Northwest Territory and subsequent states would have neither slavery nor indentured servitude, ensuring a system of free labor. The Land Act of 1820, passed after the hardships of the Panic of 1819, allowed purchase of lots of at least 80 acres for $1.25 per acre; however, it repealed an earlier credit system that had allowed homesteaders to pay in installments. An increasing number of people squatted instead, leading to further legislation in 1831 and 1841 giving the squatters an opportunity to purchase the land that they had been using.

The immigrants were not often pioneers, looking for untamed land. Instead, they often purchased land from those who had claimed it in earlier years and who now were looking for the capital to move still farther west and purchase newer or larger plots. By 1850, immigrants had become a significant portion of the population in the five states of the Northwest Territory – Wisconsin (36 percent), Illinois (19 percent), Michigan (20 percent), Ohio (14 percent), and a smaller share in Indiana (9 percent). The largest immigrant group was from Germany, with smaller numbers of Irish, Scandinavians, and, in the border areas, Canadians (Swierenga 1989).

As the country opened up to still further settlement, European immigrants followed. Some bought farms; many settled in cities. The Louisiana Purchase had opened up 800,000 square miles of land, about one quarter of the current territory of the United States, constituting all or part of fifteen states. The Oregon Territory, explored by Lewis and Clark, was formalized in 1848, after the border dispute with Britain was settled. It eventually became the states of Oregon, Washington, and Idaho. The defeat of Mexico in 1848 led to acquisition of land that extended the United States from coast to coast and incorporated new residents through conquest rather than immigration, as will be discussed in the next section. The 1849 Gold Rush ushered in a new era of immigration to California. Along with the Gold Rush and the building of the transcontinental railroad came migration from China and a resurgence of the Virginia model, as is discussed later.

Mexicans in the United States

Mexico achieved its independence from Spain in 1821, becoming a self-governing country that encompassed not only what is now Mexico but also vast territories in what is now the United States. Generally, these outposts of Mexican society had small populations. The total population of Mexico was 6 million at the time of independence, but only 50,000 lived in the frontier region (Kessell 2003: 377). Hoping to set up a buffer between its major population centers and the growing United States, Mexico encouraged Americans to emigrate to Texas, as long as the Americans agreed to abide by the terms of the Mexican Constitution (which included adopting the Catholic faith, although that provision was not enforced), pay taxes to Mexico, and forgo slavery. Similarly, Americans began to trickle into California and New Mexico, newly opened to trade now that Mexico had become independent from Spain.

At the time of independence, the Mexican population of Texas numbered only about 2,500 (Weber 1982: 160). By the 1830s, the 20,000 American settlers and slaves in Texas far outnumbered the Mexican residents (Weber 1982: 177). As the foreign population increased, concern grew within the Mexican government about the growing American influence. An 1830 law banned further admission of foreign immigrants, including Americans. Other actions sought to control the activities of Americans in Texas. Among other policy changes, new acquisition of slaves was prohibited and exemptions from customs duties were ended. As protests mounted, two Americans, William Travis and Patrick Jack, who were advocating a more militant response, were arrested, precipitating a showdown.

At this stage, most of the American leaders advocated that Texas become a separate state within Mexico and be given greater autonomy. In 1833, Stephen Austin, one of the leaders of the American community in Texas, went to Mexico City with American demands that the ban on immigration be removed and that Texas obtain statehood. He gained the first point, but Mexican President Santa Anna refused to support statehood for Texas. On his return trip, Austin was arrested for planning an insurrection. He was imprisoned in Mexico City and would not be released until 1835. In the interim, his goals shifted from Mexican statehood to independence.

Santa Anna, for his part, was consolidating power. In 1835, Mexico adopted a new constitution that centralized authority in Mexico City, dismantling the federalist system that had been patterned after the United States. A coalition of the church and military supported the new centralization, arguing that the federalist system had led to instability. The heavy-handed attempt at centralization caused violence throughout Mexico, and it caused many Mexican residents of Texas to side with the Americans in their quest for greater autonomy.

War broke out in October 1835 at the Battle of Gonzales, which, along with the next several battles, was won by the Americans. On March 2, Texas independence was declared and a constitution adopted. A few days later, though, the Mexican army won the Battle of the Alamo, creating a rallying cry for the independence movement. The Americans were further united when, on March 27, Santa Anna ordered the execution of 400 surrendered Texans at Goliad. The tide turned again at the battle of San Jacinto on April 21, in which Santa Anna was decisively defeated and Texas independence became a reality.

Texas retained its independence until December 29, 1845, when it became a U.S. state. Not surprisingly, Mexico, which had never recognized Texas independence, responded that the U.S. annexation of Texas was an act of aggression. U.S. negotiators presented the annexation as an accomplished fact and, in the spirit of America's manifest destiny, which was thought to be control of the territory from coast to coast, offered to purchase the rest of what was then Mexican land from the Texas border to the Pacific. This set off opposition in Mexico to what some saw as an American land grab. Negotiations broke down, with Mexico unwilling to give up its claim to Texas and the United States unwilling to back down and prepared to defend Texas through force. Mexico may have mistakenly believed that Britain would support its claims, not realizing that Britain had already decided to negotiate the boundaries of the Oregon territory. In April, Mexican forces crossed the Rio Grande into Texas, where they were met by U.S. forces. With the collapse of negotiations and the outbreak of violence, the United States declared war in May 1846, asserting that the Mexicans had spilled American blood on American soil.

In the meantime, dissent was also building in California. There, the Mexican population of about 10,000 outnumbered American immigrants, but immigration was growing. Even before learning of the declaration of war, American settlers in Northern California declared independence from Mexico and seized the fort in Sonoma. In July, the U.S. military arrived and forced the Mexican military from San Francisco; by January 1847, the United States controlled southern California.

The fight then moved deeper into Mexico. Despite high levels of mortality, mostly from disease, the United States won decisive victories, including one in Mexico City. Negotiations dragged on, however, until the Treaty of Gualdelupe Hidalgo was signed on February 2, 1848, and then ratified by both governments. Under the terms of the treaty, the southern Texas border was set and Mexico ceded ownership of California and the New Mexico territory, which included what are now Nevada, Utah, and parts of Colorado, Arizona, New Mexico, and Wyoming, to the United States. The United States paid Mexico $15 million and agreed to assume $3.25 million in debts Mexico owed to U.S. citizens.

For our purposes, the most salient part of the treaty of Guadalupe Hidalgo was Article VIII, which granted to the population living in the ceded territory the right to retain Mexican nationality or to take up American citizenship. The residents were required to make a decision within one year. All of those remaining in the territory after that date who had not elected to maintain their Mexican citizenship would automatically be granted U.S. citizenship. The treaty was somewhat vague, though, on what citizenship actually meant. Article IX, as amended by Congress before ratification, stated: "The Mexicans who [become US citizens]...shall be incorporated into the Union of the United States, and admitted as soon as possible, according to the principles of the Federal Constitution, to the enjoyment of all the rights of citizens of the United States. In the meantime, they shall be maintained and protected in the enjoyment of their liberty, their property, and the civil rights now vested in them according to the Mexican laws. With respect to political rights, their condition shall be on an equality with that of the inhabitants of the other territories of the United States; and at least equally good as that of the inhabitants of Louisiana and the Floridas, when these provinces, by transfer from the French Republic and the Crown of Spain, became territories of the United States" (Treaty of Guadalupe Hidalgo 1848).

Hence, for a period, a hybrid system was put in place, with Mexican residents of the new territories able to become American citizens but still subject to Mexican law with regard to many of their rights. There was no reason to believe, however, that many of the new citizens would not soon have the rights accorded citizens of the United States. As indicated in the treaty, the purchases of the Louisiana and Florida territories from France and Spain had already made French- and Spanish-speaking colonists into citizens of the new republic. By 1848, much of these territories had already become states with Florida joining in 1845 and Louisiana much earlier in 1812. Texas, of course, had become a state in 1845, so the Mexicans who remained were already citizens, and California achieved statehood in 1848.

Following the Guadalupe Hidalgo treaty, most of the Mexican landowners in the ceded territories chose U.S. citizenship. Mexicans on the Mexican side continued to cross what was now a border to work for Americans, who often paid them in coupons redeemable in company stores (Truett 2006). In the early years, however, Americans were more dependent on the Mexican economy than the reverse. As Truett (2006: 42) described, American mining camps "depended so heavily on Mexican fields, orchards, and pastures...that one had to consider southern Arizona 'a dependency of Sonora.'"

The influence of Mexican-Americans differed throughout the ceded region. In many areas, the population was so small that it would be difficult to discern any effect of Mexican-Americans. San Antonio, however, had been the center of Mexican influence in Texas before independence, and it remained a largely Mexican city. With a large enough population, San Antonio's Mexican-American citizens were able to assert political power. Their political interests often coincided with those of other members of the Democratic Party, as witnessed by the majority of Mexican voters who supported Texas secession from the United States in the 1861 election (Truett 2006: 156). Intermarriage between the large number of single male settlers from the United States and Mexican women was common, occurring especially in wealthy, influential Mexican families. Enterprising American men could increase their landholdings in this fashion, while association with the Anglos was a kind of protection for Spanish-speaking families, who were now in the minority (Dysart 1976: 371).

In other places, the Mexicans fared much worse. Camarillo's (1979) analysis of the Mexicans living in southern California at the end of the Mexican War is a story of decline. This resulted from a combination of economic factors, including expropriation of ranch lands, legal maneuvering, and discrimination by the growing non-Mexican population. Camarillo (1979) speaks of the "barrioization" of the Mexicans, with increased residential segregation and lessened economic opportunities. These differences in experience persisted through the nineteenth and twentieth centuries until the present, as is described in later chapters.

Chinese Contract Labor

If the Europeans generally came as free labor and the Mexicans became citizens through conquest and annexation, Chinese immigration to America most closely resembled the earlier Virginia model of labor migration. The Gold Rush in California occurred soon after the United States and China negotiated the Treaty of Wanghia, which opened China to American trade and missionary activity. This treaty was loosely patterned after the one that ended the First Opium War between China and Britain, which had given the British rights over Hong Kong.

The first large-scale Chinese migration came from southeastern China, the area that was most involved in trade with the rest of the world. Two provinces produced most of the Chinese emigrants during the nineteenth century – Fujian and Guangdong. They were coastal provinces with agricultural and fishing communities. Textile manufacturing and mining were their other economic activities (Mei 1979). Natural disasters, crop failures, rapid population growth, and conflict, as well as competition from imported textiles from the West, led to conditions that resulted in the emigration of 3 million Chinese from these areas in the nineteenth century, going not only to the United States but also to Mexico, South America, the Philippines, and elsewhere (Krutz 1971: 323). These migrants followed what had been an earlier emigration of settlers to Southeast Asia, where they became sizable minorities in the populations of Thailand and Malaysia.

Chinese migrants to the United States came primarily from the Pearl River Delta. As is the case with most emigration, it was not generally the poorest areas, or the hardest hit by disaster or conflict, that experienced the highest levels of mobility. Chen makes a convincing case that other regions of China experienced most of the problems found in the Pearl River Delta, but these areas often did not have the fertile soil of the delta. As it was more expensive to emigrate to the United States than to Southeast Asia, it took more resources and more information to arrange the voyage. Canton, the port with the highest levels of trade with California in the pre-emigration period, was within the delta area, thus allowing knowledge of opportunities in America to reach the residents. It was to this Chinese region that news of the discovery of gold in California came (Chen 1997: 541). Some of the early emigrants to California had been schooled by American missionaries, meaning that they had some knowledge not only of the country but also of its language.

A Chinese emigrant's decision to leave home was much like that of a European emigrant's, but it was based more on economics than on attraction to the religious or political freedom offered by the United States. Often, households determined which member would benefit the family most by migrating and sending money home. Generally, the choice fell on a man, who would emigrate alone. The expectation was that emigration would be temporary, with the men eventually returning home with their earnings. Only about one-third returned, however, so that wives and fiancés were often left behind in China.

The first large-scale Chinese immigration into the United States was to San Francisco. By 1849, the city's Chinese numbered in the hundreds. Many were merchants involved in trade with China or were proprietors of small retail operations, including restaurants, groceries, and other such establishments. The largest number came from Canton and its surrounding areas, and they arrived with the capital needed to establish their businesses (Mei 1979: 475). Some had been merchants in China. The merchants were followed by workers destined for the gold mines. The latter were generally less prosperous in China but followed the patterns of their predecessors, heading first to San Francisco and then to the mining districts. Although the Chinese were generally barred from actual mining, they provided many of the services needed by the largely male population of 49ers. By 1852, just three years after the Gold Rush began, an estimated 25,000 Chinese immigrants had arrived in the United States, most remaining in California.

A second wave of Chinese immigration occurred during the building of the transcontinental railroad. Construction of the railroad was divided between two companies, the Union Pacific, which started in Omaha and worked its way west, and the Central Pacific, which began in Sacramento and worked its way east. The Central Pacific was running well behind the Union Pacific. It had difficulties recruiting labor, especially workers willing to labor in the difficult terrain of the Sierra Nevada Mountains. The chief of construction, Charles Crocker, reported to a joint congressional committee in 1877 that he was unable to recruit more than 800 white workers, an inadequate number for the job. His solution, despite his reported initial reluctance, was to recruit Chinese laborers. He later expressed surprise that the Chinese workers proved themselves capable of doing even the most difficult work. Crocker reported on the lengths he went in order to find workers, but he noted the superiority of the Chinese in accomplishing the work:

> We went to Virginia City and got some Cornish Miners out of those mines and paid them extra wages. We put them into one side of the shaft, the heading leading from one side, and we had Chinamen on the other side. We measured the work every Sunday morning; and the Chinamen without fail always outmeasured the Cornish miners; that is to say, they would cut more rock in a week than the Cornish miners did, and there it was hard work, steady pounding on the rock, bone-labor. (U.S. Congress 1877)

Crocker also testified that the Chinese were paid $30 per month and covered their own housing, whereas the white workers were paid $35 per month plus housing. He noted that some of the white workers complained that their wages would have been even higher if the Chinese had not depressed wages. Crocker argued instead that, by doing the hard labor, the Chinese opened up other employment opportunities for white workers. He testified that about 10,000 of the 12,500 workers were Chinese, the 2,500 white workers representing a higher number than he had been able to recruit prior to the employment of the Chinese.

Other Chinese immigrated to provide services in the growing Chinatowns that had cropped up across the country. They also worked in domestic service, laundries, groceries, and small manufacturing companies. In fact, in the West Chinese men tended to be employed in many of the jobs held by women in the East. The white workforce in California was disproportionately male, so the Chinese were hired to work in woolen mills, canneries, cigar factories, and boot and shoe factories (Brown and Philips 1986: 63). By 1877, when Congress undertook its investigation of Chinese immigration, there were an estimated 148,000 Chinese residents of California.

Unlike many of the Chinese emigrants who were part of the forced labor trade to the Caribbean and South America, those who came to the United States appear to have made the choice voluntarily. A sophisticated system emerged to defray the costs of migration and to match workers with employers. If would-be migrants were unable to fund their travel, either through their own resources or the pooling of family money, brokers advanced the funds for passage (credit-tickets). The immigrants would repay the cost of the ticket, the fees for the papers needed to immigrate, middlemen's fees, and accrued interest. A $40 passage could turn into a $300 repayment when all of these other expenses were factored into the equation.

Many of the workers came as contract laborers, with employers covering their expenses in exchange for a specified period of labor. Generally the workers were paid as part of gangs, rather than as individual employees. Crocker of the Central Pacific Railroad described the process in his congressional testimony.

> They come together in gangs of twenty-five and thirty, as we need them to work on a job of work, and the account is kept with the gang, No, 1, No. 2, 25, 30, 50, 100, just as it is. Each gang has a book-keeper to keep the account among themselves. We have a foreman and he keeps the account with the gang and credits them. Every night the Chinese book-keeper, who is one of the workmen and works in the pit along with the rest, comes up with his book, and he says so many days for that gang, do you see? and they count it up and they agree, and each puts it down. Then the Chinese keep their own accounts among themselves; but we keep an account with the gang. When the pay-day comes the gang is paid for all the labor of the gang, and then they divide it among themselves. (U.S. Congress, 1877)

Although most Chinese immigration to the United States was voluntary, one form was not: the immigration of prostitutes. As Hirata (1979: 9) described, "Luring and kidnapping were the most frequent methods of procurement, particularly after 1870." Brothel owners would arrange with recruiters in Hong Kong or Canton to kidnap, entice, or purchase women, whichever means worked best. Some came under contracts, usually signed by their families, specifying that they would work for a term of 4 and one-half years for the sum of about $400, after which they would supposedly be freed. The term reflected the period that most brothels considered to be the productive one for prostitutes. Generally, it was possible to increase the period of the contract – for example, if the prostitute became pregnant or worked fewer days per year than expected, the term could be lengthened. During the term of the contract, the prostitute had no say in her working conditions.

The recruiters would turn the women over to importers responsible for arranging their travel to the United States. After restrictions were placed on departure and entry of prostitutes in the 1870s, the importers bribed U.S. officials. According to Hirata (1979: 10–11), the importers charged the brothels a fee of $40 per prostitute, $10 going to bribe the police. Brothel owners paid the passage, the fees to the recruiter and importer, and the bribes, but the returns on prostitutes' labor could be immense. Moreover, many brothel owners sold their prostitutes, making way for new ones and reaping additional benefits from the sale.

Chinese contract labor, with the exception of forced prostitution, resembled indentured service in many respects. The migration was largely voluntary, although the recruiters often exaggerated the riches that could be earned. It mostly involved men emigrating singly, leaving their families behind. But there was one major difference. Unlike the Europeans, who came as indentured servants but could aspire to full membership and family reunification, the Chinese were barred from such pursuits; and, after their contracts were over, many found themselves unwilling or unable to return home. In many cases, they had not earned enough to pay off their debts in migrating and to save enough for the return ticket and a nest egg. Because of a number of legislative and administrative actions, they were unable to bring their families to join them in the United States. Moreover, they were expressly barred from naturalization so they could not become citizens or voters. In this respect they resembled the African slaves imported in the Virginia model, consigned to a lesser status by their race.

With the completion of the railroad, the large number of Chinese workers hired by the Central Pacific joined a floating workforce in California. In the 1870s, economic recession led to high levels of unemployment. At the same time, the growing white population in California included a larger number of women who were willing to work in manufacturing at low wages. Moreover, a growing number of Chinese workers had set up their own factories, going into direct competition with their previous employers. Combined with the disgruntlement of white male workers with what they saw as the depression of wages caused by the Chinese – as well as lingering racism – these trends undercut support for continued Chinese immigration.

In 1862, the Coolie Trade Law prohibited the transport of "the inhabitants or subjects of China, known as 'coolies'... for any time whatever, as servants or apprentices, or to be held to service of labor." More fundamental curtailing of immigration from China required renegotiation of the Burlingame Treaty, which had guaranteed unrestricted immigration from China. A new treaty allowed the United States to regulate, limit, or suspend Chinese immigration. In 1875 legislation was passed barring contract labor, and in 1882 the Chinese Exclusion Act was enacted. Until then, there had never been legislation barring a whole nationality from immigrating to the United States. A series of other laws followed that prevented reentry of Chinese permanent residents who left the country on temporary visits and extended the bars to other Asian nationalities.

In effect, the Chinese immigrants were defined as expendable workers, in the best – or worst – tradition of the Virginia model. Welcomed initially to do work that was undesirable to Americans, particularly at the wages and under the working conditions offered, they were barred from full membership in their new country. When economic times worsened, the numbers grew too large for many of their critics to accept and competition with native workers worsened. The result was to bar further admission of Chinese immigrants to the United States.

Opposition to European Immigration

This focus on the Chinese exclusion policies is not meant to suggest that all European immigrants were welcomed wholeheartedly in the United States. Even as early as 1820, alarms about immigration could be heard, echoing Benjamin Franklin's concerns. An 1820 editorial in the *North American Review* returned to a familiar theme, focusing on language: "By what inconceivable perversity are these gentlemen [who seek to retain the German language] brought to think that it is an advantage to speak a language which your neighbor cannot understand, to be ignorant of the language in which the laws of the land you live in are made and administered, and to shut yourself out, be a Judaic nationality of spirit and manners, from half the social privileges of life?" (Forbes [Martin] and Lemos 1981: 63). The magazine advised Germans "instead of wishing to cherish and keep up their peculiarities of language and manners... get over and forget them as soon as possible" (Forbes [Martin] and Lemos 1981).

As the mass migration from Ireland and Germany grew, combined concerns about language, culture, and religion formed the basis for an assault on immigration. Many Protestants felt threatened by the Catholic immigrants (although they remained in the majority). Even before the mass migration of the 1840s and 1850s, the inventor Samuel F.B. Morse warned: "How is it possible that foreign turbulence imported by the shiploads, that riot and ignorance in hundreds of thousands of human priest-controlled machines should suddenly be thrown into our society and not produce turbulence and excess? Can one throw mud into pure water and not disturb its clearness?" (Morse 1835: preface). Theodore Lyman, Jr., the mayor of Boston, echoed his concerns, saying of Irish immigrants "we shall have among us a race that will never be infused into our own... Their children will be brought up in ignorance and idleness" (Steinberg 1981: 483).

Other concerns about immigration were the threat to the public welfare, public health, and public safety. Poverty was endemic among the new arrivals, prompting one New York almshouse superintendent to complain, "While towns and counties in Europe find it more economical to pay for the transport of paupers to our shores than support them at home, and hence deposit them in shiploads to our cities" (Joselit 1981: 202). This concern reflected a reality. Joselit found that the majority of those admitted to New York City almshouses in the antebellum period were foreigners.

Concerns about the threat to public health also reflected reality. Irish neighborhoods in Boston had the highest mortality rates in the city, approaching one in seven persons, compared with one in fifty-two in middle-class native neighborhoods. In 1850, foreigners accounted for 84 percent of all admissions to Bellevue Hospital in New York, although they represented less than 50 percent of all residents. Perhaps the biggest direct effects of immigration on public health were the cholera epidemics of 1832, 1849, and 1866. In each case, the disease was transmitted from Europe by a ship bringing immigrants to the United States. Most of those who died were immigrants. Yet, most commentators associated the poor health in general with conditions in Europe, the hardships of the passage, and the awful conditions in which many immigrants lived, leading to efforts to reform the slums and tenements, not necessarily to stop immigration.

That was not the case with regard to the threat to public safety. In the 1830s, *Niles' Weekly Register*, a popular journal, warned that the nation "was infested by hordes of foreign wretches, pickpockets, thieves, robbers, forgers, etc." (Steinberg 1981: 481). The inspectors of New York State Prison, commenting that 317 of 711 inmates convicted in 1852 were immigrants, noted "this large proportion of convicts furnished by that class is calculated to arrest the attention." The *Journal of Prison Discipline* offered, "crime is not of natural growth here... No. It is imported, ready made to our hands" (Steinberg 1981: 486). Politicians reminded their constituents that European countries had an explicit policy of exporting their criminals to the United States, a charge that was readily believed, given the history of convict transports.

Again, statistics bear out the charges. New York City prison data for 1858 show that 26,404 of the 35,172 prisoners were foreigners. The pattern had been much the same through the entire decade. The largest group of criminals (19, 662) was from Ireland, divided almost evenly between men (10,299) and women (9,363). A number of books on the problems caused by immigration used data from the 1850 census, plus court and prison records, to show that a disproportionately large number of criminals were foreigners. Many infractions were for minor crimes, particularly drunkenness, but for many Protestants, intemperance was an evil that was fueled by Catholicism, which was fueled by immigration. As a committee of the U.S. House of Representatives concluded, "there is a close and intimate connexion between the large influx of a bad foreign immigration, and the increase in intemperance, and all its concomitant evils" (U.S. Congress 1856).

Out of these fears emerged the first major movement to restrict immigration to the United States. The American, or Know-Nothing Party, campaigned on a platform of rigid restrictions on immigration and naturalization. Coming to political prominence in 1854, they elected 8 governors, more than 100 members of the U.S. House of Representatives, and the mayors of several major cities. Its strongest successes were in New England, New York, and parts of the Midwest, areas with large numbers of Irish or German Catholic immigrants.

The Know-Nothing Party had its origins in New York City in the 1840s. The forerunner was the Order of United Americans (OUA), a mutual insurance company (Levine 2001). Membership in the OUA was limited to Protestants who were native-born citizens and who swore to resist the insidious policies of the Roman Catholic Church (Anbinder 2002: 23). One of its key leaders and its major theorist was Thomas R. Whitney, who edited *The Republic*, a journal that became the voice of the nativist movement. Whitney had run for office as a Whig, the political party that succeeded the Federalist Party (see Levine (2001) for more information on Whitney). As with the Federalists, the Whigs were divided on immigration. The segment that wanted to build a strong capitalist economy tended to favor immigration for much the same reasons that Hamilton did, as a way to increase the population of the country. Another segment was fearful of the impact that immigration was having on American Protestant society. The Whig leadership also worried that too close an association with nativism would harm the party's chances of gaining the votes of new immigrants, not all of whom were seen as locked into the Democratic Party. The Whigs decided not to support Whitney in a run for Congress in 1854, so he ran under the banner of the new American Party.

The Know-Nothing Party was not a one-issue party. Although best known by its opposition to immigration and Catholicism, the party also espoused a form of capitalism that its members saw as consistent with republican ideals. Farmers, mechanics, and merchants were the backbone of society (Levine 2001). Not supporters of unbridled egalitarianism, the Know-Nothings supported the social hierarchy of the day. Opposing women's rights as firmly as they did immigration, they argued the cause of the industrious American worker but opposed social engineering as encompassed in minimum-hour laws and in the Homestead Act, which would have offered free land on the frontier. The Know-Nothing rhetoric was particularly appealing to artisans who felt increasingly excluded from the emerging industrial economy of the country. The party also hedged on what was to become the defining issue in American politics, the future of slavery. Although it was generally opposed to slavery, the Party was also opposed to going to war to end it.

The Know-Nothings' belief in social hierarchy extended to politics; they believed that only the "patriotic" should be able to vote. In this case, patriotism was defined by nativity, meaning native-born Americans. Echoing broader concerns about corruption in American politics, the Know-Nothings blamed immigration for bringing people with no knowledge of a republican form of government into the voting booths. They also argued that language differences were evidence of irreconcilable cultural differences between immigrants and Americans. They wanted the borders closed to all but those who already shared the prevalent American language and customs. One Know-Nothing pamphlet assailed the annexation of Mexico because it would mean "five million Papists in our midst – four millions and a half being of foreign birth and four millions speaking a foreign language – all taught from infancy to hate and detest Protestantism as a crime..." (Brownlow 1856: 71).

The Know-Nothing Party received political advantage from several attempts in the 1850s to enact legislation on behalf of the Catholic Church. One was a resurgent call by the bishops for public financial support for parochial schools. Another was a statute that would have given ownership of Catholic Church property to the bishops. Further, the Pope sent Gaetano Bedini to the United States as the papal nuncio (ambassador). Bedini had been involved in the suppression of the Revolution of 1848 in Italy, and his appointment elicited demonstrations from some of the 48ers who had left Italy for the United States when the revolutions were crushed. All of these events inflamed anti-Catholic fervor in the period leading up to the 1854 election.

As with its Federalist predecessors, the platform of the Know-Nothings focused on naturalization, not on restricting immigration. The most extreme position, held by Whitney, was to bar immigrants from ever becoming citizens. The more common proposal was a residency requirement of twenty-one years, which was even longer than that of the 1798 Naturalization Act.

Nativist sentiment manifested itself on the streets, not just in the ballot box. Immigrants were prevented from voting in a number of major cities. In 1855, riots in Cincinnati were focused on the German immigrants. Other riots against Irish or German immigrants, or both, took place in Baltimore, Maryland; Lawrence, Massachusetts; St. Louis, Missouri; and New Orleans, Louisiana. In Louisville, Kentucky, more than 20 died and hundreds were wounded in anti-immigrant and anti-Catholic violence. News of the riots and the electoral results quickly got back to Europe, where the Prussian and other German governments used the incidents to try to convince Germans not to emigrate. Cohn (2000) argues that the nativist violence and election results did succeed in reducing immigration from Ireland and Germany, and, in the case of the Germans, in redirecting immigration away from states that had supported the Know-Nothings.

The success of the Know-Nothings was short-lived and failed to achieve any significant legislative victories. Whether it would have gained more ground if slavery had not emerged as a more important issue in the 1860 election is debatable. What is known is that the Civil War diverted all attention from the issue of immigration and on to the much more fundamental issue of American unity.

Immigrant Adaptation and Integration

The level of adaptation of immigrants to the economic, social, and political contexts of the receiving society has a great impact on their own lives and on the ways in which the majority perceive them. In contrast with the much better data that began to be available in the late nineteenth century, statistical information on those who arrived before the Civil War is much scarcer. It was not until the census of 1850 that detailed data on a range of pertinent issues were collected, and it took several censuses before there was sufficient consistency in definitions to examine change over time with any assurance.

Through anecdotal information, as well as data from community and ethnic studies, it is possible to begin to put together a picture of the adaptation process. As was true for both earlier and later waves of immigrants, the human and financial capital with which mid-nineteenth-century immigrants arrived in the country greatly affected their economic adaptation as well as their notions about the American social and political system. At the risk of oversimplification, it is possible to say that German or Scandinavian Protestant immigrants who came as skilled tradesmen generally had an easier time adapting to life in America, despite their lack of English, than did Irish Catholic peasants escaping the Potato Famine. The former had skills needed by a growing economy, shared the dominant religion, and, for Germans at least, an already established community that could help them in their transition. The latter possessed few skills that they could turn into productive enterprises, had no capital for investment, and belonged to a religion that was seen by the majority as antithetical to the values of the republic. German Catholic peasants perhaps had the worst of the situation, sharing the disadvantages of the Irish but also lacking any familiarity with the majority language.

Despite these clear differences in advantage upon arrival, all of these groups adapted well to their new environment, although in different ways and with different timeframes. As we have seen, the settlement patterns also differed, with the Irish more likely to congregate in eastern cities and the Germans and Scandinavians moving westward to farms or smaller cities. As the economies of these areas differed, the economic experiences of the immigrants differed. As one analysis concluded:

> The spectacular achievement of white-collar status by first-generation Germans in Poughkeepsie is due primarily to the frequency with which they became employers in craft-related shops, notably in the food and apparel trades but also in the more specialized wood and metal manufactures. The Irish in Boston, by contrast, more often provided labor for much larger enterprises where skills were more diluted and where opportunities for achieving employer status were

far less frequent. Quite apart, then, from the advantages German immigrants had over the Irish in skill, capital or entrepreneurial propensity, there is evidence for believing that the small city, in which small craft-related shops still dominated much of the manufacturing, held obvious advantages for European newcomers. (Griffen 1972: 324)

The Irish in the large cities of the East had a particular struggle to reach middle-class status. A study of occupational mobility in Philadelphia between 1850 and 1880 found that "Even by a crude occupational rank order the Irish fare the worst of the three groups [Irish immigrants, German immigrants, and natives] in 1850, for nearly half of them were located in day labor (30.3 percent), hand-loom weaving (11.6 percent), and carting (3.3 percent). Less than a third of them worked at 'skilled' trades (excluding hand-loom weavers)" (Laurie, Hershberg, and Alter 1975: 234). By contrast, the German immigrants, who came with higher skills, were employed in more skilled occupations. Thirty years later, the Irish were still disproportionately in unskilled jobs. Their sons, however, had begun to move up the occupational ladder, especially in printing, construction, and the metal industries, but progress was slow (Laurie et al. 1975: 244). For many of the Irish, public sector employment increasingly became a popular economic adaptation strategy, particularly as they began to amass political power in urban centers. In the early nineteenth century, the Irish immigrant was stereotyped as a criminal; by the late nineteenth century, his son was likely to be the neighborhood policeman.

Language adaptation was the principal challenge for the non-Irish immigrants. To an even greater degree than is true of economic adaptation, the data of the times make it difficult to assess progress in learning English. It was not until the 1890 census that information was collected on knowledge of the English language. The growth in native-language newspapers and magazines indicated some level of native-language retention among immigrants, but this does not necessarily mean an inability or unwillingness to learn English. The earliest German newspapers dated to the colonial period. During the nineteenth century, a proliferation of Norwegian, Swedish, Danish, Dutch, and Swiss newspapers appeared (Zubrzycki 1958). These provided information about the home country but, more important, provided information about the United States. One historian has described the ethnic newspapers of this period as American newspapers written in the German or Scandinavian language (Zubrzycki 1958).

For the children of German and Scandinavian immigrants, in particular, English language acquisition and native language retention were often seen as opposite sides of the same coin. Hamre (1981: 304) notes that Norwegian immigrants eagerly sent their children to American public schools in the antebellum period because they "desired to learn English and to become acquainted with the institutions of their new homeland. They valued the contributions that the schools could make in these respects." At the same time, the Norwegian immigrants supported parochial schools in which the Lutheran religion and the Norwegian language were taught.[2]

German immigrants were also committed to native language retention; "the nineteenth-century German community in America was rent by deeply divisive religious and regional antipathies, yet the issue of native-tongue instruction drew them together more effectively for political purposes than any other" (Schlossman 1983: 144). In 1840, Ohio passed a law that made it "the duty of the Board of Trustees and Visitors of common schools to provide a number of German schools under some duly qualified teachers for the instruction of such youth as desire to learn the German language or the German and English languages together" (Andersson 1971: 428). Cincinnati developed one of the most extensive programs of German language instruction. Such programs were also common in other states and cities with large German immigrant populations. German language instruction was especially prevalent in rural areas where German immigrants predominated.

Using language that would be common today, educators that supported native language instruction argued, as did the superintendent of schools in Marathon County: "Let the child's mind have a chance to enlarge by the use of its own language and it will in time learn another language two times faster and understandingly" (quoted in Schlossmann 1971: 144). School systems also justified substantial German-language instruction as a way to encourage the immigrants to send their children to public, rather than parochial, schools. Some educators were fearful that the children would lose their knowledge of their parents' language, creating an intergenerational wedge that would disrupt family harmony (Schlossman 1971). This is not to say that there were no opponents of bilingual instruction. It was opposed on financial as well as pedagogical grounds, with particular concern expressed in some jurisdictions that native-language retention would inhibit the assumption of American values by the immigrants and their children. Rather, the point is that throughout the nineteenth century, and, indeed until World War I, German-language maintenance was a common element of public school instruction and was more often considered a vehicle of assimilation, not isolation, for the immigrant children.

Immigrants often formed voluntary associations that helped the integration process. Alexis de Tocqueville (2000: 489) commented in *Democracy in America* that "In America I encountered sorts of associations of which, I confess, I had no idea, and I often admired the infinite art with which the inhabitants of the United States managed to fix a common goal to the efforts of many men and to get them to advance to it freely." Religious institutions were, of course, important associations for immigrants in the mid-nineteenth century, as they were before and after that period. The church was a safe environment in an often hostile country, with its new customs and beliefs. It was also a place where immigrants could learn how to cope with the new realities. The

---

[2] In later years, there was more tension between the public and parochial school systems.

church itself generally underwent an Americanization process, with even the most hierarchical taking on the congregational forms of the early Protestant churches in America. English-language liturgy and sermons appeared, as did an increasing role for the laity in the management of the churches (Hirschman 2004: 1215).

Ethnic associations also played an important role in helping the new immigrants to adjust. Even sometimes-reviled Chinese societies in the United States, often referred to as the Six Companies, served an adaptation function. They provided a range of social services to immigrant Chinese communities and they offered employment services that linked immigrants to jobs. Irish, German, and Scandinavian associations also proliferated. What Diner (1983: 121) describes about the Irish applied to these other groups as well: "Like emigrants from elsewhere, the Irish in the United States actively worked to create an internal community structure of organizations of all kinds – mutual aid and benefit societies, insurance and charitable organizations, temperance lodges, nationalistic societies, fire companies, military units, building and loan associations, 'county-based clubs'. . . . " These associations provided both financial and moral support as immigrants sought to adjust to life in America. Their effectiveness was often determined by the resources available to the community and the interests of the men who ran the associations. Diner (1983) argues that the Irish civic associations did too little to address the widespread poverty of "Erin's Daughters," partly because many men did not have sufficient resources to take out memberships in the mutual aid societies, and therefore were unable to provide for their widows. On a larger scale, however, "the associational life they created reflected their concerns about politics both in the United States and back in Ireland" (Diner: 124). Where the civic associations failed to assist, the Church often stepped in, with Irish nuns particularly playing an important role in helping their secular counterparts.

Conclusion

As the United States became a nation that stretched from sea to sea, immigration played an important role in defining the new American. As in the colonial period, many different notions of immigration characterized the nineteenth-century approach to the admission and settlement of foreigners. Europeans – most of whom came from western and northern Europe – were generally seen through the prism of the Pennsylvania model, albeit with serious concerns about Irish Catholic immigrants. Seeing Catholics as much more "foreign" than even the non-English-speaking Germans and Scandinavians, Protestant Americans feared papist influences upon the new republic. Despite the pressure of the Nativist Know-Nothings, these fears did not lead to serious efforts to curtail immigration. As immigrants moved up the economic ladder and proved themselves to be loyal supporters of the Union, they became the "old immigrants" that opponents of later immigration would herald as superior examples of the benefits of the "right" immigration. In hindsight, if not at the time, the antebellum European immigrants became the symbol of the continued endurance of the American melting pot.

The same could not be said of the Mexicans or Chinese. Mexicans became American through conquest, not immigration. Although landowners fared well, the average laborer found himself marginalized economically and socially, unable to benefit from the opportunities that slowly opened up even to the reviled Irish. The Chinese immigration epitomized the essence of the Virginia model: importation as contract workers and exclusion when their labor was no longer needed. As the government took steps to prohibit further immigration of the Chinese, and barred other forms of contract labor, a new wave of European migration began that was even more suspect than that which preceded it. This is the subject of the next chapter.

7

The Golden Door

1880–1917

The 1880s ushered in a new era of immigration, with growth in both numbers and diversity of origins of the immigrants. With the advancing industrial revolution, demand for labor grew and so did immigration. From 1860 to 1880, about 2.5 million immigrants entered the United States each decade; during the 1880s, the number more than doubled to 5.2 million. In the first decade of the new century, 8.8 million entered the country, with a record of 1.285 million entering in 1907 alone. Only the decade of the 1890s saw a reduction over the previous decade's levels, largely because of the economic depression that affected much of the U.S. economy.

The origins of the new immigrants shifted with the growth in numbers. No longer were immigrants coming only from the British Isles and western and northern Europe; many of the newcomers came from southern and eastern Europe. In the first decade of the twentieth century, more than 2 million Austro-Hungarians, a like number of Italians, and 1.6 million Russians immigrated, accounting for more than 70 percent of all immigrants. Britain, Germany, and Ireland accounted for only 6.5, 4.2, and 4.2 percent, respectively. Some came for permanent residence, particularly groups, such as the Jews, who had been persecuted in Europe, whereas others were "birds of passage" who intended to work for a few years and then return home.

Attitudes about immigration and the new immigrants continued to show ambivalence. Many Americans remained optimistic about the absorptive capacity of the country. Emma Lazarus's welcome of the teeming masses might not have been universally shared, but certainly business leaders and many politicians continued to profess support for large-scale immigration. The economic case for immigration was particularly strong in the new age. Although the end of the frontier meant that immigrants would no longer be needed to fill the vast continent, the factories in many cities appeared to have an insatiable demand for workers.

That is not to say that the "golden door" metaphor was without its challenges. Just as the antebellum Germans and Irish had appeared more foreign than British immigrants, the new immigrants appeared more foreign than those in the previous wave had. They differed in other respects. In 1880, more than half of the foreign-born population of the country had come from English-speaking countries; by 1920, they represented a small fraction of the total. Rather, these years brought people who spoke languages not generally found in the United States, including Italian, Yiddish, Greek, and Slavic languages. None of these languages shared the English/Germanic roots of the earlier immigrant languages.

Echoing the Pennsylvania model was a new coalition that pressed for public and private support for the "Americanization" of the new immigrants. Although later co-opted by Restrictionists, the original Americanization movement was dominated by social reformers who focused on language training and civics education. The settlement house movement, established to help the urban poor, became an important facilitator of immigrant integration. Immigrants themselves soon established associations, schools, and other institutions to help them deal with language differences, as had immigrants in earlier waves.

Although these efforts proved fruitful in helping millions of immigrants adapt to the new country, they did not offset mounting concerns within the country about the wisdom of mass migration. The roots of the restrictionist movement, and its eventual success in curtailing immigration, are discussed in greater detail in the next chapter.

Origins of the New Immigration

The third wave of immigration, as was the case with the first two, was generated by a combination of push-and-pull factors. Timothy Hatton and Jeffrey Williamson's seminal study, *The Age of Mass Migration: Causes and Economic Impact* (1998: 250), looking at European migration from 1850 to 1914, sees continuities from the second wave:

> the story begins with two economic shocks of enormous proportions: a resource discovery in the New World and an industrial revolution in the Old World.... The two shocks produced a profound labor market disequilibrium early in the century. Wage gaps between the labor-scarce New World and the labor-abundant Old World reached huge dimensions.... But these two shocks also produced the means by which global labor market integration could, at least eventually, be achieved.

By the 1880s, wages in the principal northern and western European emigration countries had increased significantly enough to offer economic rewards to those who remained at home. The emigration of the earlier period, combined with lower fertility rates, had resulted in low rates of labor force growth, causing labor scarcity beginning in the 1880s [see Easterlin (1961) for a discussion of impact of lagged rate of natural increase and per capita income]. In the post-famine period, for example, Ireland saw what Hatton and Williamson (1998: 92) termed "the impressive rise in Irish wage rates and living standards" that allowed the economic opportunities at home to catch up with those offered by emigration, reducing the pressure to migrate. Similar gains were made in Germany and the Scandinavian countries.

At the same time, by the early 1880s, the "pull" factors in the United States had recovered from the Civil War and then from the financial panics of 1869 and 1873 that led to a prolonged depression. Recovery began in 1879, setting the scene for an expansion of the economy in the 1880s (before the cycle changed again in the panic of 1893). In contrast to the antebellum period, in which land was abundant and many of the German and Scandinavian immigrants, in particular, moved into agriculture, the primary economic activity that would draw immigrants in the late nineteenth and early twentieth centuries was occurring in the cities of America. In 1890, the Superintendent of the Census declared an end to the frontier, prompting one of the most important treatises in American history – Frederick Jackson Turner's *The Frontier in American History* (1920). Industrial cities became the new frontier, attracting labor from rural areas of the United States as well as from new source countries in Europe.

The New Emigrants

The new source countries were largely in southern and eastern Europe. Lagging behind the now industrializing northern and western European countries, the Mediterranean states and the peripheral areas of the Austro-Hungarian and Russian empires became the new sources of immigrants. Wages and living standards remained far lower in these countries than could be found in the United States or in western Europe. As Hatton and Williamson (1998: 121) say of Italy, real wages were not the determinant of emigration but "larger wage gaps [between Italy and destination countries] and lower levels of economic development drove emigration up." Although the poorest of the poor did not tend to emigrate, over time, as more and more conationals established themselves in the United States, the cost of emigration came down and became affordable for a larger segment of the population. Remittances from immigrants in the United States paid the transport costs for their relatives. Moreover, the cost of transport and the time needed to reach America had fallen dramatically with the advent of steam-powered ships and the proliferation of railroads across Europe. As Keeling (2005) notes, "by 1900 already, the total expense of moving to America (of which the oceanic fare was roughly half) had dropped to well below what an average European migrant working in the U.S. could expect to have saved, net of living costs, six months after the move." By the 1880s, steamships had replaced sailing ships, reducing the transatlantic crossing to about ten days (Gartner 1986). Moreover, the risk of a transatlantic journey had fallen as shipping safety improved (Keeling 2005).

The steamship companies played an important role in stimulating migration, even beyond cost. The larger companies, such as the Holland America Line, charged a package fare, bringing immigrants from points as far away as Russia to ports in the north Atlantic and then on to America. The Dillingham

Commission[1], charged by Congress to assess the impact of immigration, reported in *Emigration Conditions in Europe* that "next to the advice and assistance of friends and relatives who have already emigrated, the propaganda conducted by steamship ticket agents is undoubtedly the most important immediate cause of emigration from Europe to the United States" (Immigration Commission 1911b: 61). One "authority" referred to by the Commission estimated that "two of the leading steamship lines had five or six thousand ticket agents in Galicia alone" (Immigration Commission 1911b: 62). Although U.S. immigration law prohibited companies from soliciting or encouraging immigration, the companies were allowed to advertise their sailings and there was little regulation of the activities of their agents.

These lower costs of migration had profound implications for the type of migration to emerge in the late nineteenth century (see Baines 1994 for what we know and do not know about the determinants of return migration). No longer was the cost of return migration prohibitive for many Europeans who sought higher wages in the United States. Legislation passed in 1907 required the U.S. Commissioner-General of Immigration to collect data on migrants departing the United States. Between 1908 and 1910, 2.297 million immigrants were admitted and 713,356 departed (Immigration Commission 1911b: 41). The number departing per 100 admitted varied greatly by nationality. The highest proportions were from Turkey (69/100), Hungary (64/100), Northern Italy (62/100), Slovakia (59/100), southern Italy (56/100), and Croatia/Slovenia (56/100). By contrast, only 6/100 of the Irish and 8/100 of what were then termed Hebrews departed. To some extent, the departures followed economic cycles, increasing in times of economic recession, but they also reflected an increase in temporary labor migration. Italian migrants particularly fit the category of what came to be known as "birds of passage." As early as 1874, Leone Carpi wrote: "thousands of Italians go in search of work abroad, then come back within a year or two, bringing with them a small amount of savings, along with some bad habits" (quoted in Kessner 1981: 315). The Italian government data on returnees show the arrival back of more than 100,000 traveling in third class (steerage) in nine out of ten years between 1906 and 1915. A high of 240,877 returned in 1908, when the U.S. economy was beset by a recession[2] (Kessner 1981: 317).

A large proportion of the Italian migrants were men (78.6 percent) who were of working age (82 percent between 14 and 44 years) (Immigration Commission 1911b:25). The Italian government generally preferred temporary migration, seeing it as a safety valve for un- and under-employed workers and a source of

---

[1] The recommendations of the Commission are discussed in detail in Chapter 8. Given its generally restrictive leanings, it is not surprising that the commission would use such terms as "propaganda," but the general point is valid: the steamship companies had a vested interest in migrants' crossing the Atlantic.

[2] U.S. data showed the return of 167,000 in 1908. More than 80 percent had been in the United States for less than 5 years.

remittances. Kessner (1981: 323) quotes an Italian Senator: "The great current of returning emigrants represents an economic force of the first order for us. It will be an enormous benefit for us if we can increase this flow in and out of the country . . . If we can increase this temporary migration." When the U.S. Congress considered limits on immigration, the Italian government pressed for presidential veto or, failing that, exemptions for temporary workers. When it appeared likely that a literacy requirement would be imposed, the Emigration Council of Italy proposed to establish schools to prepare emigrants for the new requirement (Kessner 1981: 331).

Not all migration of this period was motivated by pure economic interests, and certainly, temporary migration was not the norm for many of the arriving immigrants. The Dillingham Commission in its exploration of emigration conditions repeatedly points to Jewish immigration as an exception to the largely economic motivation of other immigrant groups.[3] The Commission reprinted two reports on the circumstances of Jews in the Russian empire. The first was written by officials of the Jewish Colonization Society (also known as the Baron de Hirsch Fund) and the other by I. M. Rubinow of the U.S. Bureau of Labor (pp. 272–81 and 281–336). While the first dealt with legal issues and the second with economic conditions, both reports largely point to repressive policies as the underlying cause of Jewish emigration.

The reports cited restrictions in habitation, occupation, and education as contributing to economic and physical insecurity for the Jews. The Russian government increasingly restricted Jews to the towns and cities of the Pale of Settlement. The borders of the Pale included parts of what are now Poland, Ukraine, Lithuania, Belarus, and Moldova. Although the Pale was established in the eighteenth century, the requirement that Jews live only within its territory solidified in the late nineteenth century after a period of liberalization in the mid-1800s. In 1882, Jews were required to move from rural areas and villages into small towns (shtetls) within the Pale. In 1891–92, even more restrictive measures were introduced, including the expulsion of Jews from eastern Russia into the Pale, including 30,000 from Moscow and 20,000 from St. Petersburg. In addition, still more Jews were required to move from villages within the Pale into shetls.

The Baron de Hirsch Fund memorandum particularly focused on the growing number and changing characteristic of the pogroms that began after

---

[3] More recent historiography on Jewish immigration emphasizes the economic roots. See, for example, Hertzberg (1998). Others agree that emigration from Russia was largely political, emphasizing the exceptionalism of these movements in turn of the nineteenth- to twentieth-century America. For example, Friedman (2007) writes of Jewish migration from Czarist Russia: "Here, indeed, was a model case of a persecuted minority facing a hostile majority at home and finding in the United States not only a brighter economic future or a temporary source of earnings but religious tolerance, republican institutions, and the separation of church and state, all of which seemed essential to survival for many Jews in the 1880s and few of which could readily be found elsewhere. Jewish immigration would appear to be a model case in support of American exceptionalism, but for the fact that it was, well, exceptional. . . ."

Czar Alexander II's assassination in 1881 and the ascension of Alexander III to the throne: "The Government, which in every case of pogrom had displayed a remarkable indifference, in many cases clearly permitted them. During many of the pogroms, especially those of the cruelest nature, disinterested witnesses declared that the soldiers called to the spot not only failed to disperse the pogromists, but even served them as kind of escort" (Immigration Commission 1911b: 278). The pogroms of 1903–1905, after it became clear that the Czar Nicholas II was not going to reverse the policies of his predecessor, were especially devastating and led to the highest rates of Jewish emigration – some 125,000 emigrated in 1905–1906 alone. The Baron de Hirsch Fund concluded: "the Jews are emigrating, not because it is impossible for them to find sufficient earnings in Russia, but because the Government deprives them of the most elementary conditions of security of life and property" (Immigration Commission 1911b:281). Rubinow of the U.S. Bureau of Labor concurred, "The facts detailed in the foregoing pages indicate how deeply the lives of the Russian Jews have been influenced by the legal conditions under which they live.... They are of decisive influence in determining the very dimensions of the current of immigration from western Russia to the United States" (Immigration Commission 1911b:336).[4]

In one respect, Russian Jews were more fortunate than their counterparts. Czarist Russia prohibited emigration, except for Jews. Another report commissioned by the Dillingham Commission focused on Russian law and emigration, concluding "Russian law makes it very difficult for a Russian subject to leave his native land in a lawful manner, to say nothing of emigration [that is, more permanent departures], which is absolutely illegal" (Immigration Commission 1911b). In 1892, however, the Jewish Colonization Association received imperial sanction and new rules were promulgated concerning Jewish emigration. The departure of families and orphans was permitted, with the understanding that "Jews who leave Russia with outgoing certificates [from their local governors] are deemed to have left Russian territory forever" (Immigration Commission 1911b:261). These emigration rules may help explain why the demographics of Jewish immigrants differed from other groups. Jewish immigrants were

---

[4] My father and maternal grandparents were among the Jews who left Russia for America during this period. My father's family came from Milejcsicz in what is now Poland. He arrived in 1906, at age six, accompanying his mother and younger brother, to join his father who was living on Ludlow Street in the Lower East Side of New York City. They sailed from Antwerp on the *Kroonland*, arriving at Ellis Island on September 11. My maternal grandmother had come earlier that same year, accompanying her older sister, niece, and nephew, who were joining their husband and father in New York. Her family lived in Kiev, from which they traveled by train to Rotterdam to take the ship by the same name. She arrived at Ellis Island on January 24, 1906, at the age of 19. I have not found records for my maternal grandfather but he too emigrated at about this time, meeting and marrying my grandmother shortly after her arrival in New York. Like many other immigrants, they sent money back to Kiev and eventually brought her parents and younger siblings. Her oldest brother remained behind to help support the family as they awaited their opportunity to emigrate, losing his chance to join the rest of the family when World War I broke out.

more evenly mixed between men (56.7 percent, compared with 78.6 percent for southern Italians) and women (43.3 percent, compared with 21.4 percent); and they were far less likely to return home. Their occupations also reflected the legal restrictions on Russian Jews: of those who reported an occupation, only 1.9 percent listed themselves as farmers or farm laborers and 11.8 percent as common laborers while 67.1 percent reported themselves to be skilled workers.[5] For Jews as a whole, about 45 percent listed no occupation – a higher proportion than for most groups because of the larger number of women and children who immigrated. By contrast, only 23.3 percent of southern Italians listed themselves as having no occupation, reflecting the predominance of working age men.

The Italians and Jews represent two dimensions of turn-of-the-twentieth-century migration. Like Italians, others from the Mediterranean region and Balkans (e.g., Spanish, Greeks, Bulgarians, Croatians, and Serbians) tended to be overrepresented among temporary migrants. Men were a large majority of these migrants – more than 90 percent of emigrating Bulgarians, Serbians, Montenegrins, Dalmatians, Bosnians, and Herzegovinians between 1899 and 1910 and 94.5 percent of emigrating Greeks in the period 1901–1910 (Immigration Commission 1911b:376, 392). As with the Italian government, the temporary migration was seen as beneficial to the source country. A Greek commission concluded: "The Greek in departing from Greece to better his fortune not only has a firm determination to return home as soon as he shall have achieved his object, but he intends to maintain a close relation with the fatherland during his absence" (Immigration Commission 1911b:397). The Dillingham Commission estimated that $5 million was sent to Greece from the United States in 1907 alone (equivalent to $117 million in today's purchasing power). The estimate did not include money brought home by returning migrants. The Dillingham Commission hastened to point out that Greek return rates were actually lower than some of the other immigrant groups.

Jewish emigration, by contrast, was characterized by permanent migration, with very few returning to Europe. This type of migration also characterized turn-of-the-century movements from the older sources (Germany, Scandinavia, Ireland, and Britain) as well as Bohemia and Moravia in the Austro-Hungarian Empire. Polish immigration was in the middle. The Dillingham Commission's analysis of return between 1908 and 1910 showed that 30 Poles departed for every 100 who were admitted, much lower than the more than 50 return rates for the Mediterranean countries but much higher than the 7 to 11 percent found in the older source countries.

Even with high return rates, all of the countries showed net growth in the immigrant stock within the United States. The number of foreign-born from Italy in the U.S. census grew from 44,230 in 1880 to 182,580 in 1890, 484,027 in 1900, and 1,343,125 in 1910. This represented almost a fourfold increase

---

[5] Jews from the Austro-Hungarian Empire also reported a skewed occupational distribution. Of those with occupations, more than 67 percent were skilled workers.

during the 1880s and more than a two-and-a-half-fold increase in subsequent decades. The foreign-born from Poland grew at a similar rate, despite the lower return rates, from 48,557 in 1880 to 937,884 in 1910. By contrast, the foreign-born who listed Greece as their country of origin grew from only 776 in 1880 to 101,282 in 1910. Most of that increase occurred during the first decade of the twentieth century, when the Greek population grew more than twelvefold. To understand this process, we turn now to a discussion of the "pull" factors that brought immigrants to the United States and settled permanently even those who had planned to return home.

The United States at the Turn of the Century

Understanding the large growth in immigration that began in the 1880s requires an examination of the nature of the U.S. economy during this period. Using a neo-Marxism prism, Calavita (1984: 3) describes this period as dominated by capitalist immigration, which had the following characteristics: "1) the complete separation of the work force from the means of production; 2) relations of production that are based on free contract and bargaining, not outright force; and 3) an insatiable drive for increasing levels of surplus labor and surplus value."

The U.S. economy in the post–Civil War era indeed underwent spectacular growth that may well have led to the insatiable drive for labor that Calavita (1984) describes. One historian described the dual tracks of economic growth during the Gilded Age: "One path expanded the nation's agricultural base, while the other built a dynamic industrial complex. As corporations multiplied and as various industrial sectors developed, the workforce shifted proportionately toward wage labor in manufacturing, mining, sales, and services. Innovations in railroads, steam shipping, and electronic communications increasingly linked American producers to markets around the world, integrating the United States into the emerging 'global' economy" (Campbell 2002: 161–62).

The new economy was characterized by two seemingly contradictory trends – the growth in mechanization and the growth in cheap labor. The 1876 Philadelphia fair in honor of the country's centennial showcased the new technology – the telephone, power looms, sewing machines, typewriter, and new steam engines – which in turn ushered in a new era of industrialization (Trachtenberg 1982). By the 1890s, electricity had replaced the steam engine, allowing for still further growth in manufacturing, which in turn led to new efficiencies, including the assembly line. Productivity reached new heights. The completion of the transcontinental railroad had already allowed for the efficient transport of raw materials to the factories and finished products to the consumer. Large corporations grew around these new opportunities. Starting with the railroads themselves, corporate America dominated the steel industry, exploration for oil, banking, and other sectors.

While investing in technology, the American economy grew in its reliance on low-wage unskilled workers from rural parts of the United States and, increasingly, from Europe. Literacy rates were used by the Dillingham Commission as a rough indicator of the level of education of immigrants, compared with natives. About 10.7 percent of the U.S. population over the age of 10 reported themselves as illiterate in the 1900 census. By contrast, 54.2 percent of southern Italians immigrating to the United States between 1899 and 1909 were illiterate; 35.4 percent of Poles, and 68 percent of Romanians. The corporations that prided themselves on their technological advances nevertheless saw the need for unskilled labor. Moody's Investment Service, as late as 1919, argued: "We look for a heavy immigration with all that this means. For one thing, it means lower wages.... It also means lower operating costs and better control of operating ratios. It is bound to mean too some decrease in the present extraordinary power of the labor unions" (quoted in Calavita 1984: 152).

Clearly, despite – or perhaps because of – the growth in technology, corporate America wanted large-scale immigration. Hatton and Williamson (1998: 173) help explain: "immigrants filled less skilled niches in slower-growing activities while natives filled more skilled niches in faster-growing activities." The commission, in its analysis of displacement of natives, shared Hatton and Williamson's conclusion, noting that natives tended "to attain to the more skilled and responsible technical and executive positions which required employees of training and experience" (Zeidel 2004: 103).

At the other end of the skills mix, Hatton and Williamson's (1998) findings confirmed contemporary opinion that immigrants competed with unskilled natives, both displacing them and lowering wages in the sectors that remained dependent on unskilled labor. Immigration also, in their estimate, caused a geographic displacement of native workers from the northeast of the United States, where most of the immigrants settled, to the western states.

Throughout the period from 1880 to World War I, immigration followed economic cycles, albeit imperfectly. While the entire period was characterized by relatively high levels of immigration, there were ups and down determined by the state of the U.S. economy. Figure 7.1 shows the overall levels of admissions during this period.

After growing during the first three years of the 1880s, immigration dipped in 1884 and remained at relatively low levels, particularly through the recession of 1893–96, when immigration hit levels that were considerably lower than seen in the 1850s. As the economy recovered at the turn of the century, immigration increased rapidly until it reached its highest level in 1907, only to fall by 500,000 as the 1908 recession took hold. This recession was considerably shorter than those of the 1870s and 1890s, and immigration quickly resumed, again reaching levels of more than one million in 1914, when war in Europe curtailed movements. Admissions in 1915 were only a quarter of the previous year.

Some contemporaries argued that the temporary migration patterns of many of the immigrants fit the economic cycles. Not only would fewer immigrants arrive during economic downturns, more would go home when unemployment rose. Hatton and Williamson (1998: 173) concluded, however: "Migration's

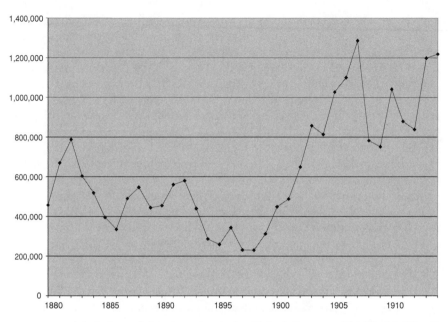

FIGURE 7.1. Admission of Immigrants to the United States, 1880–World War I.
Source: Immigration and Naturalization Service.

ebb and flow did little to ease the wide swing in unemployment associated with
business cycles and industrial crises. Immigration was simply not the effective
guestworker safety valve contemporary observers often imagined."

Immigrant Integration and Adaptation

As was the case in earlier periods, the success of immigration in the late nineteenth and early twentieth centuries was measured by the extent to which
immigrants were seen to adapt to life in the United States, as measured by
economic outcomes and well as language acquisition, health status, propensity
toward crime, and other factors. The Dillingham Commission was the first
major attempt to assess the adaptation of immigrants, amassing a large quantity of data and applying the most modern (to that date) statistical analyses.
Although the commission has been justifiably criticized for pre-judging the
results of its analysis, and ignoring data that contradicted its often racist views
on the "new" immigrants, it deserves credit for publishing forty-seven volumes
of often detailed analyses whose results the reader can judge. The commission
used existing census and administrative data and undertook its own surveys,
which collected information on occupation, sex, age, marital status, country of
birth, and "race" as defined in its own *Dictionary of Races*. To the commission,
what is often now called ethnicity was evidence of separate racial categories.
For example, Magyars were a racial group, many of whom lived in Hungary;

Hebrews were a racial group who lived in numerous states. In selected sites, the commission also asked about such topics as union membership, family structure, and charitable organizations.

While much of the Commission's research used what are now considered to be standard scientific methodologies (albeit without the statistical controls used today), some of the most controversial of the research utilized questionable techniques. For example, a large-scale study by noted anthropologist Franz Boas was based on immigrant physiology. The study examined changes in head measurements, body size, muscle strength, and physiological maturity to determine if the children of immigrants assimilated to an American standard. Boas's work undermined the racist cast of much of the commissioners' view of immigration. Boas concluded that "the adaptability of the immigrant seems to be very much greater than we had a right to suppose before our investigations were instituted," citing evidence of convergence with physical characteristics of the native-born, such as stature, even among children born abroad who immigrated to the United States at an early age (quoted in Zeidel 2004: 99).

Employment and Earnings

The heart of the Commission's analysis was its 25 volumes on immigrants in industries, including information about more than 500,000 wage earners throughout the country (see Zeidel 2004). Immigrants were involved in a wide range of industries, including construction, light manufacturing of such items as shoes, garments, and cigars and cigarettes, in food preparation, in retail sales, and in heavier industries such as mining and steel manufacturing.

The commission provided substantial data on earnings, typically showing that the immigrants coming from new sources generally had lower earnings than natives or immigrants from the old sources. Tables that compared length of residence, however, often showed that the data were capturing experience rather than origins. New evidence shows, though, that the first generation of the "new" immigrants not only started at a lower wage level but also that they took longer to catch up. Hatton and Williamson (1998: 153) concluded: "in contrast with the old immigrant groups, many first-generation immigrant groups failed to catch up with native-born." Their lower level of education and literacy caused persistent wage deficits.

Labor force participation differed by gender as well as nationality. Not surprisingly, male participation in the labor force exceeded female participation, especially among groups dominated by male immigrants. Women did work, though. As Gold (1999: 118) recounts, "During the period of great migration of Jews from 1880–1930, due to poverty and the high cost of living, Jewish women and children were often active in income generation. They frequently worked in garment assembly, an occupation that involved a large proportion of the entire population. When children were small, women often engaged in home based production, allowing them to both earn money and care for off spring." Although many small retail shops were listed as male owned, wives and children worked side by side with their husbands and fathers

(Diner 1994: 82, about Jewish immigrants in the mid-nineteenth century). Women immigrants also ran boarding houses, which served the needs of the largely male immigrant workers. Yans-McLaughlin (1982) found this was a particularly attractive option for Italian women, although Italian women would work outside the house when economic necessity required and the working environment (presence of other women in the workplace, access to child care) permitted it (Vecchio 1989).

Language and Social Adaptation

As the sources of immigration diversified, immigrants' ability to acquire the English language intensified as an issue. As we have seen, the extent and rapidity of immigrants' language acquisition had been a preoccupation since at least the mid-eighteenth century. In 1880, however, more than half of the foreign-born population came from English-speaking areas. In the 1910 census, the largest number of foreign-born residents named English (3.4 million) and German (2.8 million) as their native language, but Italian (1.4 million) and Yiddish (1.1 million) followed in third and fourth place, already reflecting the large growth in immigration of Italians and Jews (Stevens 1999: 391). With relatively less inflow from Britain and Germany, and an aging of the second-wave immigrants, the new language groups came to dominate the foreign-born population in later censuses. Large cities experienced the transformation, for example, as the once Irish-dominated area of New York became "Little Italy," but rural communities also experienced the change. In Western Pennsylvania's anthracite coal fields, for example, more than 70 percent of the foreign-born workers in 1890 had been from England, Wales, and Ireland. By 1900, "arrivals from Poland and Russia constituted more than one-quarter of the immigrant population, and a multitude of others from Italy, the Balkans, the Austro-Hungarian Empire, and the Baltic formed another fourth of the newcomers" (Dublin and Licht 2005: 21–22).

Census figures on the percentage of the population who did not speak English showed the growth of the non-English speaking population (although it is difficult to track from census to census because of differences in the ways in which the question was asked; see Stevens 1999). In 1890, when a question on language was first asked, 15.6 percent of white immigrants reported that they could not speak English; a somewhat lower percentage (12.2) reported no English in 1900. By 1910, after a decade of extremely high immigration, 22.8 percent reported that they could not speak English. A decade later, as more immigrants learned the language and fewer new immigrants arrived, the proportion of non-English speakers dropped to 11 percent.

Intent to remain in the United States appeared to have a positive effect on English language acquisition. In the 1900 census, 34 percent of those who had not applied for their naturalization papers spoke no English; 13 percent who had filed their first papers were unable to speak the language; only 3.5 percent of those who had become naturalized did not speak English (Forbes [Martin] and Lemos 1981). This finding is not surprising, in that temporary migrants would have had fewer reasons to learn English, particularly if they were working in industries dominated by non-English speaking workers.

Length of time in the United States also affected language acquisition. According to the Dillingham Commission survey of woolen and worsted goods manufacturing, 39.9 percent of those in the United States for fewer than five years could speak English whereas 87.5 percent of those in the country for more than 10 years could speak it. Age at arrival was also determinative. In the same survey, 91.9 percent of those who came before the age of 14 could speak English, while only 50 percent of those entering after age 14 could speak the language. Ethnicity affected language acquisition as well. About 78 percent of Germans spoke English among those who entered within the previous five years, but only about 30 percent of Italians, Poles, and Lithuanians acquired the language within that period. Poles appeared to be slower in acquiring English (only 60 percent after 10 years) than Italians (84 percent), perhaps because Italians who settled in after 10 years were themselves a self-selected group of the "birds of passage."

Gender also influenced language acquisition. The commission's study of households found that 67.3 percent of male immigrants spoke English but only 47.7 percent of females did so. Groups with a higher proportion of women who immigrated, such as the Poles, tended to lag behind in the overall acquisition of English. Census data from 1910 also include gender, with breakdowns by age. Until the age of 39, a higher proportion of men were unable to speak English than women, but the proportions reversed at age 40. Because many of the younger men were temporary migrants, but most of the young women and older men were permanent residents, the explanation may lie in the nature of the migration experience. This does not help to explain the larger proportion of older women with limited English proficiency although it is possible that a core of women were sufficiently isolated from American society that they never had the opportunity to learn English.

The relatively rapid English acquisition of many of the new immigrants is all the more impressive given how different their native languages were from English. The non-English speaking immigrants from Germany and Scandinavia spoke languages that shared English roots. By contrast, Italian, Greek, and the Slavic languages bore little if any resemblance to English. Immigrants from southern and eastern Europe could not draw upon common linguistic roots. They had to learn English from scratch; many needed even to learn a new alphabet.

As with previous immigrant groups, a variety of institutions catered to the new immigrants in their native language while they sought to acquire English. Foreign-language newspapers increased overall from 794 in 1884 to 1052 in 1920 (Forbes [Martin] and Lemos 1981: 66). The number of German-language newspapers declined during this period from a high of 796 in 1894 to 276 in 1920 (likely as much because of World War I as disinterest on the part of German language readers), while the number of papers in other languages grew from 176 in 1884 to 776 in 1920. In Chicago alone, there were

41 Polish-language newspapers in 1915, reflecting a variety of economic, religious, social, and political perspectives about the United States and Poland (Bekken 2000: 9). Bekken describes the orientation of the major Polish language journals as ranging from ethnic solidarity above all else, to Catholicism as the foundation of Polish culture, to class struggle as paramount, with nationalism and religion as diversions.

The foreign language newspapers served two functions. First, they allowed immigrants to receive news of the homeland. Second, they became intermediaries with the new society, helping immigrants understand America. Some papers pursued the second purpose self-consciously. The *Jewish Daily Forward*, for example, included an advice column called the Bintel Brif, Yiddish for "Bundle of Letters." Begun in 1906, the column focused on all aspects of life in America. For many years, Abraham Cahan, editor of the *Forward*, answered the letters himself. A 1910 letter asked whether the writer's husband was justified in trying to stop her from attending school two nights a week; the Forward responded that she absolutely had that right in America. A young man who was afraid of losing his job asks whether he should continue to send money to his father in Russia; the answer was yes, because he is more likely to earn a living in New York than his elderly father was in Russia. Asked whether they should return to their home countries, readers are told to give up the idea – they would no longer fit into the old ways (Metzger 1971: 28).

Interest in learning English was reflected in immigrant participation in English-language classes. As an example, in 1889 a group of Protestant women in Rochester, New York, offered English classes to Italian immigrants in the city. Ninety men enrolled immediately, out of an Italian population that numbered no more than 500. Average attendance throughout the first year was above seventy (Forbes [Martin] and Lemos 1981: 93). Yet, data indicated that schools were too few and far between to handle the number of immigrants who needed English classes. Programs for women were particularly inadequate. Emily Green Balch, a member of the Massachusetts Commission on Immigration (and later a Nobel Peace laureate), proposed the development of programs that linked basic household skills with English: "English should be taught through the medium of household activities, from the care of the stove to care of a baby, from marketing to answering the telephone" (Balch 1914: 447). Such lessons would help those who remained at home and also those who might seek employment as domestic workers in wealthier families.

The need to learn English was often linked to residential and employment patterns. When immigrants were concentrated in language enclaves, English was less essential to find employment, converse with one's neighbor, or even start a new business. Although most immigrants lived in concentrated communities, they were not necessarily segregated in ethnic ghettos. Many immigrants lived in pan-immigrant communities, in neighborhoods in which immigrants from different language origins lived in close proximity. In these neighborhoods, English generally became the common language, necessitating the more rapid acquisition of the host language.

The school was one of the most important engines of English language acquisition for immigrant children. In the late 1880s, there were fewer than 800 public schools in the United States, but by the mid 1910s, there were more than 11,000 (Jacoby 2008). One of the hallmarks of the Progressive Era was the focus on public education for all children. Laws requiring mandatory enrollment, at least until 16 years of age, were passed in many states. Yet, the concern was that too few immigrant children attended school. A Hull House study in 1906 concluded that many immigrant children left school early in order to find employment; because of their limited English ability, they could only find hard, menial jobs. Children could legally drop out of school before age 16 if they obtained a work certificate. A study by the Illinois Consumer's League found that of the more than 30,000 work certificates issued to students, almost 27,000 went to the American-born children of immigrants.

Parochial schools proliferated as well, especially among the new Catholic immigrants. The Third Plenary Council of the Catholic Church determined in 1884 that the parochial school system should greatly expand. Each parish was encouraged to open a school. Immigrants were pressured to send their children to the religious schools, rather than public schools. One German Catholic priest in 1896 warned that parents who sent their children to public school "commit major sins and cannot be absolved until they have taken their children out of that school" (Forbes [Martin] and Lemos 1981: 105). While many parochial schools were English-speaking, particularly those established in largely Irish parishes, others were deliberately bilingual, seeking to maintain the mother language of the adult congregants at the same time that the children learned English. For the Catholic Church, parochial schools protected the immigrant children from the dominant Protestant culture. For the immigrant parents, parochial schools taught the children the skills necessary to compete in American society, and they taught ethnic traditions, religious values, and the native language.

Beyond the schools, religious institutions played an important role in socializing the new immigrants to life in America. Many of the new immigrant churches and synagogues went through an Americanization process, as had the churches of the earlier nineteenth-century immigrants. They adopted organizational forms that gave more authority to congregants. Even the otherwise hierarchical Catholic Church sought ways to cater to the needs of the new immigrants, establishing parishes based on the mother tongue or ethnic origins of the congregants in addition to parishes based on location. Tensions between the largely Irish hierarchy and priesthood in the United States and the Italian, Polish, and other immigrants often forced the issue (see Vecoli 1969 on Irish–Italian relations). Non-English-speaking immigrants wanted to worship in their native language, even when the liturgy was in Latin (or Hebrew, as in the case of Jewish immigrants). As the second generation shed the native language, the churches often adopted dual services, some in the mother tongue for the first generation and others in English for the second and third. As one commentator noted about Italian immigrants (who generally did not equate religion with church attendance and lagged behind in establishing parishes), "the ultimate success of the Catholic Church among the Italians in America owes much to its capacity to abandon those characteristically Italian practices that in the eyes of the younger generation marked it as 'foreign' while at the same time retaining enough of the old atmosphere to make the old people feel that the church belonged to them" (Forbes [Martin] and Lemos 1981: 105).

Voluntary associations also played their part in helping immigrants learn English and adapt to the new society while preserving what they could of their old life. As one commentator observed, "The immigrants, who had been accustomed to a more tightly knit communal life than almost any American could now recall, were quick to adopt the fraternal form of the American voluntary association in order to bind together their local ethnic communities against the unpredictable looseness of life in America" (Berhoff, quoted in Gamm and Putnam, 1999: 531). The late nineteenth century saw a rapid growth in voluntary associations, although more often in smaller towns and cities than in the large urban areas dominated by immigrants (Gamm and Putnam 1999: 533). The new immigrants followed the pattern of the previous wave and natives, not only forming ethnic associations but joining unions, business groups, benevolent associations, savings and loan associations and other institutions that served as mediators between their members and the larger community.

Health

A recurrent theme in assessing the adaptation and impact of the new immigrants related to their health status. As discussed in the next chapter, public health concerns deeply affected the adoption of increasingly more restrictive immigration policies. For our purposes in this section, suffice it to say that for most of this period immigrants underwent multiple health screenings before their admission to the United States. The 1891 immigration bill excluded those suffering from a "loathsome or contagious disease." Initially, favus, a visible scalp infection, and trachoma, an extreme form of conjunctivitis which could cause blindness, were defined as fitting the legislative criteria. Later, tuberculosis was added to the list. In 1907 still more health restrictions were placed on arriving passengers, barring those suffering from insanity, epilepsy, feeblemindedness, and imbecility as well as loathsome and contagious diseases.

Before being allowed to board a ship bound for America, immigrants underwent a first screening, which ranged from cursory to rigorous depending on the country and steamship line. If a screener spotted one of the listed diseases, the passenger was not permitted to board. The steamship companies had an incentive not to board passagengers who were likely to be barred from entry since they could be required to return the immigrants and to pay a fine.

The secondary inspection in New York is illustrative of the next steps. Before ships could dock, officials from New York State quarantine division would board to make sure no passenger or crew member carried such contagious diseases as smallpox, typhus, yellow fever, or cholera. First- and second-class passengers would be examined on board by U.S. Public Health Service staff for "loathsome or contagious disease," and would then be permitted to disembark. Those traveling in steerage would be sent by barge to Ellis Island, established in 1892 to screen for inadmissible immigrants. The Public Health Service officials would examine the would-be immigrant's feet, gait, knees, hips, muscular development, glands, skin, scalp, and mental condition (Joselit 1981: 211). Those who passed this examination would make a sharp right turn, allowing observation of their ears, back, neck, and posture, before heading to a second physician who would examine them for trachoma. The examination increasingly used modern medical technology to spot diseases: "Commonly used instruments were stethoscopes and, after 1910, X rays, which aided in the identification of pulmonary tuberculosis. Similarly, the tools of the bacteriology laboratory, such as microscopes, slides, stains, and culture methods, were regularly used at American immigration centers during the first two decades of the twentieth century. These apparatus were crucial to the diagnosis of sexually transmitted diseases, like gonorrhea and syphilis, and parasitic infections, like hookworm" (Markel and Stern 2002: 763).

Those whose health status raised questions during these examinations would be sent to a three-person Board of Special Inquiry for another examination. If two of the three board members determined that the condition was serious enough, the board issued a certificate of ill health, which meant deportation. If the condition was not "loathsome or contagious" but the would-be immigrant might become a public charge, he or she could also be determined to be deportable. An appeal to the Commissioner General of Immigration was permitted. If a relative or benevolent association agreed to cover any costs, the deportation order might be overturned.

Very few immigrants were barred from entry on medical grounds – less than 3 percent per year between 1891 and 1924 (Markel and Stern 2002). For the most part, the new immigrants were a healthy group, despite the continuing concerns about their health status. Mortality statistics in New York, for example, showed that Russian and Italian death rates in 1910, once age and sex were taken into account, compared favorably with native-born death rates and were significantly lower than those of Irish and German immigrants. Native males in the 25–44 age group, for example, had a rate of 6.9 deaths per 1000, with Russians having a rate of 5.1 deaths per 1000 and Italians 6.6 deaths per 1000. By contrast, the Irish showed 18.5 deaths per 1000 in the same age group (Joselit 1981).

Immigrants did appear to have higher rates of hospital utilization, both for physical and mental ailments. As Joselit (1981) points out, only the very rich and the very poor tended to use hospitals at the turn of the twentieth century. Because the native-born tended to cluster in the middle-income range, compared with the poorer urban immigrants, they tended to be underrepresented in hospitals. In 1906, Thomas Darlington, president of the New York Board of Health, complained that close to half of the budgets of New York hospitals went to the care of immigrants (Joselit 1981). The primary concern of hospital authorities was the inadequate federal reimbursement for these costs, a refrain to be heard again in later periods.

Contemporary critics of the health status of immigrants generally fit into two categories. One group pointed to the hospitalization rates and other evidence of disease as evidence that the new immigrants were inherently inferior, an argument to be discussed in further detail in the next chapter. The other group pointed to environmental factors in explaining high incidence of such illnesses as tuberculosis, blaming the conditions in which immigrants lived, not any inherent weakness. Their efforts formed part of the more general Progressive and Americanization movements, discussed later in this chapter.

Crime

Few issues caused as much concern about immigrants as their supposed propensity to commit crimes. In 1888, the U.S. Census Bureau published a *Report on the Defective, Dependent and Delinquent Classes of the United States*, based on prison statistics from each state, which showed a higher proportion of criminals to total population among immigrants. The majority of crimes for which both natives and immigrants were incarcerated were minor ones, including drunkenness, vagrancy, simple assault, disorderly conduct, and breach of the peace. The release of the report generated more research to determine if immigrants, including the new groups, had greater propensity to commit crimes. Once comparisons were made that took age and sex into account, immigrants were found to be equally, and, in most cases, less likely to commit crimes. The Dillingham Commission, despite its efforts to find reasons to restrict immigration, concluded: "No satisfactory evidence has yet been produced to show that immigration has resulted in an increase in crime disproportionate to the increase in adult population. Such comparable statistics of crime and population as it has been possible to obtain indicate that immigrants are less prone to commit crimes than are native Americans" (Steinberg 1981: 542). A New York State Immigration Commission found that "a large percentage of the offenses committed by immigrants in New York City . . . are such non-criminal offenses as the violation of corporation ordinances and the sanitary code, although they swell the criminal statistics. . . . They do not imply actual criminality or criminal motivations on the part of violators" (Steinberg 1981: 560).

The statistics did show some variation by ethnic group in the type of crime committed. Census data in 1910 and 1920 and New York and Massachusetts State investigations showed that the Irish had the highest incarceration rates, but they were most often for drunkenness (82.4 percent in the Massachusetts survey). Italians had the highest proportions of crimes against persons, with the highest assault and homicide rates. Natives were more likely to be arrested for property offenses (Steinberg 1981). The native-born children of immigrants had incarceration rates that were more similar to those of the children of native-born parents than they were to those of immigrants, reflecting perhaps a negative assimilation process. This conclusion receives some support in that immigrants themselves were more likely to commit crimes the longer they were in the country (Steinberg 1981).

The Americanization Movement

Faced with new and growing immigration, the country responded in different ways. Some embraced having access to a low-wage, hard-working labor force; others sought restrictions on immigration (as discussed in the next chapter); still others focused on ways to ensure that the newcomers assimilated into American life. Not necessarily any less critical of the new immigrants, or, for that matter, any less nativist in their views, those who embraced what came to be called Americanization[6] were optimistic about the resiliency of American institutions to bring the newcomers into the mainstream. In this sense, they fit well into the Pennsylvania model. The Americanization movement ultimately was overtaken by pessimists and became immersed in restrictionism, but its early views were vindicated in the successful adaptation of the eastern and southern European immigrants and their descendants.

During the winter of 1915, two government agencies, operating independently of one another, began assessing the number and efficacy of immigrant education programs that were operating about the country. The Bureau of Naturalization in the Department of Labor undertook a letter-writing campaign aimed at ascertaining from local school districts the degree to which such programs existed. Under the title of the "Association for the Wider Use of School Houses for the Civil Education of Adults," Raymond Crist, Deputy Commissioner of Naturalization, corresponded with hundreds of local school boards, YMCAs, Chambers of Commerce, American Legion posts, and others in an effort to encourage the offering and expansion of Americanization classes (Forbes [Martin] 1981). As a follow-up, in June 1916, the Bureau of Naturalization convened a conference in Washington to discuss the question of Americanization.

By then, the Bureau of Education in the Department of the Interior had also become interested in Americanization. At a conference in New York, also in June, the Bureau of Education joined with the National Education Association to form the National Committee of One Hundred. This committee of prominent citizens organized "for the purpose of assisting in a national campaign for the education of immigrants to fit them for American life and citizenship..."
(Forbes [Martin] and Lemos 1981: 129). In the months following, the number of organizations addressing themselves to the question of Americanization multiplied dramatically. By 1918 there were more than a hundred national bodies, each claiming immigrant education as its province. The federal government had at least six agencies involved – aside from the Bureau of Naturalization

---

[6] This section is adapted from Susan Forbes (Martin) and Peter Lemos, *The History of American Language Policy*, prepared for the U.S. Select Commission on Immigration and Refugee Policy.

and Bureau of Education, there were the Committee on Public Information, the Foreign Language Governmental Information Service, an office in the Treasury Department to sell bonds to immigrants, an an office in the Justice Department to supervise their political activities.

The Americanization movement fit comfortably into the Progressive era's assumptions about the role of government and society. Believing that the country had outgrown the organic, self-regulating rhythms upon which laissez faire America had relied, the Progressives saw the assimilation of immigrants as a matter of public policy. No longer could the country assume that immigrants would be integrated into America by "catch[ing] the spirit of the country and form[ing] an element of decided worth," as a Philadelphia newspaper had written in 1888 (Forbes [Martin] and Lemos 1981: 131). Given the nature of the new immigration and its complex economic and political institutions, active governmental intervention was needed as part of a new public–private partnership.

Rejecting laissez-faire policies in a number of areas, the Progressives enacted a range of economic, social, and political reforms that they believed would harness the power of the state towards a greater good. They aimed to remove corruption from governmental systems, taking on the political machines that dominated politics in most large cities. The Progressives passed legislation at the federal level and in many states that would allow for more direct representation of the public through direct election of the Senate, the secret ballot, and initiative, referendum, and recall mechanisms that bypassed the state legislatures. To address the imbalance between corporate power and what they saw as the rights of the people, they enacted measures to break up monopolies and regulate industries. They took on issues related to child labor, compulsory education, poverty, food safety, temperance, and women's suffrage.

In all of these issues, immigrants posed a challenge. The urban political machines derived much of their support from the new immigrants who exchanged votes for help in navigating unfamiliar systems and for patronage that led to jobs and services. The large corporations also benefited from access to immigrant labor, not only to keep their costs down but also to break up unions and otherwise defy regulation (particularly by subcontracting work to smaller units that were more difficult to monitor). Urban poverty was seen most extensively in immigrant neighborhoods and child labor appeared to be rampant among many immigrant groups. Certainly, immigrants were associated with drunkenness, as witnessed by the high rates of incarceration discussed above. Achieving the Progressive agenda would be more difficult, if not impossible, without addressing the so-called immigrant problem.

The Progressives were generally sanguine in their belief that immigrants would become Americans if given the chance. Americanization built upon the work of Progressive-era institutions, particularly the settlement house. The settlement houses were started by mostly upper- and middle-class native-born women who were distressed by the lives of the urban poor. They soon realized that the majority of the poor in cities such as New York, Chicago, and Boston were immigrants from the new source countries, and their aims increasingly turned to assimilation of the newcomers. Hull House, founded in 1889 by Jane Hull and Ellen Starr, is a case in point. The West Side of Chicago was undergoing transformation from a largely native-born, Irish, and German area to one dominated by Russian Jews, Italians, and Greeks. Although the Irish and German immigrants used the settlement house's services in its first decade, by 1906–1907, Russian Jews were the largest group participating in Hull House activities; within a few years, Italian immigrants had overtaken them. The settlement house provided a range of clubs and activities that the new immigrants selectively utilized, with some favoring the educational and cultural programs and others the sports.

The early literature on the settlement houses often focused on what the authors saw as a commitment to ethnic and religious pluralism. Newer work questions this assumption, focusing instead on the assimilationist views of the leadership. Lissak (1983) questions, for example, the extent to which Hull House leadership truly understood the needs and realities of Jewish or Italian immigrants, concluding it had little influence over the ethnic communities. The settlement house movement was adamantly anti-sectarian, separating itself from the work of religious organizations, which was at odds with the interests of many of the immigrants in its neighborhood.[7] Perhaps the most important contribution of Hull House was in spawning ethnic equivalents that balanced the interests of the immigrants in retaining their ethnic and religious traditions while adapting to their new surroundings. The Chicago Hebrew Institute was modeled on Hull House, but in addition to providing English-language and civics classes and cultural activities, it also housed a synagogue, religious classes, relief societies, landsmanshaftn (equivalent to today's hometown associations) and various Socialist and Zionist groups; it effectively became the community center of the East European Jews of the West Side (Lissak 1983) Notwithstanding the criticisms leveled at the settlement houses and their largely white, middle-class leadership, they symbolized a commitment to fight the worst aspects of rampant industrialization and to help ensure that the immigrants gained access to information, services and, most important, language and civic skills needed to prosper in America.

It was within this atmosphere that the Americanization movement arose. According to the movement's leaders, only a nationwide commitment to education, the great equalizer, would give the immigrant access to American society. Faith in education was everywhere evident in the early twentieth century. "Education," pronounced one school administrator, "will solve every problem of our national life, even that of assimilating our foreign element" (Forbes [Martin] and Lemos 1981: 148). Along with education for adults, the

---

7 See Rose (1994) for the transformation of the Young Women's Union, founded by German Jews, into the Neighborhood Center, a nondenominational settlement house that in turn transformed itself into a Jewish-American community center.

Progressives wanted civics education for all children, immigrant and native alike.

The Education Bureau in August 1916 issued a press release announcing its "nationwide campaign to induce 3,000,000 non-English speaking immigrants to attend night school and learn the language of America" (Forbes [Martin] and Lemos 1981: 149). The Bureau informed its rival in the Americanization campaign, the Naturalization Bureau, that they aimed for "the education of immigrants to fit them for American life and citizenship and to assist in creating such interest as will result both in more and better opportunities for the education of immigrants and in inducing the largest number of these to take full advantage of these opportunities" (Forbes [Martin] and Lemos 1981: 149).

For its part, the Bureau of Naturalization sent out Americanization materials to various organizations working with immigrants, hoping to enlist them in the new movement, saying: "Experience demonstrates that many aliens who really desire citizenship hesitate to take any step in that direction because of lack of knowledge, or natural timidity, but that this hesitancy disappears with friendly instruction and encouragement. Furthermore, through the lack of knowledge, unscrupulous persons frequently exact exorbitant fees for the slight aid furnished aliens in filing their naturalization applications" (Forbes [Martin] and Lemos 1981: 150). The bureau reached out not only to urban institutions but also to ones in rural areas. State granges, county agricultural advisors, commissioners of schools, farmers' societies, farm papers, and the local press would also be enlisted in the campaign (Forbes [Martin] and Lemos 1981: 150).

Americanization was promoted as something that was good for the immigrants and good for the broader society. Knowing "proper" English – that is, English learned in classes – was considered essential to social, economic, and political integration. As one contemporary put it, "The alien himself, because of his inability to speak correctly the speech of the American people, feels himself a foreigner; while the native American is reminded by every uncouth sound of the foreign birth of the speaker" (Forbes [Martin] and Lemos 1981: 163). The Bureau of Naturalization offered: "Ability to use and understand a common language, making it possible for every citizen to communicate with his fellow, understand his work and the regulations made for his protection in industry, increase[s] his opportunities for entertainment and add[s] to his ability to use and enjoy the full advantages of residency in America" (Forbes [Martin] and Lemos 1981: 165).

The government agencies worked with a complex network of national and local organizations, with considerable overlap among Americanization groups. For example, the National Americanization Committee was almost identical in membership with the Immigration Committee of the U.S. Chamber of Commerce. Many of the organizations that joined the movement had already been providing English classes. When the YMCA was asked to participate, it provided a long list of testimonials from immigrants who had benefited from programs begun at the end of the nineteenth century.

Business was a particular focus of the movement. The National Association of Manufacturers encouraged its members to offer Americanization programs. Many businesses were already providing English classes, seeing "ignorance of English is a large factor in turnover" and a cause of accidents and economic loss (Forbes [Martin] and Lemos 1981: 152). Henry Ford set up classes within his plants and required attendance from his 5,000 non-English-speaking employees, outside work hours (Forbes [Martin] and Lemos 1981: 152). Detroit generally led the way in industrial Americanization programs. Crist, the Deputy Commissioner of Naturalization, described Detroit as "the banner city in this national cooperative education work.... Manufacturing concerns in Detroit are the foremost ones in the entire country in this educational work." Ford himself emphasized that "these men of many nations must be taught American ways, the English language, and the right way to live" (quoted in Barrett 1992: 1003). He had firm ideas about American ways, firing about 900 workers who took off from work to celebrate Orthodox Christmas, saying that if they were to make their homes in the United States, "they should observe American holidays."

Similar activity was common elsewhere. Chicago had some 150 factory classes a week for immigrants and a waiting list of 155 industries that were ready to start them (Forbes [Martin] and Lemos 1981: 152). One Chicago manager commented, "Our dream is that Americanization will banish foreign language foreman and interpreters in our employment office, two great barriers between us and our men. Only think what it means when I can make an announcement to them myself" (Forbes [Martin] and Lemos 1981: 152). Clearly, there was a lot of self-interest underneath the seemingly altruistic motives in offering English classes. The curricula of many of the industry courses aimed to socialize the immigrants into the corporate culture. The International Harvester Company, for example, produced its own lesson plans for non-English speaking workers. The first plan read:

I hear the whistle. I must hurry.
I hear the five minute whistle.
It is time to go into the shop....
I change my clothes and get ready to work....
I work until the whistle blows to quit.
I leave my place nice and clean.
I put all my clothes in the locker.
I must go home. (Forbes [Martin] and Lemos 1981: 153)

Partly to counteract such programs, while still advancing the educational goal, the New York State Federation of Labor sponsored a proposal for the "acquisition of a fair knowledge of the American language by continuous shop and school instruction supervised by state educational authorities, to be required of all employed foreign-language aliens as a condition of continued employment" (Forbes [Martin] and Lemos 1981: 153). Labor unions played an important role in the Americanization process, albeit with very different aims from the industrialists. In the type of "bottom-up Americanization" that Barrett (1992) discusses, labor unions tried to instill a sense of camaraderie in its immigrant members, emphasizing common interests as American workers, rather than ethnic differences. Although not always successful, many of the union organizers were able to overcome ethnic rivalries. As Barrett (1992: 1011) explains, the unions also imparted the principles of democratic governance "by relating them to practical matters: wages, hours and working conditions. For most immigrants, introduction to the American political and economic system came not through night-school classes but through discussion and debate at union meetings (with interpreters), informal conversations with fellow workers, and labor movement publications (often printed in various languages)."

This type of training in civics, of course, was not what was intended by the leadership of the Americanization movement. And, despite the extensive involvement of the private sector, more was needed than could be done through even the business sector. The public school system became the most important partner in the Americanization movement. Even as Detroit's industries took up the call, the Detroit Board of Commerce, in cooperation with Detroit's Board of Education, commenced a campaign to increase the number of night schools that would teach English (Forbes [Martin] and Lemos 1981: 156). The Los Angeles City School District enacted a program in 1917 to teach English to those pursuing naturalization. Each immigrant who filed an intent to naturalize was sent a notice by the school district: "The naturalization laws of the United States provide that no alien shall hereafter be naturalized or admitted as a citizen of the U.S. who cannot speak the English language. The free public schools of Los Angeles have undertaken to assist those who cannot speak the English language and to educate them in that regard, and in a number of schools in this city lessons in English are regularly given" (Forbes [Martin] and Lemos 1981: 157). Upon completion of the course, the student would be given a diploma that would be acceptable to the court as proof of the ability to speak English. About 600 local school districts provided such courses in 1915–16; a total of 3,500 did so in 1921 (Forbes [Martin] and Lemos 1981: 157).

In 1923, the Bureau of Naturalization announced that it had more than 250,000 immigrants in 6,632 citizenship training courses across the nation. Of these, 4,132 were in public school buildings, 1,256 in private homes, 371 in factories, and 873 in other locations. Nearly 70 percent of the attendees were men, and most were under the age of 30. Of those surveyed, 70 percent had been in the country for 10 years or less and 52 percent had been here for five years or less (Forbes [Martin] and Lemos 1981: 157).

Not all programs met with success, however. Immigrants often complained about the level of instruction. "It is childish. We keep saying all the time, 'This is a desk'; 'this is a door.' I know it is a desk and a door. What for keep saying it all the time" (Forbes [Martin] and Lemos 1981: 143). An immigrant who had dropped out of a public school program found a YMCA program more to his liking: "The public night school teaches us things we don't need, things which are good for a boy of twelve years to learn, but this school teaches us what we need, what grown people ought to know about" (Forbes [Martin] and Lemos 1981: 159).

The opportunity to learn was one of the strongest motivators for many immigrants. Not having had the opportunity to attend school in Europe, they saw the American school as a new and fascinating experience. There is even evidence that the interest in learning aroused a new awareness of education back home. One immigrant visiting Italy wrote: "One good influence which America is exerting on Italy can be seen plainly in the awakening desire for an education" (Forbes [Martin] and Lemos 1981: 160).

Although the growth in programs and participation was welcome, doubts lingered as to whether the Americanization program was reaching enough immigrants. The movement divided between those who favored voluntary participation and those who preferred compulsion. The first group thought that all that was needed was encouragement, but they also understood that there were many logistical constraints on immigrants' attending courses. They saw that earning a living, often by working multiple jobs, raising a family, and keeping a home left little time and energy for education. "I work now during the day, but my wife works at night and I have to stay at home to take care of the children" was a common explanation as to why immigrants did not attend classes (Forbes [Martin] and Lemos 1981: 159). Those opposed to coercion also questioned whether it would be effective, or whether it might even create a backlash against the programs. One contemporary commentator wrote: "the mere imposition of a language cannot automatically bring about nationalization, a fact which uncompromising advocates of compulsion in this country should note" (Forbes [Martin] and Lemos 1981: 159). A Slovak businessman warned against compulsion and haste at a 1919 Americanization conference: "Some of the propagators of the Americanization movement are getting overzealous," he remarked. "In their praiseworthy efforts they may overshoot the mark. What I mean is, that they should not try to hasten the process of Americanization in defiance of the natural laws" (Forbes [Martin] and Lemos 1981: 162).

Despite these misgivings, an increasing number of those supporting Americanization were turning in favor of compulsory English classes. Theodore Roosevelt had long favored such an approach: "I would have the government provide that every immigrant be required to learn English, with instruction furnished free. If after five years he has not learned it let him be returned to the country from which he came" (Forbes [Martin] and Lemos 1981: 158).

A somewhat more benign approach, which did not involve deportation, was taken by New York State. A law was passed in 1918 that required the establishment of night schools and of employer-maintained schools, with attendance required of every employed minor, aged 16–21, "who does not speak, read or write the English language, as is required for the completion of the fifth grade of the public or private schools of the city or school district in which he resides... Any employer may meet the requirements of this act by conducting a class or classes for teaching English and civics to the foreign-born in shop, store, plant or factory under the supervision of local school authorities." The law also recognized the barriers for adults to take classes and emphasized it was important to "make learning accessible" to them.

The outbreak of World War I had clearly intensified the pressure toward compulsion. At the third Americanization Conference, sentiments in favor of compulsion found frequent expression: "Great patience has been exercised in our efforts to convince the foreigners. In the case of those not now convinced, justice to the cause for which we fight demands a stronger measure. They must be compelled to convince themselves of the value and the justice of American ideals and this requires a knowledge of the English language" (Forbes [Martin] and Lemos 1981: 158).

At its most extreme, those advocating compulsory English spoke of the non-English speaking immigrants as a potential menace to American democracy. In the heat of war fever, the governor of Iowa prohibited the use of any language other than English in public places or over the telephone. One local post of the Veterans of Foreign Wars resolved "that this organization use its utmost efforts through legislation and other means to insist that the alien population of this country prepare to become citizens, or else prepare to leave the country" (Forbes [Martin] and Lemos 1981: 158). The Native Sons of the Golden West concurred that every foreigner "must live for the United States, and grow an American soul inside of him or get out of the country." In Senate testimony, the special assistant to the secretary of the interior, in charge of Americanization, stated: "There can be no sense of security in the land until we have met the dual menace of ignorance and non-English speaking" (Forbes [Martin] and Lemos 1981: 165). Americanization had evolved from an emphasis on helping immigrants overcome barriers to full engagement in American society to a coercive ideology that saw the unassimilated immigrant as a danger to the country.

Conclusion

Looking back a century on what was then the largest wave of immigration, it is difficult to conclude that it was anything but a great benefit to the country. Contemporaries were more critical and skeptical, though, about the new immigration. Yet, the door remained open through almost four decades of unprecedented movements – unprecedented in terms of numbers and, more significantly, in the origins of the immigrants. As we have seen, many interests were served by the new immigrants, not least those of corporate America. But fears that the newcomers would not integrate remained. Could the Pennsylvania model of a pluralistic but inclusionary country survive such differences in language, religion, and culture? Those who participated most fervently in the Americanization movement, as either purveyors or consumers of the English and civics programs, committed themselves to turn the new immigrants into Americans. They disagreed, though, as to whether immigrants should keep a hyphenated identity or be assimilated into a single American ideal. They also disagreed as to whether immigrants would participate freely and voluntarily in the Americanization process or should be coerced into learning English and becoming citizens.

There was more general agreement that "birds of passage" were bad for the country. Those coming temporarily, to return home after earning enough money, put down no roots and would never become Americans. They would retain their native identity regardless of how long they stayed in the country – and in some cases, they stayed a very long time. The Dillingham Commission saw greater problems in this form of migration and recommended that "the aliens excluded should be those who come to this country with no intention to become American citizens or even to maintain a permanent residence here – but merely to save enough – by the adoption, if necessary – of low standards of living – to return permanently to their home country" (Immigration Commission 1911: 47). Even the restrictionists were suspicious of the Virginia model of pure labor migration, divorced from participation in the broader community.

In retrospect, the voluntarists had it right. The immigrants that were so disdained at the outset of the twentieth century became the bedrock of the country as it went through the Great Depression and two world wars. By the time of the 1930 census, 93 percent of the foreign-born population reported proficiency in English. Education mattered. The children of the eastern and southern European immigrants became the professionals and the white-collar and blue-collar workers of the next generation. Much more than the Americanization movement accounts for the relative success of the new immigrants. With the outbreak of World War I, many "birds of passage" had their wings clipped and decided to remain permanently in the United States. The new settlers worked hard, married and raised families, bought homes and cars, and became the engine of the American economy even as they struggled to survive the Depression.

That they would succeed was no foregone conclusion when immigration was at its height. By the beginning of the 1920s, sentiment in favor of restricting immigration from Europe had overcome the efforts of even the most committed Americanizers. Chapter 8 turns to an examination of the forces behind the closing of the door to European immigrants.

8

The Triumph of Restrictionism

1882–1924

This chapter focuses on the growing movement to restrict immigration that culminated in the National Origins Act of 1924.[1] The chapter discusses the principal attacks on immigration, arguing that the restrictionists effectively undermined the Pennsylvania model by providing "scientific evidence" of the inability of the new immigrants from southern and eastern Europe to become Americans. A leading proponent of restriction argued that Jews were "undersized and weak muscled," Italians "possess a distressing frequency to low foreheads, open mouths, weak chins, poor features, skewed faces, small or knobby crania and backless heads." He concluded that the new immigrants "are beaten men from beaten races, representing the worst failures in the struggle for existence."

The chapter returns to the concerns about immigration highlighted in Chapter 7 – language acquisition, health, and crime. Data on these issues were used and misused by opponents of immigration to structure a seemingly irrefutable scientific argument against the capacity of the country to absorb the newcomers. The chapter reviews the progression of legislation adopted to curtail immigration. The 1875 legislation that led to the exclusion of the Chinese was the first of a series of efforts to define the attributes of desirable, as opposed to unwanted, immigrants. In 1875, prostitutes and convicts were barred. The Immigration Act of 1882 added to the classes of inadmissible immigrants, including persons likely to become a public charge. The Alien Contract Labor Law of 1885 made it unlawful to import aliens into the United States under contract for the performance of labor or services of any kind. Supported by labor unions, the legislation also addressed concerns about "birds of passage" – immigrants who worked for short periods and then returned home. The more comprehensive Immigration Act of 1891 added still other inadmissible classes

---

[1] There is a valuable body of research on this topic. See, for example, Higham's classic study, *Strangers in the Land* (1955). More recent books include Daniels (2004), Zolberg (2006), Tichenor (2002), Calavita (1984), and Ngai (2004).

of immigrants, including persons suffering from certain contagious diseases, felons, individuals convicted of other crimes or misdemeanors, polygamists, and immigrants whose passage was paid by other persons. It also made it illegal to encourage others to immigrate through advertisements.

With Ellis Island opened in 1892 to screen newcomers against these grounds of inadmissibility, language and literacy requirements took over as the battleground of immigration reform. This chapter will discuss the controversy over imposing literacy and English language proficiency on admission and naturalization. In 1906, English proficiency was made a basis for citizenship, referring to the now familiar argument, as one member of Congress put it, that "history and reason alike demonstrate that you cannot make a homogeneous people out of those who are unable to communicate with each other in one common language" (Congressional Record 1906). Efforts to impose a similar English proficiency requirement on admission failed, however, and those favoring restriction turned to a literacy requirement as a way to limit immigration. After several failed attempts, legislation imposing a literacy requirement was adopted over President Wilson's veto in 1917.

Although immigration decreased somewhat during and immediately after World War I, it resumed former levels as soon as conditions in Europe permitted. Believing that the qualitative restrictions in place were inadequate to stem the tide, those favoring restriction turned to quantitative restrictions as well as to shifts in the ethnic composition of immigration. The national origins quotas established in the Immigration Acts of 1921 and 1924 accomplished these aims. They led to substantial reductions in numbers of immigrants and severe limitations on immigration from eastern and southern Europe.

The 1920s legislation represented a repudiation of the Pennsylvania model and what was considered by too many to be a failure of Americanization. The seemingly insatiable demand for foreign labor was checked, at least in terms of European migration, but there was a resurgence of the Virginia model, with temporary immigration from Mexico in some cases replacing permanent immigration from Europe. The underlying reasons for this major shift in U.S. immigration policy is examined, as is the larger context in which the debates on immigration took place. Focusing on questions about America's place in the world following World War I, the chapter examines what became the newest manifestation of the Massachusetts model in the country's reaction to the so-called Red Scare.

Qualitative Restrictions on Admission

As immigration grew in the decades after the Civil War, many Americans reacted with alarm to the changing characteristics of the new immigrants. Initially, there were few efforts to impose numerical limits on the admission of foreigners, except for the Chinese and, later, other Asian groups. Rather, the incipient restrictionist movement focused its attention on the "quality" of the immigrants, not the quantity.

Regulating the quality of immigrants was not new. Some states with major ports of arrival had passed laws to discourage the landing of paupers and the sick by imposing bonds and head taxes. Earlier in the nineteenth century, as Motomura (2006: 23) noted, "Massachusetts required shipmasters to post a bond for immigrants deemed likely to become indigent, and to pay a head tax of $2 on all others." The state of New York also imposed a head tax on immigrants. These laws were negated by the Supreme Court in 1849 in the *Passenger Cases*, which held that regulating immigration was exclusively a federal responsibility. States continued to seek ways to protect themselves from the arrival of immigrants who would pose a financial burden, with New York requiring shipmasters to report all immigrants on board and pay fees on each arrival or post a bond to cover immigrants' use of public assistance (Motomura 2006: 23). California adopted a law that gave state inspectors discretion to refuse admission to passengers unless the shipping company posted a bond or paid a fee. The states argued that the absence of federal regulation gave them the authority to take such measures (Motomura 2006: 23).

In 1876, these laws were declared unconstitutional because they were a state infringement on the federal right to regulate immigration. In a New York case, *Henderson v. Mayor of New York*, the court held that the policies encroached on the federal power to regulate commerce with foreign powers. In a California case, *Chy Lung v. Freeman*, the bond requirement was deemed an infringement on the federal government's conduct of foreign affairs. In 1884, the Supreme Court affirmed that the federal government could regulate immigration in the *Head Money Cases*, which validated a federal head tax on ship owners to defray processing costs and provide relief to those in distress. Then, in 1889, the Court held that Congress and the executive branch have wide-reaching powers (plenary powers) to make decisions regarding the admission, exclusion, and deportation of immigrants without judicial oversight for constitutionality (Motomura 2006: 27).

With these cases, the ball was firmly in Congress' court to determine whether and how to regulate immigration. Congress' first major venture into immigration reform had occurred in 1875. In addition to the steps taken to bar Chinese contract laborers, the legislation adopted that year also designated prostitutes and those convicted of felonies as inadmissible. The legislation was aimed at placating the states that had been complaining about the high cost of incarcerating immigrants who committed crimes.

Following the 1876 Supreme Court decisions, Congress considered broader legislation to regulate admissions, passing the first comprehensive reform in 1882. This legislation gave the secretary of the treasury authority to manage immigration, shifting this authority from the Department of State's Commission on Immigration (established in 1864, during the Civil War) to the Treasury Department. The move represented a change shift from thinking of immigration as a matter primarily related to foreign relations to thinking of it as one that was at the heart of the country's commerce. The Treasury Department already had responsibility for customs and was now authorized to use existing inspectors to screen people as well as goods. The law also gave the Treasury the authority to designate state boards that would control admissions. New York had its own board and used Castle Garden for processing immigrants until the federal government began building Ellis Island.

The law further broadened the grounds under which immigrants could be excluded from entering, most notably barring those who were "likely to become a public charge." The legislation also introduced a tax of 50 cents on each passenger brought to the United States. Again, the legislation was aimed at addressing state grievances regarding the cost of immigration, establishing that those who were likely to require the use of public services would be kept out of the country. Those capable of holding a job were not deemed to be likely to be a public charge, so the restriction had little impact on the admission of would-be workers.

The first legislation aimed at workers was the Immigration Act of 1885. This statute barred admission of contract workers, going beyond the anti-contract labor provisions that had previously applied only to the Chinese. The "Contract Labor Law" made it unlawful to import aliens into the United States under contract for the performance of labor or services of any kind. A number of exceptions were made, however, either in the interest of foreign relations or at the behest of industry. Exceptions were made for aliens temporarily in the United States who engaged other foreigners as secretaries, servants, or domestics; actors, artists, lecturers, and domestic servants; and skilled aliens working in an industry not yet established in the United States. Labor unions representing skilled workers had been pressing for restrictions on contract labor for years. In 1881, the Federation of Organized Trades and Labor Unions began to advocate for abolition of foreign contract labor to stop the importation of immigrant workers as strikebreakers.

Calavita (1984) argues that this legislation was more symbolic than real. The congressional proponents clearly justified it based on the protection of American workers from unfair competition by foreign workers. Calavita identified four ways, however, in which legislation can placate supporters without having serious ramifications for those who benefit from the alternative – by incorporating loopholes, addressing only a narrow and relatively insignificant aspect of the problem, designating no enforcement procedures, or interpreting the legislation so as to render it virtually ineffective. The 1885 legislation did all of these things. Loopholes were placed in the law to ensure that relatives could continue to assist and encourage the immigration of family members, including paying their fares and arranging their employment. Since this was the main way in which immigrants entered – not through formal contracts – the legislation would not seriously reduce the numbers of persons admitted. Most strikebreakers were already in the United States, not imported from overseas, so the legislation addressed only a narrow part of the unions' concerns. No serious enforcement measures were adopted until subsequent legislation gave responsibility to the Department of Labor to enforce the law and provided that those who violated it could be expelled if identified within one year of entry. Calavita (1984) cites that at the most 8,000 immigrants were barred as contract workers out of a total of 6 million who sought entry between 1887 and 1901 as further testament to the symbolic nature of the legislation.

Although Congress was not intent on restricting overall numbers, there was continuing pressure to address concerns about the quality of the new immigrants. The Immigration Act of 1891 gave new authority to a Bureau of Immigration in the Treasury Department. This legislation added to the categories under which immigrants could be excluded. The list now included persons likely to be a public charge, persons suffering from certain contagious diseases, felons, persons convicted of other crimes or misdemeanors, polygamists, and aliens assisted by others by payment of passage. It also forbade the encouragement of immigration by means of advertisement. The deportation of persons who had entered unlawfully was mandated. Two years later, legislation was adopted to collect additional information to facilitate the screening of those who were inadmissible. Information was to be collected on occupation, marital status, ability to read or write, amount of money in possession, and facts regarding physical and mental health. The new Ellis Island screening facility would collect the information in New York, the largest port of entry.

The legislation introduced a new term, barring the admission of persons who admitted the commission of a crime involving "moral turpitude." Moral turpitude referred to "general, shameful wickedness – so extreme a departure from ordinary standards of honest, good morals, justice, or ethics as to be shocking to the moral sense of the community" (Black's Law Dictionary, as quoted in Cannato 2009: 261). The term proved difficult to interpret. It was used to bar entry of people accused of adultery. In one celebrated case, Vera, Countess of Cathcart, was denied admission after she reported being divorced. Although it is not clear how the immigration authorities learned that she had been accused of adultery, she was detained at Ellis Island awaiting deportation (Cannato 2009: 262). Ellis Island officials sometimes went to great lengths to identify those who might be barred on grounds of moral turpitude. Women traveling alone, particularly if they appeared to be pregnant, were a particular focus of attention. Officials were divided, though, as to whether pre-marital sex was an act of moral turpitude. While some ordered unmarried pregnant women to be deported, others, such as Frank Larned, the assistant commissioner of immigration in Washington, held that fornication was not punished under common law unless it was committed "openly and notoriously" (Cannato 2009: 267).

Further legislation followed in rapid order. In 1903, responsibility for implementation of immigration law was transferred to the newly created Department of Commerce and Labor. New legislation also expanded the authority of the Commissioner General of Immigration in the areas of rulemaking and enforcement of immigration laws. The Immigration Act of 1903 added political grounds for exclusion, by designating as inadmissible "anarchists, or persons who believe in, or advocate, the overthrow by force or violence the government of the United States, or of all government, or of all forms of law, or the assassination of public officials." It also toughened the public charge provisions, allowing the deportation of those who became public charges within two years of arrival because of a pre-existing condition.

In 1907 more sweeping legislation was passed. Foreign nationals arriving in the country now had to declare whether they intended to settle permanently (immigrants) or remain temporarily (nonimmigrants). The grounds for exclusion were expanded to cover imbeciles, feeble-minded persons, persons with physical or mental defects that may affect their ability to earn a living, persons afflicted with tuberculosis, children unaccompanied by their parents, and women coming to the United States for immoral purposes. Notably, a commission was authorized to study immigration and report back to Congress with its recommendations for further reform. Known as the Dillingham Commission, the panel was authorized to investigate the causes and consequences of immigration and produced the research volumes discussed in Chapter 7.

Each of these statutes addressed specific concerns about the characteristics of immigrants, generally focusing on health and criminality. Despite evidence to the contrary, Congress and the executive branch feared that lax controls were leading to the admission of the sick and the immoral. In 1902, for example, the Commissioner General of Immigration wrote that there was no reason for the United States "to become the hospital of the nations of the earth" (quoted in Joselit 1981: 213). A member of the U.S. Public Health Service remarked in 1906 that the immigrant "is afflicted with a body not only but illy [*sic*] adapted to the work necessary to earn his bread, but also poorly able to withstand the onslaught of disease. It means he is undersized, poorly developed, with feeble heart action, arteries below the standard size; that he is physically degenerate ... and very likely to transmit his undesirable qualities to his offspring" (quoted in Joselit 1981: 215).

Equally concerned about crime, Congress and the executive branch provided statistics, with none of the caveats discussed in Chapter 7, to demonstrate that steps were needed to bar the criminally motivated more effectively. The House Judiciary Committee in 1894 reported: "The total number of white convicts in our penitentiaries whose birthplace is known is 28,440, composed of 13,715 native born and 14,725 foreign born, showing that more than one-half of all our white convicts are of foreign birth" (quoted in Steinberg 1981: 536). Concerns persisted even as more stringent controls on immigration of criminals were enacted. In 1908, Police Commissioner Bingham of New York claimed that 85 percent of New York's criminals were of "exotic origin" and that half of them were Jewish (Steinberg 1981: 538).

Fears about the poor quality of the recent immigrants received support from the emerging science of genetics, or, more properly, the pseudoscience of eugenics. Believers in eugenics claimed that poverty, disease, and crime were biologically determined by inherent characteristics that were immutable. They asserted that the seemingly higher disease, crime, and poverty rates of immigrants had nothing to do with the environment in which they lived and worked. The Progressives as a whole were, in fact, split on this issue of heredity versus environment, reflecting the tension between their desire to help oppressed groups and the need to control those who were a threat to society (Leonard 2006). For the eugenicists, these were not social problems; they were biological ones and therefore not amenable to change. Madison Grant, the leading proponent of eugenics, argued: "An Anglo-Saxon by blood would always be Anglo-Saxon in quality" while "the cross between any of the three European races and a Jew is a Jew" (quoted in Joselit 1981: 221). The Nordic races, according to Grant, epitomized everything good about Americans, and Jews, Italians, and other new immigrants were unequivocally inferior (Joselit 1981: 222). Such views were not just the province of a few eccentrics. No less prominent a figure than Francis Walker, president of the Massachusetts Institute of Technology, described the new immigrants as "beaten men from beaten races, representing the worst failures in the struggle for existence" (quoted in Tichenor 2002: 78).

Language had been since the time of the Enlightenment a measure of racial and cultural hierarchy, as discussed in Chapter 4. Cultures with a largely literate population were considered to be superior in other respects to those with what were considered to be more physical styles of communication using hand movements and oral traditions. It is not surprising, then, that proponents of eugenics used the low levels of literacy among the new immigrants as evidence of their inferiority. Language differences resonated more generally with a public that found it difficult to understand or communicate with the new immigrants. Even Progressives who denied any racial inferiority of the new immigrants, such as Franz Boas, believed that language was a reflection of unconscious elements in culture. Because people group concepts together via language, an understanding of language facilitates an understanding of the underlying realities (Forbes [Martin] and Lemos 1981: 134).

It is therefore not surprising that those who wanted to restrict immigration soon took up language as the principal focus of their lobbying activities. As early as 1887, the economist Edward W. Bemis gave a series of lectures in which he proposed that the United States bar the entry of all male adults who were unable to read and write in their own language. He argued that such a regulation would reduce by half or more those who were poor and undereducated (123). In 1891, the *Nation* magazine went even further and proposed that an English language test be required of immigrants. Recognizing that such a test would limit immigration to those from the British Isles, the *Nation* declared "we are under no obligation to see that all races and nations enjoy an equal chance of getting here" (Forbes [Martin] and Lemos 1981: 125). The *Nation* allowed for the possibility of admitting the well-educated who spoke no English because they were likely to learn the language quickly.

The editorial used much the same argument as had been in support of the Americanization movement: "How a democratic state governed by opinions expressed through universal suffrage could last for any considerable length of time without a community of language, it is hard to conceive, for it is through community of language that men are able to feel and think the same way about public affairs, and cherish the same political ideals" (Forbes [Martin] and Lemos 1981: 126). In contrast to the Americanization advocates, however, the language test was to take place before the immigrant arrived.

A bill requiring a literacy test as a basis for admission was introduced in 1891 only to be defeated in Congress. In 1895 and 1896, under the leadership of Henry Cabot Lodge, Senator from Massachusetts, it passed both houses, only to be vetoed by President Cleveland on one of his last two days in office. He characterized the bill as "illiberal, narrow and un-American" (Daniels 2004: 32). Cleveland also pointed out that it was safer to admit illiterate workers than literate political agitators. The House overrode the veto but the legislation stalled in the Senate. The measure was reintroduced in subsequent Congresses and appeared to gain momentum after President McKinley's assassination in 1901, but it again stalled in the Senate, even with the support of the new president, Theodore Roosevelt. The provision was raised once more in 1906 in the context of other reforms in immigration. Although other provisions were adopted in the 1907 Immigration Act, the literacy test proved more controversial.

The Immigration Restriction League (IRL) was the leading advocate for the literacy act, as it had been in previous sessions of Congress. The IRL was formed in 1894 by three Harvard University graduates – Charles Warren, Robert DeCourcy Ward, and Prescott Farnsworth Hall. The IRL's constitution explicitly stated that its objective was to "advocate and work for the further judicious restriction or stricter regulation of immigration," clarifying "it is not an object of this League to advocate the exclusion of laborers or other immigrants of *such character and standards as fit them to become citizens*" (Immigration Restriction League n.d., emphasis added). Although the IRL's ultimate goal was to restrict the number of immigrants, the campaign for a literacy requirement fitted their objectives in the short term.

The IRL was joined by the American Federation of Labor (AFL) in support of the literacy measure. Organized labor continued to harbor concerns about the admission of unskilled immigrants who were willing to work for low wages. Opinion was not uniform among unions on the immigration question, however. Some unions were beginning to see the immigrants as ripe for recruitment into their ranks. The AFL, however, focused primarily on the unions that organized skilled workers who felt most threatened by the immigrants. The leader of the AFL, Samuel Gompers, shared many of the notions about immigrants expressed by the eugenicists. He argued that the new immigrants "could not be taught to render the same intelligent service as was supplied by American workers" (Calavita 1984, quoting Karson: 111). As Barrett (1992: 1002) notes, "exclusion from a trade might be based not simply on the question of skill but either implicitly or explicitly on race, ethnicity or gender."

By the congressional debate in 1906, the opponents of the literacy measure had become more organized. Business had been in opposition from the beginning, failing to see how a literacy requirement could do anything other than restrict access to the labor force they sought. The National Association of Manufacturers, the National Board of Trade, and other business groups lobbied against the measure. Immigrants themselves were also more organized and sought to harness the political power of newly naturalized citizens. The American Jewish Committee, which was formed in 1906 to fight discrimination against Jews and support immigrant rights, mounted a campaign against the measure (Zolberg 2006: 229–30). Speaker Joseph Cannon, who opposed the legislation, had taken firm control of the House of Representatives and had no intention of allowing the literacy test to pass. Faced with upcoming midterm elections, and fearing the loss of the immigrant vote in key jurisdictions, Roosevelt pulled his support from the measure, letting it die in Congress for that session.

Concerns about language and literacy did not die, though, as witnessed in the debate that ensued on naturalization. Representative Bonynge, one of the sponsors of new legislation on naturalization, summarized the proposed provisions: "before an alien can become naturalized, if this bill shall be enacted into law, it will be necessary that he shall satisfy the court that he is able to write either in his own language or in the English language" (Forbes [Martin] 1981: 121). Some members protested that a literacy requirement for naturalization would impose on immigrants a requirement not expected of native-born citizens. Others pointed out that a number of states gave literacy tests to prospective voters, not always for the best of motives. In 1890, Mississippi had adopted a poll tax, a residency requirement, and a literacy test that was designed to restrict the number of eligible black voters.

The majority in the House of Representatives opposed the literacy requirement for naturalization. William Alden Smith represented the opposition: "I say that any attempt to impose an educational qualification upon citizenship is an abridgement of patriotism and an unfair discrimination against unfortunate people, whose hearts may be alive to every national responsibility" (Forbes [Martin] 1981: 130). He argued that there was no relationship between learning to read and write and exercising the responsibilities of citizenship. Defining the latter as something "that lives in the heart of the American patriot as well as the head," Smith described the many men of his acquaintance who served with credit in high offices without the benefit of a common school education, concluding "any mere book learning that circumscribes [the] rights [of immigrants] or keeps them from participating in our government when they are otherwise well qualified is an act of absolute injustice" (Forbes [Martin] 1981: 131). The literacy test bill was defeated by a vote of 93–34.

The debate then turned to an English language requirement for naturalization. Bonynge spoke of the benefit: "if [an immigrant] understands the English language, whether he understood it when he came to this country or not, if he acquires a knowledge of the English language he will more readily assimilate with us than if he retained his own language and lived wholly with his own people" (Forbes [Martin] 1981: 132). He continued, "you cannot make a homogeneous people out of those who are unable to communicate with each other in one common language" (Forbes [Martin] 1981: 133). To be a good citizen, it was necessary for an immigrant to be able to read and understand the laws of the nation in the language in which they were written.

Opponents did not take exception to the importance of English but questioned whether it was a prerequisite for good citizenship. Representative Bartholdt of Missouri argued that English was not the only way to engage in civic responsibility; speaking a foreign language "is not the difference of mind or of heart or of brain, but a difference of a twist of the tongue; that is all." He further suggested that American principles could be learned in translation, citing the contributions of the foreign-language press: "take, for instance, a good American newspaper printed in the German language. That paper educates its readers in every possible way in American ideas and up to American ideals. It teaches them what the law is in this country, what our institutions are, and what it is to become an American citizen . . . " (Forbes [Martin] 1981: 139).

Representative Cockran of New York suggested that the law would discourage exactly the type of immigrants who should be encouraged: "I believe, sir, that we do not want linguists, but we do want laborers. I do not think we need men skillful in dialectics, but we do need men efficient in wielding implements of production. . . . Sir, this section might be described with perfect accuracy as a device to shut out the laborious and admit the loquacious" (Forbes [Martin] 1981: 140). The net result, argued Representative Goldfogle, also of New York, "is that these toiling masses, perfectly willing to enter the spirit of American citizenship, who love this country, who adore the flag, will be kept out because you have shut upon them the door of opportunity" (Forbes [Martin] 1981: 141).

In the end, the supporters of a language requirement won the vote. Passage of the legislation, though supported by immigration restrictionists, could be divorced from the more controversial issue of immigration itself. Requiring English fluency for naturalization could be supported by many who opposed the literacy requirement on entry as an affirmation of American values rather than a repudiation of immigration. Because there was no serious questioning of the legitimacy of English as the language of the land, knowledge of English seemed to be a fitting basis for citizenship. The final wording of the act was simple: "no alien shall hereafter be naturalized or admitted as a citizen of the United States who cannot speak the English language."

Although the literacy requirement for admission failed and was not included in the 1907 immigration bill, the concept did not disappear. President Taft vetoed a legislative provision that would have established a literacy requirement during his term of office. Congress passed such a requirement again in 1915, only to see the bill vetoed by President Wilson. Unable to override the veto, Congress took up the provision next in 1917. Wilson vetoed it once more. Wilson himself had complicated views on immigration. In his *History of the American People*, Wilson criticized the new immigration, saying that countries in southern Europe were "unburdening themselves of the more sordid and hapless elements of their population" while the immigrants of eastern Europe had "neither skill nor energy nor any initiative of quick intelligence" (Wilson 1903: 212). During subsequent campaigns for office in New Jersey and then for the presidency, Wilson backtracked from these statements to garner support from immigrants. He remained firmly opposed to the concept of hyphenated Americans, however: "I protest against speaking of German-Americans or Irish-Americans or Jewish-Americans, for these nationalities are becoming indistinguishable in the general body of Americans. Drop out the first words, cut out the hyphens and call them all Americans" (quoted in Vought 1994: 41). This view was consistent with his notion that national interest should trump group interests. He vetoed the literacy requirement precisely because of these views; he saw those supporting the literacy requirement, including the unions and members of Congress from the South, as special interests on the other side of the issue. In his 1917 veto message, Wilson argued that the literacy test is "not a test of character, of quality or of personal fitness, but would operate in most cases merely as a penalty for lack of opportunity in the country from which the alien seeking admission came. The opportunity to gain an education is in many cases one of the chief opportunities sought by the immigrant in coming to the United States, and our experience in the past has not been that the illiterate immigrant is as such an undesirable immigrant" (Wilson 1917). He further questioned a provision in the bill to exempt persons who shall prove to the satisfaction of the government that they are seeking admission to avoid religious persecution. Wilson had previously criticized the literacy test as an affront to the United States as an asylum for the persecuted, but he found this formulation troubling. It would require the U.S. government to pass judgment on the actions of another government, potentially causing "very serious questions of international justice and comity" (Wilson 1917a).

In contrast to previous vetoes, the 1917 one was overridden and the literacy test became law. All immigrants over the age of 16 years, who were physically capable of reading, would have to demonstrate literacy in English or some other language. Exception were made, however, for wives, mothers, grandmothers, unmarried or widowed daughters, and fathers and grandfathers over the age of 55. The immigration inspectors, under the direction of the Secretary of Labor, were to use uniform pieces of paper, each with no fewer than 30 nor more than 40 commonly used words, printed in plainly legible type, to test the immigrants.

The literacy test was part of a broader set of restrictive provisions. The head tax on arriving immigrants was increased to $8. The legislation also expanded the grounds for exclusion, which now included a list that ran to two full pages of text. The legislation attempted to get at all subparts to the categories that had previously been excluded. Under the category of intellectual defects, the 1917 statute listed idiots, imbeciles, feeble-minded persons, epileptics, insane persons, persons who have had one or more attacks of insanity at any time previously, persons of constitutional psychopathic inferiority, and persons with chronic alcoholism. Political grounds for exclusion barred anarchists, or persons who believe in or advocate the overthrow by force or violence of the government of the United States, or of all forms of law, or who disbelieve in or are opposed to organized government, or who advocate or teach the unlawful destruction of property; persons who are members of or affiliated with any organization entertaining and teaching disbelief in or opposition to organized government. In addition, it excluded those who advocate or teach the duty, necessity, or propriety of the unlawful assaulting or killing of any officer or officers of the government of the United States or any other organized government or who advocate or teach the unlawful destruction of property.

The legislation went into effect on February 1, 1917. On April 6, 1917, the United States declared war on Germany, entering World War I. Tensions had been mounting since 1915 when a German submarine sank the Cunard ocean liner *Lusitania* off the coast of Ireland, drowning 128 American passengers among 1,198 victims. This shocked American public opinion. Germany halted submarine attacks against unarmed passenger ships, but in January 1917 resumed unrestricted attacks. Just two days before the new immigration legislation went into effect, the *Housatanic*, a U.S. cargo ship, was sunk. Then, a German coded, top-secret telegram was intercepted and deciphered in London. Its intention was to induce Mexico to enter the war and attack the United States if the United States entered into an alliance with Britain and France. Germany offered to recognize the return of Texas to Mexico in exchange for its support. This provoked further public support for U.S.intervention on behalf of the allies.

The war succeeded in accomplishing what neither qualitative restrictions nor business cycles had achieved. In 1914, total immigration had exceeded 1.2 million; in 1915, it was only 326,700, falling to less than 300,000 in 1916 and 1917. The largest decline occurred in 1918, with just over 110,000 immigrants entering the country. This was the lowest level of immigration since 1862, at the height of the Civil War. How much the literacy test affected immigration levels, as compared with U.S. entry into the war, is unknown. As will be seen later in the chapter, however, when the war ended, immigration began to increase.

World War I significantly reduced European emigration to the United States, but it did not curtail business demand for foreign workers. As measures were taken to impose new requirements on immigrants, other steps opened the door to temporary workers from Mexico. The number of Mexican immigrants had been steadily increasing in the early 1900s. During the decade 1901–1910, more than 31,000 Mexicans were admitted; in the following decade, the number had grown to 185,000. Some commentators pointed to the political unrest in Mexico, culminating in the 1915 Revolution, as a reason for the increased interest on the part of Mexican migrants. Gamio, who interviewed Mexican immigrants during the 1920s, held that one immigrant's story was representative of many others'. Pablo Mares had arrived in 1915 from a little village in Jalisco: "I had to come to the United States, because it was impossible to live down there with so many revolutions. Once even I was at the point of being killed by some revolutionists" (Gamio 1969b: 2). Most of the Mexicans remained in the southwest American states but some sought work with the railroads and moved into the interior.

As conscription increased and more than 4 million Americans went to war, agricultural growers in the United States petitioned the executive branch to permit recruitment of Mexicans to fill the labor shortage. The Secretary of Labor agreed, exempting Mexican workers from the $8 head tax and from the literacy test if they came as part of an approved temporary worker program. When the economy took a downturn in 1919, the temporary worker program ended but the exemption stayed in place until 1921. More than 72,000 Mexicans entered the United States legally between 1917 and 1921 (Guerin-Gonzales 1994).

Other Mexicans came, without registering with the U.S. authorities, in search of wartime employment. Many Mexicans returned home when the economy worsened, but immigration from Mexico resumed in the 1920s when the economy recovered. The story of Mexican immigration in the period between the wars is told in more detail in the next chapter.

America's Place in the World

World War I and its aftermath brought about a fundamental reshaping of how Americans saw their place in the world. Wilson had tried to keep the United States out of the war. At the outbreak of hostilities, he declared neutrality in a message to Congress: "Every man who really loves America will act and speak in the true spirit of neutrality, which is the spirit of impartiality and fairness and friendliness to all concerned.... The United States must be neutral in fact, as well as in name, during these days that are to try men's souls. We must be impartial in thought, as well as action, must put a curb upon our sentiments, as well as upon every transaction that might be construed as a preference of one party to the struggle before another" (Wilson 1914). Sympathies had shifted clearly to the Allied side, though, not only because of the German attacks on U.S. interests but also stories about German atrocities against Belgian civilians.

When declaring war, Wilson went well beyond the duty to protect Americans from German aggression. He pledged nothing short of bringing American ideals to the rest of the world: "It is a fearful thing to lead this great peaceful people into war, into the most terrible and disastrous of all wars, civilization itself seeming to be in the balance. But the right is more precious than peace, and we shall fight for the things which we have always carried nearest our hearts – for democracy, for the right of those who submit to authority to have a voice in their own governments, for the rights and liberties of small nations, for a universal dominion of right by such a concert of free peoples as shall bring peace and safety to all nations and make the world itself at last free" (Wilson 1917b).

War fever soon took hold. The public supported every aspect of the war effort, including the mobilization of an army of 4 million soldiers. Corporations shifted from civilian to war production, and unions agreed to suspend all labor actions in favor of a united effort to provide the guns and matériel needed by the military. In a manner familiar during other wars, Congress passed legislation to penalize espionage and sedition. In 1918, the Entry and Departure Controls

Act authorized the president to control entry and departure in times of war or national emergency of any alien whose presence was deemed contrary to public safety. In combination with the earlier provisions regarding anarchists, the legislation was used to enforce the departure of critics of the war. Particular attention was given to supporters of the Industrial Workers of the World, seen as a radical labor organization whose members frequently condemned the U.S. war effort as a capitalist plot.

With the end of the war, Wilson tried to impose his views of democracy on the peace process through his well-known Fourteen Points. Wilson emphasized transparency in foreign relations, free trade, democracy, and self-determination. Much has been written about the negotiations at Versailles, but suffice it to say here that the compromise with British and French leaders only partially met Wilson's goals. The assignment of blame to Germany and demands for reparations were a prominent part of the final agreement. The Treaty of Versailles (1919) did lay out Wilson's vision of a League of Nations that would resolve future tensions before they resulted in open hostilities. Article 10 committed members of the League to "undertake to respect and preserve as against external aggression the territorial integrity and existing political independence of all Members of the League." Article 11 held that "Any war or threat of war, whether immediately affecting any of the Members of the League or not, is hereby declared a matter of concern to the whole League, and the League shall take any action that may be deemed wise and effectual to safeguard the peace of nations."

When Wilson returned to the United States with the treaty and the plan for a League of Nations, he found strong opposition. On a nationwide tour of twenty-nine cities in twenty-two days, he spoke in favor of the treaty (and against hyphenated Americans whose interest in foreign nations might cause them to oppose the treaty). Wilson laid out the value of the Treaty of Versailles for the ordinary American. He emphasized not only that it brought peace, but also that it helped the working man: "We added a great international charter for the rights of labour. Reject this treaty, impair it, and this is the consequence of the labouring of the world, that there is no international tribunal which can bring the moral judgments of the world to bear upon the great labour questions of the day" (Wilson 1919).

Leading the opposition was Henry Cabot Lodge, who had been a long-time advocate of immigration restriction. He viewed the League of Nations in much the same way he viewed immigration: "I have always loved one flag and I cannot share that devotion [with] a mongrel banner created for a League.... We would not have our politics distracted and embittered by the dissensions of other lands. We would not have our country's vigour exhausted or her moral force abated, by everlasting meddling and muddling in every quarrel, great and small, which afflicts the world" (Lodge 1919). Just as Lodge opposed bringing the "mongrels" to America, he opposed American interaction with them abroad. He proposed reservations to the treaty that caused Wilson, who had suffered a stroke at the end of his tour, to refuse to compromise.

Isolationism won out in the battle over the Treaty of Versailles and the League of Nations. The Senate voted against ratification, even with Lodge's reservations attached. The Republicans prevailed in the 1920 election, promising that the United States would not become entwined in the affairs of Europe. With regard to the League of Nations, the new president, Warren Harding, was clear in his inauguration address: "Since freedom impelled, and independence inspired, and nationality exalted, a world super-government is contrary to everything we cherish and can have no sanction by our Republic. This is not selfishness, it is sanctity. It is not aloofness, it is security. It is not suspicion of others, it is patriotic adherence to the things which made us what we are" (Harding 1921).

America's shift toward isolationism was intensified by concerns about the 1918–1919 influenza pandemic, which killed as many as 50 million worldwide and infected about one-quarter of all Americans. According to the U.S. Public Health Service (ND), between September 1918 and April 1919, approximately 675,000 deaths from the flu occurred in the United States alone. Unlike other flu outbreaks, this one saw the highest mortality among adults 20 to 50 years old. A resurgence of concern about the public health ramifications of immigration was fueled by the flu outbreak, as it had been by cholera and other epidemics in the past.

While influenza was deadly to the body, the infection of political radicalism could be deadly to the ideals of the country. As we have seen, from the time of Massachusetts' exclusion and expulsion of theological dissidents, through the Alien and Sedition Acts and the mid-nineteenth-century concerns about papists, the United States tempered its enthusiasm for immigration with bars on foreign political or ideological dissent. The threat of anarchism had already been addressed in the qualitative reforms of immigration law. The Haymarket Square bombings of 1886, reportedly by immigrant anarchists, drew attention, but it was the assassination of President William McKinley by the anarchist Leon Czolgosz that resulted in the 1903 exclusion of anarchists.

The Bolshevik Revolution of October 1917 raised concerns about foreign ideology to a new height. Wilson had initially heralded the overthrow of the czar as an example of the power of democratic ideals. In contrast, he and others saw Lenin's October Revolution as a coup d'etat against a democratic administration. Once in power, the Bolsheviks withdrew Russian forces from the fight against Germany, convincing many Americans that Lenin was a tool of the German government. Lenin's Communist ideology added to the fraying of relations between Washington and Moscow. The need to maintain a united front against Germany, as well as ideological concerns, led the United States to refuse to recognize the new regime and to provide material support to its adversaries in the struggle for control of what became the Soviet Union.

The menace of Bolshevism appeared to be coming to America itself when bombs aimed at high-ranking U.S. officials were intercepted in April 1919. Two of the targets were Supreme Court Justice Oliver Wendell Holmes and Attorney General A. Mitchell Palmer; other prominent figures in American politics were also targets. Further bomb plots were unveiled later in the year. Palmer responded with a series of raids, known as the "Palmer Raids," launched on November 7, 1919. Palmer enlisted J. Edgar Hoover, head of the Enemy Aliens Registration Section of the U.S. Department of Justice, to lead the effort to identify the troublemakers. Thousands were arrested and detained; most were never charged with any offense. In cooperation with the Immigration Bureau in the Labor Department, Hoover's office aimed to deport the radicals, not necessarily to try them for any criminal undertakings. The most famous deportation occurred in December 1918 when Emma Goldman and 248 other foreign-born radicals were deported to the Soviet Union on the *S.S. Buford*.

The raids went beyond the apprehension of anarchists. Hoover argued that the Communist Party and its associated organizations advocated the overthrow of the government by force, thus bringing its members under the deportation provisions of the immigration laws. Eventually, at the urging of the Labor Department, a federal judge in Boston held that the Communist Party did not advocate the overthrow of the government by force but, rather, by a general strike. The court also began an investigation of the techniques used by the Justice Department, enlisting the help of Felix Frankfurter, who was then a prominent jurist and later a Supreme Court justice. The investigation marked the beginning of the end of the Red Scares.

In the haste to round up suspected targets, citizens were swept up in the raids, as were immigrants with no ties to the Communists or anarchists. On the first day of the raids, almost 1,200 people were taken into custody and 438 were held for deportation (Schmidt 2000: 268). Decisions to deport were based on secret testimony from informants, coerced confessions, warrantless searches, and, pervasively, on "guilt by membership" in one of the organizations identified as advocating the overthrow of the government. Detainees were often interviewed with no right to counsel and detained with excessively high bail. As the agency with more resources, Hoover's Justice Department investigatory office often took the lead, with the Immigration Bureau following in its steps. These actions were aimed not only at deporting immigrant members of these organizations but also at intimidating others into dropping out of them and deterring still others from joining. In fact, the dues-paying membership in the U.S. Communist Party dropped from 23,624 in December 1919 to 1,714 in 1920.

As in the post-Independence period, in which immigrants became scapegoats for the nation's insecurity, the Red Scare reflected post–World War I insecurities and heralded a return to the Massachusetts model of ideological expulsion. The transition from a wartime to a peacetime economy had brought dislocations to many U.S. communities, which were struggling with the demobilization of 4 million soldiers within a year. Although the economy was recovering by the middle of 1919, inflation was spiraling out of control: "By late 1919 the purchasing power of the 1913 dollar [shrank] from 100 [cents] to 45. Food costs had increased 84 percent, clothing 114.5 per cent, and furniture 125 percent. For the average American family in 1919, the cost of living was 99 per cent higher than it had been five years before" (Murray 2009).

The postwar years also saw a reversal of the tenuous relationship between industry and the unions that had been achieved during the Progressive era. America's ability to galvanize its industry in support of the war effort was a large part of the Allies' success. Corporations that had bristled under the new regulatory frameworks put in place during the first part of the century demanded a loosening of those provisions. Unions, which had agreed to cooperate with industry in the war effort, were unwilling to give up what they considered hard-earned concessions from capital. In 1919 there was a swelling in the number of labor disputes; 3,600 strikes involved some 4 million workers (Murray 2009). Some commentators speculate that the Palmer Raids may have had as much to do with suppressing union activity as they did with ferreting out radicalism in America. The raids unquestionably reflected the deepening suspicion of immigration as a threat to the security of the country.

The National Origins Quotas

By the early 1920s, it became evident that neither the literacy test nor the Palmer Raids had succeeded in stopping the inflow of immigrants. In 1920, 430,000 immigrants entered; in 1921, with the full resumption of transatlantic shipping, the number almost doubled, to 805,000. Still below the highest levels of the pre-war era, the numbers were well within the range of earlier immigration trends. The resurgence of immigration convinced the restrictionists that "quality" reforms, such as the literacy test, were insufficient to address what they continued to see as the "immigration problem."

As early as the Dillingham Commission in 1911, proposals had been floated for numerical restrictions on immigration. The commission had included such an option for consideration: "The limitation of the number of each race arriving each year to a certain percentage of the average of that race arriving during a given period of years" (Immigration Commission 1917: 47). The majority of the commissioners favored the literacy test and other qualitative restrictions, so there was no follow-up to this approach although Dillingham himself introduced legislation in this regard.

The idea of national origins quotas persisted, however, among those who favored more rigorous restrictions on immigration. Although the proponents of the literacy test had proclaimed that they were not concerned about the volume of immigration, just the quality of the eastern European and southern European immigrants, it became clear that numbers mattered greatly. Even if all of the immigrants from the new countries of origin were literate, they were still considered too foreign and there were still too many of them.

Reports from U.S. State Department officials when the war ended fueled concerns about resurgence in immigration. One told of more than 2 million Germans seeking admission to the United States, most the parents of U.S. residents. Another told of 500,000 Jews seeking to leave Poland. Similarly large numbers were projected for most European countries that had not yet recovered from the ravages of the war. The consular officers were not above making conclusions about the desirability of admitting the immigrants. Writing from Poland, one consular official concluded: "the unassimilability of these classes politically is a fact too often proved in the past to bear any argument" (U.S. Congress 1921: 12).

In the legislative session of 1919–1920, some members of Congress proposed an outright prohibition on immigration, referring particularly to the difficulties of finding employment for demobilized soldiers. Not all commentators were so concerned. Frothingham (1919) of the National Security League, no sympathizer with alien notions, wrote of the capacity of American business to reabsorb the soldiers and the need to resume immigration, not stop it: "We began to suffer at once from the opposite trouble, the return of our alien population to their native lands creating labor shortage. Moreover foreign labor has always fitted into our labor demands. Such necessary work as the expansion of our railroads and the improvement of our various means of communication and our harbors will, among other things, absolutely require foreign labor, because our own people do not care for this class of work." Business also began lobbying for repeal of the literacy test, opposing any further restrictions on immigration.

An economic recession began in the summer of 1920, increasing concerns about resumption of the eastern and southern European migration. Albert Johnson, the new chair of the House Immigration Committee, suggested a temporary halt in admissions, except for farm laborers and immediate relatives of citizens. The Senate approved a plan proposed by Charles Dillingham (of Dillingham Commission fame) that would have restricted immigration for fifteen months by applying national origins quotas. A compromise was adopted that would have limited immigration to 350,000 per year, with priority given to wives and minor children of naturalized citizens and permanent residents who filed their intent to naturalize. President Wilson allowed the bill to die without signing it.

Restrictionist advocacy had thus turned to a twofold approach to immigration reform. The first approach required setting an overall quota on immigration – a quota that would be substantially lower than the levels of immigration experienced before the war. The second approach would ensure that the southern and eastern Europeans had no access to entry under the quotas while allowing the "old" immigration from northern and western Europe to regain its dominance. A congressional hearing in 1919 explored how these factors might work together. A representative of the National Committee for Constructive Immigration Legislation explained that two factors were of the essence: the degree to which immigrant groups became Americanized and the state of the U.S. economy. He outlined an extremely complex system that would have taken into account the number of naturalized citizens and U.S.-born children of immigrants from each national group and allowed for admission of between 3 percent and 10 percent of those counted in the 1920 census (U.S. Congress 1919). One of the aims of the organization was to abolish the Asian exclusion laws and institute a more objective means of determining admissions.

Congress revisited immigration reform in 1921, focusing all its efforts on the national origins quota approach. Dillingham's proposal moved quickly through Congress with the support of the incoming Republican president. The Emergency Quota Act of May 19, 1921, imposed the first numerical restriction on immigration in the country's history. The legislation limited the number of aliens of any nationality entering the United States to 3 percent of the foreign-born persons of that nationality who had lived in the United States in 1910. The formula meant that approximately 350,000 immigrants were permitted to enter each year as quota immigrants, mostly from northern and western Europe. More highly skilled or specialized immigration was exempted; actors, artists, lecturers, singers, nurses, ministers, professors, and persons belonging to any recognized learned profession could enter outside the quotas. Domestic servants were also outside the quota system. The quotas only applied to Europe, not to the Western Hemisphere. Moreover, despite the urging of the National Committee for Constructive Immigration Legislation, the Asian exclusions remained in force.

Immigration levels fell in 1922 but then started to creep back up in 1923, reaching the statutory limits. Because the national origins limits were allocated monthly upon arrival, steamships raced to reach port before the quota was filled (Zolberg 2006: 254). Visas were required but were no guarantee of admission if the quota had been met in the interim. Concerned about administrative difficulties and increasing numbers of immigrants, Congress turned once more to immigration reform. This time, Congress determined to set a lower annual limit and then allocate national origins quotas within that level.

Both houses overwhelmingly passed the Immigration Act of 1924, also called the Johnson-Reed Act and the National Origin Quotas Act. Until 1927, an annual quota was set at 2 percent of the number of foreign-born persons of the nationality who had been resident in the continental United States in 1890, with the total quota equaling 164,667. After 1927 (later postponed until July 1, 1929), the annual quota was set at 150,000. Using the 1890 census, which preceded most of the new wave of immigration, the law guaranteed that a higher number of U.S. visas would be available in Britain and western Europe and a lower number in southern and eastern Europe. Each country received a minimum allocation of 100 visas. Preferences were established within the quota for certain family members and for persons skilled in agriculture. All immigration from Asia was stopped, even the small number of visas for Japan that had survived earlier reforms. On the other hand, efforts to impose a quota on immigrants from the Western Hemisphere failed, paving the way for the growth in immigration from Mexico that is discussed in the next chapter.

Conclusion

The imposition of national origins quotas was a full repudiation of the Pennsylvania model. In contrast to William Penn's confidence that people of all nations and religions could live together in harmony, the voices of twentieth-century restriction were skeptical of the country's power to integrate its newcomers. The proponents of Americanization had failed to convince the restrictionists that with time and training, the new immigrants would indeed become Americans. Instead, the Americanization movement itself became increasingly more coercive in its techniques and, in the words of a later Americanization advocate, Barbara Jordan, who was Chair of the 1990s Commission on Immigration Reform, the movement was overtaken by xenophobia. The result was strong support for the Immigration Act of 1924.

Not only did the Johnson-Reed Act lower the overall levels of permanent immigration, it gave the largest quotas to those who were least likely to immigrate. Emigration from the British Isles and much of Western Europe largely ended because the economic pressures to leave those countries had dissipated. But the national quotas for Britain, Ireland, Germany, Scandinavia, and Western Europe were 85 percent of the total. The quotas for southern and eastern Europe were greatly reduced. Poland's quota was 5,982, Italy's was 3,845, and Russia's was 2,248, representing a mere fraction of their pre-quota levels of immigration.

9

Turning Inward

1924–1964

The legislation imposing the national origins quotas dealt a death blow to the Pennsylvania model, and the Great Depression did the same initially to the Virginia model. By the time the national origins quotas went fully into effect in 1929, any calls for renewed immigration would have been suppressed by unprecedented levels of unemployment. During the 1930s, only 500,000 immigrants came to the United States – less than one-eighth the number that had arrived in the previous decade. The Depression affected not only new arrivals but also the ability of prior immigrants to remain in the country. In 1932, emigration was almost three times higher than immigration – 35,576 entered and more than 100,000 immigrants left the United States. At the same time, there were large numbers of internal migrants, including African-Americans moving from the South to northern cities and "Okies" moving from the Dust Bowl to California.

Perhaps the most tragic victims of this restrictive atmosphere were the refugees who tried to flee repression and conflict in Europe. The German quota under the 1924 Act often went unfilled as consular officers refused to grant visas to those likely to become public charges or who fell under other exclusions. This chapter will go into some detail on the heated debate in 1939, when Congress defeated the Wagner-Rogers Act, which was legislation intended to bring 20,000 mostly Jewish children from Nazi Germany outside existing legislative limits. The language of the opposition was reminiscent of the debates over the eastern and southern European immigration of the earlier era.

As another war loomed, though, the United States executed a partial turnaround in its immigration policies, revisiting the Virginia model with a new, large-scale guestworker program with Mexico. The so-called *Bracero*[1] program was much larger than the similar program of the World War I era,

---

[1] *Bracero* derives from the Spanish word *brazo*, which means "arm." Referring to the strong arms of the agricultural workers, the term quickly became synonymous with all Mexican laborers entering under the temporary worker program.

employing between 4 million and 5 million Mexican workers over a 22-year period. The program was criticized for abusing labor standards, particularly by illegal withholding of wages from, and depressing wages for, Mexican-American workers. It also stimulated a parallel flow of undocumented workers. Approximately equal numbers of Mexicans entered the country illegally and were apprehended as entered legally during the same period.

The two sides of the Massachusetts model regained their hold as well as the Cold War intensified and the United States used a series of special bills and administrative orders to admit refugees from Nazi persecution and those fleeing Communism. At the same time, hearings were held to ferret out "un-American" beliefs and activities. In 1945, President Truman used his executive authority to admit 40,000 war refugees. In 1946, Congress acted to permit 120,000 war brides and children to enter. In 1948, Congress passed the Displaced Persons Act, approving the admission of more than 200,000 persons (later increased) by borrowing against future quotas for many of the eastern European countries of origin. When the Displaced Persons Act expired, the Refugee Relief Act of 1953, Refugee Escapee Acts of 1954 and 1957, and Refugee Fair Share Act of 1960 followed. The definition of "refugee" – those "who, because of persecution or fear of persecution on account of race, religion, or political opinion, fled from the Union of Soviet Socialist Republics or other Communist, Communist-dominated or Communist-occupied areas of Europe" – reflected Cold War ideology. Refugees harmed by the new enemy were to find sanctuary in the United States. At the same time, immigrants from Communist-dominated countries, and their children, found themselves under scrutiny as a result of the House Un-American Activities Committee and the Army–McCarthy hearings in the Senate.

In 1952, when Congress revisited immigration policy, it chose to keep the national origins quotas. Although the turn of the nineteenth- to twentiety-century immigrants had spawned a generation that prevailed through the Great Depression and World War II, bringing America to the zenith of its power and authority in the world, Congress was not ready to reverse the discriminatory measures adopted in 1924. A commission appointed by President Truman to study immigration and naturalization policies in the United States echoed Truman's own statement in vetoing the McCarran-Walter Act, concluding that the immigration laws "flout fundamental American traditions and ideals, display a lack of faith in America's future, damage American prestige and position among other nations, ignore the lessons of the American way of life." Nevertheless, Congress would not shift back to the Pennsylvania model. It overrode Truman's veto and maintained the national origins quotas for another thirteen years.

Insecurity in Europe

World War I brought about the end of empire in central and eastern Europe. The German, Austro-Hungarian, and Ottoman empires were split up by the peace treaties that ended the conflict. The czarist Russian empire collapsed in the midst of revolution and civil war. World War I itself, along with the disintegration of empires and subsequent conflicts, brought about massive population displacement. Millions were displaced by the war. Additional millions were uprooted inside and outside the Soviet Union in the early years of the Bolshevik takeover, either from fighting or, more frequently, from famine. In the early 1920s, Armenian survivors of genocide and expulsion from Turkey, who were unwilling or unable to settle in the now Soviet-controlled Armenia, began to seek refuge in Europe.

Fridtjof Nansen of Norway, who had gained international acclaim for his exploration of the North Pole, was given responsibility by the League of Nations for the repatriation of war prisoners and of those who had been displaced by the fighting in World War I. As new displacements occurred in the 1920s, his office increasingly took responsibility for them as well. One of Nansen's major contributions was the issuance of what came to be called the Nansen Passport to refugees who were unable to obtain the increasingly more important document from their own governments. As more and more countries required a passport to travel across borders, refugees had found themselves in a travel limbo, unable to return home and unable to move or even reside elsewhere.

The scale of the relief effort grew in the early years of the 1920s. In 1922–1923, an international relief effort, led by Nansen, reached an estimated 12–15 million homeless and starving refugees in the Ukraine (Marrus 2002). During that same period, Nansen was also called upon to resettle the ethnic Greeks and Turks who had been displaced by the terms of the Treaty of Lausanne, which concluded conflict between a nationalist Turkey and newly independent Greece. Nansen had conceived of the large-scale population exchanges as a way to end the fighting, but the scale of the movements and of the accompanying chaos went well beyond his expectations. A similar, if somewhat smaller, exchange occurred between Greece and Bulgaria. Defined generally by religion (Greek Orthodox or Muslim), about 2 million people were required to change homelands, often against their will and in extremely difficult circumstances.

New dislocations emerged later in the 1920s and into the 1930s as a result of fascism. With Benito Mussolini's takeover of Italy, many of those who opposed his rule fled, seeking safety outside the country. Although his fascist forces did not actually expel the opposition, Mussolini certainly did not regret their removal from the political scene (Marrus 2002). As violence intensified in the mid-1920s and the fascists consolidated their grip on the country, the number of political refugees from Italy increased. Mussolini's policies regarding these refugees also shifted as he recognized that they were continuing their opposition from abroad. His agents in France, in particular, tried to discredit the émigrés and, when that failed, to quiet them by violent means. The numbers never grew beyond about 10,000 émigrés, and the French public was generally positively disposed to them.

The situation in Germany initially followed a similar course, with the first political refugees from the Nazis finding a welcome in 1933, especially in neighboring France. This changed as the numbers of refugees began to grow. Faced with large-scale displacement from repression, the League of Nations established a High Commission for German refugees outside its own bureaucracy. Even this weak step provided the rationale for Germany's withdrawal from the League. The High Commission never had the financial means or the political support to accomplish its end of enabling German refugees to find a safe asylum.

Once the large-scale persecution of Jews began under the Nuremberg Laws, which essentially made the German Jews stateless, refugees' reception in Europe took a decided turn for the worse. As the numbers of Jewish refugees from countries under German domination increased, especially after 1938, they increasingly found a closed door. Sir John Hope Simpson, in a report issued early in 1938, tried to make the case that the number of refugees was actually quite small compared with the population exchanges that Europe had seen in the 1920s. Estimating that there were no more than 150,000 refugees from Germany, and that all but about 30,000 were settled in new countries, Hope Simpson argued that this was a manageable problem (Marrus 2002: 167). With the German annexation of Austria, however, the situation became notably worse for larger numbers of Jews. In the early months after the *Anschluss*, about 30,000 Austrian Jews joined their German coreligionists in fleeing the country.

In the meantime, the Spanish Civil War was generating large-scale refugee movements. The war began in mid-1936 when a group of generals led by Francisco Franco overthrew the Spanish republican government in a coup d'état supported by conservative and fascist groups. As Franco's forces took territory from the republican forces, widespread displacement followed. Children were evacuated by both sides, with significant numbers shipped to Britain, Belgium, the Soviet Union, and Mexico. By the summer of 1938, the republicans estimated that 2 million had been displaced. By April 1939, when Franco's forces defeated the republicans, some 450,000 Spanish citizens had crossed into France. Many were held in deplorable conditions in internment camps, able to leave the camps only if they could put up financial assurances. France encouraged the refugees to return home or move on to other countries, particularly in Latin America. Both occurred, but about 50,000–60,000 republican refugees remained in France, only to find themselves in Nazi hands when Germany occupied France in 1940.

Seeing the increasing turmoil in Europe, the United States called a conference in Evian, France, in summer 1938 to discuss the growing Jewish refugee problem. In calling for the conference, Franklin Roosevelt made it clear that he was not asking any country, including the United States, to change its refugee policy. The Evian conference was a total failure, with no government pledging to resettle significant numbers of the Jewish refugees (except for the Dominican

Republic's rather vague offer). From the beginning of the conference it was clear that not much would happen. Some delegates spent far more time enjoying the Alps than they did discussing the plight of the refugees. Although many words of sympathy for the refugees were heard, few concrete proposals came out of the conference, except for the establishment of still another international organization, the International Committee on Refugees (ICR). The ICR had a dual mandate – to encourage countries to resettle refugees and to persuade Germany to establish an orderly emigration process. If Evian and the ICR failed in its first mission – to find refuge for the Jews – it failed more spectacularly in its second. Germany responded in November 1938 with *Kristallnacht,* a country-wide attack on Jewish businesses and synagogues that was reminiscent of the Russian pogroms. When the war started, mass incarceration of Jews and others in concentration camps increased, and then Hitler launched his Final Solution – genocide – in the knowledge that other countries would do little to rescue the European Jews.

U.S. Refugee Policy

The Immigration Act of 1924 did not include special procedures or exemptions for refugees, as the 1917 legislation had. Quotas and national origins limits were to apply regardless of why people were seeking admission to the United States. As the act went into full implementation in 1929, the nation also fell into the most massive economic crisis of its history. The Great Depression was worldwide, affecting employment in countries around the globe. In the United States, almost 25 percent of the working age population was unemployed by 1933. In the absence of public safety nets, private resources were overwhelmed. Although the New Deal programs put millions back to work, the depression continued. Full recovery occurred only when World War II stimulated the economy and created new demand for labor.

America was on the move during the 1920s and 1930s. The great migration of African-Americans from the South to the cities of the North had gained impetus during World War I and the decades that followed. Partly because the pause in European immigration opened up opportunities in the steel mills, meat-packing houses, and other industries in the Northeast and Midwest, an estimated 1.5 million African Americans migrated. Cities such as Chicago, New York, Philadelphia, and St. Louis soon had large African-American communities in their midst. Immigrants also became more mobile, in some cases moving from the inner cities to new suburbs that reflected the prosperity of the 1920s. Mexican immigrants began to move north from the border regions, attracted to many of the same jobs that had appealed to the African Americans.

During the 1930s, the combination of depression and drought forced hundreds of thousands off the farms of the Great Plains. The movement from Oklahoma to California was so large that a new term was coined – Okie – to describe the migrant workers who were willing, if not eager, to work in California's fields. Dorothea Lange's iconic photograph of a migrant mother

and John Steinbeck's novel, *The Grapes of Wrath* (1939), limned the despera-
tion of those who would do anything to earn a living.

Economic crisis and domestic migration provided the subtext for the American debate on refugee policy. Until U.S. entry into World War II, the admission
of refugees into the United States was a topic of discussion in the Congress
and the State Department. Two constraints on admission stood out. First, the
national quotas restricted the number of persons to be admitted and limited
admissions to close family members of those who were already in the United
States. As discussed in Chapter 8, the National Origins Act provided for an
annual limit of 150,000 Europeans. Each nation was assigned a quota based
on the proportionate contribution of that nationality to the overall U.S. population in the 1920 census. Although the German quota was sizable (more than
20,000), the quotas for some of its annexed areas (e.g., Czechoslovakia, with
about 3,000) were very small.

In addition, the State Department maintained a rigorous policy regarding
inadmissibility, often refusing visas if a consular officer concluded that the
applicant was likely to become a public charge. This policy had general applicability; it was not specific to refugees. At the start of the Great Depression,
President Herbert Hoover had directed the State Department to find administrative ways to reduce immigration in response to worsening economic conditions
(Kraut et al 1984: 7). The consul in Germany then instructed his staff to issue
visas only to those "in possession of funds or property sufficient to support
themselves during the probably indefinite period of the present economic crisis,
i.e., funds or property yielding an income sufficient to provide their support"
(Kraut et al 1984: 7). About 99 percent of applications were rejected on this
basis.

When the Roosevelt administration took office, a number of Jewish and
liberal organizations urged a shift in policy toward refugees, but the rigorous
standards in determining "public charge" persisted, largely at the urging of
State Department officials who were openly anti-Semitic. With the German
government confiscating the financial resources of Jews, it became more and
more difficult for them to prove their economic worth. Although Secretary of
Labor Frances Perkins protested the rigorous application of public charge standards to refugees, the State Department fought back. Its consular officials alone
had the responsibility of issuing visas. Harkening back to President Wilson's
veto of the Literacy Act, the State Department argued that it would be poor
diplomacy for consular officers to make judgments as to whether other countries were persecuting their citizens. The rules were eased somewhat, however,
to allow consular officers to take into account whether the applicant had a
close family member in the United States who was willing and able to provide
financial support.

Jewish organizations asked that offers of support from more distant relatives
also be accepted. They suggested that more refugees could come in if bonds
were posted to ensure that they did not become public charges. In 1936, some of
these provisions went into effect, but for the large number of refugees without

family in the United States, there was little possibility of immigration. Further easing occurred in 1938, when instructions went out that pledges of support from unrelated persons in the United States could be accepted if they set up an irrevocable trust.

A second administrative barrier was the requirement that applicants provide legal documentation of their good moral character. Most immigrants could obtain documentation from their local police that they had not committed any crimes included in the grounds of inadmissibility. For refugees, however, requesting such documentation could be dangerous. Jews covered under the Nuremburg laws could hardly ask government offices for testaments of their worthiness to emigrate to a new country. This requirement was eventually eased; if applicants could show a good reason for not obtaining documentation, the consular official could waive the requirement – although the official was not obliged to do so. As these changes took place, the numbers entering from Germany, and then under a combined German/Austrian quota, grew. By 1936, about 25 percent of the quota was met; in 1937, almost 50 percent was met.

Even with its restrictive quotas and admission policies, the United States had the largest program for admission of immigrants in the world (Breitman and Kraut 1987). In comparison, however, with the open admissions system of the pre–World War I era, the United States was no longer the asylum for the "wretched refuse of your teeming shore," to quote Emma Lazarus's poem on the Statue of Liberty. Sadly, the quotas could not keep pace with demand as German persecution mounted. Between March and April 1938, as German repressive policies were applied to Austrian Jews, more than 40,000 Jews in Austria filled in questionnaires about admission to the United States (Kraut 1984).

After *Kristnallnacht*, Secretary of Labor Perkins of the Labor Department convinced the president to allow German and Austrian Jews on visitors' visas to remain in the United States when their visas expired. This only led the State Department to close down the processing of visitors' visas. The State Department also clamped down on what it considered to be other loopholes. For example, letters issued to approved applicants who were waiting for quota numbers to become available – which often served to keep them out of concentration camps – were no longer to be provided because they "mortgaged" the quotas. The State Department made clear, over the objections of the Labor Department, that refugees were not a priority and that a liberal refugee policy might, in fact, undermine diplomatic relations with Germany and its neighbors. Because restrictive refugee policies were also consistent with U.S. immigration policy, these views prevailed.

Two incidents – debate over the Wagner-Rogers legislation to admit refugee children and the refusal to allow a ship, the *St. Louis*, to land in the United States – exemplify negative attitudes toward liberalizing U.S. policy. Knowing that it would be exceedingly difficult to persuade Congress to open the now-closed doors to adults suffering from Nazi persecution, efforts began to bring children to the United States for safekeeping.[2] In February 1938, Senator Robert F. Wagner (D) of New York and Congresswoman Edith Rogers (R) of Massachusetts introduced a bipartisan joint resolution to authorize the granting of 10,000 immigrant visas during each of two calendar years to children 14 years of age or under who resided in Germany or German-annexed territories. It was expected that about half of the visas would go to German Jewish children while the rest would be divided among Protestant and Catholic minors. Under the terms of the legislation, the children were to be admitted outside the immigration quotas then in effect for Germany and the other affected countries.

Other provisions of the immigration law would not be waived under the proposed legislation. The children would have to show they were admissible. In particular, there had to be "satisfactory assurances that the children [would] be supported and properly cared for through the voluntary action of responsible citizens or responsible private organizations of the United States, and consequently [would] not become public charges." The Nonsectarian Committee for German Refugee Children, consisting of child-welfare experts, was organized to help implement this part of the law if it passed. They developed a comprehensive plan for the selection of children abroad, their transportation, temporary care at ports of entry, and placement in American homes. A committee of distinguished citizens was to oversee these activities.

The motivation behind the legislation was clearly humanitarian. Senator Wagner, in introducing the bill, explained: "Millions of innocent and defenseless men, women and children of every race and creed, are suffering from conditions which compel them to seek refuge in other lands. Our hearts go out especially to the children of tender years, who are the most pitiful and helpless sufferers. The admission of a limited number of these children into the United Sates would release them from the prospect of a life without hope and without recourse, and enable them to grow up in an environment where the human spirit may survive and prosper" (quoted in Forbes [Martin] and Fagen 1984: 2–3).

The proponents of the legislation also hoped to send a message to Germany that would signify U.S. condemnation of its policies of persecution. Support of the bill was widespread. A committee of forty-nine Protestant and Catholic clergymen urged all Americans, without regard to race, religion, or creed, to support passage of the legislation: "To us it seems that the duty of Americans in dealing with the youthful victims of a regime which punishes innocent and tender children as if they were offenders is to remember the admonition of Him who said, 'Suffer little children to come unto me.' And in that spirit we call on all Americans to join together, without regard to race, religion, or creed, in offering refuge to children as a token of our sympathy and as a symbol of

---

[2] This discussion is based on a report on unaccompanied refugee children prepared by the author and Patricia Fagen in 1984 for the Refugee Policy Group and preserved by the Digital Library at Forced Migration Online.

our faith in the ideals of human brotherhood" (quoted in Forbes [Martin] and Fagen 1984: 4).

Even some of those who generally favored restrictive immigration policies supported passage, usually citing the special needs of children. For example, the N.Y.-based *Herald Tribune*, in an editorial, went to some length to establish that the United States "cannot, and should not be asked to, succor all the victims of race prejudice and high politics who have been set cruelly adrift by the new barbarism. Its first duty is to preserve its own unity as a nation" (quoted in Forbes [Martin] and Fagen 1984: 4). It then went on to explain that children were a special case and urged passage of the bill. Editorials in newspapers in Richmond, Sioux City, and Pensacola, not generally seen as bastions of liberal immigration opinion, echoed similar sentiments.

Support for the bill was not, however, unanimous. A number of influential organizations actively opposed its passage, citing a variety of concerns. The president of the Allied Patriotic Societies gave several grounds for opposing the legislation, most strangely "on the humanitarian grounds on which all social agencies agree that children should not be separated from their parents and that foster parentage or institutional bringing up is prejudicial to children" (quoted in Forbes [Martin] and Fagen 1984: 5). There were more self-interested grounds as well: "These children would soon compete with American youth for jobs in this country, one-third of our unemployed being under 25 years of age" (quoted in Forbes [Martin] and Fagen 1984: 5). The legislation was suspect also because "passage of the joint resolution would inevitably lead to the further breaking down of our immigration quotas by being used as a plea that the families of 20,000 children should also later be admitted, outside of the quotas, regardless of their fitness or qualification under our immigration laws, and the separation of families produced by this very legislation would be used as an argument for increased immigration... (quoted in Forbes [Martin] and Fagen 1984: 5). Finally, "the bill violates a fundamental principle of our present immigration law, namely, the apportionment of our immigration strictly in accordance with the national origins of our population. The resolution would obviously give an unfair proportion to one European state, Germany, to the prejudice of all others" (quoted in Forbes [Martin] and Fagen 1984: 5).

The economic problems of the United States, which was very slowly emerging from the Great Depression, were also cited as a reason for opposing any increase in immigration. As a representative of the American Legion stated in hearings on the bill, "...our duty to our own citizens under the present distressing circumstances compels consideration even to the exclusion of those in foreign countries, however sympathetic we may be toward them in their present plight" (quoted in Forbes [Martin] and Fagen 1984: 5). No one, in opposing the proposed law, minimized the circumstances in which the children found themselves. All gave recognition to the serious situation in Central Europe. Some, however, asked why the framers of the joint resolution limited their concern to the children of Germany, citing problems faced by Spanish and Chinese minors. Rather than recommend expansion of the provisions of the bill, though, they used information about the plight of other children to raise the specter of unlimited immigration – or an opening of the floodgates – should special consideration be given to this first group.

The proponents of the Wagner-Rogers bill responded by making differentiations between the circumstances in these other countries and those in Germany. For example, Caroline O'Day of New York said of the Spanish situation, "That is civil war. That is not persecution" (quoted in Forbes [Martin] and Fagen 1984: 6). Opponents of the legislation then questioned whether children who had experienced the persecution cited in defense of the bill could ever adjust to U.S. life. One witness testified at a congressional hearing about the dangers of admitting the refugee children: "These refugees have a heritage of hate. They could never become loyal Americans. Let us not be maudlin in our sympathies, as charity begins at home. We must protect our own children. No society, no state can successfully assume the tremendous responsibility of fostering thousands of motherless, embittered, persecuted children of undesirable foreigners and expect to convert these embattled souls into loyal, loving American citizens" (quoted in Forbes [Martin] and Fagen 1984: 6). Others feared that the enemies of the United States would use this special legislation to bring to this country a "fifth column" of youngsters who had not, in fact, been subject to persecution, but who were really committed to an authoritarian, antidemocratic ideology.

Of these arguments, the most persuasive to Congress were those made regarding waiver of immigration quotas. Members of the Senate committee that heard testimony agreed that it would be bad precedent to authorize admissions outside the immigration quotas. They were willing to give special consideration to refugee children, but only if their admissions were counted against the number permitted entry from their country of origin. An amendment to the Wagner-Rogers bill was passed that gave refugee children first preference for admission under existing limits. Should unaccompanied minors use up the entire quota, no adults or intact families would be permitted entry that year. The drafters of the legislation, not surprisingly, were dissatisfied with this turn of events, believing that it was unfair to ask persons who had been waiting for admission, and were in similar circumstances to those of the unaccompanied minors, to wait longer than necessary. Before further consideration of the bill could take place, however, Congress adjourned. Prior to its return, war broke out in Europe, making the legislation moot – it pertained to children in Germany and German-occupied areas.

That opposition to Wagner-Rogers came at least partly because it applied primarily to Jewish refugees was clear when the war in Europe created another group of children in need of assistance – children in Britain. Many groups within the United States supported efforts to bring them to this country, if evacuation was possible. On July 13, 1940, the attorney general issued a directive permitting the entry of unaccompanied children from European countries that were subject to attack. Most of the children came from the United Kingdom (830), but smaller numbers were admitted from other countries as well. The British were admitted on temporary immigration visas, with the British crown retaining guardianship. In addition, about 450 children who had lost their parents were admitted as quota immigrants. Although the transportation of many of the children was paid by their parents, a clause in the Immigration Act of 1917 that prohibited the admission of immigrants whose way was paid by a corporation, association, or society was waived, so voluntary agencies could provide transportation to children in need.

The evacuation of children from war zones lasted for only a few months. In September 1940 an ocean liner carrying seventy-seven refugee children was torpedoed. In October, the British government halted evacuation of its children. The U.S. committee formed to support the evacuations agreed that it was too dangerous to transport children across the Atlantic, noting that "it will not take the responsibility of assisting children now abroad to run the risks of ocean passage at this time" (quoted in Forbes [Martin] and Fagen 1984: 13). In this case, humanitarian concerns for the children trumped immigration policy, even if in the end, safety trumped both considerations.

The *St. Louis* debacle dealt with another aspect of U.S. policy toward refugees. In this case, the refugees were at the actual doors of the country, not trying to enter from thousands of miles away. The *St. Louis* sailed from Hamburg on May 13, 1939. On board were more than 900 German Jews bound for Cuba. At least one passenger had been in Dachau, imprisoned on *Kristallnacht*. The passengers believed they had valid Cuban landing permits. Cuba had provisions for the admission of refugees, who were required to post a $500 bond and receive visas, and for tourists who needed a landing permit but no visa. Manuel Benitez, the Director of Immigration, had been selling the landing permits for $150. Looking like legitimate visas, with Benitez' signature, these permits were then resold at a premium to desperate refugees.

To the misfortune of the *St. Louis* passengers, a generally positive view of refugees was shifting in Cuba. The economy had declined and refugees were criticized for competing with Cubans for limited jobs. Allegedly, Frederico Laredo Bru, the president of Cuba, felt that he had not received an appropriate cut of the profits generated by the scheme. In response, a new decree was passed invalidating the landing permits. When the *St. Louis* arrived in Cuban territorial waters, the captain was told that the ship could not dock because the passengers were not eligible to land. Negotiations ensued. Initially, it appeared that the situation would be resolved by paying the $500 per passenger bond required of refugees. Representatives of the American Jewish Joint Distribution Committee, the organized relief arm of the Jewish community, were dispatched to Cuba to undertake the negotiations. After a series of miscommunications, however, Laredo Bru suspended the talks, announcing that the passengers would under no circumstances be permitted to disembark.

The captain of the *St. Louis* headed for U.S. territorial waters in the hope that the United States would accept the refugees on a humanitarian basis. Provisions were running low and the captain was under pressure to return to Germany. Complicating the situation, a crewman who worked for the German secret police had received documents about U.S. military capacities from a courier who had been permitted to come aboard the *St. Louis* in Havana. The courier pressed for a speedy return so the documents could be delivered.

Some of the passengers sent telegrams to President Roosevelt and the State Department requesting an exception to be made to U.S. immigration policy so they could enter the United States. The president never responded, but a telegram from the State Department summarized the government's position: "the passengers must await their turns on the waiting list and qualify for and obtain immigration visas before they may be admissible into the United States" (U.S. Holocaust Museum, n.d.). The U.S. ambassador in Havana appealed to the Cuban government to allow the passengers to disembark, although the United States itself was unwilling to offer asylum.

The *St. Louis* then headed back to Hamburg. The American Jewish Joint Distribution Committee was able to obtain permission from the Dutch government for the ship to land in Antwerp. After further negotiations, four countries agreed to accept the refugees: Great Britain (288), the Netherlands (181), Belgium (214), and France (224). These countries agreed to provide temporary asylum while the passengers arranged for permanent settlement. About 600 had pending visas for the United States. About 15 percent managed to immigrate before the outbreak of hostilities, but most were on the very lengthy waiting list for entry in the United States. Those admitted to Britain remained safe throughout the war, but the majority of those who went to continental Europe found only a brief refuge. Only about half survived the Holocaust.

The failure of the United States to respond more generously and effectively to the plight of the Jewish refugees was one of the darkest moments in American history. A combination of anti-Semitism, fear of economic competition, diplomatic pressures, and a general lack of political will by Roosevelt and his administration (with the exception of Frances Perkins and a few others) resulted in an exclusionary policy that could not be modified even in the face of persecution. These policies confirmed too poignantly the 1936 comment of Chaim Weizmann, the future president of Israel, that "the world seemed to be divided into two parts – those places where the Jews could not live and those where they could not enter" (Manchester Guardian 1936).

Guestworkers: Return to the Virginia Model

The Great Depression gave way to acute demand for labor when World War II began. Even before the United States was attacked at Pearl Harbor and entered the conflict, U.S. industry received a shot in the arm from the conversion program, under which peacetime manufacturing shifted to a defensive military posture, and then from the Lend-Lease program, through which the United States supplied weapons to Britain, the Soviet Union, and other countries that were fighting Germany. The civilian unemployment rate dropped from 14.6 percent of the labor force in 1940 to a mere 1.2 percent in 1944" (U.S. Bureau of Labor Statistics, n.d.).

As the military grew during World War II, the country sought a variety of sources of workers to substitute for those who had been mobilized. Women entered the labor force in unprecedented numbers. African Americans resumed their migration from the rural South to the urban North. Employment in certain sectors, particularly agriculture, remained problematic, causing Congress and the Roosevelt administration to revisit immigration issues. Restarting immigration from Europe was not possible; attention turned to the Western Hemisphere.

Immigration from other countries in the Western Hemisphere had been left outside the national origins quotas, or overall quotas, in the immigration reforms adopted after World War I. Throughout the 1920s, immigration from Mexico had been on the increase, through both legal and undocumented channels. Manuel Gamio's massive overview of Mexican immigration, completed in 1927 for the Social Science Research Council, attempted to enumerate the Mexican population in the United States mid-decade but found the data to be unreliable, in part because of the transient nature of the migration as well as the often undocumented aspects. U.S. data tended to count those who arrived legally, but there were no good estimates of those who came illegally. Mexico tried to count returnees but did not necessary know how many stayed in the United States. The Mexican Embassy estimated that the Mexican population in the United States had grown from 486,418 in 1919 to 890,746 by 1926 (Gamio 1969a: 2).

As Gamio (1969a: 11) concluded, "immigration is not only powerfully drawn from the United States but it is likewise propeled [*sic*] by conditions in Mexico." The north-central states of Mexico – the areas supplying the largest number of migrants – had suffered particularly from the political and economic insecurity wrought by the Mexican revolution of 1910–1920. The fighting destroyed property, livestock, sugar mills, and *mescal* (a distilled spirit) manufacturing (Sandos and Cross 1983: 44–45). Living conditions deteriorated and prices increased dramatically. Sandos and Cross (1983: 46) estimated net capital losses in agriculture in Zacatecas and San Luis Potosí of 50 percent in fixed assets and as much as 75 percent in variable assets. During the recovery in the 1920s, landowners shifted from a previously permanent workforce of peasant farmers to sharecropping and rentals, which gave no security to the workers. A new rebellion, the Cristero movement, broke out in 1926 and caused further destruction of lives and property.

Increased migration – both internally and to the United States – ensued. Some migrants followed the path established by the World War I–era work program. Others came legally to the United States; an increasing number crossed the border illegally. Gamio (1969a: 10) attributed the increase in illegal movements to several factors, including difficulties presented by U.S. immigration law, particularly the literacy requirement; long and complicated bureaucratic procedures; high fees for visas, compared with smuggling fees; and the ineligibility of those who had previously entered under contracts to do so again.

Gamio (1969a:4–5) examined money orders sent from U.S. postal authorities to Mexico from 1919 to 1927, finding that they had grown from 5 million pesos in 1919 to 16.6 million in 1927, reflecting the increase in population. Most of the money orders were sent from California and Texas, but Illinois and Arizona accounted for significant shares. In California, particularly, the number of money orders sent in the summer months (8,582) exceeded those sent in the winter (6,313). The number of pesos sent was also higher in the summer months than in the winter. The seasonal nature of work – again, particularly in California – contributed to this pattern. A majority of the money orders were sent to three states in Mexico with high levels of emigration – Michoacan (20 percent), Guanajuato (19.6 percent), and Jalisco (14.7 percent).

Regarding labor force activities in the United States, Gamio (1969a:43) concluded that the great majority of Mexicans were unskilled workers in agriculture: "The great part of unskilled labor in the fields is transient. During the summer and fall such men follow the crops across various states of the American union; many of them return to Mexico for the winter; a few go instead to the American southern states." Most of the seasonal workers were single men or men who left their families in Mexico. Support for keeping Mexico out of the quota system remained strong among California and Texas agricultural interests throughout the 1920s. As the *Los Angeles Times* (1928) editorialized, in opposition to proposals to apply the national origins quotas to Mexicans and Central Americans, "We need Mexican labor because we can't even begin to get enough of any other kind to handle our crops, especially at the critical time of harvest."

A smaller but more constant Mexican workforce was employed in industry. This type of labor was more likely to be found in northern states, particularly in steel mills, railroads, and automobile factories. Vargas (1991: 71) concluded that "the communities Mexicans established in the industrial Midwest became home to them. The desire for economic betterment compensated for the hardships endured by Mexicans in the North. Through hard work, they successfully made the adjustment to an industrial working-class experience."

After examining the situation of Mexicans in the United States, Gamio had a different view. He concluded that "Mexican transient immigration is beneficial to both countries, inasmuch as the United States cannot supply the need of labor which exists in certain regions for certain types of work, at a time when Mexico cannot offer better living conditions to its own workers" (Gamio 1969a:50). He was much more critical of permanent immigration, however, saying it "is harmful to both countries, especially if it takes place on a large scale.... For the United States this might be expected to make itself felt in labor struggles and perhaps in racial conflicts, whereas for Mexico it would mean the loss of its best working population, for it is exactly these that emigrate" (Gamio 1969a: 50). The sentiment was shared by proponents of Mexican migration, albeit with more racist undertones. In a hearing on Mexican migration, Harry Chandler, the publisher of the *Los Angeles Times*, "warned the committee that if Mexican labor is taken away from the Southwest, the alternative will be an inpouring of Filipinos and Porto [sic] Ricans and these, he declared, 'are less desirable if you want to call it a choice between two evils.'" Chandler went on to say that Mexicans "are quiet and law abiding and do not attempt to mingle or intermarry with Americans and then return home between seasons" (Benedict 1930b).

Although support for continued migration from Mexico continued, as the Great Depression intensified, restrictions were placed on both temporary and permanent immigration. High unemployment rates lessened the demand for Mexican workers. American workers from the Great Plains flocked to California, many to become migrant workers toiling in the fields. The factories and processing plants of the Midwest laid off workers; often Mexican immigrants were the last to be hired and the first to be fired. During economic downturns, some waited out the hard times; others moved back to Mexico; still others moved around the United States in search of jobs. Repatriation was not necessarily voluntary. Bureau of Immigration officials undertook raids in areas with large numbers of Mexican immigrants, from the Rio Grande Valley to Michigan (Valdes 1988: 7). Repatriation committees offered unemployed workers free or reduced fares to the Mexican border (Valdes 1988: 6). The Mexican government, while sometimes protesting abuses, cooperated with repatriation efforts by providing certificates that helped immigrants bring their property back to Mexico (Valdes 1988: 9).

American policies also reduced the supply of Mexican workers (Vargas 1988: 71). In November 1928, well before the State Department tightened its public charge requirements on European immigrants, and before the collapse of Wall Street, consular officials began to require that Mexicans demonstrate that they had sufficient financial resources to support themselves. After imposition of the new rules, which was undertaken at least partly to demonstrate that imposition of quotas was not needed, entries were reduced by 25 percent (_Los Angeles Times_ 1929a). By April, they had been reduced by 50 percent (_Los Angles Times_ 1929b). In February 1930, the State Department reported that visa issuance was down by 80 percent (Benedict 1930a: 4).

The Mexican government, in responding to the new U.S. initiatives, argued that these policies encouraged clandestine immigration. Mexico proposed that both countries streamline the immigration and emigration processes (Los Angeles Times 1930). Just five years earlier, the U.S. Border Patrol had been established by law to patrol the border areas between official ports of entry. The mission of the Border Patrol was twofold: to stop smuggling of goods, particularly alcohol, and to stop illegal immigration. The former mission was given more attention at first, in the context of Prohibition, and the majority of Border Patrol officers was placed on the Canadian border (U.S. Customs and Border Protection 2003).

When the United States entered World War II, American agriculture and other sectors began pressuring the government to reopen the doors to Mexican migrants. The Pennsylvania model had been abandoned; no consideration was given to offering permanent status to newly recruited foreign workers. Rather, the temporary migration so favored by Chandler and Gamio would be the norm for the new programs, representing a twentieth-century manifestation of the Virginia model.

In 1942, the U.S. and Mexican governments began negotiation about the terms of a guestworker program, which was widely called the *Bracero* program, signifying the strong arms of the Mexican workers. The United States used a loophole in legislation to set the process in motion. Although the importation of contract labor had been prohibited for decades, the 1917 legislation had given the attorney general the authority to regulate the admission and return of otherwise inadmissible persons. This provision had been used in setting up the World War I-era temporary work program with Mexico.

Mexico was initially reluctant to participate because of previous abuses against Mexican workers. Its own economic plans, however, necessitated a shift toward industrialization with accompanying changes in agricultural practices. These reforms would likely create an even larger surplus rural labor force, precisely in the locations that had been most prone to revolutionary dissent. A labor agreement with the United States could be just what was needed to provide a safety valve (Sandos and Cross 1983: 51). With a promise also of U.S. technological assistance, Mexico agreed to negotiate the terms of the labor agreement.

The original agreement to launch what came to be known as the *Bracero* program was signed on August 4, 1942, by representatives of the Mexican Foreign Affairs and Labor Ministries and the U.S. Departments of State and Agriculture.

The provisions of the agreement addressed Mexico's concerns and America's demand for labor. The United States agreed that the Mexican workers would not be engaged in military activities. The workers would be provided with transportation to and from the United States and with housing. Contracts were to be written in Spanish under the supervision of the Mexican government. The workers were to be paid wages that were the same as those paid for similar work to other agricultural laborers under the same conditions within the same area. Piece rates were set as to enable the worker of average ability to earn the prevailing wage. In any case, wages for piece work or hourly work would not be less than 30 cents per hour. Elected representatives drawn from the Mexican workers could deal with employers but they could not change the basic provisions of the contracts. To meet the concerns of American labor, which opposed the agreement, the Mexicans were not to be employed to displace other workers, or for the purpose of reducing rates of pay previously established.

Both governments were to be actively involved in the program (Calavita 1992: 20). The Farm Security Administration in the U.S. Department of Agriculture was the official employer of record, with subemployers being the companies that actually benefited from the labor. The State Department was the principal negotiator with the Mexican government. The U.S. Employment Service certified labor shortages and prevailing wages. The U.S. government would inform the Mexican government of the numbers of workers needed, and the Mexican government would make its own determination as to the numbers who could leave Mexico without negatively affecting the Mexican economy. In practice, the Mexican government chose which Mexicans could participate in the program and transported the workers to recruitment centers. The United States moved the workers from the recruitment centers to the places of employment. Mexican health authorities were responsible for clearing the migrants before they crossed the border. Mexican consular officers, assisted by Mexican labor inspectors, were to have free access to the workplaces of the Mexican workers to investigate their conditions.

During the war years, almost 220,000 *braceros* entered the United States to work in agriculture in twenty-four states. The program began with only 4,203 workers entering in 1942; it grew to 52,098 in 1943, and 62,170 in 1944. The *braceros* were employed in planting and harversting cotton, sugar beets, and fruits and vegetables, mostly in California. Mexico barred the use of *braceros* in Texas, citing abuses and discriminatory practices.

Soon after its inception, the agricultural employers sought changes to bring the program closer to their interests. The role initially taken by the Farm Security Administration was turned over to the War Food Administration, which was seen as an agency that was more supportive of employer interests. The Farm Security Administration had sought to have the wage and work guarantees in the *Bracero* program applied to domestic workers, a step that the growers opposed (Calavita 1992: 22). In the legislation that Congress passed to codify the program, still more changes were made. The state agricultural extension services, which were allied with the Farm Bureaus that represented growers, were given responsibility for setting prevailing wages – generally based on what the employers decided they were willing to pay.

The legislation also began to undermine the bilateral nature of the agreement, giving the Commissioner of the Immigration and Naturalization Service (now in the Department of Justice) the authority to waive the prohibition against contract labor for as long as would be needed. This provision was used to bypass both the Mexican recruitment process and the Mexican bar on *braceros* working in Texas by establishing a process by which employers could recruit workers at the border. The State Department intervened to stop the border recruitment in the name of good diplomatic relations with Mexico. The option remained, however, and would be used in later years (Calavita 1992: 24).

With the end of the war, Congress intended to phase out the *Bracero* program by 1947. Public Law 40 required all *braceros* to leave the country as of January 1, 1948. Very few new *braceros* were recruited in 1947, although some 55,000 Mexicans who were in the country illegally were drawn into the legal program. The U.S. government also acted unilaterally in allowing would-be *braceros* into the country. During one weekend in October 1948, immigration officials in El Paso opened the border to several thousand Mexicans who hoped to be recruited. Although Congress failed to act to extend the program beyond

January 1, the administration used its executive authority to continue importation of contract workers, with legislation coming months after the renewal took place. That legislation also expired, but the program persisted under administrative action until more formal legislation was adopted in 1951 (Calavita 1992).

As the program matured, further changes were made to accommodate the interests of agriculture. The government-to-government contracts that characterized the wartime agreement changed to direct contracting between employers and workers. Mexico still opposed recruitment at the border (that is, having would-be *braceros* travel to the border and present themselves to employers) but agreed that undocumented workers in the United States would be given preference over new arrivals for *Bracero* program slots. Although the legalization was supposed to be a one-time event, a rolling deadline made illegal migration an attractive alternative for workers and employers who did not want to go through the Mexican government process. The two countries disagreed fundamentally on ways to reduce illegal immigration. The United States asked Mexico to patrol its side of the border better, and Mexico asked the United States to impose penalties on employers who hired workers who were in the country illegally (Scruggs 1961).

In 1950, President Truman established a Commission on Migratory Labor to examine the impact of the *Bracero* program. By then, the program had grown to almost 200,000 workers per year. The volume of illegal immigration had kept pace and, in some cases, surpassed the level of legal admissions. The commission was asked to report on (a) social, economic, health, and educational conditions among migratory workers, both alien and domestic, in the United States; (b) problems created by the migration of workers, for temporary employment, into the United States, pursuant to the immigration laws or otherwise; (c) responsibilities being assumed by federal, state, county, and municipal authorities with respect to alleviating the conditions among migratory workers, both alien and domestic; (d) whether sufficient numbers of local and migratory workers could be obtained from domestic sources to meet agricultural labor needs and, if not, the extent to which the temporary employment of foreign workers might be required to supplement the domestic labor supply; and (e) the extent of illegal migration of foreign workers into the United States and the problems created thereby, and whether, and in what respect, current law enforcement measures and the authority and means possessed by federal, state, and local governments might be strengthened and improved to eliminate such illegal migration (Truman 1950). The commission held hearings in Texas, California, Arizona, Colorado, Tennessee, New Jersey, Michigan, Florida, and Oregon.

The commission determined that there were about 1 million migrant workers engaged in agriculture. About half were native-born and half were foreign-born. Of the foreign-born workers, the commission estimated that 80 percent were in the country illegally, and the rest were *braceros*. The commission found that the *braceros* actually had the highest level of labor protection among the migrant workers because of the bilateral agreement. The strong presence of workers who were illegally in the country – or "wetbacks," as the commission and others called them – depressed the wages and working conditions of the domestic workers. The commission also concluded that there was no shortage of agricultural workers in the United States, noting that wages had not risen to attract new workers and mechanization had increased productivity while reducing labor demand.

The conditions under which the undocumented worked were particularly troubling. The commission reported:

> Once on the United States side of the border and on the farm, numerous devices are employed to keep the wetback on the job. Basic to all these devices is the fact that the wetback is a person of legal disability who is under jeopardy of immediate deportation if caught. He is told that if he leaves the farm, he will be reported to the Immigration Service or that, equally unfortunate to him, the Immigration Service will surely find him if he ventures into town or out onto the roads. To assure that he will stay until his services are no longer needed, his pay, or some portion thereof, frequently is held back. Sometimes, he is deliberately kept indebted to the farmer's store or commissary until the end of the season, at which time he may be given enough to buy shoes or clothing and encouraged to return the following season.... Wages for common hand labor in the lower Rio Grande Valley, according to the testimony, were as low as 15 to 25 cents per hour. (President's Commission on Migratory Labor 2007: 433)

The commission reiterated that the value of the unauthorized workers was that they could be easily deported when their labor was no longer needed: "When the work is done, neither the farmer nor the community wants the wetback around. The number of apprehensions and deportations tends to rise very rapidly at the close of the seasonal work period. This can be interpreted not alone to mean that the immigration officer suddenly goes about his work with renewed zeal and vigor, but rather that at this time of the year 'cooperation' in law enforcement by farm employers and townspeople undergoes considerable improvement... " (President's Commission on Migratory Labor 2007: 433).

The commission made a number of recommendations to address what Edward R. Murrow would in a decade call the "harvest of shame." Most important, the commission called for agricultural workers to come under the same labor protections as industrial workers. The commission also urged increased efforts to deter illegal migration, including legislation to make it an offense to hire someone who was in the country illegally. It also called for enhanced funding for the Immigration and Naturalization Service to enforce border controls. Finally, the commission, arguing that because there was no shortage of domestic workers in agriculture and no market-driven increase in wages, the provisions to determine shortages and prevailing wages should be reassessed.

Congress rejected most of the commission's recommendations in its renewal of the *Bracero* program, arguing that the Korean War necessitated continued access to foreign workers. Yet Congress went beyond another emergency act.

In amendments to the Agricultural Act of 1949, Congress overrode the bars on contract labor, specifying the authorization of contract workers in agriculture. This meant that there no longer would be need for an executive branch override of the law. The new legislation took some of the problems identified by labor unions and the Mexican government into account,but it more often met the demands of agricultural growers. The U.S. government would be the official guarantor of the terms of the contracts under which the *braceros* worked. Only workers contracted from Mexico, Mexicans legally in the United States, *braceros* whose contracts had expired and workers who had been illegally in the United States for five years or longer would be eligible for the *Bracero* program. The Secretary of Labor would have to certify that a labor shortage existed and that the importation of *braceros* would have no adverse effects on domestic workers. The employers would have to demonstrate a good-faith effort to recruit domestic workers at comparable wages. The legislation left it to the executive branch to determine how to carry out these provisions. Most important, although the Senate version of the bill included such provisions, Congress did not enact sanctions against employers who hired workers who were illegally in the country, thus allowing the two-track system to continue.

As soon as the bill was signed in July 1951, negotiations began on renewal of the bilateral agreement with Mexico. At first, Mexico balked at signing a new agreement. Mexico had argued strongly for employer sanctions to reduce illegal immigration and increase demand for *braceros*. The Mexican government had concluded that the repeated legalizations had increased the levels of illegal movements. When the Truman administration promised to seek separate legislation to address the concerns about illegal immigration, Mexico agreed to a renewal. The workers would receive the prevailing wage for a particular crop in specific locations or a piece rate equal to that wage. As in previous agreements, the *braceros* had to be employed for at least 75 percent of the contracted period (not including Sundays) or the employer would have to provide the difference in wages. *Bracero*s could not be used to break strikes or replace striking workers but the agreement did not give them the right to unionize. In a departure from previous agreements, Mexico could not bar certain states from participating in the program, allowing Texas to join the initiative.

With the new legislation, the *Bracero* program grew from 200,000 in 1952 and 1953 to 300,000 in 1954, almost 400,000 in 1955, and more than 425,000 in the period 1956–1959. At the same time, illegal immigration continued without abatement. The *New York Times* ran articles in 1953 highlighting the problem, noting that in August there were more than 101,000 apprehensions on the United States–Mexico border. The newspaper recounted how easy it was to smuggle Mexicans across the border, citing one smuggler who stood on street corners in Mexicali offering to smuggle people across the border and provide transport to Fresno, 400 miles north of the border, for $125. The *Times* further reported the value of the "wetbacks" was not only in providing labor but also in lowering the "hypothetical 'prevailing wage'... to a level unattractive to domestic labor, making domestic labor 'unavailable' and occasioning the importation of contract labor" (Hill 1953: 65).

Initially, Congress showed little concern about illegal immigration. Having rejected the Senate proposal for sanctions on employers hiring those illegally in the country, in 1952 Congress passed a watered-down provision making it illegal "to harbor, transport, and conceal" unauthorized migrants. Congressional debate made it clear that this provision was being added to the statute because the Mexican government was balking at renewal of the bilateral agreement unless the United States took action to curb illegal immigration (Calavita 1993: 68). Congress left a loophole, however, in what came to be known as the Texas Proviso – the employment of persons illegally in the country would not be construed as "harboring." Employers did not have to fear that hiring unauthorized workers would subject them to penalties.

Congress also failed to provide enhanced resources for the Border Patrol to enforce immigration law. In fact, the number of Border Patrol officers was reduced by one-third in the period from the end of World War II until 1954 (Calavita 1992: 36). Members of Congress who were otherwise restrictionist in their views on immigration argued against increases in the budget of the Immigration and Naturalization Service (INS), noting the need for agricultural workers in the Southwest. The message from the administration was mixed at best. In December 1953, the attorney general reported to the House Appropriations Committee that the problem of illegal immigration was worsening, but he recommended a reduction of the INS budget by $3 million out of a total of about $40 million.

However, pressure was mounting on the executive branch to do something about the high level of illegal immigration. Not only were reports of depressed wages and atrocious working conditions becoming more frequent, but security concerns about a porous border were fed by Cold War political concerns. Reports of possible Communist infiltration of the border came from the administration as well as from senior legislators such as Senator Hubert Humphrey. The League of United Latin American Citizens criticized the INS for its lax enforcement, citing illegal immigration as being antithetical to the interests of Mexican-Americans.

In April, 1954, retired General Joseph Swing was appointed INS Commissioner, signaling a change in policies. As a former military officer, he determined to invigorate the enforcement capacity of the Border Patrol. In June he launched "Operation Wetback." The Border Patrol reassigned officers from the Canadian border to California to carry out a special program to deport apprehended Mexicans into the interior of Mexico; this was to disrupt what had become a revolving door of apprehension, deportation, and reentry. The Mexican government had agreed to provide trains to effect removals to the interior (*New York Times* 1954a:24). Within a month, more than 11,000 migrant workers were arrested in southern Texas and transported to El Paso for deportation. After some farmers charged that the Border Patrol seized the funds to pay for their transport from the apprehended "wetbacks," the Border Patrol confirmed that the cost of their travel had been deducted from pay the migrants received. (*New York Times* 1954b). During 1954, more than 1 million apprehensions were made, and an untold number of Mexicans departed the country voluntarily to avoid deportation. Generally, the operation was lauded, although there were criticisms over specific actions, such as use of dogs to track down migrants and deportations of U.S. citizens along with the undocumented. Swing's proposal to build a fence along the border was opposed by the State Department, the Mexican government, and many local organizations (Ngai 2004: 160).

By mid-July 1954, there was a sharp increase in requests for *braceros* from farmers in Texas and California (*New York Times* 1954c). The Labor Department announced it would hire an additional 90,000 Mexicans to fill the gap left by the deportations and requested additional appropriations. The Bureau of Prisons also asked for more funding to expand facilities to hold the arrested unauthorized workers (United Press 1954). Although the operation did not stop further illegal immigration, it convinced many employers that participating in the *Bracero* program was a more secure way to gain access to a labor force. The government was willing to provide access to the *braceros*, as witnessed by the increase in numbers admitted. In the period from 1955–1959, *braceros* represented 27 and 29 percent of California and Texas seasonal workers respectively. In New Mexico during the 1950s, they represented almost 70 percent (Grove 1996: 311).

By and large, agricultural interests supported the transition as long as enforcement was even-handed, meaning that no other employer was able to benefit from access to an illegal workforce, and the government provided enough legal workers to meet their demand. The growers had learned how to overcome some of the more nettlesome requirements of the *Bracero* program. Prevailing wages were what the farmer associations decided, rather than a product of an independent analysis. The government agreed to provide *braceros* at short notice once a farmer placed an order for workers. This meant ensuring that a larger-than-needed workforce was always available, lowering prevailing wages still further. One study of wage depression for cotton production found that during the period from 1953 to 1964, the influx of *braceros* depressed wages by 8.8 percent annually (Grove 1996: 314).

Braceros were assigned to a single employer or farm labor association so there was little turnover and even less opportunity to protest the wages or working conditions. The de facto indenture was exacerbated by government policy. The INS, much to the consternation of the Labor Department, issued documentation to workers certified to be "special" by their employers. This process effectively guaranteed that the workers could return the next year. In this way, employers could reward compliant workers and blackball those whom they considered unsatisfactory or troublemakers. Employers could request workers by name, providing further incentives for workers to comply with whatever employers expected of them. All of this gave employers access to a highly productive workforce. A study of labor productivity in the cotton harvest in Arizona found that "Mexicans harvested, on average, 6 percent more per hour [than U.S. male workers] and spent 19 percent more time picking cotton each week," resulting in 30 percent more productivity (Grove 1996: 313).

The *Bracero* program remained in place until the end of 1964. Its demise is discussed in Chapter 10 in the context of the major immigration reforms that took place during the Kennedy and Johnson administrations. Suffice it to say here that during its twenty-year reign, the *Bracero* program brought the Virginia model of immigration back to the United States. The largely Mexican workforce (*braceros* were also recruited from the West Indies) provided labor with minimal rights. While the original bilateral agreements set out a set of labor standards that actually exceeded those available to domestic workers, tolerance for illegal immigration undermined these efforts. After Operation Wetback had reduced the illegal competition, and some of the most egregious violations of rights, the program was largely designed to ensure that employers had continuing access to a low-wage-earning, compliant workforce.

Cold War Policies: Return to the Massachusetts Model

The United States emerged from World War II as a superpower with a large industrial and military base. Europe, on the other hand, was a ravaged continent, with millions of displaced persons. Many had been uprooted by the conflict itself. Now in Western Europe, they did not necessarily want to return to countries under Soviet domination. Some were ethnic Germans who had been relocated before and during the war by the Nazi formation of the Third Reich. Many of these settlers, as well as other ethnic Germans who had been long-time residents, were expelled by the newly liberated eastern European countries. Still others had been rescued from concentration and forced labor camps. In addition, there were large numbers of war prisoners who were far from their homes. In a 1945 report, the State Department estimated there were 20–30 million war refugees, 9.5 million displaced Germans, and at least 4 million who had fled ahead of the Allied and Russian advances.

Europe had neither the financial resources nor the infrastructure to handle the massive displacement. Even while the war raged, the Allied powers had recognized the need to address the looming refugee crisis. In November 1943, the Allies established the United Nations Relief and Rehabilitation Agency (UNRRA) to provide assistance to those likely to flee the counter-offensive against the Axis powers.

By 1944, the reality of the death camps could not be ignored by the Allied powers. The failures of the 1930s refugee policies became all the more certain. On January 22, 1944, President Roosevelt established the War Refugee Board (WRB) to rescue and provide relief and assistance to victims of enemy oppression "consistent with the successful prosecution of the war (Breitman/Kraut 1987: 191)." With an appropriation of $1 million from the presidential emergency fund and contributions from Jewish organizations, the WRB mostly had to use persuasion to accomplish its aims. It informed U.S. government departments that they were to take action to rescue and provide relief to Jews and other subjects of Nazi persecution (Breitman/Kraut 1987: 192) and explored the possibility of establishing temporary havens for refugees in the United States. Although they succeeded in bringing almost 1,000 refugees to a camp in Oswego, using the authority of the attorney general to waive immigration provisions in an emergency, the WRB did not make much headway in convincing the restrictionists in Congress to liberalize admission standards. Much of the work during the war was aimed at rescuing Jews who had documents from neutral countries, which would allow them to leave the country. The WRB also convinced neutral countries to provide transit visas and temporary accommodation to refugees, and, less successfully, warned countries under German domination not to cooperate with Nazi extermination plans. These efforts were too little and too late to stop the mass extermination of Jews, Roma, political dissidents, and religious activists.

Following the war, attention turned to finding permanent solutions for the displaced. UNRRA's mandate shifted from pure relief to repatriation of the displaced to their home countries. UNRRA spent more than $3.6 billion on relief and repatriation assistance until its closure in 1947. President Truman recognized, however, that some displaced persons would not be able to return. He signed a directive, on December 22, 1945, that outlined new administrative procedures to facilitate the admission of war victims into the United States. The refugees were to be admitted under the existing quotas, but efforts were to be made to give them priority, to the extent possible under existing immigration law. The president directed his administration to enlist the help of voluntary agencies to ensure that the public charge requirement did not impede admissions: "With respect to the requirement of law that visas may not be issued to applicants likely to become public charges after admission to the United States, the Secretary of State shall co-operate with the Immigration and Naturalization Service in perfecting appropriate arrangements with welfare organizations in the United States which may be prepared to guarantee financial support to successful applicants. This may be accomplished by corporate affidavit or by any means deemed appropriate and practicable" (Truman 1945). This program succeeded in paving the way for the admission of 40,000 displaced persons.

Perhaps as a result of the lesson of the failed Wagner-Rogers bill, special provisions were made for the admission of unaccompanied children who were in displaced persons camps in the American zones of occupation, even if they were later moved for safety reasons. More than 1,300 children were admitted through these provisions, the majority from Poland, Czechoslovakia, Hungary, and Germany. The program for their admission and resettlement was to be carried out through a partnership of the U.S. Committee for the Care of European Children, who identified the children and arranged sponsorships, and the Children's Bureau, which set the standards for their care.

In 1947, significant numbers of displaced persons remained in camps. By then, the Cold War had intensified and the spreading influence of the Soviet Union in eastern Europe raised questions about the viability of repatriation as a solution for all refugees. Many of the war-displaced persons refused to return to Communist countries, and the Western governments saw little reason to force that action upon them. Of greater concern were the new refugees arriving from eastern Europe, eager to get out before the door closed on them. Seen as "voting with their feet," a term used to describe later refugees from Communist countries, there was little support for returning them to the Eastern Bloc. The host countries, however, barely had enough resources for their own populations, and the occupation forces increasingly complained about the presence of displaced-persons camps in their zones of operation.

UNRRA was succeeded in 1947 by the International Refugee Organization (IRO). Although the IRO had a mandate to repatriate refugees, the "political buildup to the Cold War tilted the balance instead towards resettlement of those who had valid objections to returning home" (Loescher 1993: 25). During its operations, only about 50,000 refugees returned to eastern Europe. Rather, the IRO looked to the United States, Canada, and Australia, in particular, to resettle the displaced persons. The shift toward resettlement was both a practical and a political expedient. First, resettlement made the ideological point that people fleeing Communist countries deserved protection from persecution by the Soviet Union and its minions. Second, resettlement supported U.S. foreign policy objectives to shore up western Europe and keep it safe from Communist incursions.

Resettlement served these dual purposes, but the question was how to sell it to a Congress that still supported restrictive immigration policies. In 1947, with the support of the Truman administration, new legislation was introduced to permit the entry of 220,000 displaced persons. They were to be admitted within existing quotas, so as not to raise questions about the underlying law, but provisions were made to borrow, or mortgage, up to 50 percent of a country's annual numbers to facilitate the additional admissions. Up to 3,000 orphans, under the age of 16, could also be admitted outside the immigration quotas.

A compromise was reached with the more restrictionist members of Congress, who finally agreed to the measure if efforts were made to otherwise limit entry. They amended the bill so that it pertained to those who entered displaced persons camps no later than 1945, with the exception of 2,000 Czechs who left their country following the Communist takeover. The legislation gave special preferences to persons who had worked in agriculture in Europe and planned to be similarly employed in the United States. The legislation pertained specifically to displaced persons in Austria, Germany, and Italy. It also gave priority to persons displaced from the Baltic states. Although many supporters of the bill disliked these provisions, they accepted the changes in order to permit the entry of some displaced persons. In 1950, the proponents of more liberal immigration provisions were able to amend the Displaced Persons Act to increase the number of available visas and lessen some of the more restrictive aspects.

It was ironic that the displaced persons legislation left out precisely the refugee group that had been most adversely affected by restrictive measures – more than 250,000 Jewish displaced persons living in camps and urban centers in Germany, Austria, and Italy – and effectively gave priority to ethnic Germans who had been expelled to Germany from neighboring countries. They were more likely to have been engaged in agriculture and to have met the 1945 timeframe of the legislation. The provisions were in keeping, however, with other U.S. policies. By 1948, the United States was firmly in support of the establishment of the state of Israel as a solution to the difficulties of the surviving Jewish population in Europe. Despite British obstructions to resettlement of European Jews in Palestine, it was only a matter of time before the United Nations approved an independent Jewish state of Israel with control over its own immigration policy.

The 1950 amendments to the Displaced Persons Act increased the numbers to be admitted to 415,000, but maintained the "mortgaging" provisions. It also eliminated preferences for persons engaged in agriculture and for those from the Baltic states. It allowed admission to those who had entered displaced persons camps after 1945. By 1950, the IRO found itself with a growing population, despite the relative success in resettlement, but there was a reduced willingness of countries to foot the relief bill. "The United States was tired of financing international refugee programs. With the expensive experiences of UNRRA and the IRO fresh in their minds, U.S. policy-makers were principally interested in limiting rather than expanding their financial and legal obligations to refugees" (Loescher 1993: 43).

The IRO was left to die and a new organization established to address the refugee crisis: the office of the United Nations High Commissioner for Refugees (UNHCR). The original mandate of the UNCHR, under its 1950 statute and the 1951 Convention Relating to the Status of Refugees, focused on protection, with particular concern for repatriation and resettlement, but not direct assistance to refugees. The Refugee Convention defined a refugee as a person who "[a]s a result of events occurring before 1 January 1951 and owing to well-founded fear of being persecuted for reasons of race, religion, nationality, membership of a particular social group or political opinion, is outside the country of his nationality and is unable, or owing to such fear, is unwilling to avail himself of the protection of that country; or who, not having a nationality and being outside the country of his former habitual residence as a result of such events, is unable or, owing to such fear, is unwilling to return to it." In addition, the UNHCR could exercise its mandate on behalf of refugees previously granted status under pre-World War II agreements and the IRO Constitution.

The United States opposed providing significant resources to the new organization and did not become a signatory to the Refugee Convention (although it later signed the 1967 Protocol to the Convention). Instead, it continued to focus on its own resettlement programs, with the Refugee Relief Act of 1953 offering 205,000 entry slots, this time without borrowing from the national origins quotas. Given the still-restrictive mood of Congress, the legislation was a victory for those who supported a generous refugee response, and it demonstrated a new willingness of Congress to recognize the exigencies of refugee admissions. In the prior year, Congress had passed the Immigration and Nationalities

Act (INA, also known as the McCarran-Walter Act), which retained the national origins quotas.[3] In passing the McCarran-Walter Act over President Truman's veto, Congress had rejected the work of a presidential commission that argued that national origins quotas undermined America's standing in the world.

The Refugee Relief Act went beyond the displaced persons legislation in covering "any person in a country or area which is neither Communist nor Communist dominated, who because of persecution, fear of persecution, natural calamity or military operation is out of his usual place of abode and unable to return thereto, who has not been firmly resettled, and who is in urgent need of assistance for the essentials of life or for transportation." The legislation defined an escapee as any refugee who had fled a Communist country. The visas could be used for German expellees; escapees residing in countries that were members of the North Atlantic Treaty Organization, Turkey, Sweden, Iran, or Trieste; and refugees of Italian, Greek, Dutch, and Chinese origin. Each of these groups was given a quota, ranging from a high of 55,000 for the German expellees to a low of 2,000 for the Chinese refugees. As in the earlier programs, sponsorship by voluntary agencies was encouraged as a way to address public charge limitations on admission.

The Refugee Relief Act expired just after the country was called to respond to the next refugee crisis – the flight of refugees after the abortive Hungarian Revolution in 1956. A spontaneous uprising in Hungary, spurred by Radio Free Europe's apparent encouragement, was crushed by the Soviet Union. The Eisenhower administration decided not to confront the Soviet Union directly, recognizing Hungary as being within the Soviet sphere of influence, but did mount a major relief and resettlement effort when tens of thousands of Hungarians sought safety in Austria. The president authorized use of 6,500 of the Refugee Relief Act visas for the Hungarians before its expiration. Others would be admitted under a provision in the McCarran-Walters Act that allowed the attorney general to allow foreign nationals to enter under his own authority. Called the parole authority,[4] it was used to permit about 38,000 Hungarians to enter the United States between the end of 1956 and May 1957. Generally, parole in the immigration context was limited to the entry of individuals, particularly when circumstances (such as illness or a family emergency) required quick approval. In this case, the emergency involved the admission of thousands of persons at a time, not single individuals.

The outpouring of support for the Hungarian refugees was immense. Not only were the Hungarians justly seen as the victims of Soviet aggression, they

---

[3] The provisions of the 1952 legislation are discussed in Chapter 10.

[4] The term parole has different connotations depending on context. Although it sometimes refers to the release of immigrants from federal custody, in this context, it "refers to the practice of letting a noncitizen physically into the country for immigration law purposes" (Motomura 2006: 58). It applies in situations in which the noncitizen does not meet the requirements for admission but the attorney general determines that for humanitarian, foreign policy, or other reasons, he or she should be allowed to enter.

were also the victims of unfulfilled U.S. promises. A President's Committee for Hungarian Refugee Relief was established to coordinate the activities of the many organizations that wanted to assist in the resettlement effort. Although confusion and lack of cooperation marked the first days of the program, the operation soon became smoother and, by mid-May 1957, the President's Committee dissolved itself, most of the Hungarian refugees having been resettled.

The majority of the Hungarian refugees who were in need of resettlement were under the age of 30, with approximately 6,000 being unattached youths between the ages of 14 and 18. This age distribution is not surprising, since the Hungarian uprising had originated in the universities and secondary schools, and therefore the subsequent repression had been targeted at school-age youth. Because of their youth and high levels of education, the Hungarian refugees were seen as an easily assimilated group.

In September 1957, new legislation was passed that permitted allocation of visa numbers that had been authorized but not used in the Refugee Relief Act. This legislation, the Refugee Escapee Act, defined refugee-escapees as persons fleeing Communist or Communist-dominated countries or countries in the Middle East because of persecution or a well-founded fear of persecution based on racial, religious, or political grounds. Although using persecution criteria found in the International Refugee Convention, the U.S. legislation restricted the refugee definition to those it found ideologically compatible – persons fleeing persecution by Communist regimes.

The parole authority also continued to be used as a way to address specific refugee emergencies. The Refugee Fair Share Act in 1960 authorized its use for a limited number of refugees. When the Cuban revolution installed a Communist regime, however, the United States opened its doors to one of the largest groups admitted under the parole authority. Unlike the European refugees, the Cubans initially came on their own, often on tourist visas. American policy was to parole them into the country, and then, under the Cuban Adjustment Act of 1966, to convert their status to permanent resident. Later in the 1960s, the United States and Cuba would negotiate an airlift that brought the Cubans directly to the United States.

The exigencies of World War II and Cold War foreign policy also influenced policy reform related to the Asian exclusions. During the war, the absolute bars on the Chinese were lifted as a sign of alliance with the Chinese, who were fighting Japanese occupation. Retaining the national origins quotas, the McCarran-Walter Act lifted the bars to naturalization of Asians and their exclusion from immigration. The changes in the 1952 legislation were highly symbolic, in demonstrating that the United States no longer excluded Asians solely on the basis of race, but were mostly cosmetic because the quotas assigned to Asian countries were extremely small.

The relative openness of refugee policy, compared with immigration policy, reflected a return to the Massachusetts model. Those who shared the ideological views of the United States, and, particularly, those who were persecuted because of these views, were welcomed into the country. Fictions were created, such as "mortgaging" visas and use of the immigration parole authority, to work within the restrictive national origins quotas. But, unlike the provisions for the braceros, the intent was to resettle these ideological compatriots permanently in the country.

This is not to say that the Cold War was altogether good for American immigration policy. In fact, the exclusionary side of the Massachusetts model reemerged during this period. The refugee admissions were the positive side of the model; the McCarthy-era ideological witch hunts were its negative side. World War II had brought its own concerns about immigrants as potential security threats. As early as 1940, legislation was passed to require the registration and fingerprinting of all immigrants in the United States over the age of 14. The legislation also made past, not just current, membership in proscribed organizations a bar to admission. The Cold War, which turned a former ally, the Soviet Union, into an enemy, precipitated a new series of ideological exclusions.

In 1950, the Senate Subcommittee on Immigration and Naturalization presented a report on immigration that purported to be the most comprehensive since the Dillingham Commission. An entire section was devoted to "subversives." The committee introduced the issue in a chapter entitled "Communism as an Alien Force." It explained: "Since the rise of Soviet Russia during the past three decades, the problem of subversives has become a vital consideration in any evaluation of national immigration and naturalization policies.... As an international conspiracy, communism has organized systematic infiltration of our borders for the purpose of overthrowing the democratic Government of the United States by force, violence and subversion" (U.S. Congress 1950: 781). The subcommittee defined Communism as an alien force because, by definition, Americans would not subscribe to its beliefs. The subcommittee recommended strengthening the provisions in immigration law to make excludable and deportable members of the Communist Party, members of front organizations for the Communist Party, and others who "bring with them their subversive ideologies" (U.S. Congress: 800).

The same year, Senator Pat McCarran, who chaired the subcommittee, introduced the Internal Security Act, which passed despite President Truman's veto. The Internal Security Act barred admission to any foreigner who had ever been a member of the Communist Party or any other totalitarian party. It also allowed for the exclusion and deportation of anyone who might engage in activities "which would be prejudicial to the public interest, or would endanger the welfare or safety of the United States." The attorney general was authorized to exclude or deport someone without a hearing if the disclosure of confidential information would have been detrimental to the public interest. The attorney general was also given greater latitude in determining to which country a deportable person would be sent, but bars were placed on removing someone to a country in which he would be persecuted.

Then, in 1952, the McCarran-Walter Act codified into one statute the variety of laws that had been governing immigration, including the various grounds for exclusion and deportation. Its focus was not just on action, such as taking membership, but thought as well. In section 212(a)(27), the law barred without waiver those who wished to enter "solely, principally, or incidentally to engage in activities which would be prejudicial to the public interest, or endanger the welfare, safety, or security of the United States." In section 212(a)(28), the legislation barred entry of those who advocated "the economic, international, and governmental doctrines of world communism." The attorney general had the authority to waive the latter provision, and the legislation itself provided that those who had been unwilling members of subversive organizations, such as the Communist Party, or had opposed totalitarianism[5] for at least five years, could still enter.

The Supreme Court was asked in *Kleindienst v. Mandel* to rule on the ideological bars as an infringement of the First Amendment. The government argued that Mandel, a Belgian author who described himself as a Marxist, was denied a visa (after receiving visas in the past through waivers) because he had violated the terms of the previous visas by fundraising, not because of ideology. Those supporting Mandel argued that denying him a visa violated their First Amendment right to hear his speech. The Court found the visa denial to be constitutional because the government had a "facially legitimate and bona fide reason" for the denial. The Court found that U.S. citizens did not have a right to hear him speak, and Mandel did not have a right of entry (Motomura 2006: 90–91, Shapiro 1987). The ideological exclusions remained in the law until 1990.

Conclusion

When the United States retreated from its open immigration policies in the 1920s, it did not shut the door completely. Rather, the country shifted toward immigration policies based on the Virginia and Massachusetts models. The disdain for European temporary workers changed into a demand for Mexican temporary workers, culminating in the *Bracero* program. The roots of large-scale illegal immigration also took hold during this period, with the growth slowing only with massive enforcement that was followed by governmental efforts to meet employer demands at the expense of worker rights. By reinstating contract-based admissions, the *Bracero* program restricted labor mobility and gave employers the power to blacklist workers who demanded better wages or working conditions. Indenture was returned to the American immigration system.

---

[5] The Act stated: "the terms "totalitarian dictatorship" and "totalitarianism" mean and refer to systems of government not representative in fact, characterized by (a) the existence of a single political party, organized on a dictatorial basis, with so close an identity between such party and its policies and the governmental policies of the country in which it exists, that the party and the government constitute an indistinguishable unit, and (b) the forcible suppression of opposition to such party.

U.S. immigration from the 1920s to the 1960s reflected both sides of the Massachusetts model. The Red Scares of World War I and the Cold War led to exclusionary policies that targeted those whose ideologies conflicted with mainstream American thought. Initially anarchism was the prime target but Communism soon took over as the basis for exclusion and deportation. On a more positive side, after a tragic denial of admission to refugees from Nazism, U.S. Cold War policies gave priority to the resettlement of displaced persons who were unwilling to return to Communist countries. Extraordinary measures were taken to admit those who fled the Hungarian Revolution and the Communist takeover of Cuba. While still not ready to shed the national origins quotas, the United States was willing to circumvent them to admit those who not only shared American values but found themselves endangered by our enemies.

10

"A Nation of Immigrants"

1965–1994

In 1958, Senator John F. Kennedy published a slim volume, *A Nation of Immigrants*, which set out the case for reforming U.S. immigration policies. He argued that the national origins quotas "violated the spirit expressed in the Declaration of Independence that 'all men are created equal.'" Kennedy did not live to see legislation enacted, but, in the spirit of the civil rights movement, the 1965 Amendments to the Immigration and Nationality Act tried to revive the Pennsylvania model of immigration, attempting to put in place a universalistic vision of immigration.

This chapter discusses the new wave of immigration that followed the legislative changes. The 1965 Amendments eliminated the national origins quotas and exclusions that had restricted immigration from certain countries and regions. In their place were overall hemispheric caps on visas. At first, there were different caps for the Eastern (170,000) and Western (120,000) Hemispheres, but in 1978 a global cap of 290,000 was established. To ensure that no one country dominated, a per-country limit of 20,000 visas was instituted. Eligibility criteria broadly mirrored the 1952 law in giving priority to those sponsored by family members and employers. However, the 1965 amendments changed the employment categories and opened the door for a sizable increase in family reunification visas. Originally, only "highly skilled immigrants whose services are urgently needed in the U.S." could apply for admission. The 1965 law, however, permitted applications from skilled and unskilled workers in occupations with labor shortages. A "nonpreference" category was also established to admit applicants not covered under the other categories. Over time, this last category was eliminated because of growing backlogs in the other preferences.

The greatest growth in immigration was seen in the family categories, as the immigrants admitted for employment and other reasons petitioned for admission of their immediate families and, under numerically limited categories, their adult children and siblings. The 1965 law also paved the way for a shift in permanent immigration from its largely European roots (excepting slaves from Africa and temporary workers from Mexico) to a largely Asian and Latin

American composition. By the time that the new law went into effect, few western Europeans felt the need to apply for admission to the United States. In fact, many western European countries had become importers of workers. Moreover, the Iron Curtain succeeded in stemming the flow of potential immigrants from eastern Europe.

The chapter focuses particularly on the recommendations of the U.S. Select Commission on Immigration and Refugee Policy in 1981 and the two major legislative initiatives that followed. The Immigration Reform and Control Act of 1986 (IRCA) and the Immigration Act of 1990 expanded immigration, the former via its legalization program and the latter via its reform of the legal immigration system. Although IRCA was also intended as a way to curb the growing illegal immigration that followed the end of the *Bracero* program, it failed to provide adequate controls. This enabled the earlier two-track system of legal and illegal movements to continue.

The End of National Origins Quotas

Despite growing dissatisfaction with the national origins quotas, the McCarran-Walter Act retained most of the 1924 provisions. The 1952 law set the annual quota for an area at one-sixth of one percent of the number of inhabitants in the continental United States in 1920 whose ancestry or national origin was attributable to that area. All countries were allowed a minimum quota of 100 per year, with a ceiling of 2,000 for natives of countries in the Asia–Pacific triangle. It also set separate quotas on colonies, which had the greatest effect on residents of the British West Indies, who had been entering through the under-utilized British quota. Spouses and minor children of U.S. citizens could still enter outside the quotas. The law removed some of the gender-based constraints of earlier law, allowing husbands as well as wives of U.S. citizens to use this category.

A new category under the quota included highly skilled immigrants with skills urgently needed in the United States. Up to half of the quota was assigned to this group. Also, within the quota, preference was given to parents and adult children of citizens (up to 30 percent plus unused visas from the highly skilled category), spouses and unmarried children of permanent residents (up to 20 percent plus unused visas), and brothers and sisters of U.S. citizens (50 percent of the visas unused by the higher preferences). It also included a nonpreference category, which received the other 50 percent of visas unused by higher preferences plus any not required for siblings. In this way, a guaranteed number of visas was made available for family and skilled workers, while unused visas could go to other immigrants.

After the legislation was passed over President Truman's veto, he established a presidential commission to recommend a way forward. The commission was led by former Solicitor General Philip B. Perlman and included members from the American Friends Service Committee, Catholic Charities, and a Lutheran seminary. In its report, *Whom We Shall Welcome*, the commission took a decidedly different position on immigration than had previous commissions and committees. Recognizing the contributions the "new" immigrants had made to the country, the commission raised serious questions about the McCarran-Walter Act. They concluded that "the Immigration and Naturalization Act of 1952 injured our people at home, caused much resentment against us abroad, and impairs our position among free nations, great and small, whose friendship and understanding is necessary if we are to meet and overcome the totalitarian menace" (Commission on Immigration and Naturalization 1953).

The commission recommended the abolition of national origins quotas. Instead, a unified quota of 251,000 (about 100,000 more than under existing law) would be allocated on the basis of principles such as the right of asylum, family reunification, and labor needs of the United States. It proposed that foreign policy implications should be taken into account in allocating visas because perceptions about U.S. immigration policies abroad affect the well-being of U.S. citizens. A separate quota for refugees was recommended to allow their admission without "mortgaging" quotas. The decisions on allocation of visas within the unified quota would be made by an independent commission whose members would be appointed by the president and confirmed by the Senate. The commission also recommended that an independent Board of Immigration Appeals hear deportation cases so that immigration officials would not be "investigator, prosecutor, and, finally, judge," as one contemporary commentator described (Puttkammer 1953: 244).

Shortly after the commission released its report, Dwight D. Eisenhower became president. Although Eisenhower had also criticized the McCarran-WalterAct, reform was not high on his agenda. The Republican-controlled Congress generally ignored the report but did implement some of the recommendations, particularly a separate quota for refugees, as found in the Refugee Relief Act of 1953.

When John F. Kennedy assumed the presidency, the opponents of the national origins quotas felt they would have strong backing, not least because Kennedy published *A Nation of Immigrants* while he was in the Senate. His brother, Senator Edward Kennedy, later wrote about the circumstances in which President Kennedy became interested in immigration: "They reflected a deep personal conviction of the President, formed in part through the counsel given him by his grandfather, the late Representative John Francis Fitzgerald of Massachusetts. Grandfather believed that fair and just immigration policies, for the people of all nations, were very important to our country, and often expressed this to his grandchildren" (Kennedy 1966: 138).

Kennedy saw immigration as a key contributor to the country's success but acknowledged the challenges: "Immigration plainly was not always a happy experience. It was hard for the newcomers, and hard as well on the communities to which they came. When poor, ill-educated, and frightened people disembarked in a strange land, they often fell prey to native racketeers, unscrupulous businessmen and cynical politicians. . . . But the very problems of adjustment and assimilation presented a challenge to the American idea – a challenge which subjected that idea to stern testing and eventually brought out the best qualities in American society" (Kennedy 1964). Kennedy concluded that "Immigration policy should be generous; it should be fair; it should be flexible. With such a policy we can turn to the world, and to our own past, with clean hands and a clear conscience. Such a policy would be but a reaffirmation of old principles" (Kennedy 1964).

Moving from Kennedy's rhetoric to actual reform was more difficult. During the first two years of Kennedy's administration there was no progress on immigration reform. Francis Walter, of McCarran-Walter fame, controlled the House immigration committee and James Eastland from Mississippi controlled the Senate committee. Neither was prepared to move on elimination of the national origins quotas.

After the mid-term elections, in a press conference early in 1963, Kennedy indicated that he would be giving higher priority to immigration reform. Six months later, in a letter to Congress, he proposed elimination of the national origins quotas: "The most urgent and fundamental reform I am recommending relates to the national origins system of selecting immigrants. . . . the use of a national origins system is without basis in either logic or reason. It neither satisfies a national need nor accomplishes an international purpose. In an age of interdependence among nations, such a system is an anachronism, for it discriminates among applicants for admission into the United States on the basis of accident of birth."[1] He recommended "that there be substituted for the national origins system a formula governing immigration to the United States which takes into account (1) the skills of the immigrant and their relationship to our needs, (a) the family relationship between immigrants and persons already here, so that the reuniting of families is encouraged, and (3) the priority of registration." The president could reserve up to 50 percent of unallocated quota numbers for issuance to "persons disadvantaged by the change in the quota system and up to 20 percent to refugees whose sudden dislocation requires special treatment."

Francis Walter's death in May 1963 provided the opportunity for the reconsideration of immigration in Congress, but the efforts of the new chair, Emanuel Cellar, a long-time advocate of liberalized immigration policy, and of Philip Hart in the Senate, came to no avail. President Kennedy's assassination in November 1963 spelled the end to legislation during the remaining session.

Daniels (2004: 132) argues that the Kennedy approach would not likely have remained intact because it shifted too much authority from Congress to the president. The president would be advised, in using up to 50 percent of unallocated visas, by a seven-member immigration board appointed by the Speaker of the House (two members), president pro tem of the Senate (two members) and the president himself (three members), but the authority for allocating the numbers would rest with the president, not Congress. This process marked a distinct departure from precedent and would have reduced congressional authority over the allocation of immigration quotas.

---

[1]   http://www.presidency.ucsb.edu/ws/index.php?pid=9355&s=immigration&s1=Kennedy.

After Kennedy's assassination, the future of immigration reform was unsettled. President Johnson had voted while in Congress to overturn Truman's veto of the McCarran–Walter Act, thereby supporting the retention of national origins quotas. As president, however, he saw an advantage to supporting legislation that would reverse the discriminatory features of immigration law, particularly as he sought political support from the very ethnic groups that made up the "new" immigration of the turn of the nineteenth to twentieth centuries.

In his 1964 State of the Union message, Johnson outlined an ambitious legislative program that came to be called "the Great Society" and made clear his commitment to advancing civil rights in America: "Let me make one principle of this administration abundantly clear: All of these increased opportunities – in employment, in education, in housing, and in every field – must be open to Americans of every color. As far as the writ of Federal law will run, we must abolish not some, but all racial discrimination. For this is not merely an economic issue, or a social, political, or international issue. It is a moral issue." Johnson went on to place immigration reform squarely in this category: "We must also lift by legislation the bars of discrimination against those who seek entry into our country, particularly those who have much needed skills and those joining their families."

Although Senator Eastland, chair of the immigration committee, remained personally opposed to lifting the national origins quotas, he stood aside, allowing the young Senator Edward Kennedy to serve as acting chair of the immigration committee and shepherd legislation introduced by Philip Hart of Michigan through the Senate.[2] In the House, Emanuel Cellar, still chair of the Judiciary Committee, also introduced legislation, but he clashed with Michael Feighan of Ohio, chair of the Immigration Subcommittee, who threatened to prevent any new legislation from passing through the subcommittee.[3] Feighan eventually yielded to pressure from the White House and became a supporter of reform, claiming the eventual bill as a major part of his legislative legacy.

The resulting legislation adhered to the basic principles laid out by presidents Kennedy and Johnson, in eliminating national origins quotas in favor of more universal admissions criteria. As Senator Hart stated in testimony in support of his bill, "We should discriminate – but not with irrational concepts founded

[2] Although some commentators have cited pressure from the White House as a factor in Eastland's decision, James Ziglar, an aide to Senator Eastland and later commissioner of the Immigration and Naturalization Service, noted that Eastland frequently gave younger Senators similar opportunities when he could not promote legislation pending in his committee (personal communication, August 31, 2009).

[3] According to Lawrence O'Brien, then advisor to the president, "There's nothing worse than to have a subcommittee chairman, or committee chairman, get his nose out of joint. All bets are off in terms of common sense and judgment. It becomes a matter of principle, and he's not going to be very rational if you get into that kind of a situation. There may have been some merit to Mike's position, because whether it was overt or not, Mike at the outset and up front was not properly included in the proceedings, at least as he saw it" (http://www.lbjlib.utexas.edu/johnson/archives.hom/oralhistory.hom/OBrienL/OBRIEN12.pdf).

on the theories of ethnic superiority. Congress must enact a statute that will be discriminatory in the best meaning of the word – on the grounds of security and economic and scientific benefit; on the principles of family unity and asylum to the homeless and the oppressed" (quoted in Kennedy 1966).

The 1965 immigration bill represented a compromise on a number of other issues in order to gain broad support. Senator Edward Kennedy summarized the main areas of debate in a 1966 review of the legislative process (Kennedy 1966). First, members of Congress were concerned that the pending legislation gave too much authority to the president to allocate visas, a concern expressed earlier with regard to President Kennedy's proposal. Second, there was significant debate over setting a quota on immigration from the Western Hemisphere. The absence of a quota was a matter of concern to conservatives who feared that there would be a significant increase in migration from Mexico, now that the *Bracero* program had ended. There were also concerns about increased migration from the English-speaking Caribbean if Western Hemisphere migration was not subject to numerical restrictions; the former British colonies had been subject to quotas as colonies, but with independence, their citizens would be free to enter the United States with no restrictions. The administration opposed a quota, however, arguing that it would negatively affect foreign relations with countries in the Western Hemisphere that from the time of the Monroe Doctrine had a special relationship with the United States. Finally, labor unions expressed general support for the legislation but believed there were insufficient provisions to ensure that foreign workers did not compete unfairly with American workers.

In addressing these concerns, the 1965 legislation (Amendments to the 1952 Immigration and Nationality Act) placed responsibility for allocating visas squarely in Congress, eliminating any presidential discretion even in the area of refugee admissions. The immigration board that President Kennedy proposed was also eliminated from the final legislation. Instead, Congress established an overall annual quota of 290,000, with the exception of the nonrestricted admission of immediate family (spouses, minor children, and parents) of U.S. citizens.

For the first time, a subquota was established for the Western Hemisphere of 120,000 visas; the Eastern Hemisphere was given 170,000 visas. Based on an amendment offered by Senator Ervin, the new Western Hemisphere quota would go into effect in 1968 unless a presidential commission recommended otherwise and Congress acted to remove it.[4] The administration dropped its opposition, recognizing that this provision was necessary to passage of the legislation by a wide majority of Congress. Separate hemispheric quotas remained in effect until 1978, when a worldwide quota was adopted.

The Eastern Hemisphere quota was subject to two additional requirements that were initiallly not imposed on the Western Hemisphere. In 1965,

---

[4] The commission did recommend against the imposition of the quota but Congress did not act on its recommendation.

per-country limits were placed on Eastern Hemisphere visas, with no one country, regardless of size or demand, able to receive more than 20,000 of the quota visas. Per-country quotas were subsequently imposed on the Western Hemisphere in legislation adopted in 1976.

The 1965 amendments also established seven preferences for admission within the annual Eastern Hemisphere quotas (imposed on the Western Hemisphere in 1976). Four of the preferences were for family reunification and three were for employment purposes: First preference: unmarried adult children of U.S. citizens (20 percent); second preference: spouses and unmarried children of permanent resident aliens (20 percent); third preference: members of the professions and scientists and artists of exceptional ability (10 percent); fourth preference: married children of U.S. citizens (10 percent); fifth preference: brothers and sisters of U.S. citizens (24 percent); and sixth preference: skilled and unskilled workers in occupations for which labor was in short supply (10 percent). Refugees from Communist or Communist-dominated countries received 6 percent of the visas in a seventh preference. There was also a nonpreference category in case all of the visas were not used, a provision used in the early years of the new system until the growth in family reunification caused all available visas to be allocated to the preference categories.

The preference system was heavily tilted towards family reunification, with 74 percent of the visas allocated according to family relationship. Reflecting lingering concerns of labor about competition from immigrant workers, only 20 percent of the visas were allocated on the basis of employment and half of those went to professionals, scientists, and artists of exceptional ability. Also, to address the concerns of labor, the Department of Labor was given responsibility for certifying that an American worker was not available and that the admission of the foreign worker would not have adverse effects on the wages and working conditions of similarly employed American workers.

After almost 45 years of national origins immigration legislation, and only 13 years after McCarran Walter reaffirmed them, Congress passed the 1965 Amendments, eliminating them by a large margin in both houses. What had changed? Certainly, the general atmosphere for considering immigration reform had shifted in the context of the civil rights movement. The Civil Rights Act of 1964 and the Voting Rights Act of 1965 marked major steps in addressing long-standing racial discrimination in the United States. Rejection of national origins quotas further reaffirmed that the country valued individual contributions over racial or ethnic criteria. As President Johnson said in signing the bill, the national origins "system violated the basic principle of American democracy – the principle that values and rewards each man on the basis of his merit as a man" (Johnson 1965).

Moreover, the mid-1960s was a more optimistic era than either the early 1920s or early 1950s. In Senator Kennedy's words, national origins quotas had been adopted and confirmed in a "radical period of our history – a period when bigotry and prejudice stalked our streets, when fear and suspicion motivated our actions toward the world around us" (Kennedy 1966). The Soviet Union had blinked in the Cuban missile crisis and the Vietnam War was not yet a matter of controversy. The country could move toward eliminating what was seen by then as an anachronistic part of our history.

Equally important, by the mid-1960s, the ethnic groups that had been most adversely affected by the national origins quotas had come to amass political power. Now in their second and third generations, the "hyphenated-American" voters of eastern and southern Europe – many of nationalities that had been oppressed by the Nazis – rejected the eugenics arguments that supported the national origins quotas on immigration. Ethnic and religious organizations – such as the Anti-Defamation League (ADL), which urged John Kennedy to write *A Nation of Immigrants* – played an important role in laying the framework for immigration reform.

Passage was also supported by what was seen as the very limited nature of the reforms that were adopted. With the exception of the elimination of the national origins quotas, the legislation preserved much of what had been in previous immigration laws. The qualitative restrictions on immigration remained much as they had been in McCarran-Walter. The legislation was actually more restrictive than McCarran-Walter had been in imposing a quota on Western Hemispheric migration. The main additional change was a shift away from priority toward highly skilled immigrants (from 50 percent of the quota visas in the 1952 law to 10 percent in 1965) to family-based immigrants (from 50 percent to 74 percent). This would have ramifications that the drafters of the legislation did not anticipate.

At the signing ceremony in 1965, President Johnson made clear that he believed the legislation had more symbolic than real importance. On Liberty Island in New York, with an already decaying Ellis Island in the background, he stated: "This bill that we will sign today is not a revolutionary bill. It does not affect the lives of millions. It will not reshape the structure of our daily lives, or really add importantly to either our wealth or our power" (Johnson 1965). As the next sections will demonstrate, Johnson was wrong on all of these counts. He was more prescient in the second part of his pronouncement, that the legislation repaired "a very deep and painful flaw in the fabric of American justice. It corrects a cruel and enduring wrong in the conduct of the American Nation" (Johnson 1965). The 1965 amendments restored the Pennsylvania model by reopening immigration to those who sought to make the United States their permanent home. Although the country fully rejected neither the Virginia model nor the Massachusetts model, as will be discussed in later sections on undocumented migration and refugee admissions, the period after 1965 saw a resurgence in the immigration of legal permanent residents.

The Fourth Wave of Immigrants

Senator Kennedy noted in his 1966 article on immigration reform that some concerns had been raised about whether the legislation would affect the racial

TABLE 10.1.

Region of Last Residence	1950 to 1959	1960 to 1969	1970 to 1979	1980 to 1989
TOTAL	2,499,268	3,213,749	4,248,203	6,244,379
Europe	1,404,973	1,133,443	825,590	668,866
Asia	135,844	358,605	1,406,544	2,391,356
America	921,610	1,674,172	1,904,355	2,695,329
Africa	13,016	23,780	71,408	141,990
Oceania	11,353	23,630	39,980	41,432
Not Specified	12,472	119	326	305,406

Source: INS Statistical Yearbook.

and ethnic composition of immigration to the United States. Kennedy gave scant attention to the issue, focusing instead on the more contentious issues discussed earlier. Because the legislation favored the admission of family members of people who were already in the United States (at that time, largely those of European roots), there was little reason to believe it would significantly affect either the numbers or distribution of immigrants. If anything, the new legislation was designed to place restrictions on movements of people in the Western Hemisphere, which had been growing since the end of European migration. Less clear was the impact on Asia. Emigration pressures might increase, but it seemed unlikely that many Asians would meet the new admission criteria that were so heavily weighted toward family reunification.

The reality was different. Total immigration gradually increased in the aftermath of the 1965 Amendments, growing from almost 2.5 million in the 1950s to 3.2 million in the transitional decade of the 1960s. It increased by another million, to 4.2 million in the 1970s (a little more than a 30 percent increase) and then jumped almost 50 percent to 6.2 million in the 1980s (see Table 10.1). As in earlier waves of immigration, the immigrants tended to settle in a relatively small number of states, making the growth appear even more concentrated. Between 1975 and 1979, more than 68 percent of immigrants stated their intention to live in one of six states: California, New York, Florida, New Jersey, Illinois, and Texas.

During the 1970s, admissions under the permanent resident system began to shift noticeably toward immigrants from the Western Hemisphere and from Asia.[5] Although the intention of the drafters of the legislation was to reopen immigration to eastern and southern Europeans, events in Europe worked against this. Western European countries experienced rapid economic growth in the 1960s and many opened large-scale guestworker programs that recruited actively in the poorer European countries that might otherwise have resumed

[5] See Reimers (1981, 1992) and Rumbaut (1994) for further discussion of the impact of the 1965 Amendments on the ethnic composition of immigration to the United States.

emigration to the United States. For many Italians and Yugoslavs, working in Germany or Switzerland proved far more convenient than migrating across the Atlantic. Per capita GDP in Switzerland ($17,953) by 1973 exceeded the United States ($16,607) and Germany's was not far below ($13,152).[6] At the same time, other turn of the nineteenth- to twentieth-century countries of emigration (for example, Poland, Hungary, Czechoslovakia) had closed their borders to new emigration, effectively keeping their people behind the Iron Curtain. Other than the occasional refugee who managed to escape into Western Europe, by the mid-1960s, there were few eastern Europeans who could benefit from the lifting of the national origins quotas.

One of the characteristics of post-1965 immigration in the United States was its diversity, not its concentration in new sources. Just looking at the proportion of total immigration that the top five source countries represented makes the case.[7] During the period from 1841 to 1860, five countries (Ireland, Germany, the United Kingdom, France, and Canada) provided more than 93 percent of the country's immigrants. In the first decade of the twentieth century, five countries (Austria-Hungary, Italy, Russia, the United Kingdom, and Germany) provided more than 75 percent of the immigrants. By contrast, in the 1970s, the top five countries (Mexico, the Philippines, Cuba, Korea, and Taiwan) provided 40 percent of the immigrants.

The increase in immigration from Asia was particularly steep and steady. In 1964,[8] the quota for all of Asia was 2,290. By contrast, in 1969, the first full year of implementation of the new amendments, 54,176 Asian immigrants entered under the Eastern Hemisphere quota. More than 100,000 Asians entered under the same quota in 1978, with an even larger number (more than 142,000) entering under the numerically exempt family reunification categories. In 1978, several Asian countries were close to the 20,000 per-country limit – India (17,467), Korea (18,528), and the Philippines (18,746).

Under the new preference-driven system, countries differed in the categories under which immigrants tended to enter the United States. Overall, occupational preferences constituted 20 percent of admissions. In 1969, however, 58 percent of numerically restricted admissions from the Philippines and 52 percent from India were in the occupational categories, most of them under the third preference (immigrants in the professions). These countries had had such low levels of immigration previously that there were few relatives in the United States to sponsor their family members.[9] The pattern began to shift during the 1970s (see Table 10.2). By 1975, the majority of both Philippine

---

[6] http://www.nationmaster.com/graph/eco_gdp_per_cap_in_197-economy-gdp-per-capita-1973.

[7] This finding was already well known in the early 1980s when I constructed tables showing these data for the Select Commission on Immigration and Refugee Policy.

[8] Data on admissions are reported by fiscal year (FY), not calendar year, in this and subsequent chapters.

[9] See Boyd (1973) for a contemporary discussion of Asian immigration and occupational preferences.

and Indian immigrants entered under the family reunification categories.[10] The shift occurred largely because immigrants who arrived in the employment categories thereafter sponsored their family members for admission, who sponsored their family members in turn.

The imposition of the Western Hemisphere quota did not cause a significant reduction in admissions during the first decade of its operation. Mexican immigration averaged almost 60,000 per year during the 1970s. In 1978 alone, more than 90,000 Mexicans were admitted, 67,143 under numerical restrictions and 25,538 under the exempt immediate relative categories.[11] The Mexican number exceeded that of all of Europe (76,156) and was more than four times that of any other single country. By contrast, less than 40,000 Mexicans obtained permanent resident status in 1965, before the new measures went into effect. Jamaica (15,869) and the Dominican Republic (16,418) also had significant levels of immigration under the Western Hemisphere quotas. Cuba's numbers exceeded those of these other Caribbean countries, but the vast majority (26,365 out of 27,539) counted against various refugee classes of admission. Legislation enacted in 1976 and 1978 that brought Western Hemisphere migration into line with the requirements imposed on the Eastern Hemisphere led to a reduction in Mexican immigration, as the per-country limits brought its numerically restricted numbers into line with other countries.

A number of Caribbean countries also benefited from the changes in U.S. immigration law. The McCarran-Walters Act had imposed a quota of 100 visas per colony even in the Western Hemisphere, limiting immigration from Jamaica, Trinidad and Tobago, and the other British West Indies colonies. The advent of large-scale migration from the West Indies colonies to England is credited, at least in part, to the restrictions on access to the American labor market. In the 1960s, however, the British began to impose restrictions of their own. With independence and the lifting of the colonial quota, immigration to Britain closed down just as immigration to the United States became a possibility.

When the preference system was imposed on the Western Hemisphere, almost 60 percent of those from North America entered under the family categories (1978). Very few (4 percent) entered under the occupational preferences, with only 783 workers and their families coming in under the third preference, for professionals and 2,185 entering under the sixth preference, for

---

[10] See DeJong et al. (1986) for transformation from occupational to family categories among Filipino migrants.

[11] Only 16,000 counted against the preferences, although the preferences were imposed on the Western Hemisphere by the 1976 Amendments. The *Statistical Yearbook* of the Immigration and Naturalization Service notes that admissions differ from visa issuances because some people issued visas in one fiscal year are admitted in the next year. Because the legal requirements were due to change for the Western Hemisphere, it is likely that a large number of Mexicans sought visas under the old system but entered in subsequent years. As late as 1981, more than 100,000 Mexicans entered the country as permanent residents, with half coming under the Western Hemisphere quota that had been eliminated in 1979.

TABLE 10.2.

1971

Country	Total	Family Sponsored	Employment Based	Immediate Relatives of U.S. Citizens	Refuges	Cancellation of Removal*	Western Hemisphere	Other
TOTAL	100,879	22,254	10,012	23,773	6,060	365	26,426	11,989
Mexico	14,844	515	29	4,270	4	137	9,813	76
Philippines	7,851	2,629	2,399	2,796	0	6	1	20
Italy	5,730	4,522	48	1,107	7	23	9	14
India	5,644	779	1,585	131	1	1	1	3,146
Korea	4,687	923	827	1,515	1	1	0	1,420
Cuba	4,116	9	2	71	3,610	0	406	18
Jamaica	3,860	14	2	300	0	1	3,540	3
China	3,850	1,133	687	546	432	15	9	1,028
Canada	3,587	155	160	1,324	3	67	1,630	248
Greece	3,073	1,960	229	619	2	8	1	254

1975

Country (UN Name)	Total	Family Sponsored	Employment Based	Immediate Relatives of U.S. Citizens	Refuges	Cancellation of Removal	Western Hemisphere	Other
TOTAL	386,334	100,121	30,181	96,629	36,734	590	95,914	26,165
Mexico	60,782	2,228	81	16,595	23	211	41,541	103
Philippines	32,031	11,699	7,867	12,403	2	9	12	39
Korea	27,917	13,066	5,016	7,727	1	5	3	2,099
Cuba	27,280	23	4	345	26,423	3	435	47
China	16,707	8,811	903	3,408	1,555	18	10	2,002
India	16,033	6,071	4,932	760	3	6	5	4,256
Dominican Republic	14,087	277	12	2,120	26	2	11,644	6
Portugal	11,630	9,178	426	1,094	2	5	1	924
Italy	10,465	7,369	422	2,187	23	15	8	441
Jamaica	9,940	77	50	1,572	3	3	8,171	64

Country (UN Name)	Total	Family Sponsored	Employment Based	Immediate Relatives of U.S. Citizens	Refugees	Cancellation of Removal	Western Hemisphere	Other
				1979				
TOTAL	460,348	216,932	40,066	142,825	45,133	357	13,413	1,622
Mexico	52,096	18,022	1,297	25,736	14	95	6,816	116
Philippines	41,300	15,348	3,855	21,977	38	10	1	71
Korea	29,248	16,470	1,979	10,657	5	8	3	126
Viet Nam	22,546	1,624	65	371	20,481	0	0	5
Jamaica	19,714	14,723	716	2,911	0	9	1,217	138
India	19,708	14,343	3,110	2,176	7	8	0	64
China	17,911	10,817	1,309	4,895	866	11	0	13
Dominican Republic	17,519	13,423	82	2,473	3	1	1,467	70
Cuba	15,585	2,282	58	1,052	12,130	4	57	2
Canada	13,772	4,011	3,954	5,335	55	95	250	72

* includes individuals who are granted permission to remain in the United States on humanitarian bases.

Source: Immigration and Naturalization Service.

other workers. Even though there was substantial employment of workers from Mexico, the Caribbean, and Central America, these workers were employed in sectors, such as agriculture, in which their employers would have been unlikely to go through the new labor certification requirements to demonstrate that there were no American workers willing and able to do the job at the prevailing wage. By contrast, a significant proportion of North American, Caribbean, and Central American immigrants entered in 1978 under the nonpreference category (38 percent). By comparison, only 4 percent of Asians entered under the nonpreference category.

Temporary work and study in the United States were routes to permanent migration in both the occupational and family categories, especially for Asians. In 1965, 2,696 foreign students were admitted[12] from Taiwan and 2,558 from India, with the number growing to 4,976 and 3,904, respectively in 1978. Although more than 1,200 students came to the United States from the Philippines in 1978, up from 777 in 1965, the Philippines had developed a domestic educational system mirrored on the U.S. curriculum in such areas as nursing and medicine. Already trained in the Philippines, Filipino nurses and physicians entered under the occupational categories until the United States restricted the entry of medical personnel in 1976.

The other major source of permanent, legal admissions continued to be refugees. Although the 1965 amendments included a small quota for refugees, most came into the country under various emergency provisions, usually under the authority of the attorney general. The Kennedy and Johnson administrations tried to introduce a flexible process for setting refugee admissions that would have given the president emergency powers to respond to refugee crises, but this proposal for executive branch authority failed along with the immigration board. In the meantime, refugees entered the country in numbers that exceeded those available in the seventh preference of the immigration quota system. In 1966, the Cuban Adjustment Act was passed, which permitted Cubans paroled into the country to adjust their status to permanent resident alien one year later. In 1975, the attorney general used his parole authority to admit about 130,000 Indochinese refugees who fled the Communist takeover of South Vietnam. Special legislation was passed to adjust the status of these refugees as well. The recurrent use of the parole authority eventually led Congress to reconsider the earlier proposal for a more flexible system of refugee admissions, as is discussed later.

Although the changes in U.S. policies were important, immigration patterns during this period were also affected by economic and political factors in home countries. The three major sources of East Asian immigration –Taiwan, Korea,

---

[12] The admission of people coming for temporary stays is reported as an event (inspection at the ports of entry). Ten admissions may represent ten individuals coming once and staying or one individual coming ten separate times during the course of a year. In the case of foreign students from Asia, it is unlikely that students frequently left and reentered the country during the course of the year, so the number of inspections is likely to be close to the number of students.

and, to a lesser extent, the Philippines – were experiencing rapid economic growth, leading to an expansion of resources and opportunities for the middle class. Because of the low level from which their economic growth began, however, it was still difficult for the educated population to reap the same financial rewards at home that emigration offered. Taiwan's GDP experienced an average annual growth rate of 9 percent in real terms between 1952 and 1980. South Korea's growth rate was comparable. Per capita GDP increased in South Korea from $876 in 1950 to $2,840 in 1973 and in Taiwan from $922 to $3,669 during the same period. The Philippines did not experience the same sustained economic growth, beginning at a higher per capita GDP in 1950 ($1,293) and lagging behind South Korea and Taiwan in 1973 ($1,956). Even with the increase in per capita GDP, these Asian countries had far less wealth than the United States, with a per capita GDP of $9,573 in 1950 and $16,607 in 1973.

Liu (1992) explains that expanding access to education was a key goal in the reconstruction of selected Asian countries after World War II and the Korean War. The investment in primary and secondary education led to increasing numbers of students who sought university education in the professions. In Liu's analysis, "as highly educated persons crowded the domestic labor market, both credential inflation and underemployment occurred. Many professionals and technically skilled people were underemployed (1992: 676–77)." Emigration served three purposes, according to Liu (1992). First, it served as a safety valve, reducing protests from discontented professionals. Second, immigration allowed professionals to keep up their skills, which might have been lost had they become unemployed at home. Finally, the immigrants became a reserve source of labor who could help the source countries in their development when they returned with skills acquired in the United States.

These skilled migrants were welcomed in the United States, which was building up its own capabilities in science and engineering. After the Russian launch of Sputnik, the United States feared it was falling behind in scientific achievements. The Kennedy administration's pledge to put a man on the moon within 10 years furthered the commitment to rebuild the country's scientific capacities. Demand for health professionals also grew in the period immediately after the 1965 amendments, especially with the enactment of the Medicare and Medicaid programs. Health professionals from India, the Philippines, and other countries provided what was considered needed labor, at least until 1978, when concerns about the qualifications of foreign physicians and nurses, combined with fears of competition, led to a tightening of admissions criteria.

Networks were also at work in stimulating migration from selected Asian countries. The Philippines, South Korea, and Taiwan, in particular, had special ties to the United States that created opportunities for immigration. Philippine links to the United States may have been the strongest. Even after the Philippines achieved independence in 1946, it remained closely allied with the United States, providing air and sea bases for the American military. The United States also had a strong military presence in South Korea during this period, following the Korean War. Until the Nixon administration established diplomatic ties with mainland China, the United States recognized Taiwan as the legitimate government of China, also maintaining military bases to protect the island from attack by the mainland forces. Even during the period of national origins quotas, many spouses of members of the U.S. military immigrated as immediate relatives, outside the numerical restrictions.

Economic and political conditions at home and ties to the United States also help explain growing migration from Latin America and the Caribbean. The situations in the three largest sources of labor and family immigration – Mexico, the Dominican Republic, and Jamaica – highlight similarities and differences in the push-and-pull factors. As we have seen, Mexican migration into the United States had been significant in the period leading up to the 1965 amendments, but most Mexican migration was through the *Bracero* Program or else undocumented. Although undocumented migration continued after the *Bracero* program ended, as will be discussed in the next section, Mexico also became a source of permanent immigration, especially through family reunification. Although most Mexicans entered as temporary workers, some had established permanent residence, mostly in the border states and Chicago. With no numerical quotas, the main constraint on larger permanent immigration from Mexico had been the financial requirements imposed on visa applicants. By the 1970s, though, many Mexican-Americans had amassed sufficient resources to sponsor their families.

As was true for the Asian countries discussed earlier, this immigration accelerated during a period of economic growth in Mexico. The 1960s are sometimes described as the Mexican Miracle, when the economy grew at a rapid rate. Gutierrez (2004), however, writes that economic growth did not keep pace with population growth, leading to high levels of underemployment. This resulted in "an increasingly unstable and economically polarized situation in Mexico in which the already wide gap between the rich and the poor steadily increased" (Guttierez 2004: 63). The networks that would allow migration to take place were already well established, permitting thousands of Mexicans to migrate legally to join family members in the United States, where the demand for low-wage workers continued. The Mexican economy faltered in the 1970s and fell into crisis in the early 1980s, so northward migration became attractive to an increasing number of Mexicans.

After the Communist takeover of Cuba, U.S. foreign policy focused on ensuring that its Caribbean neighbors did not follow suit. The Dominican Republic was of particular concern since it too was run by an authoritarian regime. Following the 1961 assassination of Trujillo, the strongman who had ruled the country since the 1930s, a pent-up demand for visas to the United States supported what the American ambassador saw as the potential for riots (Mitchell 2004: 96). Trujillo had restricted emigration, fearing that a diaspora would organize opposition to his rule (Guttierez 2004: 234). Long lines of Dominicans seeking visas formed around the U.S. embassy. Some had the intent to travel and return and others were hoping to escape political and economic instability. The embassy responded by approving a backlog of applications that had been pending, seeing access to the U.S. labor market as a safety valve. In the aftermath of the U.S. military intervention in the Dominican Republic in 1965, the process accelerated. Although immigration was not a prominent part of the agenda of either the United States or the new administration in the Dominican Republic, "northward migration provided both real and symbolic assistance to President Balaguer's regime and to its successors, while gradually creating strong ties linking the Dominican Republic to the society and economy of the United States" (Mitchell 2004: 104). In a familiar pattern, the Dominican Republic experienced rapid economic growth in the late 1960s but failed to produce sufficient jobs for its growing population.

In the case of Jamaica, emigration pressures remained relatively constant during the period from 1950 to 1980, but the destination of most migrants shifted considerably during this period (Cooper 1985). In the early period, the large majority of Jamaican immigrants went to the United Kingdom, benefiting from their colonial ties to the motherland. With independence and new restrictions imposed by the British on immigration from former colonies, Jamaican emigration declined significantly from 1963 through 1965 but it resumed in 1966, with a majority now heading to the United States. The early 1960s saw an expansion of Jamaica's economy, when it became the largest exporter of bauxite and alumina (*Encyclopedia of the Developing World*, p. 889) and built a robust tourism industry. However, the 1970s saw economic decline, with the collapse of the sugar industry, Jamaica's other major export. Violence and environmental problems during the same decade also reduced Jamaica's tourism industry. As unemployment grew, Jamaican migration increased. Middle-class professionals especially sought opportunities abroad when they were unavailable at home, leading to significant concerns about a Jamaican "brain drain."

In examining the shifting origins of the post-1965 immigration, it becomes apparent that neither of the "new" immigration streams was truly new. Rather, Asia and North America had been largely seen as the source of temporary workers – Asians (from China, Japan, and the Philippines, in particular) in the mid-nineteenth century and North Americans (Mexicans in particular, but also some 100,000 British West Indians admitted between 1956 and 1965) in the mid-twentieth century. The 1965 amendments differed in that they provided the opportunity for would-be immigrants from Asia and the Americas to settle permanently in the United States.

This transformation was achieved primarily by the priority given to family reunification in both the nonquota system and the preference system. What was seen as potentially restrictive in the drafting of the legislation, in that it favored the ethnic groups already in the United States, turned out to be expansive in practice. Asians, having been excluded for decades, resumed immigration largely through the occupational categories, but, having settled, many of the immigrants brought their families to join them. Many would-be Western Hemisphere immigrants had more recent relatives in the United States but others, who had no family members to join, used the nonpreference categories.

TABLE 10.3. *Apprehensions of Migrants: 1961–1979*

1961	88,823	1972	505,949
1962	92,758	1973	655,968
1963	88,712	1974	788,145
1964	86,597	1975	766,600
1965	110,371	1976	875,915
1966	138,520	1976 TQ*	221,824
1967	161,608	1977	1,042,215
1968	212,057	1978	1,057,977
1969	283,557	1979	1,076,418
1970	345,353	1980	910,361
1971	420,126		

* TQ is third quarter (July–September). The fiscal year shifted from July–June to October–September.
Source: Immigration and Naturalization Service.

The expansiveness of the family categories allowed a single immigrant to sponsor his or her spouse and children, and, upon naturalization, parents, siblings, and members of their immediate families. The siblings' spouses could in turn sponsor their own parents, children, and siblings who could in turn bring their families, setting off a chain migration that soon increased the numbers of applicants from a core of Asian countries that included China and Taiwan, India, Korea, and the Philippines. Others came initially as refugees (e.g., from Vietnam, Laos, and Cambodia) and then sponsored their families for admission through the refugee resettlement program and, later, the family admissions categories.

Undocumented Migration and Temporary Workers

After the *Bracero* program came to an end, undocumented migration from Mexico accelerated. Although the numbers apprehended are an imperfect measure of unauthorized migration, since they are affected not only by the number of persons attempting illegal entry but also the human and financial resources directed to catching them, the steady growth in the numbers apprehended in the 1960s and 1970s point to increased pressures at the border. Apprehensions were less than 90,000 per year on average during the last years of the *Bracero* Program; they were more than 200,000 by 1968 and more than half a million by 1972. In the second half of the 1970s, apprehensions were averaging more than 1 million per year. See Table 10.3.

As was discussed in Chapter 9, the *Bracero* program itself did not stop unauthorized immigration, but in combination with tighter enforcement and incentives for employers to hire legal temporary workers, it had reduced what had been a growing phenomenon in the 1950s. Ngai (2004) attributes the regrowth of unauthorized migration not only to the end of the *Bracero* program but also to the imposition of Western Hemisphere and per-country quotas. She argues that the 1965 amendments were restrictive with regard to Mexican migration as well as to migration from other countries in the Americas. However, Mexico represented the largest country of legal permanent admissions at the same time that it dominated the unauthorized migration flow. As in the 1950s, both legal and illegal migration occurred in tandem.

Demand for low-wage labor remained in the post-*bracero* period, but many employers of Mexican and other foreign workers were unwilling to participate in the temporary worker programs that succeeded the *Bracero* program. In part, the reluctance was related to the labor standards included in the new programs. A series of bills enacted during this period evidenced a shift in attitudes and policies regarding workers' rights. In 1961 and again in 1966, minimum-wage provisions were extended to new industries, including many that had hired *braceros*, such as agriculture, nursing homes, laundries, and the construction industry. Title VII of the Civil Rights Act of 1964 prohibited employment discrimination based on race, color, religion, sex, or national origin. The Equal Pay Act of 1963 protected men and women who perform substantially equal work in the same establishment from sex-based wage discrimination. Individuals who are 40 years of age or older are protected against employment discrimination in the Age Discrimination in Employment Act of 1967. In 1970, legislation was passed to enforce occupational health and safety provisions. Although foreign workers were not specifically targeted in these laws, they provided a framework for acceptable practices with regard to all workers.

Given the climate that supported passage of these laws, employers in the mid-1960s and 1970s were unlikely to win the kinds of concessions that were critical parts of the *Bracero* program in the 1950s. In fact, the 1965 amendments tightened labor standards for both the permanent and temporary admissions programs. The McCarran-Walter legislation had authorized admission of temporary workers under Section 101(H): "an alien having a residence in a foreign country which he has no intention of abandoning (i) who is of distinguished merit and ability and who is coming temporarily to the United States to perform temporary services of an exceptional nature requiring such merit and ability; or (ii) who is coming temporarily to the United States to perform other temporary services or labor, if unemployed persons capable of performing such service or labor cannot be found in this country; or (iii) who is coming temporarily to the United States as an industrial trainee." The 1965 Amendments required that admissions under the H (ii) (better known as H-2) program, as in the permanent occupational preferences, be permitted only upon "certification from the Secretary of Labor... that qualified persons in the United States are not available and that the employment of the beneficiary [of the visa] will not adversely affect the wages and working conditions of workers in the United States similarly employed." The resulting regulations required employers to file an application with the state employment service that included a job offer for U.S. workers and certified that the employer met wage, working conditions, housing, transportation, and other provisions of the program.

Wages were determined by an "adverse effect rate" published annually by the U.S. Department of Labor. The state employment service would notify the federal Department of Labor's Employment and Training Administration, which made the final decision on the application. The attorney general, delegating his authority to the Immigration and Naturalization Service, would make the determination as to whether the worker was admissible. If the application was approved, a visa could be issued (Congressional Research Service 1980).

During the late 1960s, about 50,000 persons were admitted each year under the H-2 program. The largest group (with the exception of Canadians working in the logging industry along the United States–Canada border) was from the West Indies. The workers were spread across several occupations. In 1969, 13,800 were farm workers, 10,564 were laborers, 8,255 were craftsmen, and 7,514 were professionals (mostly artists, athletes, and musicians). Smaller numbers came as service workers, private household workers, and operatives. By the late 1970s, the number of H-2 workers had been cut in half. The largest group remained from the West Indies. In 1978, H-2 workers were employed as professionals (8,400), farm workers (8,300), laborers (1,580), and craftsmen (2,845).

Most of the farm workers who entered under the H-2 program were employed on the east coast of the United States. They were employed disproportionately in the apple harvest and in sugarcane cutting. A Vermont apple grower explained the dependence on the H-2 program: "southern domestic migrants and local groups have been tried, but we have never been able to successfully pick a crop without the use of H-2 workers for a substantial period of time" (Select Commission on Immigration and Refugee Policy 1981c: 268). Sugar cane workers had been coming into the country on temporary visas since 1943 when a program began with the Bahamas and was extended to the other British West Indies.

Western growers never utilized the H-2 program to any sizable degree, even after the end of the *Bracero* program. A Congressional Research Service report in 1980 concluded: "The limited number of Mexican H-2's has been the result of administrative determinations by the U.S. Labor Department, either that domestic workers have been available in the areas and occupations for which Mexican workers have been requested, or that employers have failed to meet the requirements of the regulations governing the importation of H-2's" (Congressional Research Service 1980: 62).

Initially, in the absence of a secure temporary foreign workforce, Western growers agreed to concessions demanded by the United Farm Workers union, ushering in what agricultural economist Philip Martin (2001) terms "the golden age for farm workers." The expectation was that farm workers, without competition from *braceros*, would be able to negotiate on the basis of other seasonal occupations, such as construction work, and provide hiring halls that would ensure that workers received just compensation. According to Martin (2001), "Cesar Chavez and the United Farm Workers seemed to prove this theory of inevitable and desired labor market evolution true when in 1966 the union won a 40 percent wage increase for grape pickers, raising their wages from at least $1.25 to $1.75 an hour." A combination of factors undermined this progress, however. The United Farm Workers, after having successfully led a national boycott against table grapes, were unable to sustain contracts they won with the grape producers. Internal disputes undermined the united leadership that the union had provided and growers invited the Teamsters Union to represent their workers, leading to conflicts between the two unions. A change in leadership in California state politics in the early 1980s brought in Republican governors who were less sympathetic than their Democratic predecessors to the plight of farm workers.

Perhaps most important, however, was the resurgence of undocumented migration in providing a supply of workers who were willing to pick crops and do other 3D (dirty, dangerous, and demeaning) jobs at the wages and under the working conditions offered. With this ready supply of labor, often drawn from the same communities and sometimes including the same people who had been *braceros*, there was little need to hire domestic workers or to use the H-2 program. The president of the Association of General Contractors testified at a federal hearing in San Antonio in 1979 about undocumented migrants: "Employers would dislike being deprived of willing [illegal] workers who generally exhibit a very high attitude" (SCIRP 1981c: 269). A California farm manager claimed that domestic workers do not want the jobs that undocumented workers hold while "undocumented workers need the jobs and do not feel exploited" (SCIRP 1981c: 269).

In 1980, the Census Bureau estimated there were between 3.5 and 5 million, and no more than 6 million, undocumented immigrants in the United States (Siegel et al. 1980) based on a review of more than a dozen relevant studies of the issue. About half of the undocumented population was estimated to be from Mexico. On the basis of apprehensions and survey data, it appeared that the majority came from the Mexican states that had contributed most heavily to the *bracero* Program – Guanajuato, Jalisco, Michoacan, San Luis Potosí, and Zacatecas in central Mexico (SCIRP 1981b). The remaining undocumented migrants mainly came from other parts of Latin America, the Caribbean, and parts of Asia, especially the Philippines (SCIRP 1981b). The undocumented were believed to settle in the same locations as those residing legally. Mexicans tended to go to the southwestern United States and non-Mexicans to urban areas throughout the country. By the late 1970s, evidence also supported the growing movement of Mexicans out of agricultural work and into urban areas (SCIRP 1981b). The demographic profile of the average undocumented migrant was male and young, between the ages of 15 and 45. North and Houston (1976) argued, however, that these profiles were often based on apprehensions data and that a higher proportion of the undocumented migrants was female than was estimated by border apprehensions. An INS study of visa abuse indicated that women were more likely to enter and then overstay their visas. Undocumented immigrants came, overwhelmingly, for employment. Studies of apprehensions and surveys conducted in Los Angeles and New York determined that unemployment and, particularly, underemployment in source countries accounted for the majority of the undocumented population. Wages in the United States were low relative to U.S. standards but high relative to home country opportunities.[13]

Labor and Hispanic groups opposed any return to the *Bracero* program or expansion of the H-2 program to address unauthorized migration. In the words of a representative of the United Farm Workers, "H-2 undermines equal opportunity for domestic workers and violates civil rights to organize a strong labor movement (SCIRP 1981c: 270)." In 1978, the Hispanic Ad Hoc Committee on Immigration stated unequivocally its opposition "to any and all proposals that would, in effect if not name, reestablish the Bracero program" (SCIRP 1981c:270). David North and Marion Houston's 1976 report to the Department of Labor summarized the problem: "Thus, like the de facto admission of illegals, not only would the de jure admission of significant numbers of nonimmigrants provide cheap labor at the cost of depressing the labor standards in the secondary market and displacing the nation's most disadvantaged workers, their role in the nation would similarly contravene its democratic values, despite the fact that in this instance it represented a policy enacted in law. At bottom, a decision to use aliens – nonimmigrants or illegals – as a supply of cheap, low-skill labor is an attempt to acquire that labor and to adjure its economic and its social costs. That is, of course, a form of exploitation, the de jure or de facto institutionalization of inequities" (quoted in CRS 1980: 115).

These groups were less sure what should be done about undocumented migration and eventually split over the issue. Labor unions generally supported the imposition of sanctions against employers who hired unauthorized workers, a position long held by labor and endorsed by the United Farm Workers as late as 1980. Hispanic groups were divided in opinion. Although the Labor Council for Latin American Advancement supported employer sanctions, most of the Latino organizations opposed them because of potential discrimination against Hispanics. The lynchpin of effective sanctions would be a requirement that employers verify employment authorization, probably by looking at an identity document. The president of the Mexican American Legal Defense and Education Fund summarized the concern: "[W]e know that employers will not question everyone. Only those who look 'foreign' will be asked to present an ID card" (SCIRP 1981c: 254).[14]

There was greater agreement between labor and Hispanic groups on the need for some type of legalization that would enable undocumented workers to press for their rights. On this front, they were joined by civil rights groups and representatives of religious organizations. Opposition to any "amnesty" came from

---

[13] This discussion of the characteristics of undocumented migration comes from my 1981 review of the literature for the Select Commission on Immigration and Refugee Policy. See SCIRP staff report (SCIRP 1981b).

[14] See Tichenor 2002: 230–39 for interest group politics on immigration during this period.

a nascent immigration restrictionist movement, led by the new Federation for American Immigration Reform (FAIR), under the leadership of Roger Conner, an avowed environmentalist who opposed population growth in the United States. Joining the opposition to amnesty were such groups as the American Legion, which argued that it would induce a surge in illegal immigration and would provide legal status to an excessive number of people (see SCIRP 1981c and Tichenor 2002). Business reiterated that its sole interest was in ensuring access to workers and that any program of employer sanctions would have to be reasonable in its administrative requirements and hold harmless employers who inadvertently hired unauthorized workers (SCIRP 1981c). Business representatives also emphasized that a tightening of undocumented migration would necessitate the introduction of a new temporary worker program to fill likely shortages arising from the enhanced enforcement.

The Select Commission on Immigration and Refugee Policy

Congress met the same impasse in determining what should be done about illegal immigration into the country. President Carter pushed the issue by advancing a plan in 1977 that included employer sanctions, the use of the Social Security card as identification for determining employment eligibility, and an amnesty for undocumented migrants who had entered prior to 1970. Reflecting the views of Secretary of Labor Raymond Marshall, who steadfastly opposed any large-scale guestworker program, the proposal notably included no expansion of the H-2 program.

Congressional Democrats were in a quandary. With some of their major constituencies (labor, Hispanic groups, environmentalists) in disagreement over immigration reform, they found a time-honored way to delay action while setting the stage for change – the establishment of the Select Commission on Immigration and Refugee Policy (SCIRP). Even more high-powered than the Dillingham Commission had been, SCIRP was composed of four Cabinet officers, four Senators, four members of the House of Representatives, and four members of the public. The commission was first chaired by Reuben Askew, former governor of Florida, and then the Reverend Theodore Hesburgh, president of Notre Dame University, after Askew resigned to be the U.S. Trade Representative. As head of the Civil Rights Commission for its first fifteen years, Hesburgh was committed to a nondiscriminatory immigration policy, and as a university president, he made clear that he wanted the best research to guide the commission's deliberations. Askew set the tone for the commission by ruling that only members – not delegated representatives – could vote on commission recommendations. This provision, endorsed by Hesburgh, ensured the active participation of the Cabinet officers and members of Congress.[15]

---

[15] Lawrence Fuchs described an incident in which Secretary of State Vance was called to testify before Congress on the day of a commission meeting. Askew told him that it would be embarrassing for the Deputy Secretary of State Christopher because he would not be allowed

The Commission staff director was Lawrence Fuchs, Professor of American Studies at Brandeis University. Fuchs brought together a staff drawn from government agencies, academia, and interest groups whose knowledge of the administrative intricacies of immigration, as well as the politics of the issue and the experiences and impacts of immigrants, enabled the development of a concrete set of options for the commission's consideration.[16] Fuchs himself came to his expertise on immigration through his study of ethnic group politics. He had written books on *The Political Behavior of American Jews* (1955) and *American Ethnic Politics* (1968). In his early years at Brandeis, he had team-taught courses with Eleanor Roosevelt and had become an advisor to John Kennedy when he was still in the Senate. Fuchs' understanding of politics was summarized in the first sentence of an article he wrote in 1956: "The understanding of American politics rests upon two facts of American life: ideological unity and group pluralism" (Fuchs 1956: 270). Continuing this theme, he wrote that the "historic American policy of welcoming immigrants has shaped the pluralistic character of American politics" and advocated a liberalization of immigration as a way to "sustain the contribution which ethno-religious group interests have made in shaping the American party system" (Fuchs 1956: 270). He pointed to the historical consistency with which immigration groups adopted the ideological unity of the country (that is, respect for constitutional principles) in arguing that there was no reason to fear increased immigration.

SCIRP differed significantly from its predecessor, the Dillingham Commission, in the ethnic composition of its members. Whereas all of the Dillingham Commission's members were descendents of longer-term British immigrants, SCIRP's members were of more diverse ethnic makeup, including children and grandchildren of Italian, Irish, German, Japanese, and Mexican immigrants. The public members included Rose Matsui Ochi, whose parents had been interned in Japanese camps during World War II, and Judge Cruz Reynosa, whose father had been deported in one of the mass expulsions of Mexicans in the 1930s.

As Tichenor (1992: 250) points out, "the SCIRP report... helped frame policymakers' basic assumptions about the effects of international migration on the United States...." Chairman Hesburgh described the basic tenets of the commission's recommendations: "The emphasis in our recommendations, which are themselves complex, can be summed up quite simply: we recommend closing the back door to undocumented/illegal migration, opening the front door a little more to accommodate legal migration in the interests of this country, defining our immigration goals clearly and providing a structure and mechanism to implement them... " (SCIRP 1981a).

to participate in the discussions, leading Vance to request that the congressional committee reschedule his appearance (Fuchs 1983).

[16] In the interest of full disclosure, I served as research director of SCIRP from October 1980 to the completion of its work in June 1981 and wrote large segments of the commission report and staff supplement to the report.

In reconciling the diverging views of its own members and the public interest groups who testified, the commission voted 14–2 in favor of employer sanctions but split on the type of identification to be required – a new identification card or a combination of existing forms of identification.[17] Some commissioners opposed any identification requirement as a potential infringement on civil rights and civil liberties, fearing that employers would discriminate against foreign-appearing or foreign-sounding persons who had the right to work in the United States. The majority agreed that some form of identification was necessary but were reluctant to recommend a specific document. Commission member and Secretary of Health and Human Services Patricia Roberts Harris, who headed the federal agency that included the Social Security Administration, was strongly against using the Social Security card as a national identifier: "Anything that makes it desirable to counterfeit or duplicate the social security number will make it very difficult to maintain the integrity of our records for people whose benefits depend on payments made in their behalf" (SCIRP 1981c). The staff recommended the development of a single-purpose work eligibility card that would be used in the hiring process but failed to convince a majority of the commissioners that this would be a good approach (SCIRP 1981b).

SCIRP rejected a large-scale guestworker program but recommended that the H-2 program be streamlined to address some of the objections of business and labor. In particular, SCIRP voted 14–2 in favor of improving the time-liness of decisions regarding the admission of H-2 workers. The commission recommended streamlining the application process; removing the economic disincentives to hire U.S. workers by requiring that employers pay Social Security and other taxes and unemployment insurance for H-2 workers; maintaining the labor certification process in the Department of Labor; and providing incentives for government, employers, and labor to cooperate to end the dependence of any industry on a constant supply of H-2 workers. The commissioners made clear that their recommendations did not preclude a "slight expansion" of the program, but they were clearly opposed to a major expansion in numbers.

The commission was unanimous in recommending legalization of those who were in the country illegally. Avoiding the term "amnesty," SCIRP Chair Hesburgh argued that legalization would have many benefits for the country, not the least of which was because it would help bring immigration under control (SCIRP 1981c). In combination with the enforcement measures recommended by the commission, legalization would enable the government to redirect its attention to curbing future illegal migration.

The second component of SCIRP's recommendations was to "open the front door," but in Father Hesburgh's terms, using a cautious approach: "This is not the time for a large-scale expansion in legal immigration ... because the first order of priority is to bring illegal immigration under control while setting

---

[17] The vote on existing forms of identification was 9 to 7 in favor; on a more secure method, the vote was in favor by 8 to 7 with one abstention.

up a rational system for legal immigration" (SCIRP 1981c). The commission recommended a modest expansion in numbers, to 350,000 numerically limited visas plus 100,000 per year to clear the more than 1.1 million backlogged applications (SCIRP 1981b: 377). The commissioners rejected (by a 9–6 vote, with one commissioner not voting) the idea of establishing an immigration advisory committee to assess domestic and international conditions and recommend changes in the visa levels. They recommended instead that the House and Senate subcommittees, with input from the executive branch, provide an annual report on conditions affecting immigration.

The commission recommended a three-pronged approach to legal admissions, one not too dissimilar to the provisions of the 1965 Amendments. Priority would be given to family reunification, to what the commission called "independent" admissions, and to refugees. Within the family reunification category, the relatives not subject to numerical restrictions would be expanded to include adult unmarried sons and daughters of U.S. citizens (a heavily backlogged preference, approved 14–2) and grandparents of adult U.S. citizens (a group not covered by the 1965 law, approved 13–3).

It was proposed that the largest number of numerically restricted preference visas be reserved for spouses and unmarried children of legal permanent residents, with no per-country limits applied to this category (9 votes in favor plus 4 votes for shifting them into the numerically exempt category). Married adult children would also be admitted under the preference system. Most divided was the vote on siblings of U.S. citizens (9 votes to maintain it, 7 votes to include only unmarried siblings) but the commission unanimously rejected the proposal to eliminate this category.

The independent category would substitute for the occupational categories in the 1965 Amendments, which were also badly backlogged by the time of the SCIRP review. Small, numerically limited preferences would be established for those with exceptional qualifications and for investors. The remainder of the category would be determined by labor market requirements, but the commission split on whether to use a streamlined labor certification procedure with a job offer (7 votes) or a new process in which applicants would be admitted unless the Secretary of Labor ruled that their admission would be harmful to the U.S. labor market (7 votes). Two commissioners voted for a point system, similar to the mechanism used in Canada and Australia, which would consider a broader set of criteria. Refugees would be admitted under the terms of the new Refugee Act (discussed later).

SCIRP recommended a phasing in of its recommendations, with initial adoption of the enforcement measures followed by legalization and the clearance of backlogged applications for immigrant visas. Only then would the new legal admissions system be phased in and immediate relatives of the legalized immigrants who were living outside the country be admitted. In this way, the enforcement measures would deter future illegal migration. The legalization program would address the already resident population, while the backlog clearance would ensure that those who had been patiently awaiting visas were not disadvantaged by the legalization program. Once the past problems came under control, the country would be ready for the new legal admissions system.

The commission thus affirmed the Pennsylvania model, stating clearly that legal immigration was in the national interest of the United States while firmly rejecting illegal immigration as an acceptable response to the demand for low wage labor.[18] The commission's research (twenty-two reports undertaken by outside experts, research commissioned from executive branch agencies, and in-house research) supported its conclusions on the benefits of immigration to the country. Of particular concern was the labor force adaptation of immigrants. Research by the economist Barry Chiswick, quoted in the commission's staff report (SCIRP 1981b),[19] found a U-shaped pattern of occupational mobility and earnings, with immigrants initially experiencing downward mobility but catching up and often surpassing native-born workers over time. Julian Simon, in research commissioned for SCIRP, found that it took only two to six years for immigrant families to catch up to and then surpass the earnings of the native-born. David North found that immigrants entering in the occupational categories generally did better economically than those entering as family members or refugees (SCIRP 1981b). Economic success was clearly related to education and English-language ability, as demonstrated in research presented by Tienda and Niedert (SCIRP 1981b). Research on the children of immigrants showed that after an initial period of educational disadvantage, children of immigrants tend to accumulate more years of schooling than did native-born Americans (Schultz referenced in SCIRP 1981b). Equally important, immigrant children soon adopted the civic culture of their new country. Fuchs spoke of no incident during the commission's field hearings and site visits that affected him more than his encounter with a Vietnamese-American child who had been in the country for only six months, but identified George Washington as "the father of our country."[20]

Some of the commission research addressed the concerns of environmentalists and groups interested in population stabilization as to the likely fertility patterns of immigrants. Recognizing that immigrants generally came from countries with higher fertility, demographer Frank Bean and his colleagues found that Mexican women initially had more children than native-born American women but that their fertility lowered with time in the country, to levels well below that of Mexicans remaining at home. Therefore, although immigration might increase the U.S. population, it would reduce worldwide population growth (SCIRP 1981b).

---

[18] See Tichenor (2002) for a similar analysis of SCIRP's legacy.

[19] In a chapter that I wrote as research director (SCIRP 1981b).

[20] This anecdote made it into the SCIRP final report and Fuchs often spoke of it during his tenure as vice chair of the U.S. Commission on Immigration Reform whenever critics of immigration spoke pessimistically about the capacity of the new immigrants to become "Americans." (personal observation)

The commission's staff report concluded that "the extent of ... adaptation seems to [be] more closely related to a combination of rising socioeconomic status, usually measured by education, and length of exposure to U.S. society than it is to the immigrant's country of origin" (SCIRP 1981b: 328). The 1965 Amendments might have changed the geographic origins of immigration, but they did not necessarily change the capacity of immigrants to adapt to life in the United States. Regarding broader impacts, the commission's final report concluded: "Immigrants, refugees and their children work hard and contribute to the economic well-being of our society; strengthen our social security system and manpower capability; strengthen our ties with other nations; increase our language and cultural resources and powerfully demonstrate to the world that the United States is an open and free society" (SCIRP 1981a: 6).

In contrast, the commission concluded that illegal immigration had pernicious effects on the country. It rejected the Virginia model's argument that illegal immigration should be tolerated, even encouraged, because undocumented workers did jobs that Americans were unwilling to do, although the commission did recognize that the immigrants themselves were often "hard working, highly creative people who, even if they remain in this country, aid rather than harm US society" (SCIRP 1981a). In detailing the problem with illegal immigration, SCIRP noted that "[s]ome U.S. citizens and resident aliens who can least afford it are hurt by competition for jobs and housing and a reduction of wages and standards at the workplace. The existence of a fugitive underground class is unhealthy for society as a whole and may contribute to ethnic tensions. In addition, widespread illegality erodes confidence in the law generally, and immigration law specifically, while being unfair to those who seek to immigrate legally" (SCIRP 1981a: 40).

Toward New Legislation

SCIRP made its recommendations in January 1981 before the change in administration resulting from Ronald Reagan's election to the presidency. When it issued its final report in March 1981, four new Cabinet members had assumed their responsibilities as commissioners without having been actively involved in the commission's deliberations. After receiving the report, the new administration formed an inter-agency taskforce to review the recommendations and develop a considered response.

Other political changes occurred as well. Representative Romano Mazzoli, who had not been on the commission, was the new Chair of the Immigration Subcommittee in the House, taking over from Elizabeth Holtzman, who had lost her bid for a Senate seat. Mazzoli was a graduate of Notre Dame and clearly held Father Hesburgh, the president of his alma mater, in high regard. Although he was not an official member of SCIRP, he sat in on its deliberations, knowing that he would be assuming the chairmanship.

Senator Alan Simpson, who had served on SCIRP, was the new Republican chair of the Senate immigration subcommittee. Simpson's experience on SCIRP had influenced his decision to assume the chairmanship from Senator Edward Kennedy, who remained on the subcommittee as ranking minority member. Rounding out the team that would move the SCIRP recommendations toward enactment, Senators Dennis DeConcini and Charles (Mac) Mathias remained on the Senate immigration subcommittee, as did Representatives Peter Rodino, Robert McClory, and Hamilton Fish in the House.

Omnibus legislation to reform the immigration system was introduced by Simpson and Mazzoli in 1982.[21] The provisions related to illegal migration were faithful to the commission's view but the ones related to legal admissions departed considerably from SCIRP's recommendations. Simpson had been in the minority in the vote on elimination of the siblings category but included provisions toward that end in the bill. He and Mazzoli also agreed on a cap on all family admissions, including immediate relatives who had been numerically exempt. Their numbers would have been subtracted from an annual quota, leading to reductions in other family admissions if the immediate relative numbers increased.

The only serious debate in the Senate revolved around legalization of those who were residing illegally in the country. Simpson blocked amendments to remove legalization and to add a large-scale guestworker program. The major dissenter to other provisions was Senator Kennedy, who had grown concerned about employer sanctions and the potential for discriminatory actions against foreign-sounding and foreign-appearing workers. He regretfully joined the minority in both the subcommittee vote and the final Senate vote of 81–19 (Fuchs 1983).

The House debate saw far greater opposition to the bill. An unlikely coalition of business groups, Hispanic and other ethnic organizations, and civil liberties groups came together under the umbrella of the National Immigration Forum to work toward stopping employer sanctions and the changes in the legal admissions system. The White House did little to support the legislation, wary of the impact employer sanctions might have on business interests. The administration introduced its own plan, which had a weakened form of employer sanctions and a large-scale temporary worker program. With other legislative priorities awaiting action, immigration reform died in the House.

The legislation was reintroduced in the next Congress. Again, it passed the Senate with relatively little debate. And, again, passage through the House was more problematic. By now, though, the coalition in opposition to the bill was coming apart as the various different interests pursued their own objectives. Agricultural growers proved willing to compromise if some of their priorities were addressed in the legislation. The Senate passed an amendment requiring that warrants be issued before raids could take place in open fields. Representatives from western states proposed a new seasonal agricultural workers program. Committees other than the immigration subcommittee added

[21] See Tichenor (2002), Zolberg (2006), Fuchs (1983), and Schuck (1998) for the political machinations surrounding Simpson-Mazzoli and its successor, Simpson-Rodino.

provisions designed to make the legislation more palatable to civil rights and ethnic and religious groups, including new antidiscrimination protections and services for legalized migrants. Negotiations continued into 1984, when the House narrowly approved the measure by a vote of 216–211. The bill died in conference committee before it could be enacted. Simpson was dejected but vowed to reintroduce the legislation in the next Congress.[22]

When the bill was reintroduced in 1985, the dynamics in the Senate had shifted somewhat. Senator Wilson of California gained sufficient backing to pass an amendment establishing a temporary agricultural workers program that would have admitted 350,000 such workers per year. Simpson had opposed such a plan but now saw it as essential to ensure passage of the bill in the Senate. Opposition to legalization continued but he had the votes to overcome any attempt to delete it from the bill. The changes in legal admissions had been dropped from the bill, with agreement that they would be considered only after the illegal immigration issue was addressed.

In the House, Peter Rodino, chair of the Judiciary Committee, assumed a more important role in the legislation that would eventually bear his name along with Simpson's. He authorized two younger members, Charles Schumer of New York and Howard Berman of California, to negotiate a substitute plan that would address agricultural growers' interests without instituting a new *Bracero*-style program. An unlikely pair who represented districts in Brooklyn and Los Angeles, Schumer and Berman produced a plan that would give permanent residence to farm workers who had been engaged in seasonal agricultural work and provide for replacement workers if the newly legalized left agriculture. Termed the Seasonal Agricultural Workers (SAW) and Replacement Agricultural Worker (RAW) programs, the new provision passed muster among the agricultural interests as well as among Hispanic and labor groups opposed to a guestworker program. The attraction to the former was having a continuing source of labor and to the latter of providing labor mobility to workers who could more easily assert their rights.

When the bill went to conference committee in October 1986, the House measure on agricultural workers prevailed over the Senate version. Two other major differences led to compromises. First, the House and Senate agreed that the General Accounting Office would investigate any discriminatory effects of employer sanctions and report on them to Congress. Then, Congress could act by joint resolution to end the program. This provision replaced a three-year automatic sunset provision that had been in the House bill. Second, in response to administration concerns about the costs of the legalization program, as well as concerns of states and localities that they would be left with the financial burden, the conferees agreed to restrict the access of the newly legalized to a range of public benefits while providing State Legalization Impact Assistance

[22] Personal communication with Simpson and his chief aid, Richard Day, on the evening that the bill died in Congress.

Grants (SLIAG) to help them in dealing with state and local costs attributable to legalization.

On November 6, two days after the election, the Immigration Reform and Control Act (IRCA) was signed into law. It largely followed the SCIRP recommendations but with some notable differences. As in the SCIRP report, the intent was to reduce future illegal immigration through a combination of improved border enforcement and sanctions against employers who knowingly hired persons without a work authorization, while bringing those who were illegally in the country out of the shadows and onto a path to citizenship. For the first time, IRCA made it illegal to hire an illegal alien but imposed sanctions only if the employer knew the worker was in the country illegally. Employers would be required to ascertain their workers' legal status by checking two forms of documentation – one that showed identity and one work authorization. The legislation named a number of acceptable documents. Passports issued to citizens and "green cards" issued by the Immigration and Naturalization Service to legal immigrants would show both identity and work authorization. To establish identity, new hires could show a driver's license or, as stated in the IRCA, "similar document issued for the purpose of identification by a state, if it contains a photograph of the individual or such other personal identifying information relating to the individual." To establish work authorization, the new hire could show a Social Security card, a birth certificate, or other documents authorized by the attorney general. IRCA authorized pilot programs to test more secure forms of employment eligibility, but the default program effectively offered a " Chinese menu" of possible documentation. Interestingly, it was this approach that the SCIRP staff warned against as too likely to lead to the use of fraudulent documents (which was just what happened, as discussed in Chapter 11).

To address concerns about discrimination, IRCA authorized a new office within the Justice Department to investigate "unfair immigration-related employment practices." IRCA prohibited employers from discriminating "against any individual (other than an unauthorized alien) with respect to the hiring, or recruitment or referral for a fee, of the individual for employment or the discharging of the individual from employment (A) because of such individual's national origin, or (B) in the case of a citizen or intending citizen (as defined in paragraph (3)), because of such individual's citizenship status." It was considered an unfair practice to seek different or additional documents from any newly hired employees, a provision designed to dissuade employers from setting up special procedures for foreign-appearing workers.

The legalization provisions included two separate programs. One program focused on undocumented immigrants who had been in the country since January 1, 1982. Initially, they obtained conditional legal status upon demonstrating their continued presence in the United States. After eighteen months, they could apply for legal permanent resident status upon showing that they had successfully completed a course in the English language and civics or had passed an examination that was comparable with the naturalization test. To be legalized, the immigrants also had to demonstrate they were not otherwise excludable under U.S. law. The second program was the SAW program. Under its terms, persons who could demonstrate that they had worked unlawfully in agriculture for ninety days during the twelve-month period ending on May 1, 1986, were eligible to be legalized. After demonstrating that they continued to work in agriculture during the following three years, they could become permanent residents.[23] For both programs, the legislation authorized the attorney general to designate qualified voluntary organizations to receive applications, a measure taken to encourage those who feared government authorities to come forward and be legalized.

IRCA barred the newly legalized from most public benefit programs for the first five years after they received legal status. Exceptions were made for education and training programs, especially those, like Head Start, that helped children. A program of assistance to states was authorized in the amount of $1 billion. Some of the funds could be used to provide the language and civics training required for adjustment to permanent residence.

While the major provisions of IRCA related to illegal immigration and legalization, it also reorganized the existing temporary work programs. It enacted an H-2A program specifically designed for agriculture. As in earlier legislation, IRCA required the Department of Labor to certify "(A) there are not sufficient workers who are able, willing, and qualified, and who will be available at the time and place needed, to perform the labor or services involved in the petition, and (B) the employment of the alien in such labor or services will not adversely affect the wages and working conditions of workers in the United States similarly employed." Housing and transport requirements were also codified.

A final provision in IRCA authorized a new Commission for the Study of International Migration and Cooperative Economic Development (referred to as the Ascencio Commission after its chair, former Ambassador Diego Ascencio). This commission was to focus on the source countries of undocumented migrants. More specifically, IRCA specified that "in consultation with the governments of Mexico and other sending countries in the Western Hemisphere, [the Commission] shall examine the conditions in Mexico and such other sending countries which contribute to unauthorized migration to the United States and mutually beneficial, reciprocal trade and investment programs to alleviate such conditions." Although Congress had rejected proposals for a bilateral admissions program, as in the *Bracero* program, or any special consideration for Mexico and other Western Hemisphere countries, the Ascencio Commission recommended a provision that would gain traction in the 1990s – a free-trade agreement with Mexico that would build its economy and, in the long

---

[23] IRCA also included the RAW program and authorized a commission to investigate whether it should be triggered. The Commission on Agricultural Workers concluded that the RAW program was not needed, largely because employers had found enough unauthorized workers to fill the gap when the SAW program recipients left agriculture.

term, reduce emigration pressures (Commission for the Study of International Migration 1990).

In the years after enactment of IRCA, 1.6 million immigrants who were in the United States illegally were found eligible for legalization under the pre-1982 program and 1.1 million were found eligible under the SAW program. These numbers represented 90 percent of pre-1982 applicants and 86 percent of SAW applicants. About half a million changed to permanent residence status in 1989, with another 881,000 in 1990 and 1.13 million in 1991. The number of pre-1982 applicants was consistent with estimates of the eligible population. The number of SAW applicants, on the other hand, greatly exceeded expectations. The number of applications far exceeded estimates of the seasonal agricultural workforce. Several explanations have been offered for the wide discrepancy. SAW applications could be made from outside the country, meaning that people who had worked previously in agriculture (perhaps not during the period included in the law) could apply even if they had left the country. More seriously, there appeared to be many fraudulent applications by people who had never worked in agriculture but found someone to provide an affidavit or counterfeit documents showing that they had put in ninety days in the fields.

Among the pre-1982 applicants, males accounted for almost 54 percent of the applicants. More than three-quarters were between the ages of 15 and 44, and about half were married. By 2001, about one-third of those legalized had been naturalized, with a higher proportion of pre-1982 applicants becoming citizens than was true of the SAWs. Mexicans had lower naturalization rates than did legalized immigrants from other countries, which is consistent with the pattern found among other permanent residents.

Two immediate issues were raised by the IRCA legalization program. First, it did not cover undocumented immigrants who had entered after January 1, 1982, unless they were seasonal agricultural workers. IRCA thus led to a large residual population that was still in the country illegally. Second, IRCA made no accommodations for the admission of the families of legalized immigrants. Once legalized immigrants had the opportunity, they began to petition for their spouses and children to obtain permanent residence. Some of these family members were in the home country while others were in the United States but did not meet the IRCA requirements for legalization or had entered after their "anchor" relative gained legalized status. Because the immigrants whose status was legalized under IRCA came from so few countries, and the per-country limits applied to immediate relatives of legal permanent residents, the backlog of applications began to grow exponentially.

IRCA made no significant changes in the legal permanent admissions system. Its only provision related to non-legalization-related admissions was a small program aimed primarily at the admission of European immigrants. At the urging of Irish-American lobbying groups, which recognized that would-be immigrants from Ireland generally did not meet the family reunification requirements of existing law (Tichenor 2002: 268), the legislation afforded

5,000 nonpreference visas in 1986 and 1987 "to qualified immigrants who are natives of foreign states the immigration of whose natives to the United States was adversely affected by the enactment of [the 1965 Amendments]." Labor certification requirements were waived for these visas.

In 1988, action began on reform of the legal admissions system.[24] Initially, the key members of Congress devising reform were Senators Kennedy and Simpson. Kennedy generally supported expansion of legal immigration, noting the benefits that SCIRP had found. He had also been instrumental in enacting the IRCA provision that provided additional visas for the Irish and other Europeans. Simpson wanted to enact an overall cap on admissions and, within the cap, redirect visas away from family and toward the highly skilled. They merged their interests in a new independent category (so named by SCIRP in its earlier recommendations) for which admissions would be based on a combination of education, job skills, English language fluency, and diversity of immigration source countries. To keep numbers within levels acceptable to Simpson (about 600,000 per year), the bill would have limited the number of family visas and restricted the admission of siblings to those who were never married.

The bill passed the Senate, but it ran into difficulties in the House. The coalition that had derailed Simpson-Mazzoli came together again in opposition to the Kennedy-Simpson approach. Although business was generally favorable toward the expanded skills-based admissions, they understood that a firm cap on admissions could end up being detrimental to their interests if the number of applications for immediate relatives of U.S. citizens increased to displace other categories. Ethnic and religious organizations were not only worried about the cap, but also about what they saw as an assault on family, particularly with the restrictions on the admission of siblings.

In 1989, Kennedy and Simpson reintroduced their bill in the Senate, indicating a willingness to negotiate key elements. Amendments in the Judiciary Committee restored the family preferences that had been reduced or eliminated. On the floor of the Senate, a number of liberalizing amendments were passed, including a mechanism by which the annual cap could be pierced if the number of immediate relative applications increased. The cap itself was increased to 630,000 visas per year. Recognizing the precarious situation of the immediate relatives of newly legalized immigrants, an amendment was passed to allow their spouses and minor children to remain in the country while their petitions were adjudicated, in the name of "family unity."

Representative Bruce Morrison, the new chair of the House subcommittee on immigration, favored liberalization as well. The House bill that emerged from committee had no cap on overall admissions, instead expanding the number of family and employment visas. Morrison particularly promoted a diversity program, similar to one that had passed in the previous Congress, allocating visas on the basis of a lottery. While the principal constituency for such a program

[24] See Tichenor (2002).

was European ethnic groups, the program was designed to allow immigration from other continents (notably Africa) with very low levels of immigration and therefore few family ties with immigrants already in the United States. The House bill was more liberal in other respects, particularly in its elimination of many of the exclusions to admissions based on ideological grounds and sexual preference.

The legislation that emerged from the conference committee between House and Senate generally expanded immigration. Under the Immigration Act of 1990, the flexible cap remained, but the number of visas was increased to 700,000 per year for the first three years and 675,000 per year thereafter. During the transition period, 55,000 visas per year were allocated to the spouses and minor children of legalized immigrants, who could enter outside the preferences. Family- and employment-based immigration each had its own quota. After 1994, the cap on family admissions would be set at 480,000. An estimated 254,000 immediate relatives would be admitted each year, but no restrictions were placed on their admission, so the number could be higher. Regardless of the number of visas for immediate relatives, no fewer than 226,000 visas would be available for the numerically restricted family admissions. Four family preferences received allocations: 1) unmarried adult children of U.S. citizens (23,400); 2) spouses and unmarried children of legal permanent residents (114,200); 3) married adult children of U.S. citizens (23,400); and 4) brothers and sisters of adult U.S. citizens (65,000). Although per-country limits would apply to the other family preferences, they would not apply to the spouses and minor children of legal permanent residents, which received a sub-allocation of 80,000 visas in the second preference.

Employment-based immigration received an annual quota of 140,000 visas. There were five preferences: 1) workers with extraordinary skills (sometimes called the Einstein visas) and executives and managers of multinational corporations (40,000); 2) workers with exceptional skills and those with advanced degrees (40,000); 3) professionals with bachelor's degrees and workers with needed skills (40,000) within which was a small sub-cap for other workers (10,000); 4) special immigrants and religious workers (10,000); and 5) investors (10,000). Unused visas in higher preferences would be carried to lower preferences. No labor certification was required for those entering under the first, fourth, or fifth preferences. Labor certification could also be waived for other applicants whose admission was deemed to be in the national interest. Most second- and third-preference workers were subject to a labor market test in which the employer had to demonstrate that there was no minimally qualified U.S. worker to take the job.

The final category was diversity immigration, which received a quota of 55,000 visas. After a transition period, the diversity program was restricted to natives of foreign states from which less than 50,000 immigrants had been admitted over the preceding five years, weighted by region. Generally, only countries in Europe and Africa qualified because of the high levels of immigration from Asia and the Americas. To be eligible for a diversity visa, an applicant had to have at least a high-school education or its equivalent or two years of work experience in an occupation requiring at least two years of training or experience. The most interesting aspect of the program was that visas were to be allocated through a lottery system. At first, applicants could send in as many applications as they wished (initially, a postcard sufficed), but after the State Department was inundated with millions of applications with many duplicates, the rules were changed and each applicant could submit only one postcard.

The 1990 legislation was more restrictive on temporary worker programs. It revamped what was then called the H-1B program for the admission of professionals with at least a bachelor's degree. While there was no recruitment requirement and employers could attest to meeting the wage requirements, Congress placed a numerical limit of 65,000 visas per year on admissions. The bill also allowed H-1B workers (and intracompany transfers under the L visa) to come into the country with dual intent (to stay or to return), thereby giving them a route to obtaining permanent residence. The labor certification requirements were maintained on the H-2 programs (H-2A for agriculture and H-2B for other temporary jobs) and a ceiling of 66,000 visas per year was placed on the H-2B program.

The bill also streamlined the naturalization process. The federal district courts had the final authority for naturalizing immigrants, after the Immigration and Naturalization Service approved the applications. There were long waits, however, for court action in many busy districts. The legislation conferred authority to naturalize upon the attorney general, allowing administrative ceremonies. It also provided an appeals process for those who were denied naturalization.

Finally, the bill addressed one of the gaps in humanitarian protection remaining after passage of the Refugee Act. It provided for temporary protected status for individuals if their countries were adversely affected by conflict or natural disasters. At the insistence of Representative Moakley, the legislation included a specific provision for Salvadorans displaced by the civil war in their country. It also included a more general authority for the attorney general to grant what was effectively a stay of deportation and work authorization to those affected by humanitarian crises.

Conclusion

The Immigration Act of 1990, and the massive legalization program under IRCA, effectively implemented the full set of SCIRP recommendations. With the Refugee Act of 1980, these developments culminated a 25-year period in which there was a substantial return to the Pennsylvania model of immigration. The 1965 Amendments reversed the discriminatory national origins quotas, but the architects of the reform did not extol the benefits of immigration. Rather, they argued that national origins quotas were an anachronism in a period in which civil rights were flourishing. Eliminating the discriminatory provisions would enhance American prestige around the world, but they would not necessarily open the United States to increased immigration. By contrast, the 1990 legislation was promoted precisely because its supporters thought an expansion in immigration was in the national interest. Even those who favored controls on overall numbers, such as Senator Alan Simpson, were persuaded by the need to expand highly skilled immigration to meet the needs of a global economy. Moreover, Congress chose permanent admissions over temporary workers. In the spirit of the Pennsylvania model, immigrants would be welcomed as proto-citizens rather than as indentured laborers. IRCA had legalized millions of undocumented immigrants, putting them on a road to citizenship if they learned English and civics.

The 1990 legislation was intended to facilitate family reunification, with family unity visas and the lifting of per-country limits on spouses and minor children of legal permanent residents. This is not to say that everything about the 1990 legislation should be seen within this context. The legislation also expanded the grounds for deportation, including the creation of a category of aggravated felons that would become problematic in later years. On balance, though, the Immigration Act of 1990 favored a form of immigration that valued family, skills, and humanitarian interests and provided immigrants the opportunity to join the American community.

The consensus that led to passage of the Immigration Act of 1990 was short-lived. Within a few years of its passage, the reemergence of illegal immigration and concerns about the fiscal impact of legal immigration challenged the Pennsylvania model, as discussed in Chapter 12. Before addressing those issues, however, Chapter 11 discusses the evolution of U.S. refugee policy from the mid-1960s to the mid-1990s.

11

A Nation of Refuge

Just as the civil rights movement affected attitudes toward immigration, notions about the universalism of human rights eventually affected refugee policy, with the adoption of the international definition of a refugee in the Refugee Act of 1980. The Cold War definition, in contrast, had been related specifically to those fleeing Communist or Communist-dominated countries. As early as 1948, the United States had subscribed to the idea that all people, regardless of where in the world they lived, had certain inalienable rights. Eleanor Roosevelt chaired the United Nations conference that drafted the Universal Declaration of Human Rights and lent her considerable prestige to the endeavor. During the height of the Cold War, however, U.S. leadership in the field of human rights diminished as U.S. foreign policy increasingly relied on *realpolitik*, which included support for authoritarian regimes as long as they allied themselves with the west against the Communist threat.

During the 1960s, however, as the civil rights movement took hold domestically, the United States also became more active internationally in setting out human rights standards. After almost two decades of logjam in the General Assembly over the primacy of civil and political or economic and social rights (with the United States and its allies supporting the former and the Soviet Union and its allies the latter), separate treaties were drafted. In 1966, the International Covenant on Civil and Political Rights (ICCPR) and the International Covenant on Economic, Social and Cultural Rights (ICESCR) were adopted, although it took a decade longer for them to enter into force. Although the United States was active in the drafting, particularly of the ICCPR, the treaties did not go to the Senate for ratification until the Carter administration; in the end, only the ICCPR was ratified, and not until 1992. The covenants marked only the beginning, however, in international activity on human rights.

Several months after the General Assembly completed work on the covenants, it finalized the 1967 Protocol to the 1951 U.N. Convention Relating to the Status of Refugees. The Protocol removed references in the convention to its origins as a treaty for the protection of those displaced by events in

Europe that occurred prior to 1951. The United States ratified the Protocol in 1968, thereby becoming a party to the Convention. Domestic U.S. law did not change, though, until the Refugee Act of 1980 adopted the U.N. definition and also a process through which annual decisions would be made on the number and composition of the refugee population to be admitted for resettlement. This legislation also established an asylum system for the protection of refugees who arrived on their own and a domestic assistance program to help refugees adapt to life in the United States.

In the decades before passage of the Refugee Act of 1980, U.S. refugee policy reflected the Cold War priorities of the 1950s and early 1960s described in Chapter 9. The 1965 Amendments adopted the ideologically bound definition of earlier legislation, creating an Eastern Hemisphere quota for refugees fleeing Communist and Communist-dominated countries. The refugee resettlement program continued to fit perfectly into the Massachusetts model for most of the rest of the century. The United States gave highest priority to the admission of those who risked harm because they shared the country's democratic values and preferred living in a market-based economy. Between 1965 and 1980s, the United States admitted record numbers of refugees, especially from Cuba and Southeast Asia, using the parole authority of the attorney general since the refugee quota was inadequate to the task. These resettlement efforts continued after enactment of the Refugee Act. With a more universal definition of a refugee, though, pressure mounted for a less ideologically driven policy that would favorably consider applications from persons fleeing other types of repressive governments and situations. This tension will be discussed in the context of policies regarding recognition of Haitians, Salvadorans, and Guatemalans as refugees.

This chapter concludes by examining how the end of the Cold War affected refugee policy and admissions decisions. By the time the Berlin Wall fell, the resettlement program had been sufficiently institutionalized that there was an expectation that the United States would continue to bring refugees to the country. In the absence of strong ideological support for a generous refugee policy, and an uncertain foreign policy in a new unipolar world, the refugee program had to find a model different from the Massachusetts model it had largely been following.

Pre-1980 Refugee Resettlement

During the signing of the 1965 Amendments to the Immigration and Nationality Act, Lyndon Johnson addressed the issue of Cuban refugees. As was discussed in the previous chapter, Cubans began to seek refuge in the United States after the Cuban revolution and, particularly, after Fidel Castro's embrace of Communism. Johnson announced: "I declare this afternoon to the people of Cuba that those who seek refuge here in America will find it. The dedication of America to our traditions as an asylum for the oppressed is going to be upheld." Just a few days before, Castro had announced that any Cuban with relatives in the United States would be free to depart the country after October 10, 1965. Since the Cuban missile crisis, leaving the island had been difficult. The controversial Operation Pedro Pan program (December 1960–October 1962) that brought unaccompanied children to the United States had been effectively terminated during the missile crisis and had not been resumed (Forbes [Martin] and Fagen 1984). Some Cubans went through third countries to the United States and others crossed the waters between the two countries by raft.

Castro's announcement led to the first major sealift of Cubans, from the port of Camarioca. Some departed in Cuban boats but many others were brought to the United States by Cuban émigrés who had already settled in Florida. Faced with the prospect of much larger numbers of boats and the danger of even the short sea crossing during hurricane season, Johnson planned to negotiate an orderly departure program. With the aid of the International Committee of the Red Cross, the United States proposed a regular airlift from the island. The agreement between the two countries allowed for two chartered flights per day (dubbed Freedom Flights by the United States). The flights continued more or less consistently between 1965 and 1971 and then with less frequency between 1971 and 1973. Priority was to be given to Cubans with immediate relatives in the United States. U.S. efforts to obtain the release of political prisoners generally failed. In all, almost 300,000 Cubans departed Cuba through the airlift.

Johnson announced that the federal government would provide supplementary funds to support the new Cuban arrivals. He called on voluntary agencies, which had done most of the post-World War II resettlement of displaced persons (Hungarians and the earlier wave of Cubans), to assist the new arrivals, pledging help from the government. Johnson also acknowledged the particular impact of the Cubans on Florida, where the largest numbers lived, and called on other states to receive the Cubans as well.

The Cuban program had been established several years before Johnson's announcement. The Migration and Refugee Assistance Act of 1962 provided the statutory authority for the program and appropriations. The federal government provided grants to voluntary agencies for the reception and placement of the Cubans, particularly for those who were resettled out of Florida. States received funds to help with unanticipated costs related to education, health care, and social services. Many first-generation Cuban refugees were middle-class professionals and business persons who brought human and financial capital with them. Others, though, would probably have been excluded had the requirement to show they would not become public charges not been waived. With federal funding, these refugees were able, even encouraged, to access cash and medical assistance programs. Given that Florida had one of the most restrictive welfare policies in the country, the federal program offered a higher level of aid to the refugees than was available to many native-born Americans – a point raised in testimony about the propriety of the program (Loescher and Scanlon 1986: 66). Special programs were also implemented to help professionals, particularly physicians, to receive retraining needed to pass qualifying examinations. Federally financed business loans also helped Cuban entrepreneurs to establish new businesses, helping to make Miami the financial capital of Latin America. By 1980, the total tab for assistance to the Cubans had grown to about $1.4 billion (Reimers 1992: 160).

Johnson's declaration of refuge for the Cubans came just as the 1965 Amendments set a specific quota for refugee admissions from the Eastern Hemisphere. Of course, the Cubans were from the Western Hemisphere so the preference system did not apply during the airlift. But the issue also did not arise because the attorney general continued to use his parole authority under the Immigration and Nationality Act to admit the Cubans. With the anticipation of large numbers of Cubans arriving each day, and the prospect for return dwindling as Castro consolidated power, the United States could no longer ignore the question of what would happen to the Cubans in the longer term. In 1966, the Cuban Adjustment Act was passed. Under this legislation, Cubans who had been paroled into the country since January 1959 would be eligible for permanent resident status one year after their parole. Unlike the legislation that had applied to the Hungarian refugees, the Cuban law differed in being open-ended. The Hungarian adjustment act applied only to those who had entered prior to the date of enactment, whereas the Cuban legislation could be used to adjust the status of future arrivals. It remains in force to this day.

Although U.S. refugee policy continued to favor the admission of persons fleeing Communist countries, the first movement toward a more universal definition of refugees came with U.S. ratification of the 1967 Protocol to the UN Convention Relating to the Status of Refugees. The United States had not signed the original 1951 Convention, which pertained to European refugees who had been displaced prior to 1951, but it did ratify the Protocol that eliminated the geographic and time limitations. Ratification of the Protocol made the United States a party to the Convention. The U.N. Convention definition of a refugee was similar to that of the United States, specifying that a refugee is a person fleeing a well-founded fear of persecution on the basis of race, religion, nationality, membership in a particular social group, or political opinion. The U.N. definition did not mention particular ideological factors, however, and did not restrict its applicability to persons fleeing Communist countries.

When ratification of the Protocol went before the Senate, the administration made clear that it would not affect who would be admitted to the United States. Parties to the Convention were not obliged to bring refugees to their shores; that decision was purely within the discretion of the government. Rather, the Convention required that state parties not "expel or return (*refoule*) a refugee in any manner whatsoever to the frontiers of territories where his life or freedom would be threatened on account of his race, religion, nationality, membership in a particular social group or political opinion." A separate part of U.S. law dealt with that issue, barring deportation to a country where a person's "life or freedom would be threatened on account of race, religion, nationality, membership in a particular social group or political opinion." The administration, asserting that this provision was consistent with obligations under the treaty, recommended ratification with no changes to domestic law.

It was be another twelve years before these first steps resulted in a full shift in U.S. refugee law. In the meantime, the United States used the parole authority to admit refugees outside the seventh preference quota. The next major challenge was Vietnam in 1975.[1] The fall of the South Vietnamese government in April 1975 precipitated a flow, during the following decade, of more than one million Indochinese refugees from Vietnam, Cambodia, and Laos. The United States, recognizing its responsibility for assisting these refugees because of its long military involvement in Southeast Asia, mounted a resettlement program that brought about 600,000 Southeast Asian refugees to the United States.

The first wave of Indochinese resettlement occurred with the evacuation from Saigon and other parts of Vietnam. Because of the large numbers of refugees and the shortness of the time during which they left Vietnam, the federal government played an unprecedented role in resettlement. The refugees were brought to processing centers in the Pacific, with the majority going to Guam (with a peak refugee population of 50,000 in May) and Wake Island (with 15,359 processed). From these processing centers, the refugees were flown to the United States. Between April and December 1975, more than 130,000 Indochinese refugees entered under the attorney general's parole authority. Once in this country, the refugees were sent to one of four camps – Camp Pendleton, California; Fort Chaffee, Arkansas; Fort Indiantown Gap, Pennsylvania; and Eglin Air Force Base, Florida.

Responsibility for the refugee program resided with the Interagency Task Force for Indochinese Refugees (IATF), housed in the State Department and composed of twelve federal agencies. The IATF had responsibility for allocating funds and coordinating activities; for the evacuation, processing and resettlement of refugees; and for consultations with public and private agencies involved in the program. At the camps, the military was responsible for providing food, clothing, housing, and logistical support. The INS processed applications for admission, conducting security checks on all adult refugees. The Department of Health, Education and Welfare conducted medical screenings, assigned Social Security numbers, determined if those requesting release without sponsors had sufficient resources, and provided some educational services. Voluntary agencies and a few state agencies, under contracts with the State Department, interviewed refugees to match them with American sponsors or sponsoring agencies. The agencies received $500 per refugee to cover the costs of placing and receiving refugees in local communities. The Southeast Asian refugees were eligible for a range of public benefits, similar to but generally not as generous as those afforded their Cuban predecessors.

The first wave of Indochinese refugees was similar to the first wave of Cubans in that it included professionals and business persons. Priority was

---

[1] The discussion of Indochinese refugees was adapted from Forbes [Martin] and Fagen 1984. Also, see Loescher and Scanlon (1986), Zucker and Zucker (1987) and Bon Tempo (2008).

given to evacuating those who had worked for the U.S. military or other U.S. organizations. Although the war in Vietnam had been extremely controversial in the United States, admission of the refugees could be easily justified on both foreign policy and humanitarian bases.

A second wave of Southeast Asian departures had fewer individual links to the United States but provoked equal or greater foreign policy and humanitarian interest. By 1977, it was apparent that thousands of people were continuing to flee the Communist take-over of Laos, Vietnam, and Cambodia. The numbers seeking asylum in Thailand had grown enough that the United States feared the destabilizing impact it might have on one of its sole remaining allies in the region. The United States admitted several thousand refugees in 1977 and 1978. The expectation was that this would effectively end the Indochinese refugee program, prompting the Department of Health, Education and Welfare to notify states that they should begin phasing out their assistance to refugees.

Late 1978 and 1979 saw even larger refugee flows from Southeast Asia. The Vietnamese invasion of Cambodia enabled hundreds of thousands to flee the killing fields of the Pol Pot regime across the border into Thailand. The Pathet Lao government increased its reprisals against allies of the United States, forcing hundreds of thousands of Hmong and lowland Lao across the Laotian border into Thailand. At the same time, the Vietnamese government enacted repressive policies against ethnic Chinese, prompting large-scale departures of refugees toward Thailand, Malaysia, Indonesia, Hong Kong, Singapore, and the Philippines by boat. Pirates in the South China Sea made the trip extremely dangerous, leading to countless rapes, other physical attacks, and the sinking of ships with all aboard.

By mid-1979, more than 27,000 refugees were arriving in "first asylum" countries each month. More than 300,000 were in camps in June 1979 and there appeared to be no let-up in emigration. In response, Thailand and Malaysia announced the closing of their doors. In June, about 42,000 Cambodians were forced back across the border, and Malaysia and Thailand began systematic pushbacks of boats arriving in their territorial water (Stein 1979). These actions prompted the calling of an international conference to address the refugee problem. In sharp contrast to the disappointing showing of the United States in the Evian conference, the U.S. government participated in the Geneva Indochinese conference at the highest level. Vice President Walter Mondale, representing the U.S. government, chaired the meeting. The U.N. High Commissioner for Refugees presented a plan of action that included pledges of 260,000 resettlement slots and increased funding for the camps. In exchange, the countries of first asylum in Southeast Asia agreed that all refugees would be allowed entry and placed in holding centers until they could be resettled. Although neither Laos nor any of the Cambodian factions participated, the Vietnamese government agreed to institute an orderly departure program and dissuade boat departures. The United States pledged to admit 14,000 refugees per month. Canada, Australia, and France also pledged large resettlement quotas and dozens of other countries agreed to smaller ones.

The new Indochinese arrivals had far fewer personal and financial resources than the 1975 refugees. The Cambodians had suffered through four years of killings and dislocation, escaping as famine and conflict engulfed the country, causing still more suffering. Many of the Cambodians had no more than a few years, if any, of education. A disproportionately large number of women-headed households were resettled, the men not having survived the Khmer Rouge years. The Hmong from Laos came from a society that had no written alphabet until one was created for them in the 1950s. The vast majority of the Hmong who entered the United States were illiterate. Coming with large families from the hills of Laos, where they had practiced slash-and-burn agriculture, most Hmong refugees had no skills that could be transferred readily to an urban or rural American context (Castle 1993). Although the Vietnamese refugees tended to have higher levels of education than the Cambodians or Laotians, the second wave brought far less human capital with them than had the professionals and civil servants who preceded them.

A large proportion of the first wave of Southeast Asian refugees settled in California, some going there directly, especially from Camp Pendleton, and others moving there from their original resettlement locations. Other major settlement sites included northern Virginia (not surprisingly, since many of the 1975 refugees had ties to the U.S. military and were familiar with the location of the Pentagon). Chicago, Houston, and Seattle also received large numbers of Southeast Asian refugees. By and large, the refugees were more dispersed than other immigrants had been because of the network of voluntary agencies that placed them with affiliates throughout the country (Forbes [Martin] 1983, 1984). Initially, employment rates were significantly lower for the Southeast Asian refugees than was true of immigrants admitted because of family ties or occupation (Forbes [Martin] 1985). Public charge restrictions were waived when they were admitted. Because they had special eligibility for public assistance through the Indochinese Refugee Assistance Program, with federal reimbursement of state costs, and large families that could be supported only poorly by entry-wage jobs, rates of welfare utilization were also higher than average.

The 1970s also saw a resurgence of immigration from the Soviet Union. With most emigration from the Soviet bloc having been cut off after World War II, lifting the Iron Curtain had become a central tenet of U.S. foreign policy. Within the Soviet Union, a growing number of Jews, ethnic Germans, Christian Pentecostals, and others were seeking permission to leave the country. The plight of the Soviet Jews was particularly poignant because of rising anti-Semitism in areas that had seen centuries of pogroms and persecution. Most of the Jews who sought to leave the Soviet Union in the 1970s intended to go to Israel. Once they applied for exit permission, they were often subject to further repressive acts, including the loss of jobs and housing. Some Soviet Jews – called refuseniks – had been denied exit for many years.

Beginning in the early 1970s, the emigration of Soviet Jews became a matter of quiet diplomacy, in the context of the movement toward détente, and then more open action developed. After it became clear that Congress was likely to pass legislation barring a trade agreement, the Soviet Union lessened some of its restrictions on exit, allowing about 35,000 Soviet Jews to exit in 1973. In 1974, Congress passed an amendment introduced by Henry Jackson and Charles Vanik that forbade "most favored nation" (that is, normal, permanent) trade relations with a country if the president determined that that country did not comply with the freedom of emigration requirements of the amendment. At the end of 1975, the Soviets backed out of trade negotiations, partly because of the Jackson-Vanik requirements but also because of other congressional provisions. The number of Soviet Jews who were allowed to emigrate declined from 21,000 in 1974 to 13,000–14,000 in 1975 and 1976 (Bon Tempo 2008). During the course of the 1970s, about 250,000 Soviet refugees entered the United States (Remennick 2007). Although Soviet emigration waxed and waned through the rest of the 1970s, it was not until the late 1980s, when the Gorbachev government sought better relations with the West, that large-scale movements resumed.

The Soviet refugees were, on average, better educated than most refugees. Gold described the situation of the Soviet Jews as follows: "recent Jewish immigrants find themselves among the upper echelon of all migrants due to their largely European origins, high levels of education, legal status, connections to established coethnics, and white skin" (Gold 1999: 124). They were also more likely to live in a household with the potential for multiple wage-earners. In contrast to the Indochinese women, who had very low levels of education and literacy, Gold (1999: 128) reported, "sixty-seven percent of Soviet Jewish women in the United States were engineers, technicians, or other kinds of professionals prior to migration." This proportion is higher than that for native-born Americans.

Refugee Act of 1980

As the use of parole grew in the 1970s, Congress revisited refugee policy. Recognizing that the seventh preference visa numbers were inadequate to address even routine refugee movements, and that there was no statutory authority to address crises except for parole, congressional attention turned toward devising a more flexible mechanism for the admission of refugees. The leading proponent of reform was again Senator Edward Kennedy, now chair of the Judiciary Committee, who had been working on reform of the refugee system throughout the 1970s. He was joined in 1979 by Congressman Peter Rodino, chair of the House Judiciary Committee since 1973, and Elizabeth Holtzman, chair of the House immigration subcommittee. Holtzman was known for leading the movement to uncover and expel Nazis and other persecutors who had entered the country after World War II.

The impetus for reform came from two agendas. First was a desire to place U.S. refugee policy more squarely in line with international human rights principles. This perspective was shared by the congressional reformers and the

Carter administration, which had established a new State Department bureau focused on human rights. The second impetus was to gain greater congressional control over refugee admissions. Kennedy described the twin goals as follows: "In the Refugee Act of 1980, Congress gave new statutory authority to the United States' longstanding commitment to human rights and its traditional humanitarian concern for the plight of refugees around the world. But it was also attempting to assure greater equity in the treatment of refugees and more effective procedures in dealing with them" (Kennedy 1981: 142).

Most of the negotiations focused on devising a mechanism that allowed congressional input but did not force the hand of the president in the conduct of foreign policy. Key members of the executive branch recognized that the ad hoc nature of the refugee program was problematic. Former Senator Dick Clark, the U.S. Coordinator for Refugee Affairs, testified in 1979 that "We can no longer merely react to refugee situations as they arise, in an ad hoc fashion. The nature of the current, extended refugee crisis requires that we make realistic projections of our program needs and that we plan our resource allocations and assistance activities in a coordinated way" (quoted in Gallagher et al. 1985: 17).

The administration did not want its hands tied, however, by too much congressional control over refugee admissions. Senior officials argued that refugee admissions were within the president's foreign policy making authority and chafed at the idea that Congress would have a veto over presidential actions. Members of Congress complained, for their part, that they were repeatedly called upon to provide funding and adjust the status of parolees *after* the refugees were already in the country. This process gave Congress little input into the actual decision to admit the refugees. Also, states and voluntary agencies often incurred costs during the early phases of an emergency with no guarantee that Congress would reimburse their expenditures.

The legislative solution was to establish a "normal flow" refugee program of 50,000 admissions per year and a special mechanism by which the president could exceed that number after holding consultations with Congress. The normal flow program was authorized for FY 1980–1982. The special mechanism had no statutory time frame. Rather, the president would send a report to Congress at the beginning of the fiscal year, specifying the number of refugees to be admitted and the geographic distribution of the admission slots, with supporting documentation about the need to exceed the normal flow. Consultations would be held between the responsible Cabinet officers (the secretary of state and the attorney general) and the congressional committees responsible for immigration and refugee policy, but Congress had no veto authority over admissions. In an emergency, the president could hold consultations mid-year on an expansion in numbers of refugees to be admitted. Attorney General Griffin Bell noted the importance of investing the president with this authority, rather than the attorney general, as was the case with parole: "The transfer of policy making authority to the President recognizes that these decisions are of such importance to the United States that they should be made only at the highest level" (quoted in Gallagher et al. 1985: 18).

The Refugee Act of 1980 changed the definition of a refugee to remove the ideological biases in the 1965 Amendments. Senator Kennedy stated clearly that a major goal of the legislation was to "repeal ... the previous law's discriminatory treatment of refugees" (Kennedy 1981: 143). The legislation adopted the U.N. Convention definition, which covered persons outside their country of origin, but Congress broadened the scope to include persons still within their own countries who had a well-founded fear of persecution on the basis of race, religion, nationality, membership in a particular social group, or political opinion. This provision would allow orderly departure programs to function as a mechanism to bring people into the country without requiring them to risk their lives to escape first to a neighboring country. The legislation barred admission of those who had persecuted others, an issue of considerable concern given the large-scale resettlement of Cambodians who had lived through the Khmer Rouge period. Congress wanted to admit the victims but also to ensure that the perpetrators of the violence did not slip into the United States in the guise of refugees from current Vietnamese authorities.[2]

As defined in the Refugee Act, the decision to admit refugees from abroad was a purely discretionary decision on the part of the government. The legislation's preamble made clear that admission would be granted only to refugees of special humanitarian concern to the United States. The refugees would be admitted conditionally, and their status could be changed to that of permanent residence one year after entry. This provision would give the government time to undertake security checks if emergent circumstances precluded doing such checks before admission.

Of particular interest to states and voluntary agencies was the legislation's provision of statutory authority for the domestic refugee resettlement program. Two forms of assistance were authorized. The Department of State would provide reception and placement grants to voluntary agencies that assisted in the initial phase of resettlement. These grants would cover the costs of meeting refugees upon arrival, finding them housing, helping enroll their children in school, obtaining needed health care, assisting adults to find jobs, and similar activities. Then, the Office of Refugee Resettlement in the Department of Health and Human Services would provide grants to state offices of refugee resettlement to cover the longer-term costs of cash and medical assistance, language and vocational training, and other services provided to the refugees.

In addition to addressing issues related to resettlement of refugees from abroad, the Refugee Act included a new provision for adjudication of

---

[2] This issue came up in the mid-1980s when an increasingly large number of Cambodians in Khao-I-Dang camp were placed on hold, neither accepted for resettlement nor denied, because suspicions that they were Khmer Rouge surfaced but could not be proven (personal observations 1984).

applications for asylum in the United States. Although U.S. law had had provisions to stay the deportation of someone fearing serious harm, it did not have an affirmative process for granting refugee status to a person who requested asylum after arriving in the United States illegally or on a temporary visa. The new law applied the same definition in determining whether an individual qualified for asylum as would be used in determining eligibility for resettlement. Those granted asylum, as was the case with the resettled, would be admitted on a conditional basis. After one year, they would be eligible to have their status adjusted to permanent residence. Unlike the resettlement process, however, Congress set a cap of 5,000 adjustments per year for those who applied through the asylum program.[3]

The Refugee Act was signed on March 17 and went into effect on April 1, 1980. This legislation accomplished a number of important reforms. It provided a permanent authority for admission of refugees, recognizing the recurrence of these crises. Rather than act in an ad hoc manner, the government would have a flexible mechanism that respected presidential powers while recognizing congressional prerogatives. Countries of asylum and other countries of resettlement had a more consistent partner in dealing with refugee emergencies. Moreover, the voluntary agencies and state and local governments that helped refugees to resettle into American communities would have a better idea as to the amount and type of resources that the federal government would provide.

Cuban–Haitian Crises

The refugee resettlement provisions mirrored several decades of experience well enough to have been implemented rather smoothly, even though the law came into effect at the height of the Indochinese refugee program. The asylum provisions were more problematic, especially when Fidel Castro announced within a few weeks of enactment of the Refugee Act that any Cuban who wished to leave the island was welcome to do so through the Mariel port. Initially, President Carter responded much as President Johnson had in announcing that the United States would welcome the Cubans. What followed, however, was an exodus of unprecedented proportions that was handled largely outside the parameters set by the Refugee Act of 1980.[4]

Relations between the United States and Cuba had been improving. In 1977 each country opened an "interest" section in the other's capital. Operating through the Swiss government, the "interest" sections allowed the two governments to explore a range of issues. Reflecting the improved relations, the Castro

---

[3] Jerry Tinker, Senator Kennedy's principal staff member, remembered having done a "back of the envelope" calculation of the average number of persons granted the equivalent of asylum during the previous ten years and doubling that number to arrive at the 5,000 limit. Personal conversations with Tinker during the 1980s.

[4] See Zucker and Zucker (1987), Loescher and Scanlon (1986), and Daniels (2004) for further discussion of the Mariel Boatlift.

government authorized the release of political prisoners and permitted Cubans residing in the United States to visit their relatives in Cuba. As more and more political prisoners were released, it became apparent that the United States and other countries were not keeping pace with the need for resettlement. To some extent, this reflected suspicions on the part of U.S. authorities that Castro was releasing criminals, not political prisoners. At the same time, economic conditions in Cuba were deteriorating, with housing and food supplies short. More Cubans who had seen the wealth of their U.S. relatives sought escape from the economic deprivations. Political tensions between the United States and Cuba were renewed and increased. The United States was concerned about Cuba's support for Angolan and other rebel groups, and Cuba complained about the slow pace of resettlement and continued economic embargo.

Cubans seeking to leave the country began to take matters into their own hands. Throughout 1979 into 1980 small numbers of Cubans sought entry into foreign embassies to claim political asylum. On April 1, 1980, a group of six Cubans stormed the Peruvian embassy, killing a guard. At first Castro reinforced the guards at the embassy, but a few days later, he removed the guard and announced that those who wanted to leave could go to the embassy. About 7,000 Cubans took him at his word. On April 6, Castro reestablished the security force at the embassy, effectively locking the would-be émigrés into the embassy. The United States responded by offering to take about half of the Cubans, who would be transported to Costa Rica, screened there, and then sent to the United States and other countries.

The evacuation was slow; by April 18, fewer than 2,000 Cubans had departed for Costa Rica. Conditions in the embassy were deteriorating, prompting a flotilla of boats to leave Miami with provisions for those awaiting resettlement. When the boats reached Mariel port on April 20, Castro announced that Cubans could leave the country. As more boats arrived from Miami to pick up family members, Castro put in place a quota system. About 30 percent of the passengers would be relatives but the remaining persons would be demonstrators from the embassies and others to whom he granted exit permission (Zucker and Zucker 1996). It was the latter group who would prove the most controversial; a small but noticeable number were released from prisons and facilities for the mentally ill.

By May 1, about 5,000 Cubans had arrived in Florida. The State Department proposed issuing stern warnings of the criminal penalties that might apply if Cubans from Miami brought relatives into the country illegally, but on-the-ground INS officials knew such threats would do little to deter the boats from leaving. Instead, local officials reminded Cuban-Americans to inform Customs and INS about departures and arrivals so that the newcomers could be registered (Engstrom 1997).

On May 5, President Carter made an unequivocally positive statement about the boat lift: "We'll continue to provide an open heart and open arms to refugees seeking freedom from Communist domination and from the economic deprivation brought about primarily by Fidel Castro and his government" (quoted in Zucker and Zucker 1996). Although Carter reversed this position several days later, calling for an orderly departure program along the lines of the Freedom Flights, the damage was done. By the end of September, when Castro finally closed the port, about 125,000 Cubans had arrived by boat in the United States.

U.S. policies regarding what to do with the Cubans after arrival were as confusing as were those about the boat lift itself. During the first days of the boatlift, tent cities were set up in Miami. The Orange Bowl received the first group and then a camp was located under Interstate 95 and another one at Eglin Air Force Base. As the numbers increased, the so-called Marielitos were moved to Fort Chaffee in Arkansas, Fort Indiantown Gap in Pennsylvania, and Fort McCoy in Wisconsin.

The administration was reluctant to use the emergency provisions of the new Refugee Act in addressing the crisis. Seeing those provisions primarily as a mechanism for resettlement abroad, despite Senator Kennedy's assurance that it was designed precisely for this type of crisis, the Immigration and Naturalization Service initially took individual applications for asylum from the new arrivals. As the numbers grew, however, and it became clear that the Cubans would not be returned even if their asylum applications were denied (which might be the case, given the strong economic motivations that many of the Marielitos described), the administration determined that other approaches were needed to deal with the situation. Parole was problematic because the Refugee Act had barred its use in admitting large numbers of people, reserving its use for individuals rather than groups.

The alternative that the administration came up with was a pure fiction. The Immigration and Naturalization Service (INS) labeled the Cubans "Special Entrants: Status pending." The government would screen the Marielitos to identify those who could not be released into U.S. communities (that is, felons and persons with serious mental diseases) and then have voluntary agencies and state and local governments provide assistance toward their resettlement. Congress acquiesced. Having only recently demanded a measure of control over refugee admissions, Congress passed the Fascell-Stone Amendments to the Refugee Education Assistance Act in October 1980. Under the terms of the amendments, Cuban (and Haitian, as discussed later) special entrants would be treated as if they were resettled refugees.

Release from the camps took longer than expected because of the difficulties in screening the Cubans who had no relatives in the United States. Conditions deteriorated and rioting occurred in some of the camps. The situation at Fort Chaffee, Arkansas, was especially dire when about 1,000 Marielitos rioted, setting fires to two buildings. A young governor, Bill Clinton, learned an important lesson about the political volubility of refugee crises when he lost the next gubernatorial election, largely because of dissatisfaction with the events in Fort Chaffee. It was a lesson he would apply when the next major boat lift occurred during his tenure as president.

The vast majority of the Marielitos were eventually released from the camps. Even most of those who had acknowledged having been in jails were determined to be admissible. Some had committed offenses in Cuba that would not be considered criminal acts in the United States (e.g., criticizing the government) and others had committed minor crimes that did not bar their admission. About 1,200 Cubans who had committed serious criminal acts (often known because of their own admission) and 600 patients with serious mental health problems remained when the initial processing ended. All but about 200 were eventually released, with these remaining Cubans turned over to federal prison authorities.

Resettlement of the Marielitos was generally more difficult than it had been for Cubans admitted in earlier years. A larger number had no relatives in the United States who would provide assistance in finding jobs and otherwise adapting to their new home. A majority were men who came without their families. The Cuban community in the United States was highly ambivalent about the Marielitos. The reports of criminals and mental patients affected the treatment of the Marielitos as a whole. Moreover, racism impeded the resettlement effort. While the already established Cubans were largely white, a sizable number of the Marielitos were black or of mixed race. In addition to these factors, the agencies that undertook resettlement were already overwhelmed with the resettlement of the Southeast Asian refugees. Many had shifted to hiring Indochinese staff in order to have the language and cultural expertise needed for the Southeast Asian refugees. These newcomers did not necessarily have the knowledge to work effectively with the Marielitos. Finally, the ambiguity of the Marielitos' status made the situation all the more complicated. Unlike the earlier arrivals, it was not certain when and if the Marielitos would obtain permanent resident status.

The Cuban situation, however, was nowhere near as problematic as was that of Haitians who came to the United States. Haitian immigration had begun in the late 1950s when political dissidents and largely middle-class Haitians left the country to settle in the United States as the dictatorship of François "Papa Doc" Duvalier began a reign of terror. Boat arrivals began in the early 1970s, when Jean-Claude "Baby Doc" Duvalier took over from his father and a broader swath of Haitian society fled the country to escape a deteriorating economic and political situation.

Corruption was endemic during the Duvalier regimes. The general public saw little of the international aid that came into the country. Twenty million dollars from a grant from the International Monetary Fund to help Haiti recover from hurricanes and rising oil prices in 1979–1980 was diverted to the presidential palace (Bethell 1990: 567). When Baby Doc married in 1980, he spent a reported $5 million – 7 million on the wedding (Stepick 1987). His wife reportedly drew a salary of $100,000 per month for her official duties. The Duvaliers also controlled most industry in the country, setting excessively high prices for common merchandise. Maingot (1987) reports that a pound of rice cost sixty cents in Haiti when the same bag cost only twenty cents in the neighboring Dominican Republic. During this same period, income disparity grew. One percent of the population controlled 44 percent of the national wealth, while 90 percent of the population lived on less than $150 per year (Coupeau 2008).

Although Baby Doc had announced his intention to abide by human rights standards, the reality never met his stated aspirations. In 1974, the U.S. Senate Appropriations Committee concluded that "the grim visible terror of Francois Duvalier's regime may have subsided, [but] it seems that autocratic rule characterized by an unflinching willingness to suppress people had not" (quoted in Stepick 1987: 146). American human rights organizations were blunter in their assessment. Amnesty International, reporting on prisoners held without charge, found that "the variety of torture to which the detainee is subjected is incredible: clubbing to death, maiming of the genitals, food deprivations to the point of starvation, and the insertion of red-hot pokers in the back passage" (quoted in Stepick 1987: 143).

In 1979, Duvalier, who had inherited his father's title of President for Life, took steps to repress political opposition, making it a crime to insult the President for Life, his wife, or his father's memory. During 1980, human rights activists, political opponents, and members of the independent media were systematically targeted. Some of the atrocities were carried out by the official police and military. Regional officials called prefects "engaged in physical elimination of actual or suspected opponents, summary arrests and incarceration without trials, abductions, secret torture, and selective and random murders" (Coupeau 2008). Still other abuses were carried out by the National Security Volunteers, called the *Tonton Macoutes*, a paramilitary group that the Duvaliers had established as a counterpoint to the military to ensure their continued control over the government (Maingot 1987).

The U.S. government consistently designated the Haitian boat people as economic migrants, entering illegally, rather than as refugees. A combination of factors created a vastly different response to the Haitians than was seen in U.S. policies toward the Cubans. First, the United States supported the Duvalier regime, seeing it as a bulwark against Communism. Foreign policy precluded an admission that a U.S. ally persecuted his country's citizens or even seriously harmed them through his policies. Second, the Haitians did not fit the definition of refugee in use at the time. In the years before the Refugee Act, refugees were defined as persons who were fleeing Communist or Communist-dominated countries. Haiti may have been governed by an authoritarian dictatorship, but it was clearly not Communist. Third, elements of racism and class bias no doubt entered into U.S. policies. Although the United States had opened itself to Asian and Latin American immigration under the 1965 Amendments, and even admitted a sizable number of Jamaicans and others from the British West Indies, the Haitians presented different issues. Educational levels were very low, they did not speak English as did the British West Indians, some practiced unfamiliar African religious rites, and they came from a country that had gained its independence through a slave rebellion.

The United States was not the principal destination for most Haitians seeking to leave the country. A far larger number went to the Dominican Republic. Grasmuck (1982) cites estimates of 200,000 Haitians in the Dominican Republic in 1980. Most had entered to work in the sugar cane industry. Although the conditions in which sugar cane cutters worked were extremely difficult, Grasmuck explains that the Haitians "consider suffering on the Dominican side of the border to be more attractive than suffering on the Haiti side" (Grasmuck 1982: 365). Although some of the Haitian workers returned periodically to Haiti, others remained illegally in the Dominican Republic, seeking work in other sectors.

Still other Haitians migrated to the Bahamas, which had become a destination for Haitian workers after World War II. By the 1960s, more than 40,000 Haitians lived in the Bahamas, representing almost 20 percent of the population. Despite periodic attempts by the Bahamian government to deport Haitians who lived in the islands illegally, Haitian migrants still sought entry via small boats. In 1978, however, the Bahamas began more systematic apprehension and removal of Haitians. Reports of beatings and rapes of Haitians by Bahamian immigration officials provoked protests by human rights groups and the U.N. High Commissioner for Refugees, but did not slow down Bahamian efforts to deport the Haitians.

As human rights conditions in Haiti deteriorated in the late 1970s, and the Bahamian government adopted increasingly restrictive measures, the number of Haitian asylum seekers in the United States increased (Loescher and Scanlon, 1984: 341). By 1979, about 9,000 Haitians had applied for asylum, but only 55 had received it (Zucker and Zucker 1996: 46). The number of applicants grew in 1980, reaching new heights in the months leading up to and during the Cuban boat lift crisis.

Initially, the Haitians did not have a constituency in the United States willing to use its political power on their behalf. In light of the Mariel boatlift, however, that situation changed. Even earlier, African Americans in Miami had complained about the preferential treatment accorded to Cubans. The Catholic Church also raised questions about the disparity in treatment of Haitians and Cubans. Legal aid groups took up the Haitian cause. The National Council of Churches prevailed in a legal challenge that required the government to reconsider many Haitian asylum claims (UNHCR 2000: 176). The Haitian Refugee Council won an important decision in 1980, in which the presiding judge, James Lawrence King, rejected the government's argument that the Haitians were economic migrants, finding that the Duvalier government's policies were the issue.

The involvement of the congressional black caucus in Congress finally led to changes, albeit short-lived ones, in U.S. policy toward the Haitians. When President Carter announced that Cubans would be accorded Special Entrant status, he gave about 40,000 Haitians the same status. Under the Fascell–Stone Amendment, they were granted access to federal refugee benefits along with the Marielitos. For the first time, Haitians received equal treatment with Cubans, although the government skirted the crucial issue as to whether the Haitians were refugees.

In September 1981, the new Reagan administration offered its own response. First, the new U.S. administration tried to deter continuing Haitian movements by detention and mass exclusion hearings. Facing new legal challenges, the Reagan administration negotiated an agreement with the Duvalier regime to interdict boats leaving Haiti before they arrived in U.S. territorial waters. Under the agreement, Haitians onboard would be asked by the U.S. Coast Guard if they wished to apply for asylum. If they answered in the affirmative, an INS official would determine if there were grounds to admit them to the United States to pursue the claim. Otherwise, they would be returned to Haiti.

In October 1981, the Coast Guard interdicted 168 Haitians, but the number fell to 18 in November. During 1982, the Coast Guard interdicted fewer than 200 Haitians, but the pace increased in 1983 to 762 and then quadrupled in 1984, to 2,942. It remained at an average of about 2,500 well into 1991. From 1981 through 1990 only six Haitians were admitted to the United States to pursue an asylum claim. This period included the later years of the Jean-Claude Duvalier regime when repression and corruption grew, until he was forced to leave the country in 1986. After Duvalier's departure, Haiti experience political instability. Planned elections in 1987 were marred by violence when the headquarters of a number of candidates were stoned and shot. The violence culminated on Election Day, Sunday, November 29, 1987 (Bloody Sunday), when the Haitian military and the Tonton Macoutes harassed and shot would-be voters, many of whom waited for ballots in vain. In the capital, the Macoutes "machine-gunned unarmed voters in the courtyard of the Argentine-Bellegarde school. After emptying their guns, they hacked off limbs and heads with machetes..." (Pezzullo 2006: 110). A rigged election followed, in which the military's handpicked candidate, Leslie Manigot, was elected, only to be deposed a few months later when he tried to rein in his military supporters. Still more violence followed, and attacks against the members of the democratic opposition grew throughout 1988. In one attack against Father Jean Bertrand Aristide in his church, thirteen parishioners were killed and seventy-seven were wounded (Pezzullo 2006). The military then installed Papa Doc's chief aide, General Prosper Avril, in the presidency, but he too ran afoul of his sponsors when he cooperated with a U.S. anti-narcotics campaign. Avril averted a coup, but his days were numbered. Avril resigned in March 1990, leaving the government in the hands of a caretaker, Supreme Court Judge Ertha Pascal-Trouillot, until elections could take place. At the end of 1990, Father Aristide, Haiti's first democratically elected president, took office.

Aristide's tenure was brief and stormy. Even before his inauguration, there was a coup attempt, led by Roger Lafontant of the Tonton Macoute. After it was suppressed, mobs of Aristide supporters took to the streets in revenge against suspected Macoutes. After Aristide took office, his economic policies (raising taxes on the wealthy and the minimum wage for workers) created animosities between his administration and the business community. The military also remained suspicious of Aristide's populism. On September 29, 1991, the acting commander in chief of the army, General Raoul Cédras, led a coup that deposed Aristide.

Beginning in November 1991, Haitian interdictions rose dramatically to an approximate total of 36,500 from then through May 1992. The overthrow of Aristide and the resulting suppression of the supporters of the populist priest precipitated the new movements. In contrast to the 1980s, a higher proportion of those who were interdicted were found to have legitimate claims to asylum. This was caused partly by changes in asylum processing in the United States. In light of long-standing criticisms of asylum policies, to be discussed in greater detail in the next section, the George H. W. Bush administration had instituted reforms at the Immigration and Naturalization Service. Most important, a new corps of asylum officers was established that was separate from the immigration services and enforcement divisions of the INS. Heretofore, asylum decisions were made by INS officials with little training in the intricacies of refugee law. The new corps, recruited from outside INS, included people who had worked in overseas refugee camps and who had knowledge of the political conditions in the source countries from which asylum seekers came.

The timing was good and bad – ultimately, more bad than good from the perspective of those seeking to protect refugees. As more of the new asylum officers were deployed onto Coast Guard cutters, the numbers of Haitians referred for a full asylum hearing grew. This was initially seen as promising. The administration was unwilling to admit large numbers of the Haitians into the United States to pursue their claims, however, fearing that this would signal "a new Mariel" crisis. At first the Bush administration tried to keep pace, sending larger ships than Coast Guard cutters to house the asylum seekers. When the numbers were too large to be accommodated at sea, the administration looked for alternatives. The Guantanamo naval base in Cuba – controlled by the United States under a long-term agreement that Castro had not been able to abrogate – initially appeared to be a solution. As the numbers brought to the base grew, however, the Navy argued that it could not accommodate the growing numbers and the Bush administration agreed. Entreaties were made to other countries to accept the Haitians but no one volunteered.

On Memorial Day weekend, the situation came to a head. In response to the largest single monthly exodus that occurred in May 1992, when 13,053 Haitians were interdicted, President Bush issued Executive Order No. 12,807 (the Kennebunkport Order) on May 24, 1992,[5] instructing the Coast Guard to interdict Haitians and return them directly to Haiti without any determination of refugee status. Although the original agreement with Haiti had specified that the United States would abide by its international commitments as a party to the Refugee Convention, the new proclamation appeared to contradict not only our treaty obligations but also domestic law.

---

5 57 Federal Register 23,133 (1992).

That at least was how most experts on refugee law saw the situation. The U.N. High Commissioner for Refugees stated, in very direct terms: "This policy of summarily repatriating Haitian refugees whose lives or freedom would be threatened in Haiti is contrary to the terms of the 1951 Convention and the internationally recognized principle of *non-refoulement* (UNHCR 1994: 86)." Citing Article 33 of the Refugee Convention, UNHCR argued that state parties were prohibited from "the involuntary return of refugees 'in any manner whatsoever' to the frontiers of territories where their lives or freedom would be threatened" (UNHCR 1994: 86). Although not condoning the actions of other countries in closing their borders to refugees, UNHCR pointed out the United States "has gone a step further and effectively prevented the Haitian refugees from fleeing either to the United States or to any other country in the same general direction" (UNHCR 1994: 101). In effect, because the Coast Guard interdicted Haitians while they were still near Haiti, they were denied the opportunity to seek asylum anywhere in the region, not just in the United States.

The U.S. Supreme Court did not accept these arguments. In a landmark decision, *Haitian Refugee Centers v. Sales* (then Acting Commissioner of INS), the Supreme Court held that, in the exercise of foreign policy, the president had the authority to return persons interdicted on the high seas without offering them the right to seek asylum. According to this interpretation, the Refugee Act pertained only at the borders and within the United States. Although the majority recognized that the Haitian policy violated the spirit of the Refugee Act, they held that it did not violate the letter of the law. In a stinging dissent, Justice Harry Blackmun argued: "The refugees attempting to escape from Haiti do not claim a right of admission to this country. They do not even argue that the Government has no right to intercept their boats. They demand only that the United States, land of refugees and guardian of freedom, cease forcibly driving them back to detention, abuse, and death. That is a modest plea, vindicated by the Treaty and the statute. We should not close our ears to it" (Blackmun 1994: 84).

The interdiction and immediate return policy stayed in effect until May 1994, when President Clinton reversed the policy in light of a deteriorating human rights situation in Haiti. Boat interdictions had been climbing through 1993 despite the return policies. A number of prominent civil rights leaders sent public and private communications to President Clinton decrying his maintenance of what they considered the reprehensible return policy.[6] The Clinton administration initially focused on diplomatic efforts at the United Nations to

---

[6] For example, Barbara Jordan, then chair of the U.S. Commission on Immigration Reform but communicating privately with the president in her personal capacity, urged him to provide a safe haven for the Haitians to stop the direct returns. Jordan had special credibility with the president. She had been a keynote speaker at the presidential convention that nominated Clinton in 1992 and was also trustee of the legal defense fund that had been established to help the Clintons prepare their defense in the Whitewater investigation.

restore Aristide to the presidency. With pressure mounting to do something about the increasing number of Haitians fleeing the island, President Clinton announced that requests for asylum would once more be heard at sea. Processing began on the USNS *Comfort*, a converted Navy hospital ship docked in Kingston, Jamaica, on June 16, 1994 (U.S. Committee for Refugees 1995: 180). Of the 2,294 people interviewed by INS during the next three weeks, 596 (26 percent) were granted refugee status. By early July, the outflow of migrants from Haiti had increased to more than 3,000 per day and quickly overwhelmed the processing capacity of the USNS *Comfort*.[7]

On July 5, 1994, it was decided to provide safe haven for Haitians at the U.S. military base on Guantanamo Bay, Cuba (Gordon 1994). This time, the Navy was ordered to accommodate as many Haitians as needed protection. The Clinton administration had, in fact, decided that a new paradigm was needed in addressing the mass movements from Haiti. Experts within the administration argued that protection was paramount, but protection had to be divorced from admission into the United States (Martin et al. 1998). In effect, all Haitians who fled the island would be guaranteed protection against return, but none would be allowed to enter the United States.

This policy addressed a challenge that Representative Mazzoli posed at a hearing on Haitian asylum seekers: "How can we protect the lives of Haitians who are being victimized by the current military leaders? How can we prevent problems at sea of the Haitians who have left their country? And, at the same time, how can we prevent what some would call an uncontrollable exodus of Haitians to the United States?" (U.S. Congress 1994: 1). The U.S. Coast Guard brought some 20,000 Haitians to Guantanamo. Not long after the policy was changed from processing and resettlement to temporary safe haven, the numbers of Haitian migrants rapidly decreased. In July more than 16,000 Haitians were interdicted, but only about 300 were interdicted in August and even fewer thereafter.

The numbers declined for a variety of reasons. Those who left Haiti intending to work and send money home to support their families were probably deterred by the realization that they would not be given the chance to enter the United States. An important reason for the decline, even among those who might have left because of fears for their safety, was the change in U.S. foreign policy that occurred at the same time. President Clinton had resolved to use military intervention, if necessary, to restore the Aristide presidency. Not only did boat departures decline; returns to Haiti increased. On September 19, 1994, U.S. military forces entered Haiti and returned President Aristide to power on October 15, 1994. Most of the Haitians in Guantanamo then chose to repatriate voluntarily. On December 29, 1994, the U.S. authorities told the remaining Haitians (less than 5,000) that they should return to Haiti by January 5, 1995. Only about 15 percent did so. Except for some 800 Haitians

---

7 See Table 3, U.S. Dept. of State, Bureau of Population, Refugees and Migration, *Daily Interdiction of Haitian Boat People by U.S. Coast Guard and U.S. Navy, 6/15/94–10/6/94.*

who were allowed to remain in Guantanamo, largely for humanitarian reasons, including 300 unaccompanied minors, the rest (3,765) were returned to Haiti (U.S. Committee for Refugees 1995: 180).

A similar policy was put in place when the next mass migration from Cuba occurred. During the summer of 1994, civil unrest began in Havana; in August, Fidel Castro responded to dissent as he had done in the past, by opening a port and telling Cubans they could leave without restriction (Zucker and Zucker 1996). The numbers of interdicted Cubans increased dramatically. On August 18, the administration held a Cabinet-level meeting where the decision was made to reverse long-standing policy toward Cuban boat arrivals. On August 19, 1994, President Clinton announced that interdicted Cubans would be brought to a safe haven on Guantanamo and those who reached the United States would be detained.

A number of factors contributed to this sudden change in policy. The administration did not want invidious comparisons to be made between its policies toward Haitians and its policies toward Cubans. Moreover, a new precedent had been set with the creation of safe haven for Haitians. Other factors that allowed implementation of the new policy included a shift in the views of the Cuban-American community and the actions of Florida Governor Lawton Chiles. For many years, the Cuban-American community, particularly in Miami, had welcomed the flow of Cubans, viewing it as an embarrassment to the Castro regime and as proof of the regime's problems. That opinion changed, however, as many Cuban-Americans were now more concerned about domestic economic issues and about the effect a new refugee crisis would have on Florida.

Governor Chiles was also determined not to have a repetition of the Mariel boatlift, particularly when he was trying to win reelection in a tight race. Prior to the administration's change in policy, he threatened to declare a statewide immigration emergency and take state action to resolve the situation, not a desirable precedent given the number of other states grappling with immigration problems. President Clinton, who remembered the riots at Fort Chaffee and U.S. Attorney General Janet Reno, formerly state's attorney for Dade County, were also sensitive to concerns about a repeat of Mariel.

Federal action was decisive. The INS immediately initiated harbor patrols in the Miami area, sent a strong warning message to those who might use their boats to bring Cuban rafters to the United States, and seized boats headed toward Cuba to pick up rafters. The U.S. attorney in Miami prosecuted individuals who disregarded the warning.

Some 32,000 Cuban migrants were interdicted by the Coast Guard and brought to Guantanamo (Zucker and Zucker 1996). About 9,000 of these Cubans were transferred to a U.S. military-run safe haven near Panama City (U.S. Committee for Refugees 2006: 187). Although the safe-haven policy had significantly decreased the number of Haitians who sought protection outside Haiti, the number of Cubans interdicted after the announced policy change continued to increase until the weather created rough conditions for boats and rafts toward the end of August. The number of rafters picked up again significantly when the weather permitted new boat departures, but began to decline in early September. The flow stopped almost completely when the United States and Cuba entered into a migration agreement that included Castro reimposing constraints on departures and the United States promising to increase legal immigration channels for Cubans. In contrast to Haiti, there was no intention on the part of the United States to change the Cuban government. As a result, the concept of temporary protection was meaningless because return of thousands of Cubans was unlikely. On May 2, 1995, the Clinton administration announced that most of the Cubans in Guantanamo would be paroled to the United States, but that all rafters henceforth would be interdicted, put through an abbreviated shipboard screening procedure, and repatriated to Cuba unless they met the screening criteria (U.S. Committee for Refugees 1996). The only Cubans who would be admitted into the United States were those with so-called dry feet, that is, those who eluded interdiction and made it onto U.S. land. The United States encouraged those seeking refuge to apply for recognition at the U.S. Interests Section in Havana. Ultimately, most of the Cubans (28,450) on Guantanamo or in Panama were paroled into the United States. Some six hundred returned voluntarily through official channels, while about a thousand Cubans jumped the fence at Guantanamo to return spontaneously to government-controlled Cuba. About three hundred fifty found ineligible for parole to the United States were returned involuntarily to Cuba (Martin et al. 1998).

Central American Asylum Seekers

Prior to the outbreak of civil war in El Salvador, Nicaragua, and Guatemala, small numbers of Central American migrants trekked northward to the United States. In 1978, almost 6,000 Salvadorans, 4,000 Guatemalans, and 2,000 Nicaraguans obtained permanent residence, largely in the family and nonpreference categories. An unknown number of Central Americans entered illegally, but few studies of undocumented migration attempted to enumerate them.[8] The situation changed dramatically in 1979 with an escalation of violence in the three Central American countries.

The Nicaraguan conflict generated the first movements requiring U.S. response. The early migrants were political dissidents who opposed the regime of Anastasio Somoza. They came to the United States only in small numbers, with more of them going to neighboring countries. In July 1979, the United States offered extended voluntary departure (EVD) to the Nicaraguans who feared return to Nicaragua. This allowed persons living without status in the United States to remain temporarily when conditions in their home countries were unstable or insecure. A nationality could be designated as eligible for EVD if the secretary of state and the ttorney general agreed, generally taking

---

[8] An exception is Guy Poitras' (1981) study for SCIRP of return migrants in El Salvador.

account of a combination of foreign policy and immigration considerations. EVD offered beneficiaries relief from deportation and the right to work, but it did not lead to permanent status. Beneficiaries were not eligible to bring their families to the United States. Previously, EVD had been granted to Cubans, Czechs, Southeast Asians, Ethiopians, Ugandans, and Iranians.

When EVD was granted to Nicaraguans, the government assumed it would be used primarily by opponents of the Somoza regime; but shortly after the designation, Somoza was overthrown. The designation stayed in force until September 1980 and it was mostly the opponents of the new regime, controlled by the Communist-leaning Sandinistas, who benefited from the program. Although the Nicaraguans who came to the United States fit the Cold War profile of fleeing a Communist-dominated country, the government decided not to renew the grant of EVD status. After Mariel, the U.S. authorities feared EVD would encourage larger numbers of Nicaraguans to come to the United States. Instead, the United States provided financial and military support to the rebels, called contras, who opposed the Sandinistas. The United States also encouraged Honduras and Costa Rica to open their borders to the contras and to refugees fleeing the emerging conflict. As fighting between the Sandinistas and their opponents intensified in the 1980s, between 350,000 and 500,000 Nicaraguans were displaced, most internally or to neighboring countries. An estimated 40,000–80,000 Nicaraguans had come to the United States by 1985 (Zolberg et al. 1989: 212). Most arrived too late to benefit from EVD.

In 1979, there was also an intensification of conflict in El Salvador when a coup against President-General Romero's military dictatorship shifted power to a reformist junta. The junta's leadership was torn, however, between its left and right wings, particularly over economic reforms. There were also disagreements on how to handle the long-standing rebel movement, which would come together in 1980 as the Farabundo Martí National Liberation Front (FMLN), with the apparent backing of Cuba. What resulted was a weak national government that relied heavily on right-wing extremists in its fight against the FMLN. The civilian population was caught between the two sides: "The continued high level of political violence was attributable not only to the actions of the death squads and the security forces but also to the decision by the left to shun cooperation with the junta in favor of a call for armed insurrection" (www. globalsecurity.com n.d.). In 1980, a series of events brought the violence to the attention of the United States. These included the assassination of Roman Catholic Archbishop Romero in September and four churchwomen in December. The United States had backed the junta, providing it with modest amounts of military aid, but the Carter administration suspended the aid in light of the assassinations. Aid was resumed, however, when FMLN attacks intensified in early 1981 and the new Reagan administration determined to back the Salvadoran government against what it saw as the FMLN Communist threat.

Violence and displacement in El Salvador took many forms. The civil war precipitated large-scale internal displacement as well as international migration. Right-wing death squads precipitated still further movements. Young men often fled the threat of conscription into the national army or the rebel forces. The prolonged conflict destroyed homes and livelihoods, making it difficult for rural Salvadorans to survive. An estimated 1.2 to 1.8 million Salvadorans had been displaced by the mid-1980s, with an estimated 500,000–850,000 Salvadorans coming to the United States (Zolberg et al. 1989).

Major displacement in Guatemala began somewhat later than it did in the other countries. The Guatemalan military had a long-standing and unsavory reputation for committing human rights violations against citizens, with particular focus on the indigenous population. In 1977, the Carter administration suspended military aid to Guatemala. A growing insurgency, involving middle-class opponents of the regime and indigenous groups, provoked an extremely violent counterinsurgency campaign in the early 1980s. Involuntary displacement of potential supporters of the insurgency was an explicit aim of government policy. As a result, an estimated 100,000–250,000 persons were displaced inside Guatemala and an equal number became refugees in Mexico. An estimated 100,000–200,000 Guatemalans came to the United States by mid-decade (Zolberg et al. 1989).

With a new refugee definition and the rudiments of an asylum process in place, many of the Central Americans applied for refugee status upon arrival in the United States. Few applications from Salvadorans or Hondurans were granted, and the numbers of actual approvals of Nicaraguans remained small relative to the number of applicants.

The explanation for the low number of approvals is complex. Certainly, as the government agreed in a class action suit that it settled in the 1990s, foreign policy considerations were at work. Although the actual decisions about asylum were made by the INS, the State Department provided advisory opinions that were generally determinative. In almost all Salvadoran and Guatemalan cases, the State Department held that economic causes, not a well-founded fear of persecution, had motivated flight and the unwillingness to return. Unwilling to label governments that were by then allied with the United States in the fight against Communism as persecutors, the State Department effectively dismissed the claims, often in one-sentence opinions that did not even consider the information presented in the application.

Foreign policy considerations do not fully explain what happened in the Nicaraguan situation. Throughout the 1980s, it appeared as if a very high proportion of Nicaraguan applications were approved. Data released by the INS often showed that 80 percent or more of cases that had reached final decisions were approved. These data convinced many observers that Cold War foreign policy indeed continued to exert a positive influence on asylum decisions if the applicants came from a Communist-dominated country. The reality was somewhat different. The INS reached final decisions in only a fraction of the Nicaraguan cases. When it appeared that the applicant did not meet the criteria for refugee status, the file was stored away for further consideration. Only in a few cases were denials published. Many of the Nicaraguan cases in the 1980s were heard in Miami, and the INS district was concerned that large numbers of denials would inflame the Cuban community who saw the Nicaraguans as fighting a common enemy.[9] Washington decision makers had no interest in reversing the decision to defer asylum decisions (indeed, some officials actively encouraged it) since it was consistent with U.S. foreign policy interests to permit the Nicaraguans to remain in the United States.

The small number of approvals in Central American cases also resulted from the narrowness of the definition used in adjudicating claims for asylum. Asylum seekers had to demonstrate that they had a well-founded fear of persecution that was related to a specific characteristic – race, religion, nationality, membership in a particular social group, or political opinion. The determination has two aspects. First, the adjudicator must determine how well founded the applicant's fear of persecution is – whether the fear is grounded in some objective reality that the person would be subject to serious harm that rises to the level of persecution. Second, the adjudicator must determine if the persecution was because of the applicant's specific characteristics (that is., race, religion, nationality, membership in a social group, or political opinion).

Persons fleeing well-documented violence might not be able to meet this definition if the violence was not directed at them as individuals. Fighting during a civil war might cause serious harm, but the violence may well be so generalized that the individual victims could not demonstrate that they had been harmed because of one of the specified characteristics. They might have a well-founded fear of death from the fighting, but not a well-founded fear of persecution from an actor who specifically targeted them.

Recognizing that both foreign policy and legal technicalities prevented the use of asylum as the best way to offer protection to the Central Americans, advocates for the Salvadorans and Guatemalans[10] adopted a two-pronged strategy. First, they focused on Extended Voluntary Departure to provide immediate relief from deportation for the majority of asylum applicants. In addition, they took the government to court to force reforms in the asylum system.

In December 1981, Representative Ted Weiss introduced a resolution requesting that the secretary of state recommend to the attorney general "that extended voluntary departure status be granted to aliens who are nationals of El Salvador and grant such status to such aliens until the situation in El Salvador has changed sufficiently to permit their safely residing in that country (Gallagher et al. 1989). The House passed the nonbinding resolution but there was no action from the executive branch. In the meantime, Senator Edward Kennedy criticized the administration for its current policy on EVD, noting

[9] Personal communications with INS officials in Miami. On a visit to the district office, I was shown a storage room with boxes of Nicaraguan applications that had been filed, pending a final decision.

[10] This was less of an issue for the Nicaraguans since few were threatened with deportation, particularly after President Reagan encouraged them to vote with their feet against the Sandinista regime.

that EVD had been granted in similar situations in the past. In April 1983, under the leadership of Representative Joseph Moakley, eighty-six members of Congress wrote to the secretary of state asking that EVD be granted to Salvadorans because of the widespread destruction and civil strife in their country. Several other congressional resolutions passed both Houses, often attached to appropriations bills to demonstrate the seriousness with which Congress took the issue.

In April, the State Department responded to this congressional action, arguing that "While civil strife and violence in El Salvador continue at distressing levels, conditions there do not warrant the granting of blanket voluntary departure.... Moreover, Salvadorans now present in the U.S., estimated at 500,000, who were not involved in political or military activities would not, upon their return, be in greater danger than other non-combatants in El Salvador" (quoted in Gallagher et al. 1989: 37). The policy remained throughout the remainder of the decade, with the State Department explaining that "the extent of civil unrest alone does not determine the Department's view towards the granting of EVD to nationals of a particular country (Gallagher et al. 1989: 37)." Rather, immigration considerations needed to be considered because "a grant of extended voluntary departure to the Salvadorans undoubtedly would encourage the migration of many more such aliens." Even a request from President Duarte of El Salvador that his nationals be granted EVD was denied. Duarte had argued that their remittances would increase the economic stability of the country and thereby increase its political stability.

In 1984 and then again in subsequent Congresses, Representative Moakley and Senator DeConcini introduced bills to halt the deportation of Salvadorans already in the United States. First the Reagan and then the George H. W. Bush administrations opposed enactment, reporting that the human rights situation had improved in El Salvador. In the meantime, the administration stopped using EVD as a means of protection, refusing to grant it even in cases where it was unlikely that many people would be able to reach the United States.

Little progress on EVD was made until 1990 when Representative Moakley, then the Chair of the Rules Committee, threatened to derail the Immigration Act of 1990 if something were not done about the Salvadorans in particular and victims of civil war more generally. The legislative solution was Temporary Protected Status (TPS). On a purely discretionary basis, as stated in the Immigration Act of 1990, the government could provide temporary relief from deportation to persons "in the United States who are temporarily unable to safely return to their home country because of ongoing armed conflict, an environmental disaster, or other extraordinary and temporary conditions." To address concerns about the immigration-magnet effect, TPS applies only to persons already in the United States at the time of the designation. It is not meant to be a response to an unfolding crisis in which people seek admission from outside the country. The reluctance of the administration to use its discretion in favor of Salvadorans was known; the Immigration Act of 1990 required that TPS be granted to them for an 18-month period.

While the legislative process unfolded, the courts were hearing a range of suits related to the asylum system. Some of these would affect all asylum applications (and are discussed in the next section), whereas others more specifically pertained to Central Americans. The most important was the suit by the American Baptist Churches (ABC) on behalf of Salvadoran and Guatemalan asylum seekers. Litigation began in 1985, when a class action lawsuit was filed on behalf of the asylum seekers against the INS, the Department of State, and the Executive Office of Immigration Review, which heard appeals from INS decisions. The suit accused the government of discriminatory treatment of asylum claims made by Guatemalans and Salvadorans.

In 1990, the government and attorneys representing the Salvadorans and Guatemalans settled the class action lawsuit, and a federal court approved the agreement in January 1991. The ABC settlement provided that all Salvadorans who had been physically present in the United States on or before September 19, 1990, and all Guatemalans who had been physically present in the United States on or before October 1, 1990, were eligible for a new review of their asylum applications. Those whose applications had been denied were eligible as well as those who had chosen not to apply previously, knowing how few applications were approved. The government agreed to hear the cases using asylum regulations promulgated in 1990, which significantly reduced the reliance on the State Department and its consideration of foreign policy ramifications, as is discussed in the next section.

Asylum Reform

In 1990 the Cold War came to a screeching halt. The tearing down of the Berlin Wall in November 1989 signaled a fundamental shift in international relations. Soon, the countries of Eastern Europe asserted their independence from Soviet authority, throwing out Communist governments and instituting democratic reforms. Soviet experimentation with *glasnost* (openness) and *perestroika* (rebuilding) under the Gorbachev regime loosened the controls that the old Soviet state had imposed, leading to even more significant political changes with the election of Boris Yeltsin and the breakup of the Soviet Union.

Dissatisfaction with the asylum system had been building throughout the 1980s, and the altered geopolitical environment provided new opportunities for fundamental reform. The INS had taken initial steps in the late 1980s to reform the system through training the officers who heard asylum claims. The first training showed how difficult it would be to professionalize asylum adjudications within existing INS structures.[11] Most of the trainees had been hearing asylum cases along with many other petitions for some type of immigration benefit. None of them were experts on asylum, and most came from district

---

[11] This discussion is based on my own observations. In 1989, INS engaged the Refugee Policy Group to develop and implement the training program. I served as project director and principal trainer.

offices that gave low priority to these cases. On average, an asylum interview took longer than most adjudication interviews, placing pressure on already overworked staff. In some cases, the leaders of the district offices in which they worked were hostile to asylum-seekers, seeing asylum as an abusive end run around immigration processes. The situation was complicated by the fact that INS had never promulgated final regulations on asylum and the officers were still using interim regulations published in 1980.

Although most immigration adjudication required little knowledge of country conditions, the asylum decision generally depended on the credibility of the applicant in describing his or her fear of persecution in the home country. Since few asylum seekers had a letter from their country's dictator expressing the intent to persecute them, deciding cases often required research to test the validity of the claim against what was known about human rights violations in a country. Few INS officers had that information or the time to conduct such research. Therefore, they had relied heavily on the State Department advisory opinion. Legal scholar David Martin, summarized the situation: "while 'the trend is clearly toward assigning the [asylum] adjudication task to specialists, well-trained in refugee law and highly knowledgeable about conditions in source countries..., the United States has been one of the last to see the wisdom...' of such specialization" (quoted in Beyer 1992: 456).

In fact, the need for a more specialized corps of asylum officers had been recognized as early as 1981 when SCIRP (1981a) recommended the establishment of the position of "asylum admissions officer" who should be "schooled in the procedures and techniques of eligibility determinations." Proposals for a specialized corps were included in a number of proposed regulations, but generally those rules were derailed over other, more controversial issues (particularly related to the appeals process for denied asylum applications and the weight to be given to State Department advisory opinions).

In July 1990, permanent asylum regulations were finally promulgated. The regulations addressed a number of the most pressing concerns regarding asylum. First, the regulations created a new corps of professional asylum officers, who would report to the INS Assistant Commissioner for Refugees, Asylum and Parole (CORAP) rather than to INS district directors (Beyer 1992). In this way, asylum decision-making would be insulated from immigration enforcement priorities. Second, the regulations created a separate Resource Information Center (RIC) that would provide independent information about countries' political, economic, and social conditions. The regulations emphasized that the asylum officers were to use a wide range of documentation in making their decisions. The State Department advisory opinions became one among a number of sources of information. Making a decision on asylum was defined as a nonadversarial process in which the asylum officer would probe for information that both supported and undermined the asylum claim.

During the next year, the Asylum Corps was put in place under the leadership of Gregg Beyer, formerly with the U.N. High Commissioner for Refugees. As Beyer described the corps, "Over 45 percent of the Asylum Officers, all U.S.

citizens, were recruited from outside the INS while the remaining 55 percent had either previous INS or other U.S. government experience. Some of those selected had come to the United States as immigrants themselves, and a few had come as refugees or been granted status as asylees. Almost 15 percent were ex-Peace Corps volunteers" (Beyer 1992: 471).

The asylum corps was overwhelmed from its very beginning. Not only did it inherit a large caseload of applications submitted prior to the new regulations, but it also soon began to receive the ABC case applications. In February 1992, INS headquarters estimated that there would be more than 184,000 cases to be adjudicated from 1993 to 1995, taking into account current receipt of applications, the backlog, and the ABC cases (Beyer 1992). This number of cases was well above the projected number of completed applications, even before many of the asylum officers were diverted to Guantanamo. By 1993, when the asylum system once more came under policy scrutiny, the backlogs had grown to 425,000 cases, raising serious concerns that are discussed in Chapter 12.

Refugee Resettlement in the Post–Cold War Era

While the end of the Cold War marked an opportunity for reform in an asylum system accused of placing foreign policy interests above refugee protection, it marked a different type of challenge for the refugee resettlement system. Cold War policies and anti-Communist ideology had provided a rationale during the post–World War II era for generous refugee admissions from abroad, even when immigration policies were at their most restrictive. That situation did not change markedly during the more liberal immigration of the 1980s. Although the Refugee Act eliminated the ideological underpinnings of the refugee definition, resettlement tended to focus on refugees who had been displaced by the various proxy conflicts that marked the Cold War. The United States continued to admit large numbers of refugees from Southeast Asia but smaller allocations were made for Ethiopians, Afghans, Iranians, Iraqis, Poles, and Romanians. As late as 1994, well after the end of the Cold War, 80 percent of resettled refugees were from Southeast Asia and the former Soviet Union (U.S. Commission on Immigration Reform 1995).

In fact, the geopolitical changes initially led to an increase in refugee admissions from the Soviet Union and its successor states. Jews and members of other religious minorities, particularly Christian Evangelicals, had a new opportunity to leave when the Soviet authorities began to loosen restrictions on movement. As the numbers mounted, however, many of those seeking admission to the United States were denied admission as refugees because of the very changed circumstances that had allowed them to exit. Yet, there were significant concerns that the political instability in Russia and its neighbors would lead to a new outburst of anti-Semitic activity, as had occurred historically. Senator Frank Lautenberg introduced an amendment to the 1990 Foreign Operations Appropriations Bill that required that the attorney general, in consultation with the secretary of state, develop standard profiles "which would identify applicants with a strong likelihood of qualifying for admission as refugees due to well established histories of persecution." These profiles would apply to "Soviet nationals who are Jews or Evangelical Christians or Ukrainian Catholics or Ukrainian Orthodox, and holders of Letters of Introduction in the Orderly Departure Program in Vietnam." The Lautenberg amendment, which has been reintroduced in subsequent Congresses, gave a strong presumption of refugee status to the listed groups, specifying that persons in this group could demonstrate "acts of persecution committed against other persons in his or her standard profile, in his or her geographical locale, or acts, regardless of locale, which give rise to a well-founded fear of persecution." Historical patterns of persecution against the group, rather than the individual, could thus be used as evidence to support a future well-founded fear, allowing persons from the listed groups to qualify for admission to the United States.

Although the Lautenberg Amendment meant that refugees from the Soviet Union and Vietnam would continue to enter the United States, questions arose as to what criteria for admission would be used in the post-Cold War period. Not surprisingly, the responses generally came in reaction to specific refugee crises. Most notably, in the aftermath of the first Gulf War, the United States admitted Iraqi refugees who were in camps in Saudi Arabia. In fact, in the first years of the 1990s, admission ceilings went up, reaching a high of 142,000 in 1993. Then began a steady decline, however, reaching new lows in both ceilings and actual admissions in 2002, following the terrorist attacks on the World Trade Center and the Pentagon. That story is told in Chapter 12.

Conclusion

The 1980s marked an eventful era in U.S. refugee and asylum policy. For most of the decade, the United States struggled between a commitment to a universalistic notion of refugee protection, based on international human rights standards, and lingering foreign policy and domestic constituency interests that defined who would be admitted. In keeping with the Massachusetts model, the United States accepted with great generosity refugees who were fleeing from Communist regimes or had been allied with the United States in conflicts rooted in the Cold War. Refugees from Cuba, Southeast Asia, and the Soviet Union were welcomed on this basis. President Reagan's recall of John Winthrop's phrase in calling the United States "a shining city on the hill" gave testament to the Massachusetts model's continuing endurance (Farewell Address).

The response was anything but welcoming, however, to those who stood outside the model. Haitians, Salvadorans and Guatemalans found a mostly closed door. Leaving countries that were closely allied with the United States, their admission served no foreign policy interest. More pointedly, these would-be immigrants came from countries in close proximity to the United States, with histories of illegal immigration. Concerns about immigration surges overrode concerns about human rights and refugee protection in formulating official policy. Echoing the policies of the 1930s, the U.S. decision to return Haitians, without even giving a cursory examination of their reasons for flight, marked a low point in modern asylum policy.

Unlike in earlier periods, however, advocates of refugee protection were more successful in reversing the policies. A broad coalition of civil rights and civil liberties groups, allied with religious institutions, pressed in the courts and in Congress for more consistent standards in adjudicating asylum applications and for at least temporary protection for persons fleeing conflict – regardless of foreign policy interests. The promulgation of asylum regulations in 1990 and the establishment of a specialized asylum corps marked a major step toward delinking refugee protection from ideology. As with the legal immigration reforms of 1990 discussed in Chapter 10, some of these advances would be severely challenged in the next decade as national security concerns overcame human rights standards in the implementation of U.S. refugee policy.

12

The Pennsylvania Model at Risk

1993–2009

Within a few short years of the 1990 changes in immigration and refugee policy, the country was turning away from the Pennsylvania model of immigration. This chapter begins with a discussion of the renewed growth in unauthorized migration after the IRCA legalization and the failure of the United States to address it. In many respects, the high level of tolerance for unauthorized migration represents a return to the Virginia model of disposable workers with few rights. But that tolerance came at a price when numbers increased. Illegal immigration became a divisive issue in the 1994 elections when California adopted Proposition 187, which would have restricted the access of unauthorized immigrants, including children, to basic emergency services and education. The chapter discusses continuing efforts at the state and local levels to address unauthorized migration, including Arizona's passage of legislation in 2010 that sparked widespread opposition and efforts by the federal government to preempt implementation.

As the economy boomed in the late 1990s, Immigration and Naturalization Service officials indicated that they would not conduct workplace raids. In part, this decision reflected frustration with the overall inadequacy of sanctions on employers as a mechanism for enforcing immigration laws. However, the hands-off policy was also based on recognition that aggressive workplace enforcement resulted in attacks from powerful constituencies when the unemployment rate was the lowest in decades. Worksite enforcement remains a controversial issue, with periodic announcements from the successor agency to the INS, Immigration and Customs Enforcement in the Department of Homeland Security, about new measures, but little in the way of sustained attention to factors that attract unauthorized workers. This chapter discusses the failures of repeated Congresses to make reforms in immigration policies that would either address the situation of those already in the country illegally or stem future movements of unauthorized workers.[1]

[1] For an excellent set of essays on the contemporary debate on immigration policy in the United States, see Swain (2008).

Also discussed is the growth in temporary worker programs, a further manifestation of the Virginia model. The United States has a complex set of temporary worker programs, each referred to by the subsection of the law that authorizes the admissions. The most prominent programs are the H-1B program for professionals and the H-2A and H-2B programs for farm workers and unskilled workers in nonfarm work, respectively. The chapter focuses in particular on the growing reliance of the information technology industry on the H-1B program in the later 1990s and early 2000s, and on the growing backlog of persons awaiting visas for permanent admissions. This chapter discusses the debate in Congress about reforms proposed, but not enacted, to augment still further the use of temporary worker programs.

The chapter then presents changes in the rights of legal permanent residents, focusing on the 1996 antiterrorism, immigration, and welfare reform bills. With regard to due process rights, two pieces of legislation are at issue: the Antiterrorism and Effective Death Penalty Act and the Illegal Immigration Reform and Immigrant Responsibility Act (IIRIRA). Although most of the provisions of these two laws are directed to controlling illegal aliens, both made significant changes in the rights of legal immigrants as well. Of most concern is the curtailment of due process in removal hearings involving aliens, whether they entered legally or illegally. In combination with the Personal Responsibility and Work Opportunity Reconciliation Act (Welfare Reform Act), IIRIRA also reduced substantially the access of legal immigrants to public benefit programs that are available to citizens. Although parts of these laws have since been amended, the reversals generally pertain to retroactive application of the new standards to immigrants who were in the United States at the time of passage. The significant derogation from the social rights of legal immigrants entering now and in the future has not changed. These changes marked a major shift in policy. In previous periods of U.S. history, legal immigrants had access to most social benefits on the same basis as citizens. The Pennsylvania model generally saw immigrants as presumptive citizens, with most of the same rights held by citizens except for the franchise; the new legislation placed legal permanent residents at a distinct disadvantage relative to citizens.

A final section reviews post–September 11 developments that have put further pressure on notions of immigrant integration and belonging. Among the issues covered are the actions taken immediately after the terrorist acts to detain and apply special registration requirements to foreign nationals from Arab and Muslim countries. The chapter also examines provisions of the Patriot Act that eased deportation and restricted admission of refugees and others accused of providing material support to terrorists, even when that support was coerced.

Illegal Immigration

The problem of illegal immigration erupted in 1993 with a series of events that brought national attention to the issue just after the change in administrations. The so-called nanny-gate fiasco derailed the first two nominees for attorney general, when prominent attorney Zoe Baird and federal judge Kimba

Wood admitted to having hired undocumented workers as nannies for their children. Three further incidents linked illegal migration to broader security concerns. Mir Aimal Kasi, who opened fire outside the headquarters of the Central Intelligence Agency on January 25, had entered the country with false documentation. Then, Ramzi Yousef, one of the architects of the World Trade Center bombing in February 1993, was found to have been apprehended at Kennedy Airport but released from detention when he applied for asylum. Finally, in June 1993, the ship *Golden Venture* ran aground in New York with almost 300 Chinese migrants attempting illegal entry. This proved to be the tip of a much larger global smuggling and trafficking problem.

In California, the concerns about illegal immigration were taking the shape of a political movement. The United States–Mexico border appeared to be a free entry zone with no controls over illegal migration. Photos of large numbers of migrants racing by foot up Interstate Highway 5, the major route which runs from the Mexican to the Canadian border, became stock footage on U.S. news reports. Reflecting growing dissatisfaction with the federal government's apparent inability to control the border, California activists responded by introducing Proposition 187. The preamble summarized their concerns: "The People of California find and declare as follows: That they have suffered and are suffering economic hardship caused by the presence of illegal aliens in this state. That they have suffered and are suffering personal injury and damage caused by the criminal conduct of illegal aliens in this state. That they have a right to the protection of their government from any person or persons entering this country unlawfully."[2] Proposition 187 required state and local law enforcement agencies to cooperate with federal authorities in administering immigration law. Several California jurisdictions had pointedly refused such cooperation, arguing that it impeded the ability of the police to protect immigrant communities that would not report or cooperate in investigating crimes if they thought it might lead to deportation.

Proposition 187 also barred undocumented immigrants from a range of public services, with the exception of emergency medical assistance. In what may have been the most controversial provision, the bar extended to public primary and secondary education. A 1982 Supreme Court decision, *Plyler v. Doe*, guaranteed the right of all children, including undocumented immigrants, to public education. The Supreme Court had determined that children should not be punished for the decisions of their parents to come to the United States illegally. Supporters of Proposition 187 felt they were sending a powerful message to the federal government to gain control over illegal immigration. Opponents saw the proposition as a mean-spirited assault on undocumented immigrants but not a serious effort to get at the underlying factors at work.

By the early 1990s, unauthorized immigration was indeed on the rise. After levels of illegal immigration had tapered off in the late 1980s, mostly because of the IRCA legalization discussed in Chapter 10, it was becoming apparent that

---

[2] http://www.usc.edu/libraries/archives/ethnicstudies/historicdocs/prop187.txt.

IRCA's laxly implemented enforcement measures were doing little to deter new arrivals from crossing the border or from gaining employment. Using methods similar to those pioneered by the Census Bureau in its 1980 analysis, the INS estimated that at the end of 1992 there were about 3.9 million persons living in the United States without authorization. The agency estimated that the net population of unauthorized persons was increasing by almost 300,000 each year. The majority were from Mexico, but other countries that contributed sizable populations included El Salvador, Guatemala, Canada, and Haiti (Haines and Rosenblum 1999). California was the principal destination of the undocumented, followed by Texas, New York, Florida, and Illinois.

During the 1990s, as is the case today, unauthorized entry occurred in a number of different ways. Most of those illegally in the United States were believed to have entered clandestinely, largely across the land border with Mexico although others arrived by sea, often in makeshift boats or rafts. A sizable minority (estimated as high as 40–45 percent) entered through recognized ports of entry. Many did so having obtained legitimate visas, often as tourists, and then overstayed the period that the visa covered. Some obtained a border crossing card or longer-term visa that did not permit employment, and then worked in contravention of the terms of their admission. In still other cases, migrants entered as temporary workers but failed to leave when their period of work authorization ended. In some cases, migrants sought visas knowing that they planned to violate the terms. In other cases, the migrants had no initial intention of overstaying or working illegally, but circumstances changed, their stay was prolonged, and they entered into irregular status.

Some of those who entered after having been inspected by immigration officials used fraudulent documents, including counterfeit passports, visas, and other identity documents. Still others entered with "impostor" documents that belonged to people who bore a superficial likeness to their own appearance. These included documents possessed by family or friends who were legally in the country, and documents purchased for the specific purpose of gaining admission. As with those who came clandestinely, the migrants who entered with inspection often obtained their documents through smugglers.

IRCA had attempted to deal with all of these forms of illegal migration, focusing on the one common element – the employment magnet. Employer sanctions had done little to curb employment of undocumented workers, however, because of a faulty employment verification system. As discussed in Chapter 10, workers had to present documents demonstrating identity and work authorization. Most workers used a combination of drivers' licenses to show their identity and Social Security cards to demonstrate they had work authorization. Neither form of documentation was particularly secure. Many drivers' licenses had no photographs and the Social Security card was a paper document that was issued at birth or during childhood to most citizens. These forms of identity were easily forged, shared, or stolen.

The proliferation of fraudulent documents allowed employers to hire unauthorized workers with little risk of sanction. Employers were not expected to weed out the counterfeits if the documents looked valid on their face. In fact, if an employer requested additional documentation, he or she faced penalties imposed to ensure that employers did not discriminate against foreign-looking or -sounding workers.

U.S. Commission on Immigration Reform (CIR)

As public outcry about the loss of control over immigration grew, a new federal commission began its investigations. The Immigration Act of 1990 had authorized the Commission on Legal Immigration Reform, which was mandated to examine the impact of the changes in legal admissions on the U.S. economy and society. The legislation specified that the chair would be appointed by the president (then George Herbert Walker Bush) and the remaining members would be chosen by the House and Senate majority and minority leadership.[3] The congressionally appointed members would serve for the duration of the commission (till December 31, 1997), but the chair would serve at the discretion of the president, which gave President Clinton the opportunity to name his own chair to succeed Cardinal Bernard Law, Catholic Archbishop of Boston. Susan Martin who had been research director of SCIRP, was appointed staff director of the commission. With the change of administration, Cardinal Law indicated an interest in remaining as chair, but it was months before the Clinton administration focused on appointments to federal commissions. After hearing nothing from the White House for several months, Cardinal Law submitted his formal resignation.

Even before the commission began its work, its mandate was broadened by Congress. Dropping "Legal" from its title, the commission was asked to examine the issue of illegal immigration. In the meantime, the Clinton administration was taking initial steps toward addressing the problem. The White House had nominated Doris Meissner, an expert on immigration affairs who had a great deal of inside experience with the agencies responsible for immigration, to serve as commissioner of the Immigration and Naturalization Service. She had served in the Justice Department in the Carter administration and in the INS during the Reagan administration. The vice president headed a taskforce assigned the responsibility of recommending new policies. The taskforce primarily tackled the problems raised by the Golden Venture episode and proposed legislation to bring the racketeering statutes to bear on human smuggling operations.

As the immigration issue heated up, the appointment of a new commission chair was seen by the administration as a way to demonstrate how seriously it

---

[3] The congressional choices did not follow clear partisan lines. The Senate Democrats chose Lawrence Fuchs, who had directed SCIRP, and Nelson Merced, the first Hispanic to hold statewide office in Massachusetts. The Senate Republicans chose Michael Teitelbaum, a demographer who had long worked on immigration issues, and Richard Estrada, associate editor, *Dallas Morning News*; neither identified themselves as Republicans. The House Democrats chose Bruce Morrison, former chair of the immigration subcommittee, who had lost his bid for governor of Connecticut, and Warren Leiden, the president of the American Immigration Lawyers Association. The House Republicans chose Harold Ezell, a former regional commissioner of the INS, and Robert Charles Hill, a practicing attorney who had worked on asylum issues in the Bush administration.

regarded the problem. A decidedly short list of potential candidates was narrowed by the White House to Barbara Jordan, the former member of Congress from Texas who had galvanized the country in her keynote address at the Democratic conventions in 1976 and 1992. As a young House member during the Watergate hearings, she had spoken eloquently of her view of American civic values as the first African American woman in Congress:

> Earlier today, we heard the beginning of the Preamble to the Constitution of the United States: "We, the people" It's a very eloquent beginning. But when that document was completed on the seventeenth of September in 1787, I was not included in that "We, the people." I felt somehow for many years that George Washington and Alexander Hamilton just left me out by mistake. But through the process of amendment, interpretation, and court decision, I have finally been included in "We, the people."

Jordan was committed to bringing other minorities into the American fold. She was particularly proud of having introduced federal legislation that extended the Voting Rights Act to Hispanic Americans.

Despite initial reluctance, Jordan accepted nomination as chair of the commission because of her concern that the issue of immigration was threatening to divide the country.[4] President Clinton summarized what she brought to the debate: "I have chosen Barbara Jordan, one of the most well respected people in America, to chair this Commission because immigration is one of the most important and complex issues facing our country today.... I am confident that Congresswoman Jordan will use her prodigious talents to thoughtfully address the challenges posed by immigration reform, balance the variety of competing interests, and recommend policies that will be in our country's best interests."[5]

Soon after the commission commenced work under its new leadership, the Clinton administration adopted new border-control strategies to try to halt unauthorized entries. Operations "Hold the Line" in El Paso and "Gatekeeper" in San Diego succeeded in slowing movements in these locations, but the illegal crossings just moved to other parts of the border. Crossings became more expensive and, in some locations, more dangerous, but most of those who were serious about entering the United States succeeded in doing so. The enhanced border enforcement also resulted in greater use of professional smugglers who, in turn, developed more elaborate operations to bring migrants through rugged terrain that remained beyond the scope of the Border Patrol's fences and personnel.

In its first report to Congress, issued on September 30, 1994, the commission supported the new border measures but determined that "reducing the employment magnet is the linchpin of a comprehensive strategy to reduce illegal immigration. The ineffectiveness of employer sanctions, prevalence of fraudulent

---

[4] Personal communication with Barbara Jordan prior to her appointment. During the conversation, Jordan evidenced increasing interest in learning just what role the commission might play in providing a reasoned analysis to combat what she feared would be growing xenophobia.

[5] http://www.presidency.ucsb.edu/ws/index.php?pid=46238.

documents, and continued high numbers of unauthorized workers, combined with confusion for employers and reported discrimination against employees, have challenged the credibility of current worksite enforcement efforts" (U.S. Commission on Immigration Reform 1994: xii). The commission recognized that if employers could easily hire unauthorized workers, with no fear of effective sanctions, the jobs they offered would lure increasingly larger numbers of unauthorized workers. Many employers would not knowingly break the law to hire unauthorized workers, but they would take advantage of weaknesses in the law to get the workers they sought.

Crucial to reducing illegal immigration, then, was the implementation of a more secure form of employment verification. Since experts reported that all document-based systems were vulnerable to increasingly sophisticated technology, such as color copiers, CIR concluded that an electronic verification system was needed to double-check the validity of the information provided. The commission recommended pilot-testing various approaches to determine the best mix of documents and electronic verification.

The commission's recommendations were met with controversy. The arguments heard during the IRCA debate resumed. Fears that electronic verification would lead inevitably to a national ID card were raised although CIR had pointedly excluded a new document-based system from its recommendation and made clear that the electronic system should be used for no purpose other than employment verification. Legitimate concerns about data protection, privacy, and quality had led to the recommendation for pilot-testing, with the commission acknowledging that there were no systems in place to ensure the accuracy of the verification process.

The 1994 report also addressed the issues under consideration in Proposition 187. The discussion among the commissioners was tricky because a number of them had made known their views on the proposition, with Barbara Jordan and several other commissioners publicly opposing it and Commissioner Harold Ezell of California actively supporting it (*Migration News* 1994). The language of the commission's recommendations enabled it to navigate a pathway through the political minefield that could have destroyed its consensus on other issues. Ezell agreed that with the reforms recommended by the commission, Proposition 187 would not be needed. He voted with the majority on a broad set of criteria to govern eligibility of unauthorized immigrants for public benefits: "illegal aliens should not be eligible for any publicly funded services or assistance except those made available on an emergency basis or for similar compelling reasons to protect public health and safety (e.g., immunizations and school lunch and other child nutrition programs) or to conform to constitutional requirements." The last phrase referred to children's education, a focus of Proposition 187. *Plyler v. Doe* had held that children's education was protected under the Fourteenth Amendment of the Constitution.[6]

---

[6] Texas tried to argue that undocumented children were not "persons" under the Fourteenth Amendment's equal protection clause. In the 5–4 majority decision, Justice Brennan cited earlier

By the time of the commission's 1994 report, the eligibility of *legal* immigrants for public benefits was also on the public policy agenda. The impetus to restrict eligibility was largely budgetary, but there were also concerns that post-legalization immigrants, because of lower skills and wages, would mean higher demand for programs that were aimed at the working poor, such as food stamps. Moreover, policies in the 1980s that encouraged poor elderly immigrants to apply for Supplementary Security Income, if they were ineligible for regular Social Security payments, had resulted in a notable increase in their enrollment in the program. In contrast with Social Security, which required that participants or their spouses work at least 40 quarters before gaining eligibility, SSI determined eligibility on the basis of need, not work experience. Most U.S. citizens qualified for Social Security by the time they reach 65 years of age, but a sizable proportion of immigrants, particularly those arriving at more advanced ages, never qualify for the regular program.

The commission was unequivocal in its recommendation on this issue: "The Commission recommends against any broad, categorical denial of public benefits to legal immigrants. The United States admits legal immigrants with the expectation that they will reside permanently in the United States as productive residents. Therefore, the Commission believes that . . . the safety net provided by needs-tested programs should continue to be available to those whom we have affirmatively accepted as legal immigrants into our communities" (U.S. Commission on Immigration Reform 1994). The commission rejected unequal treatment of citizens and legal immigrants in access to public programs, but did recommend a tightening of the affidavit of support that families signed before their relatives could be admitted so that fewer immigrants would need public assistance. Nevertheless, the commissioners understood that there were unanticipated events that might impede an immigrant's ability to support him or herself, or a sponsor's ability to offer help to an indigent immigrant.

Jordan was particularly concerned about the debasement of citizenship if social rights were tied to citizenship. In testimony before the Ways and Means Committee of the U.S. House of Representatives, she stated: "I believe firmly that citizenship in this country is something to be cherished and protected. I want all immigrants to become citizens. I want them to seek citizenship because it is the key to full participation in our political community, to know first hand and understand the American form of democracy. I want unnecessary barriers to naturalization – and there are many of them – to be removed. *However, I do not want immigrants to seek citizenship because it is the only route to our safety nets. To me, that would be a debasement of our notions of citizenship*" (Jordan 1994).

The commission also emphasized that responsible immigration policy meant a system of mutual obligations that the welfare reform changes would undermine: "Immigrants must accept the obligations we impose – to obey our laws, to

---

cases that had determined that aliens within the country were covered under the amendments due process provisions. He concluded that there "is simply no support for [the] suggestion that 'due process' is somehow of greater stature than 'equal protection'. . . . " (Olivas 2005: 209).

pay taxes, to respect other cultures and ethnic groups. At the same time, citizens incur obligations to provide an environment in which newcomers can become fully participating members of our society" (U.S. Commission on Immigration Reform 1997). The commission thought it especially hypocritical to admit low-wage workers and then deny them access to programs designed for the working poor. This stance – that legal immigrants should be eligible for the same social rights as citizens – influenced the commission's thinking throughout the rest of its term.

The commission further emphasized that enforcement of immigration laws, especially as they related to removals, should comply with due process. The commission recommended initiatives to expand legal representation for immigrants and to test alternatives to detention. Although highly critical of the failure of the Immigration and Naturalization Service to identify and remove immigrants with final orders of deportation, the Commission concluded that the problem was in how the programs were managed, rather than an excess of legal protections for the undocumented. Thus, although the commission supported increased deportations, particularly of those who committed criminal acts, the commission believed such removals could be accomplished without reducing the right to due process under the law.

Having launched its recommendations on illegal immigration, the commission turned to legal immigration. The CIR members had been largely in agreement that illegal immigration was problematic and came to ready agreement in 1994 on most of its recommendations. The same was not true regarding legal immigration, on which views ranged from expansive to restrictive. There was agreement, however, on two points. The first was that immigration embodied American values in a number of important ways. In the letter of transmittal of the report to Congress, Jordan summarized the overall view of the commission: "The United States is the most successful multiethnic nation in history. It has united immigrants and their descendants from all over the world around a commitment to democratic ideals and constitutional principles. Those ideals and principles have been embraced by persons from an extraordinary variety of religious and ethnic backgrounds, partly because they permit and protect religious and cultural diversity within a framework of national political unity" (U.S. Commission on Immigration Reform 1995). Even if there were differences among the commissioners on appropriate levels of immigration, there was no disagreement that, on balance, immigration was in the national interest of the United States.

The second agreement was that priorities should drive numbers and not the reverse. This was a surprisingly new perspective on immigration. Since 1924, annual quotas were established first and the preference system helped determine who would be admitted within those quotas. The 1990 legislative debate had taken place within that context, with Senator Alan Simpson wanting a firm quota and agreeing reluctantly to one that could be modified in the interests of family reunification.

The commission found the quota approach problematic because it meant managing migration through backlogs and waiting lists in almost all categories.

The members were particularly concerned about the multiyear wait in the second family preference (for spouses and minor children of legal permanent immigrants). At the time of the commission's deliberations in 1995, there were more than one million applications in the backlog but only about 90,000 visas per year for this category. The fourth family preference, for siblings of U.S. citizens, was even more backlogged, with 1.6 million on the waiting list and only 65,000 visas per year.

The commission did not propose eliminating quotas altogether but recommended redefining priorities and setting quotas to match the priorities. The commission recommended a backlog clearance program to admit all of the spouses and minor children over five years. Added to existing quotas, the commission's recommendations would have led to increased immigration during that period. Thereafter, visa numbers would be lower but still set so that all immediate relatives of U.S. citizens (spouses, minor children, and parents) and all spouses and minor children of legal permanent immigrants would be admitted within one year of the "anchor" immigrant's application. The commission concluded that 400,000 visas, plus backlog clearance, would accomplish that goal during the next five years. Quotas for employment-based admissions and refugees would also be set to match demand in priority categories. The commission recommended that the diversity program be eliminated altogether and those visas transferred to the backlog clearance program.

There were three especially controversial areas in the CIR recommendations. The first was that the commission defined family more narrowly than existing law did and urged eliminating the sibling and adult children categories. The commission gave spouses and minor children a clear priority over other family relationships, arguing that "no adult child or sibling should enter while someone's spouse and minor child is waiting" (U.S. Commission on Immigration Reform 1995). To the commission, the waiting periods in the sibling category, in particular, showed the deficiency of a legal admission system that offered a promise of admission to many more than could be accommodated. Because of preference and per-country limits, the siblings admitted in 1995 from the Philippines – the country with the worst backlog – had applied for admission in 1977. To proponents of a broader definition of family reunification, elimination of the categories for adult children and siblings of U.S. citizens was a violation of basic principles of family reunification. Asian ethnic organizations, in particular, argued that in many cultures siblings were as important as spouses and age had no bearing on basic family values. If it was desirable to speed up reunification of immediate relatives, and many agreed it was, this process should not come at the expense of adult children and siblings.

The commission's recommendations on labor migration were also controversial. After clearance of backlogs from the old third preference system in 1993 and 1994, admissions had settled to a level well below the quota of 140,000. The commission found "requests from employers averaged about 90,000 per year; our review of FY 1995 data indicate no increase during this past year." Reflecting demand, the commission recommended that employment-based admissions be set at 100,000 visas per year. The commission also recommended a new way to test the labor market's demand for visas. Instead of labor certification, a cumbersome system in which employers had to recruit for a minimally qualified U.S. worker, often to fill a job already filled by the foreign worker for whom the employer was petitioning, the commission recommended a market-based approach. Demand would be tested by the willingness of an employer to pay a substantial fee to gain access to a foreign worker. The logic was simple. If an employer had to pay more to hire a foreign worker than a comparable domestic worker, there would be no incentive to hire the foreign worker over the domestic one. The fee would then be used to increase "the competitiveness of U.S. workers, for example through education and training"(U.S. Commission on Immigration Reform 1995). Business interests opposed these changes on two grounds. One, they did not want any lowering of admission levels; even if many of the visas were not now used, they might be in the future. Second, although they were highly critical of the labor certification process, it was a known evil that companies and their legal representatives had learned to use. The new labor market test might be more efficient, but it was considered too risky.

In addition, with regard to labor migration, the commission came out strongly against an expanded agricultural workers program. In perhaps the strongest language used in its 1995 report, the commission said that "revisiting the 'bracero agreement,' is not in the national interest and unanimously and strongly agrees that such a program would be a grievous mistake" (U.S. Commission on Immigration Reform 1995). Speaking more broadly, the commission concluded: "guestworker programs are predicated on limitations on the freedom of those who are invited to enter and work. Experience has shown that such limitations are incompatible with the values of democratic societies worldwide."

The third controversial area surrounded refugee admissions. The Refugee Act of 1980 had established a "normal flow" number of 50,000 admissions per year that could be admitted without consultation between the president and Congress. Only if the president wanted to exceed the normal flow would the consultation process be triggered. The provision applied only during the first three years of the Refugee Act's implementation. During that period, the admission levels greatly exceeded the normal flow level. The commission recommended reverting to the normal flow concept for regular admissions. The consultation process would remain if the president deemed it necessary to admit more than 50,000 refugees per year, and the emergency consultation process would remain unchanged if a mid-year crisis occurred.

In recommending a return to a normal flow concept, the commission sought to remove the links between refugee admissions and the foreign policy and domestic constituency interests that still dominated the consultation process. As late as 1995, 80 percent of refugee admissions continued to be from Southeast Asia and the former Soviet Union. When these programs ended, the residual number of admissions each year would be far below the 50,000 level that the sponsors of the Refugee Act had anticipated. Reestablishing a normal flow would guarantee a floor on refugee admissions. CIR also attempted to set out a post–Cold War logic to resettlement, recommending that "resettlement criteria should take into account the protection of refugees who otherwise would be endangered in a country of origin or asylum and who would have no other alternatives" (U.S. Commission on Immigration Reform 1995).

Most organizations that advocated on behalf of refugees disagreed with the Commission's recommendations regarding refugee admission numbers. They saw the 50,000 "normal" flow as a derogation of U.S. commitments because the actual number of admissions still exceeded that level. Realists among them argued that only by linking refugee admissions to foreign policy interests would there be sufficient support for resettlement to maintain sizable admissions levels. They saw the consultations as a positive process because it raised the visibility of refugee admissions and provided the opportunity for voluntary agencies and religious groups, in particular, to advocate in favor of generous refugee policies.

One of the commission's recommendations generated very little notice at the time. In keeping with its belief that priorities should generate numbers, CIR recommended that immigration quotas be reassessed and revised, if needed, every three to five years. The 1952 quotas remained in place for 13 years and the 1965 annual quotas had remained essentially the same for 25 years before the 1990 law set higher limits. Yet, economic and other conditions had changed during these lengthy periods. CIR concluded "an effectively regulated system requires some flexibility with regard to numbers so as to permit adjustment as circumstances in the United States change" (U.S. Commission on Immigration Reform 1995).

The commission released its report on legal immigration on June 7, 1995. After a meeting between President Clinton and Barbara Jordan, the White House released a statement of support for the recommendations: "Consistent with my own views, the Commission's recommendations are pro-family, pro-work, pro-naturalization. As with the Commission's first report on illegal immigration, which we are now aggressively implementing, the Commission has again laid out a roadmap for the Congress to consider. It appears to reflect a balanced immigration policy that makes the most of our diversity while protecting the American workforce so that we can better compete in the emerging global economy."[7] During the briefing, the President seemed in particular agreement with the Commission's view, articulated strongly by Jordan, that the number of immigrants to be admitted was less crucial as the measure of a generous immigration policy than the rights and opportunities accorded to the newcomers.[8]

The commission's recommendation to launch a new Americanization program fit into this category. Recognizing that the term Americanization retained negative connotations, Jordan (1995b) acknowledged "that word earned a bad

---

[7] http://www.presidency.ucsb.edu/ws/index.php?pid=51453&st=Commission&st1=Immigration.

[8] This is based on my observations during the briefing.

reputation when it was stolen by racists and xenophobes in the 1920s. But it is our word, and we are taking it back." Jordan summarized the essence of the new Americanization approach in testimony before Congress in July 1995: "Cultural and religious diversity does not pose a threat to the national interest as long as public policies ensure civic unity. Such policies should help newcomers learn to speak, read, and write English effectively. They should strengthen civic education in the teaching of American history for all Americans. They should lead to the vigorous enforcement of laws against hate crimes and of laws to deter and to punish discrimination. Of course, such policies should encourage the naturalization of immigrants as the path to full civic participation" (Jordan 1995b). The commission further defined Americanization as the "process of integration by which immigrants become part of our communities and by which our communities and the nation learn from and adapt to their presence" (U.S. Commission on Immigration Reform 1997). In its 1997 report to Congress, the commission expanded on these notions, recommending a public–private partnership to support enhanced language training and civics courses for immigrants, along with programs to help communities address local challenges deriving from settlement of immigrants.[9]

In many respects, the Commission on Immigration Reform reiterated the views that had underpinned the policies of the 1980s. Along with its predecessor, the Select Commission, CIR recommended closing the back door on illegal immigration and keeping the front door open. Like SCIRP, it favored permanent immigration over temporary admissions, providing a strong endorsement of full membership of immigrants in American society. In formulating its recommendations, however, CIR took on many of the most controversial issues in immigration reform in a manner that the more politically attuned SCIRP commissioners had rejected. Of particular concern to critics of CIR's recommendations was the elimination of three categories of family-based immigration – adult unmarried children, adult married children, and brothers and sisters of U.S. citizens.

Hence, although CIR recommended an expansion in legal immigration for five years, with an additional 150,000 visas for backlog clearance and a mechanism to adjust the numbers thereafter, its report on legal admissions was widely touted by supporters and opponents alike as supporting restrictionist policies. Its basic argument – that priorities and rights are more important than numbers – failed to persuade policymakers or immigration interest groups.[10]

---

9   The commission's 1997 report also made recommendations for structural change in the federal agencies responsible for immigration, to be discussed later in this chapter. The recommendations on Americanization are discussed in greater detail in Chapter 13.

10   Daniel Tichenor (2002: 276) placed Barbara Jordan in the category of "nationalist Egalitarian" in his analysis of attitudes about immigration numbers and alien rights. Members of this category believe that alien admissions should be restricted but alien rights should be expanded. Although it is debatable whether Jordan supported restrictions in numbers (as discussed below, the commission actually recommended an increase in immigration), she clearly gave higher priority to rights than she did to numbers.

Most of its recommendations on combating illegal immigration were adopted administratively, and, in the case of verification of work authorization, through legislated pilot programs. Its legal immigration recommendations and its views on the eligibility of legal immigrants for public benefits were soundly rejected, however, in the round of legislation that went through Congress in 1996, as discussed later.

The Legislative Debate in 1996

The 1994 election heralded a major shift in congressional politics when the Republicans secured control of the House of Representatives after years of being in the minority and regained control of the Senate. The new chairs of the immigration subcommittees were Alan Simpson in the Senate and Lamar Smith in the House. Both chairs repeatedly referred to the CIR's recommendations although their legislation differed and, in some cases, repudiated the commission in a number of ways, not least of all in treatment of the rights of legal immigrants.

The legislation introduced by both chairs addressed illegal immigration and legal admissions in one omnibus bill.[11] On illegal migration, although in somewhat different forms, they authorized additional border patrol agents and provided for other enhancements in border enforcement, such as fences and technology. They ratcheted up penalties against human smuggling and document fraud. Electronic verification of employment authorization was mandated.

In both cases, the provisions on legal immigration proved more controversial than those on illegal entries during committee and full floor debate. Smith initially proposed reductions in family, employment, and refugee admissions, but offered to leave the employment numbers unchanged if business interests would support the bill. Simpson's bill would have reduced employment visas to 90,000 per year. It also included the fee that the commission had proposed, but added it to the existing labor certification procedures rather than substitute it for what the commission had seen as an unworkable system. Simpson belatedly also offered to delete his employment provisions to gain business backing. Both bills proposed an annual cap on refugee admissions and elimination of the diversity program. The bills also tightened sponsorship requirements for legal immigrants admitted in the family categories.

A coalition of libertarians, business interests, immigration attorneys, and liberal ethnic and civil rights groups (sometimes called the left–right coalition) joined together to block the changes that would have affected the legal admissions system. Their strategy was to decouple the two parts of the bills, arguing that they raised different issues and should be addressed separately. The argument gained momentum in the Senate when Republicans Spencer Abraham and Michael DeWine joined with Senator Edward Kennedy to kill the legal immigration reforms that Simpson had introduced. On the floor of the House,

[11] For a detailed discussion of the legislative debates and processes in 1996, see Gimpel and Edwards (1999).

a bipartisan amendment offered by Democrat Howard Berman and Republicans Dick Chrysler and Sam Brownback accomplished the same purpose.

Once the legal admissions provisions were stripped from the bills, they moved more readily through Congress. The House bill was approved in March and the Senate bill in May 1996. The two houses approved a number of different measures that had to be reconciled, both with each other and with the administration's preferences for immigration reform. Perhaps the most controversial was an amendment offered by Elton Gallegly to the House bill that would have barred undocumented children from public schools, a measure that was opposed by a majority in the Senate and was the subject of a threatened presidential veto. The House bill also had more restrictive asylum measures that included time limits on applications and procedures for expedited removal of persons entering with fraudulent or no documentation. In 1995, the administration made regulatory changes in the asylum system that had succeeded in slowing abusive applications without restricting the access of bona fide refugees, and the administration argued that further restrictions were not needed. Both houses had adopted provisions to ensure that sponsors' income was taken into account in determining eligibility for public benefits but they differed in terms of time frames and income requirements. The Senate pilot projects to test employment verification mandated business participation in selected locales; the House made participation voluntary.

With Republicans holding both houses of Congress, the effort to work out differences mainly involved members of their party, with occasional discussions with emissaries from the administration. Senate and House Democrats were effectively left out of the process although there had been bipartisan cooperation during the committee and floor debates. The president continued to threaten a veto if the Gallegly amendment remained in the bill. Republicans were split on whether to call his bluff in an election year. Republican candidate Dole would have retained it in the hopes that Clinton would indeed veto legislation to curb illegal immigration, losing votes in California as a result (Gimpel and Edwards 1999). Members from California and other states in which immigration had become a hot political issue did not want to risk failing to enact tough legislation over an issue that the courts had already determined was unconstitutional. The latter view prevailed and the amendment was stripped from the legislation. Compromises were reached on the other major issues, allowing the legislation to go to a formal conference committee vote in September. Democrats complained about having been left out of the real negotiations, but there was little that they could do about it. The House passed the final version on September 28 and the Senate on September 30. The president signed it into law on October 1, 1996, well in advance of the November election.

The Illegal Immigration Reform and Immigrant Responsibility Act (IIRIRA) was actually the third significant bill enacted in 1996 that addressed immigration issues. Prior to its passage, Congress had passed and the president had signed the Anti-Terrorism and Effective Death Penalty Act and the Personal Responsibility and Work Opportunity Reconciliation Act of 1996 (better known as welfare reform). Although the Congress professed to being concerned only about illegal immigration, and the opponents of changes in legal admissions won in both Houses, taken together, these bills represent a distinct shift in U.S. law on the rights of legal immigrants. In contrast to the Jordan Commission's stance that rights are more important than numbers, Congress, with the acquiescence of the President, determined to maintain significant levels of immigration at the expense of the rights of legal immigrants.

IIRIRA, in combination with the Anti-Terrorism Act, included provisions that weakened the due process rights of legal permanent residents. Passed in the aftermath of the Oklahoma City bombing, with the 1993 bombings of the World Trade Center still fresh in memory, the law went well beyond terrorism, including sections on the removal of immigrants who committed crimes. The Immigration Act of 1990 had dealt with this issue, adopting provisions to ease removal of "aggravated felons," defined as persons who committed such serious crimes as murder and rape. Immigration judges had the authority to weigh various factors in determining whether to enforce removal, including the seriousness of the crime, when it was committed, at what age the immigrant had come to the United States, whether subsequent behavior showed a change, and whether the immigrant had family in the United States.

The Anti-Terrorism law redefined crimes of "moral turpitude" to include those punishable by imprisonment for one year or more, rather than those for which the alien is actually sentenced to imprisonment for one year or more, and expanded the list of crimes that could be considered aggravated felonies. IRRIRA revised the definition of an aggravated felony to include far less serious crimes than those covered by the 1990 legislation or the Anti-Terrorism Act. Just about any offense that could result in a potential – not necessarily actual – custodial sentence of one year or more could render the alien deportable. The new rule was applied retroactively; crimes committed many years ago, even if there was no evidence of subsequent criminality, qualified as grounds for removal. The "one strike and you're out" policies applied even to those who had come to the United States as young children and were likely to have acquired their criminality in their new country. The law eliminated the discretion that immigration judges could use in weighing mitigating factors, such as ties to U.S. citizens, before ordering deportation. Also curtailed was the right to appeal decisions to the federal judiciary. Mandatory detention was required until removal took place. If the government claimed certain national security interests, the evidence upon which the removal decision was made could be withheld from the immigrant.

Some of the most profound changes to occur in immigrant policy found their way into law through the welfare reform legislation passed in 1996. The Welfare Reform Act, in combination with IIRIRA, reduced substantially the access of legal immigrants to public benefit programs available to citizens. Although parts of these laws have since been amended, the reversals pertain to retroactive application of the new standards to immigrants in the United States at the time of passage. The significant derogation from the social rights of legal immigrants entering now and in the future has not changed.

Until 1996, no federal benefit program denied eligibility to permanent resident aliens solely on the basis of alien status. During the course of the 1970s and 1980s, however, the courts held that Congress (but not individual states) could make distinctions among different immigration statuses and between aliens and citizens, paving the way for the 1996 changes. The Supreme Court held that as long as distinctions between citizens and aliens were not wholly irrational, Congress could draw them. Through legislative and regulatory actions, distinctions were then made between aliens residing permanently and legally in this country and undocumented aliens. The former were generally determined eligible for federal assistance; the latter were generally barred from these programs.

The welfare reform bill moved the line. Now, the major distinction was between immigrants, regardless of their status, and citizens. The welfare act made legal immigrants ineligible for Supplementary Security Income (SSI) and food stamps until citizenship or until the immigrant had worked 40 qualifying quarters and had not received any federal means-tested program assistance during any such quarter. Exceptions were made for refugees during their first five years (now seven for some programs) in the country and for veterans and active duty service personnel and their immediate families. The legislation applied retroactively, which meant it would have removed many indigent elderly immigrants from the Supplemental Security Income rolls. Many of these elderly immigrants would have found it very difficult to pass the naturalization test. President Clinton called for changes in his State of the Union speech in January 1997. Legislation was passed that relaxed the provision applying the SSI bar only to legal immigrants who had been admitted after enactment of the 1996 law. Legislation in 1998 restored eligibility for food stamps to some elderly and disabled immigrants who had lost food aid as a result of the welfare reform legislation.[12]

Legal immigrants were made ineligible for federal, means-tested benefits during their first five years after entry. Exceptions were made for emergency Medicaid, emergency disaster relief, a range of public health programs, and certain housing benefits if the immigrants were receiving them on the date of enactment. Other exceptions were made for programs aimed at children and students, including foster care and adoption assistance, school lunches, and Head Start. The act also authorized states to decide if they would permit legal immigrants to receive temporary assistance for needy families (the principal cash assistance program for needy families with dependent children), certain social services, and Medicaid (a need-based health insurance program).

Under IIRIRA, all immigrants admitted under family-based categories must be sponsored by a relative who signs an affidavit of support and who can demonstrate an ability to support the immigrant and members of his or her

---

[12] A 2002 law gave eligibility for food stamps to immigrants who had been working for at least five years in the United States, but the law allowed them to receive the assistance for only two years. Citizens are eligible without regard to time limits.

immediate family at 125 percent of poverty level. The affidavits would be legally enforceable against the sponsor by the sponsored immigrant, the federal government, and state and local governments that provide means-tested public benefits. The sponsor must agree to support the alien and submit to the jurisdiction of any federal or state court for reimbursement of government expenses. The income of the sponsor would be taken into account in determining the eligibility of immigrants for federal programs (called "deeming") until the immigrant became a citizen or had worked 40 qualifying quarters without having received aid from any federal means-tested program during any such quarter. These provisions would apply to current recipients of federal programs when they went through the normal eligibility review process. The income was considered available to the immigrant even if the sponsor did not, in fact, provide any financial assistance to the immigrant.

A "right–right" coalition of free marketeers, libertarians, and immigration restrictionists joined together in the successful effort to reduce the access of legal immigrants to public benefits, much to the chagrin of the ethnic, religious, and generally socially liberal members of the left–right coalition that had fought changes to legal immigration. In fact, proponents of the welfare restrictions included many pro-immigration members of Congress who had been persuaded by the left–right coalition. Senator Spencer Abraham, who successfully fought restrictions in 1996 on the number of immigrants to be admitted, was a staunch supporter of the welfare changes and one of the architects of an "Immigration Yes, Welfare No" campaign. He also introduced the aggravated felony provisions discussed earlier. Rick Santorum, one of the senators responsible for managing the debate on the Senate floor, countered proposals to retain eligibility for immigrants already in the country with the following words: "I am pro-immigration.... I believe immigration is important to the future of this country ... If we clean up [the abuse of welfare programs] I think we improve the image of immigration and there is less pressure on lowering those caps and doing other things that I think could be harmful with respect to the area of immigration and, I think, save the taxpayers a whole bundle of money in the process" (Congressional Record 1996).

In effect, the 1996 legislative activities turned out to be pro-immigration but anti-immigrant, in the best tradition of the Virginia model. At a time when the United States was admitting record numbers of immigrants, and a sizable proportion lived and worked in poverty, restricting eligibility for safety-net programs made it clear that immigrants were welcomed as workers, but not as full members of the community. The welfare reforms said, in effect, that all obligations were one-sided: immigrants must continue to pay taxes, contribute to the U.S. economy, obey U.S. laws, and otherwise contribute to the public weal, but the broader society had no reciprocal obligations toward them. In its final report to Congress in 1997, the Commission on Immigration Reform (then chaired by Shirley Hufstedler, a former federal judge and first secretary of education, who succeeded Barbara Jordan after her death in 1996) once more tried to evoke a different message in renewing its call for an Americanization model that was a two-way street with mutual obligations, including an obligation to provide social safety nets to needy immigrants. However, by then the battle had largely been lost.

Immigration and Economic Boom

Any interest in restricting legal immigration levels or in making serious efforts to curb illegal migration disappeared during the economic boom of the late 1990s. The IIRIRA reforms may have helped members of Congress and President Clinton win reelection, by letting them be seen to "do something about illegal immigration," but they did little to stem the flow of unauthorized workers into an economy that appeared to have an insatiable demand for low-wage workers. Even more so than welfare reform, the most striking example of a return to the Virginia model of labor migration without membership may well have been the tacit acceptance of high levels of unauthorized migration, as long as the newcomers were gainfully employed.

In 1998, INS officials announced a significant curtailing of workplace raids. In part, the shift in focus reflected frustration with the overall inadequacy of sanctions on employers as a mechanism for enforcing immigration laws. This inadequacy persisted after IIRIRA, which authorized pilot programs but made no significant changes in employment verification. The hands-off policy also reflected recognition that aggressive workplace enforcement brought attacks from powerful constituencies at a time when the unemployment rate was the lowest in decades. The INS undertook some publicized raids at the height of the harvest on farms growing Vidalia onions in southeastern Georgia. This led to protests even from members of Congress who voted for tough controls on illegal immigration. Although the INS took pains to emphasize that shifting enforcement activities away from workplace raids should not be taken as a green light by employers to hire unauthorized workers, the message nevertheless was noted that the agency's focus would be elsewhere.

By the time of the economic recession of the early 2000s, the number of unauthorized U.S. immigrants had grown to an estimated 8 million. Most unauthorized immigrants continued to come from Mexico (about 56 percent) and Central America. The states that saw large numbers in earlier decades remained principal destinations, but during the 1990s there was a significant dispersal of unauthorized immigrants throughout the country, with large numbers of undocumented immigrants living in relatively new settlement areas in the South and Midwest. States such as North Carolina and Georgia showed the greatest growth in immigration between the 1990 and 2000 censuses, largely fueled by unauthorized workers in the food processing and construction industries (Gozdziak and Martin 2005). Many live in mixed households, with legal permanent resident spouses or parents and U.S. citizen children. As in previous periods, on average, the unauthorized migrants were less educated than either native-born Americans or legal immigrants. They worked primarily in perishable crop agriculture, food processing, construction, and light manufacturing, and in services, such as cleaning, landscaping, and gardening.

A further manifestation of the Virginia model's resurgence was the expansion in temporary worker programs during this period. After having taken steps to restrict use of the H-1B program by setting numerical restrictions in the 1990 legislation, Congress passed laws to expand it during the economic boom. Demand for the H-1B visas had grown rapidly, largely reflecting demand in the expanding information technology (IT) sector. Employers sought foreign-born IT graduates of U.S. colleges as well as those trained in newly emerging centers of excellence in India and China. Repeatedly, the 65,000 cap on H-1B visas was reached early in the fiscal year.

In response, Congress raised the cap twice before the end of the decade. In 1998, primarily as the result of lobbying by the information technology industry, the U.S. Congress passed the American Competitiveness and Work Force Improvement Act (ACWIA). Beginning in October 1998, the number of available H-1B visas was increased from 65,000 per year to 115,000 per year in 1999 and 2000, and to 107,500 in 2001. Although employers welcomed the increase in the H-1B cap in ACWIA, the numbers proved to be insufficient because of backlogs carried over from prior fiscal years and ever-growing demand. In response, Congress once again passed legislation, the American Competitiveness in the Twenty-first Century Act of 2000 (ACTFA), which increased the ceiling to 195,000 until FY 2003 and exempted certain categories of employers, including universities and research centers, from numerical limits. With the so-called dot-com bust of the early years of the twenty-first century, Congress did not extend the higher numbers under the cap when ACTFA sunset. As of this writing, the number has reverted to 65,000, although the exemption for universities and research centers remains, along with an additional 20,000 visas set aside for foreign graduates of U.S. universities.

ACWIA adopted CIR's proposal regarding labor market-testing and linked the expansion in numbers to the imposition of a fee that would be used to fund training programs for U.S. citizens and lawful permanent residents. The funding provided scholarships for low-income students as well as grants for mathematics, engineering, or science enrichment courses administered by the National Science Foundation and the Department of Labor.

Significantly, Congress did not take steps to reform the employment-based permanent system, although its weaknesses were becoming apparent. Unlike other temporary workers, H-1B workers were admitted without regard to whether they intended to return home or to remain in the United States. If an employer wanted to retain them, they could petition for a permanent visa. In most cases, the employer still had to demonstrate to the Department of Labor that there was no minimally qualified U.S. worker for the position, which was a time-consuming process that flew in the face of most business's desire for the best worker at the lowest cost (as compared with the minimally qualified worker). The Department of Labor's certification process could take years, and if the application was approved, the processing at INS was also lengthy. Unless an employer petitioned as soon as a worker was hired, it was unlikely that the green card would be issued within the six years that H-1B visas were valid. Rather than address these problems in the permanent system,

Congress extended the period during which the H-1B visas remained in force, allowing workers to renew the visas yearly if they had a pending application for permanent status. Although the H-1B workers ostensibly had the right to change employers, making such a shift could put the green card at risk, so few would take the risk. Essentially, they remained indentured to the employer throughout the lengthy period.

Also growing during the economic boom were the H-2A and H-2B programs for less skilled workers. The H-2A program had no numerical limit, but the H-2B program was capped at 66,000 per year, and the jobs and the workers had to be temporary ones. In the mid-1990s, fewer than 15,000 visas were issued each year in the H-2A and H-2B programs. By the end of the decade, the numbers had gone up to 30,000 in the H-2A program and to 45,000 in the H-2B program. The numbers in the H-2A program then leveled off until 2007; they jumped to more than 50,000 that year and reached 64,000 in 2008. The H-2B program numbers continued to grow through 2002, when they were approaching the cap. Beginning in 2003, legislation allowed the cap to be pierced by exempting certain categories of work and not counting returning H-2B workers against the numerical limit. In FY 2007, almost 130,000 H-2B visas were issued to new and returning workers.

Ramifications of September 11

When President George W. Bush had his first meeting with President Vincente Fox of Mexico early in 2001, the two leaders pledged cooperation in solving the problem of unauthorized migration from Mexico to the United States. A series of high-level meetings, including presidential summits, began to outline a set of policies to be adopted by both countries. Mexico would enhance border controls to dissuade its nationals from exiting the country illegally, while the United States would provide a mechanism through which Mexicans could enter as temporary workers or regularize their status within the United States or both. Called "earned legalization," the idea was that Mexicans who had been working in the United States and paying their taxes had proven themselves worthy of regularization.

What was referred to as a "Grand Bargain" soon ran into problems when members of Congress questioned whether the components of the agreement would reduce illegal movements or just reward persons who had entered or worked illegally. They pointed to the amnesty adopted in 1986 that had legalized more than 3 million unauthorized migrants, only to see the numbers of undocumented migrants grow even higher in subsequent years. In addition, other governments questioned why Mexicans should get special treatment when their citizens were also contributing to the U.S. economy.

The negotiations between the United States and Mexico came to an almost complete halt after the terrorist attacks of September 11. Although some security experts claimed that it would be beneficial to bring the very large – some 8–9 million – illegal population into the open, most political observers believed it impossible to get approval for a legalization program or an expanded temporary worker program in the aftermath of the terrorist attacks by foreign nationals. Attention turned instead to legislative and administrative actions to ensure that foreign terrorists did not pose a danger to the United States. Action focused on four principal issues: issuance of visas to terrorists, tracking foreign nationals in the United States, bars on entry and removal of suspected terrorists, and organizational roles and responsibilities.

Visa Issuance

From the beginning it appeared that the September 11 hijackers had entered the United States with visas issued by U.S. consulates abroad. Almost 10 million foreigners applied for visas to enter the United States in 2000, and about 75 percent of these visa applicants received the visas they requested. Some 1,100 consular officers – mostly young people at the start of their careers – dealt with visa applications in more than 200 consulates and embassies worldwide.

The National Commission on Terrorist Attacks Upon the United States (9/11 Commission) found in its report on the attacks that "had the immigration system set a higher bar for determining whether individuals are who or what they claim to be . . . it could have potentially excluded, removed, or come into further contact with several hijackers who did not appear to meet the terms for admitting short-term visitors" (2004: 384). A number of plotters had failed to obtain visas, largely because, as Yemeni citizens coming from a poor country, they were considered at high risk of overstaying their visas. By contrast, the Saudi applicants were considered good prospects for admission because they came from a wealthier country with many economic and foreign policy ties to the United States.

Visa officers had long been criticized for being too cautious, using country and economic profiling to deny visas to many people with legitimate reasons to travel to the United States. Still, the 9/11 Commission had grounds for concern. Consular officers had only a limited time to review visa applications, as had immigration inspectors at U.S. ports of entry in reviewing the documents presented by those seeking entry. The 9/11 Commission found that a number of the hijackers had requested new passports so as not to show that they had been previously in Pakistan, with access to Afghanistan. Others had altered passports. Yet, even with additional time, the consular officers and inspectors would probably have been unable to identify the suspected terrorists because they did not have access to needed information in the law enforcement and intelligence databases.

At the time of the terrorist attacks, the INS maintained the National Automated Immigration Lookout System, or NAILS, and the INS, Customs, and the State Department used NAILS to screen foreigners seeking visas or entry to the United States. NAILS was a name-based system that was effective only if an applicant used a name that had been entered into the database; false names, supported by fraudulent documentation, could help an individual to evade identification with NAILS. Moreover, the intelligence services had been reluctant to enter data from classified sources, fearing the identification of those who provided the information. In all too many cases, there was no action-able intelligence about visa applicants whose terrorist activities had not come to the attention of government authorities. Without this sensitive information, the look-out system could never function effectively in preventing known terrorists from entering the country.

In the aftermath of the attacks, the State Department took steps to tighten issuance of visas. All applicants from countries where visas were required had to come to embassies and consulates for a hearing. Most of the terrorists had obtained their visas in Saudi Arabia, where an expedited process had waived an interview for many applicants. Members of Congress debated whether to eliminate a visa waiver program that allowed mostly Western Europeans to enter without visas, but it would have been very expensive and diplomatically difficult to reinstate visa processing in those countries. Moreover, the program operated on a reciprocal basis and American citizens might have been subject to visa requirements when traveling to Europe.

The government also took steps to help ensure that the visa look-out systems received more timely law enforcement and intelligence information. This was part of broader measures to enhance information sharing among agencies responsible for counter-terrorism activities.

Identification of Terrorists

A second prong of the response to 9/11 focused on identifying terrorists who might still be in the country. In the days following September 11, the government detained more than one thousand foreign nationals from Arab and other Muslim countries that have been linked to terrorism. Most of the detainees were found to have no ties to terrorist organizations. More than 750 were turned over to the Immigration and Nationalization Service, though, because they were found to have violated immigration laws.[13] Federal authorities identified another five thousand young men from these countries as potential subjects of interviews to determine whether they had any pertinent information about terrorist activities. About half were located in the United States; the whereabouts

---

[13] The Office of the Inspector General of the Justice Department (2003) subsequently issued a critical report of the lengthy detention and sometimes abusive treatment of these foreign nationals in a report entitled *The September 11 Detainees: A Review of the Treatment of Aliens Held on Immigration Charges in Connection with the Investigation of the September 11 Attacks.* After investigating conditions in a Bureau of Prison (BOP) facility, the Inspector General (2003: chapter 7) concluded: "We also believe that the BOP instituted excessively restrictive policies on the detainees, particularly regarding telephone privileges. In addition, the BOP did not provide adequate information about the location of the detainees to the detainees' attorneys or their family members. These policies hindered the detainees' ability to obtain and consult with legal counsel and were more appropriate for detainees who had attorneys prior to arriving at the MDC. We also believe that some of the detainees were subject to physical or verbal abuse. Finally, we believe that some of the conditions of confinement were unnecessarily severe, such as two lights constantly illuminated in the detainees' cells. While the chaotic situation and the uncertainties surrounding the detainees' role in the September 11 attacks and the potential for additional terrorism explain some of these problems, they do not explain or justify all of them."

of the rest (whether they had left the country or were at another location within the United States) was unknown (Martin and Martin 2004).

The administration then introduced a new registration system for nationals of more than 30 countries that are largely Arabic or Muslim, the National Security Entry–Exit Registration System (NSEERS) (Jachimowitz and McKay 2003). NSEERS was composed of a registration program conducted at various ports of entry and a special registration program for certain foreign nationals already in the country.

In testimony given before the Senate Committee on Finance, a senior INS official stated that the NSEERS program promotes several important national security objectives:

> It allows the United States to run the fingerprints of aliens seeking to enter the U.S. or present in the U.S. against a database of known terrorists. It enables the INS to determine instantly whether such an alien has overstayed his/her visa. It enables the INS to verify that an alien is living where he said he would live, and doing what he said he would do while in the United States, and to ensure that he is not violating our immigration laws. (Williams 2003)

Critics of the program were especially concerned abou the targeting of Arab and Muslim foreign nationals for registration. According to a report of the Migration Policy Institute, the special registration program implicitly assumed that all citizens of the stated countries were suspected of participating in ter-rorist activities. It also pointed out that there was little consultation with Arab and Islamic communities prior to the implementation of the registration sys-tem, leading to an increase in tensions between members of these communities and government officials. Critics also pointed to the small number of suspected terrorists who were actually identified by the program, raising questions as to the effectiveness of nationality and religious profiling.[14] In fact, cooperation of the Arab and Islamic communities in the United States is a key ingredient in the intelligence gathering needed to identify actual threats. To the extent that special registration makes such cooperation harder to achieve, it was thought by some that it might harm national security and reduce the likelihood of apprehending terrorists.

Recognizing the controversy surrounding the special registration provisions, the administration moved forward with a universal entry–exit program, which had been mandated in IIRIRA but postponed because of the fears of businesses along the border between the United States and Canada that it would impede commerce. US–Visit (United States Visitor and Immigrant Status Indicator Technology) allowed the automated capture of basic information about each arriving and departing passenger. All arriving foreign visitors would have their photograph and fingerprints taken upon arrival and departure. The system would be introduced at air and sea ports of entry and then extended to the

---

[14] The INS had testified that as of January 23, 2003, "NSEERS has led to the identification and apprehension of 7 suspected terrorists" (Jachimowitz and McKay 2003).

land ports of entry, which had far more crossings each day. As of this writing, US–Visit is operational on entry but exit controls have still not been introduced.

Because several hijackers had received student visas, movement in introducing a tracking system of foreign students and exchange visitors also accelerated. The Student and Exchange Visitor Information System (SEVIS) became operational in 2003. Schools report electronically to the Department of Homeland Security on the arrival of foreign students and exchange visitors and on the students' and visitors' change of address, changes in program of study, and other pertinent information.

Bars on Entry and Grounds for Removal

The third area receiving post 9/11 attention related to bars on entry and grounds for removal of persons suspected of being foreign terrorists. At the time of the attacks, the United States had several special policies and procedures that applied to all foreign nationals, including permanent residents. The Immigration and Nationality Act specified that a foreign national who had engaged in a terrorist activity, or about whom there were reasonable grounds to believe was engaged or likely to be engaged in such activity, could be deported from the United States. The section also applied to a person who, indicating an intention to cause death or serious bodily harm, incited terrorism. Terrorist activity was defined to include hijacking or sabotage of conveyances, violently attacking protected persons, assassinations, the use of biological, chemical, or nuclear weapons or devices, and other similar activities. Engaging in such activities included planning, providing material support, soliciting funds, and soliciting individuals to conduct such activities. The law also allowed the removal of an alien who was a member of a foreign terrorist organization, as designated by the secretary of state, which the alien knew or should have known, was a terrorist organization.

The 1996 antiterrorism law had contained special removal procedures to be used when the government case required the use of classified information to prove that the defendant is a foreign terrorist. The legislation established a removal court, composed of five U.S. district court judges appointed by the chief justice of the Supreme Court, as well as a panel of special attorneys who have security clearances that afford them access to classified materials. Neither the foreign-national defendant nor his or her attorney would be permitted to see the classified information. The special attorney would assist the defense by reviewing the materials and challenging, if appropriate, the veracity of the information. The special attorney was not authorized to reveal the information to the defendant or his or her attorney. The defendant might only see an unclassified summary of the information (if such a summary was available). At the time of the September 11 attacks, this provision had never been used.

The USA Patriot Act, passed after September 11, expanded the definition of terrorist activity to include persons who have used positions "of prominence within any country to endorse or espouse terrorist activity, or to persuade others to support terrorist activity or a terrorist organization, in a way that the Secretary of State has determined undermines United States efforts to reduce or eliminate terrorist activities." The USA Patriot Act also expanded the grounds for detaining aliens who were barred from entering or could be removed because of suspected terrorist activities or membership. The Justice Department may detain an alien for seven days without charging him or her for either an immigration or criminal offense. If the attorney general certifies that an alien is excludable or removable on one of these grounds, the alien must remain in detention until removed from the country. When removal is not possible, the alien may continue to be detained upon a determination by the attorney general that his or her release "will threaten the national security of the United States or the safety of the community or any person."

In most cases, determinations did not need to be made as to whether a foreign national was a terrorist because the foreign national had committed some violation of immigration law. The use of immigration law as the basis for apprehending, detaining, and prosecuting suspected terrorists had both advantages and disadvantages. Law enforcement officials noted the difficulty of proving criminal charges against terrorists. Immigration violations are generally treated as a civil rather than a criminal matter, and there is usually no question that the immigration laws have indeed been violated. In the meantime, potentially dangerous persons are taken off the streets. However, immigration law provides relatively few long-term benefits to law enforcement against terrorism. If someone accused of entering illegally, overstaying his or her visa, or even falling within one of the excludable or removable terrorism-related categories volunteers to be removed from the United States, there may be no other grounds to keep him or her in custody. If removed from the country, the person may be free to pursue terrorist activities abroad – bombing a U.S. embassy, for example, rather than a domestic U.S. target.

One group affected by the new bars on entry and grounds for removal has been refugees. Immediately following September 11, the U.S. refugee resettlement program was suspended. Reportedly, a planeload of Afghan refugees arrived at Kennedy Airport soon after it was reopened, raising questions about whether terrorists might be infiltrating the resettlement program. The resettlement program indeed admitted nationals of known state sponsors of terrorism (for example, Afghanistan, Sudan, and Somalia) but these countries were also known for persecution of their citizens. Although many refugee advocates pointed out that refugees went through more scrutiny than immigrants, reports of fraud in the resettlement program operating in Nairobi made it difficult for the State Department to dismiss questions about the bona fides of the refugees being admitted.

The resettlement program might not have been suspended had it not been so visible. The September 11 attacks came shortly before the consultations on refugee admissions. Unlike immigration programs that operate deep within the bureaucracy, refugee admissions required a presidential determination on the number of refugees to be admitted and public statements by the secretary of state and attorney general in defense of the numbers and allocations to different nationalities. The Jordan Commission's fears that this process would undermine refugee protection had been proven prescient. Even when the resettlement program resumed, the number of admissions remained well below 50,000 per year through 2007.

Complicating the situation was the bar imposed by the USA Patriot Act on the admission of foreign nationals who provided material support to terrorist organizations. Terrorist organizations are defined broadly to include "groups of two or more individuals, whether organized or not," which engage in proscribed activities. There is no exception for providing material support under duress, which is particularly problematic for refugees. Even minimal support is prohibited. As Schoenholtz and Hojaiban (2008) write: "The material support bar . . . uses events associated with the very basis of refugee claims – persecution by an armed group – to deny admission to refugees. Many victims of persecution provided support to armed groups under duress simply in order to stay alive or save another family member." Georgetown University Law Center students conducted interviews with Colombian refugees in Ecuador, identifying specific examples of duress in more than fifty cases, including the forced digging of trenches to bury civilians killed by paramilitaries (Georgetown University Law Center 2006). In other cases, applications are on hold because the applicant paid a ransom for the release of relatives kidnapped by insurgents or had been forced to cook for, clean for, and provide sexual services to the insurgents that had captured them (Sridharan 2008). In effect, what gives refugees a well-founded fear of persecution becomes the basis for denial of admission and, if they are already in the country, the potential for deportation. The legislation permits admission only if the secretary of state and secretary of homeland security specifically waive the application of the material support bar.

As applied, the law has had an unintended effect. The bar also applies to organizations that are working to overthrow governments that the United States has opposed militarily. On this basis, Hmong, Burmese, Iraqi, and other refugees who would be threatened on return to their home countries because of their association with the U.S. government have been barred from entry. The waiver that permits entry of those providing material support to U.S. allies does not even apply to those who actually fought alongside U.S. forces.

Organizational Changes

The fourth major change resulting from September 11 affected the organizational arrangements for implementing immigration policy. The Immigration and Naturalization Service was the principal federal agency responsible for immigration, with district offices that handled both enforcement and immigration services. The Commission on Immigration Reform had pointed out in its 1997 report that "[i]mmigration law enforcement requires staffing, training, resources, and a work culture that differs from what is required for effective adjudication of benefits. . . . " CIR recommended that the two functions be separated, with the Justice Department retaining authority for enforcement and the State Department gaining authority, not only for visa issuance, but also for other immigration-related services.

Although the recommendation led to some administrative efforts to address the overlapping and sometimes conflicting responsibilities, it was not until the

creation of the Department of Homeland Security after 9/11 that serious attention was given to the organizational structures. The legislation that created
the massive department moved most immigration functions out of the Justice Department into the new Cabinet-evel agency, giving responsibility for
enforcement and services to different bureaus. U.S. Citizenship and Immigration Services had responsibility for benefits adjudication while enforcement
was divided between two bureaus: Customs and Border Protection, which had
responsibility for border-related immigration issues, and Immigration and Customs Enforcement, which had responsibility for interior enforcement. Each of
the enforcement agencies would address the movements of people and goods
into the country. The new organizational arrangements came into effect in
2003.

Half-Hearted Efforts at Immigration Reform

George W. Bush campaigned for the presidency in 2000 with a pledge to make
immigration reform a top priority of his administration. President Bush had
served as governor of Texas, a border state with close ties to Mexico, where
more than one-third of the population is of Hispanic origin. Texas also depends
heavily on cross-border trade with Mexico for its economic livelihood, especially after the launch of NAFTA in 1994. Familiarity with issues involving both
the United States and Mexico thus predisposed the new Bush administration
to place immigration at the forefront of the political agenda.

In the aftermath of September 11, serious discussion of immigration reform
languished in the United States although some progress was made in achieving
agreements with Canada and Mexico on border security strategies. The Summit
of the Americas, held in Monterrey, Mexico, January 12–13, 2004, provided
the opportunity for President Bush to return to the issue of immigration reform.
Less than a week before the summit, he unveiled his proposal for a new temporary worker program, titled the "Fair and Secure Immigration Reform." The
temporary worker program outlined by President Bush on January 7, 2004,
sought to provide a broad framework for resolving some of the many problems that plague the U.S. immigration system. Chief among these was the need,
in his words, to better "match willing foreign workers with willing American
employers, when no Americans can be found to fill the jobs" (White House
2004).

Before delving into the specifics of the president's January 2004 proposal, it
is important to note that no substantial progress toward its implementation was
made before the U.S. elections. Harsh public criticism of his plan came from
both liberal and conservative camps, effectively blocking any comprehensive
immigration reform. The dynamics of a presidential campaign year further
impeded the immigration reform agenda. Efforts to curry favor among voters
in the battleground states of the upper Midwest refocused the political debate
on issues other than immigration, most notably on the war in Iraq and the U.S.
economy, for fear of alienating critical undecided voters.

After the presidential election, the Bush administration indicated it planned to return to the issue of immigration reform. Secretary of State Colin L. Powell and Secretary of Homeland Security Tom Ridge announced on November 9, 2004, while attending meetings of the United States–Mexico Binational Commission in Mexico City, that moving forward with a temporary worker program was a "high priority" for President Bush in his second term. Still, Secretary Ridge cautioned that disagreements within Congress could block achieving such reform in the near term (*New York Times* 2004).

The president's proposal for "Fair and Secure Immigration Reform" at its most basic was an uncapped temporary worker program. Although the program would provide status as a temporary worker, it would not lead directly to citizenship. Temporary workers would be eligible to apply for permanent residency, but only through the existing application process and without any preferences over other applicants for citizenship. De-linking the temporary worker program from citizenship status was designed to deflect criticism of President Bush's proposal from conservative political groups that oppose amnesty for immigrants illegally in the country. Instead, program participants would be eligible to work in the United States for an initial period of three years, with the possibility to renew their temporary worker visa for an unspecified number of three-year periods. Return to the country of origin otherwise would be required at the end of three years.

The primary incentive for individuals to come forward and participate in the guest worker program was the guarantee of the right to live and work in the United States. It would eliminate the risk of deportation for three years. A related benefit of the temporary worker program, according to the proposal, was that it would ensure "circularity," or freedom of travel between the United States and the temporary worker's country of origin. Program participants no longer would have to fear being barred reentry to the United States after a visit to their home community.

The Bush proposal was criticized widely. At the conservative end of the political spectrum, critics voiced concern that the temporary worker proposal amounted to an amnesty for unauthorized migrants. Although the Bush proposal did not provide an automatic path to citizenship to unauthorized aliens currently in the United States, it nevertheless would have allowed temporary workers participating in the program to apply immediately for a green card if they had an employer's sponsorship for the very limited number of visas available for less-skilled workers (World Net Daily 2004).

Equal criticism of President Bush's proposal emanated from the liberal side of the political aisle. After the plan was unveiled in January, Senator Edward Kennedy disparaged the temporary worker proposal as grossly inadequate to resolve the nation's broken immigration system.[15] Senators Tom Daschle and Joe Lieberman specifically criticized the proposal for failing to offer guest

---

[15] Subsequently, he and Senator McCain introduced their own version of comprehensive immigration reform.

workers a direct path to citizenship, such as through an earned legalization process (CNN 2004).

An additional concern was that most of the onus of reforming the immigration system was placed on the immigrant guest worker, not on the employer that hired the worker. Despite calls for increased workplace enforcement and verification of compliance with other labor laws, the proposal earmarked very little funding to verify that employers were hiring only those individuals with temporary worker cards and were complying with fair labor standards. Whereas the president's proposal designated $2.7 billion for border security inspections in the FY 2005 budget, the funding for worksite enforcement was increased to a mere $25 million (U.S. Department of Homeland Security 2004). The AFL-CIO asserted that the president's proposal did nothing to strengthen protections for wages, benefits, and other rights for either immigrant or domestic workers. Instead, the proposal would create a permanent, and larger, underclass of workers in the U.S. economy. The plan allegedly would reward large corporations and employers with a steady stream of vulnerable and underpaid workers, while weakening the rights of workers and exacerbating disrespect for individual's rights within the immigration system, according to the AFL-CIO (Sweeney 2004).

Several legislative alternatives to President Bush's temporary worker proposal were introduced but not enacted during the 108th to 110th Congresses. Two bills, AgJOBS and the DREAM Act, had bipartisan sponsorship in Congress. AgJOBS, introduced by Senator Larry Craig, was the principal legislative effort to reform the system for admitting temporary agricultural workers. It focused on reform of the H-2A visa category and proposed two basic reforms. First, it would grant legal residence, on a one-time-only basis, to unauthorized migrants who had worked in the agricultural sector for the equivalent of 100 workdays, during any 12 consecutive months, of the 18-month period ending on August 31, 2004. This would apply to approximately 500,000 foreign farm workers in the United States at the time of the bill's introduction and to their spouses and minor children. Adjustment to permanent residency (green card) would be possible if the migrant performed an additional 360 days of agricultural work over the following six years. Second, AgJOBS would streamline the H-2A temporary, nonimmigrant guest worker program. It would make the hiring process more like expedited hiring for H-1B high-tech workers. The H-1B process only requires an "attestation" that the employer has complied with the requirements, as opposed to the much lengthier certification process that is required to obtain an H-2A visa.[16]

The DREAM Act (Development, Relief, and Education for Alien Minors Act), originally sponsored by Senator Orrin Hatch of Utah, sought to facilitate the entry into institutions of higher education of those illegal immigrant minors who have obtained a high-school diploma. These students were barred legally from seeking employment and were constrained from pursuing additional education because of the high costs of out-of-state tuition. The DREAM Act

---

[16] "AgJOBS Legislation," Issue Briefing, Senator Larry Craig, craig.senate.gov.

would authorize states to determine residency for higher education purposes, regardless of an individual's immigration status. It also would suspend removal of students who were admitted to an institution of higher education or joined the military. After a six-year wait, the immigrant could gain permanent residence status.

Despite their bipartisan support, AGJobs and the DREAM Act languished as Congress considered more far-reaching reform. In the 109th Congress, the Senate and the House of Representatives took very different approaches to the issue. The House focused primarily on enhanced enforcement while the Senate tried for comprehensive reform. The Border Protection, Antiterrorism, and Illegal Immigration Control Act of 2005, which passed the House in December 2005, was roundly criticized because it included what were widely seen in immigration circles as draconian measures and lacked any legal alternatives to unauthorized migration. The bill's border security provisions included increased staffing and training for the Border Patrol, technology to be deployed along the border, and physical infrastructure to deter unauthorized crossings. The bill also required development of a national strategy for border security. It expanded the scope of, and enhanced the penalties for, smuggling and trafficking offenses.

In an especially criticized provision, the bill increased the penalties for "harboring" an unauthorized migrant in a manner that would risk the imprisonment of staff of religious and social services organizations that assist immigrants. As described by the American Immigration Lawyers Association, "This incredibly overbroad definition of smuggling would criminalize the work of social service organizations, refugee agencies, churches, attorneys, and other groups that counsel immigrants, treating them the same as smuggling organizations. In addition, family members and employers could be fined and imprisoned for "harboring," "shielding," or "transporting" undocumented family members or employees, filling our prisons with people who have done nothing more than try to reunite their families, or help a worker, friend or client" (American Inmigration Lawyers Association 2005).

In an equally criticized provision, the bill created a new felony offense – unlawful presence in the United States. Traditionally, simple violations of immigration law have been treated as civil offenses, not criminal ones. Other provisions enhanced the use of mandatory detention, expanded still further the definition of aggravated felonies that would result in mandatory removal, put into place new definitions of terrorist-related reasons for inadmissibility and removal, and eliminated or reduced access to the courts to hear certain immigration related cases. It also made changes in the burden of proof for an asylum seeker. It required such a person to establish that "his or her life or freedom would be threatened in the country in question, and that race, religion, nationality, membership in a particular social group, or political opinion would be at least *one central reason* for such threat." A number of these provisions overturned federal court rulings.

In addressing the work magnet for unauthorized migration, the bill required the secretary of homeland security to implement an employment eligibility verification system, building on the pilot program already in use to verify work authorization. The system would become mandatory for employers. Employers would need to verify not only new hires but also their existing workforce.

The House-passed legislation created an uproar among immigrant advocacy organizations, businesses, and civil rights and civil liberties groups. Opponents argued that enforcement-only approaches would not solve the immigration problem, just further criminalize individuals whose main purpose in violating immigration law was to work. Demonstrations across the country showed the depth of concern within ethnic communities with large immigrant populations. These demonstrations, along with the concerns of business that immigration reform must address their legitimate need for foreign workers, paved the way for a radically different approach in the Senate.

The Secure America and Orderly Immigration Act was introduced by Senators John McCain and Edward Kennedy and Representatives James Kolbe, Jeff Flake and Luis Gutierrez. The bill addressed a wide range of issues ranging from legalizing unauthorized migrants and creating temporary work programs to increased border security and new employment verification provisions. It attempted to provide answers to three aspects of reform: 1) what to do about the existing unauthorized migrants; 2) how to meet the legitimate needs of employers for foreign labor and families for reunification; and 3) how to deter future unauthorized migration. A competing bill, the Comprehensive Enforcement and Immigration Reform Act of 2005 was introduced by Senators John Cornyn and Jon Kyl in the Republican-controlled 109th Congress. It too provided a mechanism to legalize the status of unauthorized migrants in the United States, but it was far more restrictive than the McCain-Kennedy approach. A compromise was then negotiated by Senators Chuck Hagel and Mel Martinez that paved the way for passage of the legislation by the Senate. There was no prospect for agreement with the House enforcement-only approach and the bills died with the elections and the turnover of Congress to Democratic Party leadership.

In the 110th Congress (2007–2008), immigration reform once more came on the political agenda but again died before enactment of legislation. The Senate and the House once more took different approaches although both bodies were under the control of the Democratic Party. In the Senate, closed-door discussions between Senators from both parties and the administration led to introduction of a bill that lifted elements from each of the previous legislative attempts and introduced new policies not previously encompassed in any of the legislative packages. The bill was comprehensive in scope and radical in many of its strategies for curbing unauthorized migration and reforming legal admissions. The House, by contrast, held numerous hearings on immigration reform issues but the leadership decided to take a wait-and-see attitude and defer action until the Senate debated its legislation. When the Senate failed to end debate on the bipartisan bill supported by the president, the House also deferred action.

The most controversial element of the Senate bill was its legalization provisions. The legislation included what was called an earned regularization program (Z visa) that was at the same time more generous and more restrictive than previous versions. It was more generous in its scope, providing a route to legal status for all unauthorized immigrants in the country as of January 2007. Eliminating a tiered system used in previous legislation, the provision would treat all unauthorized immigrants similarly. They would regularize their status with a new nonimmigrant visa that could be renewed every four years, with additional fees and with English and civics testing requirements applied at the renewals. Although it made unauthorized immigrants eligible for eventual permanent residence and citizenship, the Senate bill put new restrictions on access to these benefits. The persons granted the new Z visa would be at the back of a long waiting list, estimated to take about eight years to clear. Moreover, the Senate bill would require what is referred to as a "touch back" – the heads of all regularized families would have to return home to reenter as permanent residents. They would also have to meet the requirements of a point system. Although unauthorized migrants would immediately find relief from deportation, the full regularization program would only go into effect when certain benchmarks were met in the enforcement of immigration laws.

The Senate bill also included a new temporary worker program (Y visa) that would introduce a rotational requirement. Workers would be granted an initial two year visa, renewable twice. What made the Senate version of a temporary worker program a radical departure was the requirement that workers return home for one year between each renewal. After three rotations, they would not be eligible to reenter. A ceiling of 200,000 Y visas was approved by amendment on the floor of the Senate, but a mechanism remained to permit increases in the ceiling if demand was high.

Also included in the Senate legislative initiative were major changes in the program for permanent admission. After clearing the backlog of current applicants, the legislation would eliminate the extended family, employer-petitioned, and diversity visa categories for admission. Although immediate family (spouses, minor children, and parents) of U.S. citizens and permanent residents would still be eligible for the visas, all other immigrants would be admitted on the basis of a point system that would reward education, English language ability, and qualifications in occupations with a shortage of workers. A small number of points would be awarded for family ties if the applicants amassed a minimum number of points in these other areas.

Most of the enforcement provisions were lifted in their entirety from previous bills or represented a variation on the themes of already negotiated provisions. The legislation emphasized both border security and interior enforcement. With regard to worksite enforcement, the bill included provisions for mandatory electronic employment verification, as well as increased penalties for illegal hiring of unauthorized workers.

As negotiations over the Senate bill continued, provisions were added that troubled the proponents of comprehensive reform without satisfying the opponents. The agreement began to unravel in its own bipartisan way, with some Democrats peeling off because of concerns about the open-endedness of the temporary worker programs and its lack of labor protections, the new enforcement measures, and the elimination of many family categories. Many Republicans remained opposed, and they were joined by some newly elected Democrats from Republican-leaning districts, because of what they called an amnesty program that, to their supporters, signified a reward for illegal activity. When the Senate leadership tried to end debate over the legislation, it failed to garner the 60 votes needed to bring the legislation to a vote. With the 2008 elections looming, few members expected immigration reform to regain any momentum until a new administration was in place.

State and Local Initiatives

As the prospects for federal reform diminished, a number of states and localities took action to address what they perceived as the growing problem of illegal immigration. The National Council of State Legislators documented the trend: "State laws related to immigration have increased dramatically in recent years: In 2005, 300 bills were introduced and 38 laws were enacted. In 2006, activity doubled: 570 bills were introduced and 84 laws were enacted. In 2007, activity tripled: 1,562 bills were introduced and 240 laws were enacted" (NCSL 2009). Some of these laws attempt to implement at the state level provisions that were debated at the federal level. For example, in 2008, nineteen laws were enacted in thirteen states to enforce sanctions against employers who hire unauthorized workers and to impose employment eligibility verification requirements and penalties (NCSL 2009).

Perhaps the most controversy was generated by an Arizona law (S.B. 1070) "requiring that a [law enforcement] officer make a reasonable attempt to determine the immigration status of a person stopped, detained or arrested if there is a reasonable suspicion that the person is unlawfully present in the United States, and requiring verification of the immigration status of any person arrested prior to releasing that person."[17] The law, enacted in April 2010, further made it a criminal act if an unauthorized immigrant sought employment or failed to carry federal alien registration documents. It also allowed warrantless arrests "where there is probable cause to believe the person has committed a public offense that makes the person removable from the United States." And the legislation allowed people to sue local government or agencies if they believe the law is not being enforced. S.B. 1070 followed other Arizona initiatives to curb illegal immigration, including legislation that required employers in the state to use the E-Verify program to determine authorization to work and made it a state offense to knowingly hire an unauthorized immigrant.

In signing the law, the Arizona governor called it a "tool for our state to use as we work to solve a crisis we did not create and the federal government has refused to fix" (Brewer 2010). Proponents of the legislation cited what

---

[17] *United States of America*, Plaintiff, vs. *State of Arizona; and Janice K. Brewer, Governor of the State of Arizona, in her Official Capacity*, Defendants, judgment issued by federal district court Judge Susan Bolton on July 28, 2010.

they described as increasing crime and border violence related to illegal immigration. The law was condemned immediately by civil rights and other groups that feared it would lead to racial and ethnic profiling. The governor's assurances that law enforcement could be trusted to implement the law in a nondiscriminatory manner did little to quell these concerns.[18] The law was also criticized as an overreaction to concerns about border violence and crime, with opponents pointing out that crime rates had actually gone down in Arizona. Law enforcement officials were split, some favoring the legislation and others concerned that it would drive a wedge between the police and the communities they served. A number of legal suits followed, including one by the federal government challenging the constitutionality of the law. The federal government argued that the power to regulate immigration is vested exclusively with the federal government, and that the provisions of S.B. 1070 were preempted by federal law. On July 28, 2010, a federal judge enjoined Arizona from implementing several provisions of the law, including those cited above, stating that the federal government was likely to prevail in its preemption arguments in reference to those provisions. As of this writing, the governor of Arizona pledged to appeal the ruling to the 9th Circuit Court of Appeals, and several other states indicated interest in passing similar legislation if Arizona prevailed.

Conclusion

Just a few years after the liberalizing reforms of the Immigration Act of 1990 were enacted, immigration was in crisis. The country reacted with ambivalence. Public backlash against illegal immigration fueled efforts such as Proposition 187, but economic and humanitarian interests kept the back door open. The tension inherent in these two positions led to a return to the Virginia model. Foreign workers would be tolerated, even encouraged, but within restrictive frameworks that often precluded full membership in American society. An underclass of undocumented immigrants would pick the crops, process the food, garden and landscape, construct homes, manufacture garments, clean homes, take care of children and the elderly, and provide myriad other services. The immigrants benefited from higher wages than they could expect at home but were without the legal protections afforded to citizens in the labor market. Middle- and upper-class Americans benefited from having a workforce willing and able to do these jobs at low wages and under working conditions that most Americans would not accept.

At the same time, industries employing highly skilled workers benefited from the growth in temporary worker programs. A broken permanent immigration

---

[18] The legislation had been amended to prohibit law enforcement from taking race, color, or national origin into consideration in implementing the law (HB 2162). The training developed for Arizona law enforcement who would be implementing the law emphasized the problems with racial profiling but also specified that such issues as dress, demeanor and English language ability could be taken into account in determining if there was a reasonable suspicion that the person was unauthorized (http://www.azpost.state.az.us/SB1070infocenter.htm).

system could not keep up with demand for foreign science, information technology, and engineering professionals. Rather than fix the permanent program to benefit from this human capital, Congress repeatedly tinkered with the H-1B program, increasing numbers and allowing workers to remain tied to an employer for longer and longer periods. As of July 2010, second-preference applicants (that is, persons with advanced degrees) from India and China must have applied before October 2005 because of large backlogs. The waiting times for family reunification for adult children of U.S. citizens, spouses, and minor children of Mexican legal permanent residents, and siblings of U.S. citizens, were even longer.

The Massachusetts model also had a resurgence in the aftermath of the World Trade Center bombings in 1993 and 2001. Although most of the impetus for the 1996 Anti-Terrorism legislation was the Oklahoma bombings that were carried out by native-born U.S. citizens, Congress took the opportunity to institute restrictive measures affecting the rights of immigrants. September 11 quickly led to ethnic and religious profiling in the form of the NSEERS program. With passage of the USA Patriot Act, new ideological bars to admission were adopted, the most problematic being the provisions on persons providing material support to terrorist organizations even under significant duress. With an end to the Cold War, the ideological underpinnings of the refugee program disappeared, making it the first victim of the new preoccupation with terrorism.

The Pennsylvania model is not dead, but it is under severe challenge. Permanent immigration, with a route to citizenship, remains substantial but during the first half of the 2000 decade, the increase in unauthorized migrants exceeded the net increase in legal immigrants (Passel and D'Vera 2008). This situation appears to be shifting as a result of the economic recession. In 2008, net growth in the unauthorized migrant population slowed down considerably because of fewer new arrivals. Demographers have found no evidence, as of the time of this writing, that returns to Mexico (the largest source of unauthorized migration) have increased significantly (Passel and D'Vera 2009).

Public concerns about immigration have not disappeared, however. As discussed above, recent years have seen a proliferation of initiatives at the state and local level to curb illegal immigration. Proponents argue that the federal government has abdicated its responsibility to manage movements of people into the country, creating a vacuum to be replaced by state and local efforts to deal with unresolved issues. Moreover, systemic problems in U.S. immigration policy remain, as do the underlying causes of migration. With economic recovery, illegal immigration is likely to resume at least at the same levels as were reached in the past decade. The question will be whether the country will resume the pro-immigration, fundamentally anti-immigrant, policies of the past fifteen years or renew the covenant with immigrants, with mutual obligations, that long characterized the Pennsylvania model.

13

Looking Ahead

On January 20, 2009, Barack Obama was sworn in as president of the United States. His election marked a turning point in American history. An African American man had been elected president of a country that had ended officially sanctioned racial discrimination only a few decades earlier. No less noteworthy is President Obama's heritage as the son of an African immigrant. Only six presidents have had parents who came as immigrants to the United States. None came from non-European heritage.

On June 25, 2009, President Obama hosted a summit with congressional leaders to lay out the contours of immigration reform. The president described the areas of agreement during his remarks after the meeting: "I think the consensus is that despite our inability to get [immigration reform] passed over the last several years, the American people still want to see a solution in which we are tightening up our borders, or cracking down on employers who are using illegal workers in order to drive down wages – and oftentimes mistreat those workers. And we need an effective way to recognize and legalize the status of undocumented workers who are here." Members of Congress made clear, as in previous efforts at reform, the battle will be over the details.

Even more important, as the country debates the specifics of immigration reform, is the need to decide just what model of immigration will provide the framework for legislative change. Whatever the specific policies adopted, the United States will remain a country of immigrants. Given our history, traditions, and economic realities, it is highly unlikely that the United States will cut off immigration, even if the government were able to obtain control over movements across the border. Rather, the question is whether immigrants will be admitted as exploitable workers, as tools of U.S. foreign policy and ideology, as presumptive citizens with full membership in the society, or in some combination of these three models.

This chapter sets out an agenda for restoring the Pennsylvania model that would afford full membership to legal immigrants. The United States has benefited the most from immigration when its policies underscored the equality and rights of immigrants and treated newcomers as presumptive citizens. To that effect, the chapter makes recommendations regarding U.S. admissions and enforcement policies to address the problems identified in Chapter 12. It will also include discussion of ways to curb unauthorized migration, shift it into legal channels, and enact measures that reduce exploitation and the growth of an underclass. Particular focus will be given to changes needed in legal admissions policies, to reduce the excessively large backlogs and long waiting periods for family- and employment- based categories, which delay the integration of immigrants while they await permanent residence. This chapter also suggests ways in which the United States can regain leadership on refugee issues within a revitalized Pennsylvania model.

Above all else, restoring the Pennsylvania model requires renewed attention to the integration of immigrants in the United States. A large segment of immigrants in the United States enter with very low levels of education. Although that has been true of past waves of American immigrants, the nature of the U.S. economy has changed. Low-skilled immigrants face significant challenges in an information-age economy that rewards education rather than brawn. Many immigrant households live in poverty and there are few prospects for upward mobility. High drop-out rates for Latino youth, in particular, are troubling. As in the past, many first-generation immigrants are prepared to make sacrifices to give their children better opportunities. When those opportunities are not available to the second generation, they and the broader community suffer.

This chapter makes the case for a renewed public–private partnership to support immigrant integration. The federal government provides limited support toward integration, including assistance to refugees to adapt to their new society and funds to school systems to help teach English to children with limited proficiency in the language. The chapter will set out additional areas in which the federal government, in combination with the private sector, could help to ease the future integration of immigrants and, most important, of their children.

Four prerequisites for an immigration system that fulfils the aims of the Pennsylvania model will be addressed. First, there will be a discussion of ways to curb illegal immigration. The next section focuses on the revitalization of legal immigration. The third section addresses U.S. refugee and asylum policies. The final section focuses on a new Americanization movement aimed at the full integration of immigrants into American society.

Curbing Unauthorized Migration

Despite public outcries against unauthorized migration, there has been little political will during the past two decades to tackle the problem in a serious manner. The status quo and its high level of tolerance of unauthorized immigration serve many political and economic interests. Much of the research on the impact of legal and illegal immigration on the U.S. economy demonstrates that the principal beneficiaries are employers and consumers (Smith and Edmonston

1997). Immigrants to the United States tend to fall into one of two educational categories; most are either worse or better educated than the average American. They thereby either fill positions that most U.S. workers do not want because of low pay and poor working conditions or they take positions for which most U.S. workers do not have the skills. Unauthorized immigrants tend to fall into the first category and those admitted under the legal employment-based programs fall into the second.

The presence of unauthorized migrants is attractive to the businesses that demand their labor and to consumers who benefit from lower prices. At present, the family and community networks that provide these workers are far more efficient than the bureaucratic processes that approve applications for the admission of foreign workers. Typically, unauthorized migrants get jobs through referrals by relatives or friends. As long as they have documents – counterfeit or real – that can satisfy government requirements to show work authorization, they are able to obtain jobs in a wide array of businesses. These businesses risk few penalties for hiring the unauthorized workers as long as they fill out the proper paperwork.

As long as the status quo continues to serve the economic interests of business and consumers, reform of the immigration system will be difficult. There appear to be some signs of fraying, however, in the current situation. After reform failed in the Senate during the 110th Congress, the executive branch began to enforce provisions of the law that had long been dormant, including prosecution of unauthorized migrants for using counterfeit or borrowed or stolen documents. Large-scale worksite raids received substantial publicity, apparently as part of an effort by the Department of Homeland Security to demonstrate that the failure to enact comprehensive reform also has a cost. A number of states and localities passed new enforcement measures, citing the failure of the federal government to control illegal immigration as the reason that they are taking unprecedented action.

There is also growing recognition that illegal migration undermines support for legal immigration and exerts a heavy human toll on the migrants themselves. The Commission on Immigration Reform (1994) posited that credible immigration policies must meet a simple yardstick: "People who should get in, do get in; people who should not get in are kept out; and people who are judged deportable are required to leave." When destination countries tolerate high levels of irregular migration, they undermine their own legal immigration systems. There is little credibility to immigration law if migrants and, particularly smugglers, are allowed to circumvent the policies in place to determine who enters, for what purposes, and for what period of time. Often, the public reacts negatively to migration because it feels that the government no longer has control over who is to be admitted. High levels of illegal migration can then create a backlash that extends to legal immigration as well.

Illegal migration also undermines the rule of law. Generally, smuggling operations cannot function effectively without the aid of corrupt officials in source, transit, and destination countries. It also thrives when there is access to counterfeit and fraudulently obtained documents, which in turn create opportunities for identity theft. Many unauthorized migrants work in the underground economy, allowing unscrupulous employers to violate labor laws with impunity because the undocumented workers are unlikely to complain to authorities.

Added to these concerns is the human cost to the immigrants who enter through unauthorized channels or who remain illegally in the country. Clandestine migration is dangerous. When migrants cross deserts, are packed in containers, or cross oceans in unseaworthy boats, they put themselves at risk of serious harm or even death. When they use the services of professional smugglers who are only interested in profit, their lives are at considerable risk. Even if the unauthorized immigrants are able to arrive safely at their destination, they find themselves in very vulnerable situations as they attempt to elude authorities and work illegally. They have few rights and face the risk of apprehension and removal. These immigrants find it difficult to maintain contact with their families because they are not eligible for family reunification unless they are able to obtain legal status.

All in all, for the rule of law and for the sake of humanity, reduction in illegal migration is highly desirable. Its reduction is also a necessary precursor to reinvigorating the Pennsylvania model. Unauthorized migrants are unable, by definition, to participate fully in American society. They are an underclass, unable to take part in the political process and having no prospects – as do legal immigrants – for future participation.

Border Enforcement

In preventing illegal migration, countries tend to fall into two camps: those that follow an "island" model, focusing enforcement activities on the border, and those that follow an interior model, focusing enforcement on activities inside their countries. The island model is generally characteristic of the English-speaking[1] countries (whether they are islands or have contiguous neighbors) that tend to eschew national identity documents, sweeps of immigrant neighborhoods, buses and subways, or businesses that employ immigrants. The emphasis is on keeping unauthorized migrants out, not on finding them after they have entered. By contrast, continental European countries tend to focus more heavily on interior enforcement, with a greater willingness to ask foreign-looking residents for identity documents and stronger systems for enforcing sanctions against employers who hire irregular workers. These two systems are not, of course, pure types, with most countries practicing elements of both types of enforcement.

The United States has tended to deal with prevention through border enforcement. Visa issuance has generally been considered to be the first line of defense against illegal migration, by preventing the admission of security risks

---

[1] This particularly applies to the United States, Canada, United Kingdom, Australia, New Zealand, and Ireland.

and keeping those likely to overstay their visas from obtaining permission to travel to the United States. Inspections at air, sea, and land ports of entry are a backup to identify those who may have obtained visas fraudulently, as well as to prevent entry of inadmissible persons among those who do not require visas to enter. The United States has also invested heavily in efforts to police the long land borders with Mexico and, to a lesser degree, Canada, and to interdict boats attempting illegal entry. Antismuggling operations are a further part of the U.S. border enforcement strategy.

Border enforcement alone, however, has had little success in curtailing illegal immigration. Unauthorized immigrants mostly come for jobs, and as long as the prospects for employment remain promising, they will take financial and physical risks to reach the U.S. job market. Erecting fences and deploying additional personnel and technology, as has been done at the border, may increase apprehensions, but they do not deter those who are determined to enter. When Janet Napolitano, secretary of the department of homeland security, was the governor of Arizona, she famously said, about efforts to deter illegal immigration by constructing walls on the border, "Show me a 50-foot wall, and I'll show you a 51-foot ladder."[2]

Worksite Enforcement

Preventing or at least curbing unauthorized immigration requires measures that get at the push-and-pull factors that motivate people to migrate. From the pull side, reducing the job magnet is crucial. This is not a new conclusion. From the Mexican government in the 1950s to the U.S. federal commissions of the 1980s and 1990s, observers of illegal immigration have emphasized the importance of employment in encouraging illegal migration.

A one-size-fits-all approach, however, does not fit the realities of unauthorized employment. Employers differ in their reliance on and propensity to hire unauthorized workers, requiring different worksite strategies. Many employers seldom if ever hire unauthorized migrants. Their workforce may be mostly professionals and highly skilled workers, and the companies do a variety of background checks to verify credentials and past work experience. Or, they may be located in geographic areas with small numbers of unauthorized immigrants.

Other employers hire unauthorized workers unwittingly (at least as far as the law is concerned). These employers generally hire workers referred by existing employees or by recruitment agencies. They scrupulously fill out the required paperwork and examine, at least cursorily, the documents provided. They may even participate in the electronic verification system in current use, submitting the names and Social Security numbers that the new employees present. The documents are forged or borrowed, however. The names and Social Security numbers may match, but they do not belong to the worker who

[2] http://www.tucsoncitizen.com/ss/border/116207.php.

has just been hired. These employers would not knowingly break the law to hire unauthorized workers, but they are pleased to have access to a low-wage workforce willing and able to do the jobs offered.

Still other employers hire unauthorized workers knowingly to exploit their labor. Such employers are likely to violate a number of labor standards. They may require employees to work long hours at less than minimum wage. They are unlikely to pay Social Security and other taxes, even if they withhold them from the employee's paycheck. These employers often violate occupational and safety standards and may employ child labor. They seek unauthorized workers precisely because they are less likely to complain about ill treatment.

The system of employment verification that has been in place since IRCA requires employers to verify the identity and work authorization of all new hires. An employer fulfills this obligation by completing the federal I-9 form and requesting that the employee present a combination of documents from a list that includes more than twenty approved documents. Most employees provide a driver's license to document identity and a Social Security card to document work authorization. Employers are not required by law to verify that the documents are legitimate; in fact, requesting additional or different documents from some employees, but not others, is a violation of the employer sanctions law.

Employers who violate IRCA's verification provisions face different civil or criminal penalties, known as employer sanctions, depending on whether they committed paperwork violations or knowingly hired unauthorized workers. Penalties range from fines to criminal prosecution depending on the severity and frequency of the offense. The Office of Investigations in the Immigration and Customs Enforcement (ICE) arm of the Department of Homeland Security (DHS) enforces these provisions.

In 2007, my colleagues at Georgetown University and I released a report on worksite enforcement based on interviews with employers, workers and government officials. We also observed conditions in places of employment (including garment factories during a California Department of Labor raid). We identified key factors limiting the effectiveness of the I-9 process, including 1) the proliferation of counterfeit and fraudulent documents; 2) unfamiliarity and confusion regarding the verification procedures and employer responsibility; 3) outright abuse by employers; 4) a growing reliance on labor subcontractors to protect the company benefiting from the work from any penalties attached to hiring the workers; and 5) low penalties for violations, which left the benefits of hiring unauthorized workers greater than the risks. None of these problems were new (Lowell et al. 2007).[3]

---

[3] Lowell et al. (2007) concluded: "counterfeit documents have long been a problem with estimates indicating that as much as half of all unauthorized workers were using fraudulent documents two years after IRCA's implementation. Improvements in secure document technology since IRCA have been readily matched by counterfeiting operations. And several reports have concluded that it is relatively easy to obtain genuine documents, such as birth certificates or drivers licenses, by

Following on the Commission on Immigration Reform's recommendations to pilot-test new models to determine work authorization, the INS launched an electronic verification system that has since become known as E-Verify. It is now operated by one of INS's successor agencies, the Bureau of U.S. Citizenship and Immigration Services (USCIS) in the Department of Homeland Security. E-Verify is a voluntary program for most businesses. Since September 2009, though, all federal contractors are required to use the electronic verification process. Employers who participate are not guaranteed immunity from employer sanctions penalties but if they follow the proper procedures, they generally are able to demonstrate that any hiring of unauthorized workers was inadvertent.

In our 2007 project, we concluded that E-Verify was not ready to become a mandatory program for all employers because of errors in verification (Lowell et al. 2007). The errors were in two directions. The system failed to verify authorization for eligible workers when names or Social Security numbers were misspelled or mistyped or, more seriously, when immigration authorities or the Social Security Administration (SSA) had errors in their databases (false negatives). The system also authorized ineligible workers when they provided a legitimate name and matching Social Security number that belonged to someone else (false positives). Since then, USCIS and SSA have taken steps to improve the data systems. New databases have been added to reduce the number of false negatives. For example, SSA did not have timely access to naturalization records, which resulted in mismatches when workers claimed to be citizens. Once USCIS added its naturalization database to E-Verify, the mismatches decreased. USCIS has also been experimenting with ways to enable employers to verify the photographs of workers when they check their names and Social Security numbers, which would reduce false positives (Ayres 2009). In July 2009, USCIS reported that 97 percent of requests for verification were approved within seconds. It is still questionable, however, that E-Verify would be able to achieve an acceptable level of accuracy if the program were expanded from the 137,000 employers who used the system in July 2009 to the millions of companies with employees in the United States.

The E-Verify program, despite these problems, is still the most promising approach to employment verification. It provides a simple tool to businesses in the first and second categories – that is, businesses that intend to comply with hiring requirements. To be more effective, however, USCIS and SSA will need to continue to correct errors in their databases to reduce false negatives and to

fraudulent means. The Government Accountability Office (GAO) has reported that the practice of using genuine documents obtained from friends, relatives or the underground market is on the rise. This leads to some hiring of undocumented workers without employers knowledge and dishonest employers (and employees) using false documents or others' identities (Lowell et al., 2007)." A 2008 report of the Government Accountability Office also found that E-Verify is "vulnerable to acts of employer fraud and misuse, such as employers limiting work assignments or pay while employees undergo the verification process, that can adversely affect employees queried through the E-Verify program."[3]

develop a process to allow workers to verify and correct information before they go through the hiring process. The agencies will also need to develop better systems to guard against identity theft, probably through the use of a biometric (most likely, photos or fingerprints). Making these changes will require a significant increase in resources. As the Government Accountability Office (GAO) concluded, "A mandatory E-Verify program would necessitate an increased capacity at both U.S. Citizenship and Immigration Services (USCIS) and SSA to accommodate the estimated 7.4 million employers in the United States" (Stana 2008).

Whether E-Verify remains voluntary or becomes mandatory, steps are also needed to ensure that the privacy and rights of employees are protected. To ensure that employers do not discriminate against workers who appear foreign, it is important that employers be required to undertake the same verification procedures for all workers, not just those whom they believe are illegally in the country. Universal application is also important to guard against fraud; if only noncitizens are required to provide documentation or undergo electronic verification, unauthorized workers would claim to be citizens. IRCA in fact made it an unfair employment practice to require more or different documents from some workers than from others. As resources are targeted on employment verification, it will be important to ensure that a comparable increase is made in resources to ensure against discriminatory use of the new procedures.

Privacy of data is another concern. Electronic data must be secure when transmitted over the Internet and there must be ongoing evaluations of data security. There must be better mechanisms to notify individuals if their identity is compromised or the databases have inaccurate information. Education on the use of the system will be necessary, given what we know about existing levels of employer confusion and misuse. In view of the pitfalls of the current system, the implementation of an electronic employer verification system should be gradual, taking into account issues related to expanding the scale, education, user management, and data quality and control, as well as privacy. These cautions should not be taken as reasons to delay making the necessary improvements. After all, in 1994, when the Jordan Commission recommended pilot testing, its best estimate of the time needed for full implementation was seven to ten years. It would be unfortunate if fifteen years from now, the GAO and other observers are still concluding that the system was not yet ready to be made mandatory.

An improved verification system alone will not address the third category of employer – those who knowingly hire unauthorized migrants to exploit them. In fact, some employers use immigration enforcement as a way to dissuade workers from organizing in pursuit of better pay or working conditions. They threaten to report undocumented workers to Immigration and Customs Enforcement (ICE) if the workers try to form unions or even complain too publicly about their work situation. A 2002 Supreme Court decision left unauthorized workers with even less protection. The Court held in *Hoffman Plastic*

Compounds v. NLRB that unauthorized workers are not entitled to back pay when they are illegally fired from their jobs because of their union activities (Fisk and Wishnie 2005).

Addressing the exploitative use of unauthorized workers requires a comprehensive enforcement approach that combines sanctions for illegal hiring with penalties for violation of labor standards. During the past decade, the resources available for enforcement of labor standards have shrunk significantly. The Wage and Hour Division of the Department of Labor experienced a drop in staff of 13 percent between FY 2001 and FY 2008. The overall budget for the Department of Labor remained effectively constant from 2006 to 2008, growing from $11.5 billion to only $11.7 billion during this period. Spending is expected to increase to $12.7 billion in FY2009. President Obama has requested an appropriation of $13.3 billion in FY2010, with another $4.8 billion to come from the Economic Recovery Act, which includes additional support for the federal payment of unemployment benefits. About $500 million is for the Employment Standards Administration, which is responsible for investigating labor abuses. This represents an increase of $64 million over FY 2009 levels. By contrast, ICE requested $2.5 billion for detention and removal of persons illegally in the country. There is a clear disparity between the level of resources targeted at detaining and removing unauthorized migrants and those targeted at the employers who hire and exploit them. Redressing this disparity should be one of the aims of immigration policy.

To ensure further that unscrupulous employers can no longer use immigration status to frighten workers into accepting substandard wages and working conditions, Congress should also take steps to overturn the *Hoffman* decision, thereby requiring employers to pay back pay when they illegally fire unauthorized workers who are involved in union activities; clarify that employers are also responsible for paying back wages when they violate wage and overtime provisions; and make it an immigration-related unfair employment practice to use worksite verification or enforcement actions as a means of retaliation against workers who petition for improved wages or working conditions. These steps would level the playing field and ensure that unscrupulous employers gain no advantage from hiring an exploitable workforce.

Addressing the Push Factors
These steps will help address the pull factor of employment, but reducing illegal immigration also requires steps to address the push factors. Today, as during previous waves of immigration, it is not the poorest of the poor who emigrate from their home countries. Rather, most people who migrate have relatively greater resources than their neighbors. It is for this reason that there are no simple solutions to addressing the push factors, just as there are no simple ways to address the pull factors. Certainly, economic development of source countries will not immediately alleviate the circumstances that cause people to migrate. Indeed, some economists posit that economic development will increase

emigration in the short to medium term until there is sufficient reduction in wage disparities between source and destination to eliminate the push factors. They refer to this process as a "migration hump" that can be charted as an inverted-U shape. With greater economic development, more people have the money, information, and skills needed to move to another country where they can earn more than they would at home. This increases migration – the upward slope of the inverted U. In the long term, economic development reduces emigration pressures significantly, as has been seen in such countries as Ireland, Italy, Greece, and South Korea. This leads to the downward slope of the inverted U. It takes time for income to equalize, however, so the process can take decades. Investment in economic development is beneficial for many reasons, not least because of the increased opportunities that higher income affords. However, it should not be seen as a panacea for solving immigration problems.

Mexico is now, and has been for some time, the largest source country of immigration to the United States. Mexico is also one of the largest trading partners of the United States. The economic context of Mexican migration changed fundamentally with the advent of the North American Free Trade Agreement (NAFTA) in 1994. In accordance with the "migration hump" projections, the greater integration of the Mexican and the U.S. economies did lead to increased migration. As we have seen, the economic boom of the late 1990s in the United States reinforced labor demand for Mexican workers. At the same time, "although population growth diminished in Mexico, the working-age cohorts still expanded by between 2.5 and 2 percent per annum until the year 2000, and economic conditions did not progress rapidly enough to off-set the pull of U.S. jobs and wages (Escobar Latapi and Martin 2008: 239)." The economic recession in the United States appears to have reduced demand and slowed immigration from Mexico, but the underlying push factors are still present and will likely resume when economic recovery once more creates demand. The trajectory is positive for Mexico in the long term, however, particularly when the lowered fertility of the past twenty years results in a smaller work force and the economic reforms of the past fifteen years lead to sustained economic growth. In the meantime, the billions of dollars in remittances that Mexican families receive from their relatives in the United States represent an important contribution to economic stability in Mexico.

Working with Mexico to manage migration across our shared border during this transition period is in the interests of both countries. Since the mid-1990s, immigration and border issues have been discussed in a binational working group that focuses specifically on ways that the two countries can cooperate to manage migration and border security. During the immediate post-NAFTA period, the workgroup met frequently and regularly to ensure continued momentum in discussing areas of both agreement and disagreement. With the summits of the early Bush and Fox presidencies, the working group was eclipsed. After September 11, Mexico–United States discussions focused primarily on border security, not labor migration. The binational working group should be revitalized as a mechanism for coordination and cooperation in identifying mutually supportive policies to deter unauthorized migration and promote legal avenues for Mexican migrants.

Revitalizing Legal Immigration

A second priority in renewing the Pennsylvania model is the revitalization of legal immigration as the principal avenue for new entries into the United States. Curbing illegal immigration will be impossible without addressing the demand for foreign workers, but legal admission policies should be constituted in a manner that is consistent with broader American values and traditions. There are two aspects to be addressed. The first set of issues pertains to future admissions to the United States through both the permanent and temporary systems. The second set of issues pertains to the legalization of those who are already in the country, outlining ways to bring the underclass of unauthorized migrants into full membership.

Future Admissions
Perhaps the most important recommendation to be made with regard to future admissions is the need for flexibility. Predicting demand for foreign workers even three to five years in the future is difficult. Congress often gets it wrong. The 1990 expansion in legal immigration was enacted just as the country was plunging into the 1991 recession. The cap on H-1B admissions was increased to 198,000 just before the dot-com bust that reduced growth in the information technology industry, and the 65,000 cap was restored just as the economic recovery took hold in 2003. Demand for family visas is more consistent because economic cycles do not tend to affect applications. Chain migration can cause substantial increases in applications for visas in certain family categories, however, creating large waiting lists when demand far exceeds supply of visas. Managing migration through inflexible quotas and resulting backlogs just raises expectations for admission without serving national interests in a credible, well managed immigration system.

How flexibility should be accomplished is the relevant question. In this regard, Congress should set priorities for admission and derive admission numbers from those priorities. This would mean elimination of firm quotas in most admission categories. Rather, there should be a guarantee that all applicants who meet the highest priorities set by Congress will receive visas within one year of application if they fulfill all other admission requirements. Admission numbers would increase or decrease depending on the demand for visas in the priorities that are set. Congress would in turn examine, on a continuous basis, whether there are grounds for adjusting the priorities because of changed national interests, which would in turn affect admission numbers. In doing so, Congress should not attempt to follow short-term economic cycles (since they will generally miss the trends, as discussed above). Rather, Congress should set priorities by assessing the medium-term interests of the United States in reuniting families, building human capital, meeting employer demand for workers in specific occupations, and fulfilling humanitarian obligations. These interests broadly define current immigration categories of family-based, employment-based, and refugee admissions.[4] The issue for Congress to address is which groups within each of these broad areas should be given priority for admission within a specified time frame. The time frame may well differ depending on the category. For example, an emergency consultation mechanism for refugee admissions makes sense given the difficulty of anticipating new crises. On the other hand, family admissions are more predictable because they are based on prior levels of immigration. Employment visas are somewhere in the middle because of economic cycles and changing demand.

Deriving numbers from priorities means Congress would have either to raise annual admission levels significantly to provide a sufficient number for all current preferences or to choose from among the many categories that are now given visas. If Congress chooses the latter option, in the interest of fairness to those who have been patiently waiting in backlogs in most of the current preferences, the waiting lists should be cleared before the new priority system is implemented. This would mean short-term increases in overall admissions until backlogs are eliminated. To ensure that the waiting lists do not continue to grow, new applications should be taken only in the categories that are designated as future priorities.

Of most concern are the delays for immediate relatives of permanent residents. Spouses and minor children of legal immigrants who applied in January 2005 became eligible for admission in August 2009 – a waiting period of four years and seven months. Because the demand is higher from Mexico than other countries, the wait for the spouses and minor children from that country is almost seven years. Few U.S. natives would tolerate such long separations. Not surprisingly, many family members instead wait for their visas in the United States. The stock of unauthorized immigrants could be significantly reduced by clearing these backlogs immediately. Eliminating numerical quotas on these close family members would help reduce the flow of future unauthorized immigrants who are only seeking to be with their spouses and parents. Reducing waiting times in this category would be beneficial to the broader society as well. Delays in receiving permanent residence impede integration, particularly for the children awaiting legal status. Rather than spending their formative years in the United States, where they could be learning English and other skills needed to compete in the American economy, their only choices are to remain in their home countries or to immigrate illegally. In either case, they lose valuable time and the United States risks losing valuable members of

---

[4] I have not included the diversity program in this listing. It is the only part of current admissions that would merit a firm quota. In FY 2009, there were more than 13 million applications for 50,000 slots. If Congress determines that encouraging immigration from new destinations remains a priority, a lottery may be the only fair way to manage a program aimed at accomplishing that purpose.

our society when they are unable to take full advantage of opportunities for integration.

In the context of the Pennsylvania model, admitting legal immigrants as permanent residents is preferable to admitting them through temporary worker programs. By definition, temporary workers do not have full membership in U.S. society, nor are they able to exercise full rights. This is particularly the case if temporary workers are tied to a specific employer. Mobility – that is, the ability to change employers – is a powerful protection against abuses in the labor market. Moreover, if immigrants know that they have the opportunity to remain in the United States, they are more likely to learn the language, buy homes, invest in businesses, and become involved in civic activities. U.S. history shows that a large number of persons admitted temporarily remain in the United States, delaying their integration is in neither their interest nor that of the broader society.

Although permanent admissions should be the norm, there may be situations in which temporary workers are more appropriate. If the work to be done is truly temporary – for example, seasonal jobs or a project with a clear end date – then admitting immigrants for the duration of the work may make sense. This is the case in some U.S. temporary worker categories, such as the H-2A program for seasonal agricultural workers and the H-2B program for nonagricultural workers in temporary jobs. It is far from the case in others, such as the H-1B program for professionals, which admits workers for six years or longer if there is a petition for permanent residence. When the jobs are of indefinite, long duration, using temporary worker programs flies in the face of the realities of the labor market. Employers do not want to lose workers who are providing valuable service and employees do not necessarily want to stop working just because the visa expires. Both often find ways to prolong the employment. This situation leads to the old adage that "there is nothing as permanent as a temporary worker."

Using temporary worker programs to regularize the status of unauthorized workers is fraught with difficulties. Only a minority of unauthorized workers are employed in agricultural or other seasonal labor. The majority are in urban labor markets doing year-round work. In some of the industries that are most dependent on unauthorized workers, the jobs they do are of indefinite duration. At present, the unauthorized workers remain in these jobs as long as it is mutually beneficial to them and their employers. In fact, under current policies, unauthorized workers have an advantage over many temporary workers because they have greater labor mobility. If they can earn higher wages from another employer or in a different occupation, there is little to stop them from seeking other employment. This situation would change if there were effective verification processes, but shifting the unauthorized workers into temporary worker programs would not be the ideal solution (see the following discussion for more on legalization).

Even in situations in which the jobs truly are temporary, caution must be taken in the design of temporary worker programs. There must be incentives for temporary workers to return to their home countries at the end of the admission period. If the stay is too short or the pay is too low, or both, the immigrant will be unable to recoup the cost of migration and will be tempted to overstay. An effective verification system would help prevent overstay but temporary workers might be driven into underground employment if their economic goals in migrating are not met. There must also be safeguards to ensure that employers fully meet U.S. labor standards.

A second caveat relates to how demand for temporary workers is measured. Economists point out that there is no such thing as a true shortage of labor. If there were too few workers to fill jobs, businesses would compensate by raising wages and improving working conditions to attract new employees or by finding alternative ways to accomplish the work – for example, by using technology or outsourcing the jobs. As economist Philip Martin (2006) argues, access to temporary foreign workers can distort these economic processes. Businesses may not make investments that would be in their longer-term interests if, in the short term, they are able to hire foreign workers with less immediate expenses. Interviews that Philip Martin and I conducted with raisin grape farmers in California illustrated this point. We visited one grower who had invested in machinery that picked the grapes, laid them out to dry, and then collected them. The machine greatly reduced his labor needs at a time when his competitors feared that the Mexican farm workers who picked their crop might not be able to get past new border controls. When we asked why other farmers did not invest in the labor-saving machinery, we learned that it would take several years to amortize the costs. The other growers were not prepared to make the investment as long as low-wage labor was available.[5]

To avoid creating unnecessary dependence on temporary foreign workers, measures are needed to test labor demand. As CIR recommended, it is preferable to use market forces to test demand, rather than cumbersome bureaucratic processes. Fees could be imposed that would make the hiring of foreign workers at prevailing wages more expensive than alternatives, such as raising wages for domestic workers. The fees could go towards research and development on mechanization and other means of reducing dependence on low-wage foreign workers.

Legalization

The future status of the unauthorized workers already employed in the United States has been one of the most controversial issues in immigration reform. The debate has been between opponents and proponents of legalization. Opponents tend to use the term "amnesty" to describe any efforts to legalize the status of those who entered or work illegally. They argue that rewarding those who violated immigration law with legal status is a travesty of the rule of law.

---

[5] Philip Martin reports that many of the growers subsequently made the investment, not because of a shortage of Mexican workers, but because of competition from China. Chinese labor was so much cheaper than Mexican labor that a low-wage strategy could not compete.

Proponents tend to use the term "regularization" and to emphasize that the unauthorized immigrants are otherwise law-abiding. I prefer the term "legalization" because I stand somewhere between these two groups. Although the rule of law argument is important, and is a principal reason for combating future unauthorized migration, the benefits to accrue from legalizing those who came to work illegally far surpass arguments against it.

Most important, in keeping with the Pennsylvania model, it is crucial that immigrants become fully participating members of our society. At present, about 11 million long-term residents of this country are precluded from such membership because they are without legal status. As an underclass, they are vulnerable to exploitation and abuse. Many of them live in households with children who are U.S. citizens and spouses who are permanent residents. Removing so large a number of persons with such close ties to the United States would be inhumane. It would also pose insurmountable practical problems. There is neither the capacity nor the resources to undertake the type of detention and deportation that such a large-scale removal program would require.

Failing to legalize the current unauthorized workforce would also hamper efforts to curb future illegal immigration. The key to reducing illegal migration is the implementation of a more effective system to deter employment of unauthorized workers. Implementing such a system requires the cooperation of employers, particularly businesses in the second category described above – those who would not deliberately break the law to hire unauthorized workers. These employers are much less likely to cooperate with new verification procedures if it means they will lose their current workforce. Legalization offers them, as well as their workers, the opportunity to operate under the new rules.

The situation works in the reverse as well. Legalization without effective steps to deter future illegal immigration is foolhardy. It sends the message that if one is able to circumvent border controls and gain access to the U.S. labor market, eventually the U.S. government will offer legal status. This only encourages more illegal immigration. Hence, enforcement and legalization must go hand in hand. Neither works effectively without the other.

The legalization implemented under IRCA provides a number of lessons for how best to implement such a program. On the positive side, IRCA succeeded in encouraging undocumented migrants to come forward and apply for legalization, despite suspicions within the immigrant community that it was a ruse to apprehend and remove the applicants. The government worked with non-governmental organizations, ethnic associations, religious groups, and others to publicize the program and convince immigrants that the aim truly was legalization. The government made it clear that most enforcement efforts would be suspended during the implementation of the program to further reassure the intended beneficiaries. A future legalization program would benefit from similar measures.

IRCA worked less well in other regards. First, it left too large a residual population of unauthorized immigrants because the principal program applied to those who had been in the country prior to January 1982, about five years before implementation of the program. For legalization to clear the slate on illegal immigration, it needs to be as expansive as possible in providing options for all of those in the country without legal status.

Second, the rules encouraged use of counterfeit documents even by those who met the requirements. Proving that one had arrived prior to January 1982 was difficult, even for those who had been in the country for the entire time. Some applicants resorted to using counterfeit documents because they did not have employment records or rent or utility receipts to prove their residency. This is not surprising; many were employed in jobs that paid in cash and they rented rooms or even beds in houses that were not zoned for large groups. The Seasonal Agricultural Workers program was especially rife with fraud. Some of the fraud involved outright lies by those who never worked in agriculture, but in other cases, workers did not have evidence of employment or had worked in years not covered under the law's requirements. In each of these cases, applicants used counterfeit documents or bought affidavits from unscrupulous contractors and employers. The more complicated the requirements, and the further they are removed from the realities of life as an undocumented migrant, the harder it will be to deter fraud. Some of the legalization provisions under consideration in previous Congresses included requirements that applicants show they had paid taxes in order to demonstrate they had "earned" the right to regularize their status. Piecing such information together, even for those who have had taxes withheld, will be very difficult since most unauthorized immigrants work under false names and Social Security numbers.

A third problem arose because legalization applied only to the person already in the United States and not to his or her spouse and children. Immediate relatives of the legalized applied within a short period after the sponsors gained legal status, creating the backlogs that have continued to slow down admission of spouses and minor children. A new program of legalization should plan for these family members so as not to create unnecessary waits for all immediate relatives of permanent residents.

Refugee and Asylum Policies

Renewal of U.S. leadership as a nation of refuge is a third priority. Since the end of the Cold War, the United States has not had a fully articulated refugee policy. In some respects, the removal of Cold War ideological under-pinnings to refugee policies proved beneficial, allowing decisions on asylum applications and refugee resettlement to be made on humanitarian, not foreign policy, grounds. The United States offered protection to a broader range of persons who were fleeing fear of persecution in their home countries. In other respects, however, it has left refugee policy, which had been steeped in the Massachusetts model, in a vulnerable state. Most tellingly, since September 11, concerns about terrorism have led to the unfortunate situation raised by the material support restrictions in the USA Patriot Act. In the fight against terrorism, the United States has abandoned some of the most vulnerable victims of the very acts it deplores. In some of the most egregious cases, refugees have been kidnapped because of their association with the United States but refused admission because they paid a ransom for their release.

To address these issues, Congress should amend the USA Patriot Act to allow admission of individuals who can demonstrate that they provided material support under duress. In determining refugee status, adjudicators must already make difficult decisions about the credibility of applicants. Deciding that someone has a well- founded fear of persecution requires that the adjudicator consider both subjective and objective factors in determining if the applicant truly has grounds to fear return to the home country. Deciding whether material support had been offered voluntarily or under duress requires similar assessment of facts and should not prove any more difficult for adjudicators than the refugee status decision itself. Congress should also mandate that the secretary of state develop a list of organizations that can be exempted from the material support ban because of their close association with the U.S. government. This list should also include groups that can more properly be termed freedom fighters than terrorists because they oppose illegitimate government authorities but do not resort to violence against civilian populations to accomplish their goals.

These measures would help revitalize the resettlement program and ensure that *bona fide* refugees receive asylum when they apply from within the United States. In the longer term, however, the United States must define more clearly why it is in the national interest to admit refugees now that Cold War ideology no longer drives these policies. It is all the more important to define the principles behind U.S. refugee policy because displacement is a growing global problem that requires U.S. leadership.

Displacement, as a subset of migration, includes persons forced from their homes by a complex array of factors. Some fit the definition of the 1951 U.N. Convention and the 1980 U.S. Refugee Act of a refugee as someone with a well-founded fear of persecution. A larger number of those who are generally referred to as refugees have fled more generalized conflict and, as was discussed in Chapter 11, do not necessarily meet the persecution standard. Still others have been displaced by natural disasters and cannot return to homes destroyed by hurricanes, earthquakes, volcanoes, and other natural events. Even countries as wealthy and technologically advanced as the United States have difficulty addressing large-scale destruction of habitat by these events, as witnessed in hurricane Katrina. Looming on the horizon is displacement from climate change, as rising sea levels and increasing drought drive millions from communities that can no longer support lives and livelihoods.

Although most people who are displaced by conflict and environment seek safety and resettle within their own home countries, the scale of these events is likely to cause some spillover to other countries. In some of the worst-case scenarios, entire countries may disappear as rising sea levels engulf island states in particular. Deciding who among the displaced should be admitted for temporary protection or permanent resettlement will be a difficult matter. No one country is likely to have sufficient resources to address the problem alone. An international response will be needed. U.S. leadership will be particularly important given our role in world affairs.

How the United States handles its current refugee and asylum policies will provide a context for thinking through appropriate future responses. The lesson of the twentieth century is that U.S. policies matter to other countries. When we failed to pledge to resettle Jews from Nazi Germany, the Evian conference failed. By contrast, U.S. leadership in the 1979 Indochinese refugee conference led to resettlement pledges from countries around the world. It is hard to overemphasize the importance of U.S. policy as a model for other countries. In 1992, as I took up the responsibilities of executive director of the Commission on Immigration Reform, I visited Kenya to examine the growing Somali refugee crisis. In conversations with Kenyan government officials about their reluctance to continue to admit Somalis who were crossing the border, I heard references repeatedly to U.S. interdictions of Haitians. The message was clear: how could the United States ask more of Kenya than we were willing to offer to Haitians? As the international community addresses the complex displacement of the future, other governments will continue to judge U.S. policy prescriptions by the nature of our own admissions policies.

Americanization Revisited

The test of an effective immigration policy is the integration of immigrants. I use the term integration as did the Commission on Immigration Reform. Integration is a two-way street: "Immigrants become part of us, and we grow and become all the stronger for having embraced them" (Commission on Immigration Reform 1997: 27). In some respects, immigrant integration is a one-generation issue. Birthright citizenship – the granting of citizenship to all of those who are born on the territory of the country – means that being an immigrant – a foreigner – is time-limited. Unlike the policies of many other countries, it cannot be inherited. There are no second-generation immigrants in this country. This is not to say that members of the second generation will not experience discrimination on the basis of race or other factors, but they will not have the added problem of exclusion from citizenship. In another respect, though, birthright citizenship makes it all the more important that immigrants and their children have opportunities to succeed. Whatever the model of immigration followed, they will be the new Americans as the generation of immigrants is succeeded by their citizen children.

More than fifteen years after CIR issued its call for a new Americanization program, the need is still there. CIR saw Americanization as a covenant between the newcomer and the broader society. The covenant is voluntary, in that immigration is not an entitlement and integration cannot be forced. It is mutual and reciprocal. "Immigrants must accept the obligations we impose – to obey our laws, to pay taxes, to respect other cultures and ethnic groups. At the same time, citizens incur obligations to provide an environment in which newcomers can become fully participating members of our society" (Commission on Immigration Reform 1997: 28).

During the past two decades, the United States has moved away from this ideal. We imposed few obligations on immigrants, and, even more important, we imposed few obligations on ourselves. With the upsurge in unauthorized immigration, most newcomers entered outside the legal framework. Their labor was valued but their membership in U.S. society was not. Legal immigrants were denied access to basic social safety nets, even though many were among the working poor who most needed the help that food stamps and Medicaid, in particular, provide. According to the U.S. census, foreign-born families were more likely to be living in poverty (15.7 percent) than the families of native-born Americans (9.3 percent). This is not surprising given the low levels of education and low-wage employment of many immigrants.[6]

Reforming immigration policies as discussed earlier will help restore the covenant, but closing the back door to unauthorized immigration and opening the front door to legal immigration is just a first step. There is also need for a public–private partnership that would help ensure that immigrants have the opportunity to succeed. Immediate steps would focus on orientation and education for both immigrants and receiving communities. Orientation would include welcoming materials for newcomers as well as information clearing-houses to help receiving communities learn about the new immigrants and prepare for their integration. The Bureau for Citizenship and Immigration Services took up some of the recommendations of the Commission on Immigration Reform in this regard, and now provides a welcoming packet of information to immigrants who obtain permanent residence.

More needs to be done, though. Given the dispersal of immigrants throughout the country and the growth in new settlement sites, the need for information and best practices in integration has grown dramatically. It is no longer just in the traditional gateways for immigrants – New York, Chicago, Los Angeles – that integration takes place (Gozdziak and Martin 2005, Singer et al. 2008). It is now just as likely that immigrants will come to Rogers, Arkansas, or Westchester, Virginia (sites of some of our research at Georgetown University). These communities have had little experience in settling newcomers and they have few institutions with knowledge about the newcomers in their midst. Yet, there are many innovative programs in these communities, aimed at health, education, language acquisition, small business development, community relations, and so on (Gozdziak and Bump 2008). The challenge is to share the best practices.

Integration of the children of immigrants is perhaps the most important challenge. Although recent research indicates that most children of immigrants do well in American schools, an alarmingly large number do not complete high school. Portes and Rumbaut (2006) found in their longitudinal survey of the children of immigrants in California and Florida that "members of

---

[6] See census data at http://factfinder.census.gov/servlet/STTable?_bm=y&-qr_name=ACS_2005_EST_G00_S0602&-geo_id=01000US&-ds_name=ACS_2005_-ST_G00_.

the new second generation ... are ... performing better academically than their native-parentage peers, graduating from high school and going on to college (where many are still enrolled), speaking accentless English, working hard at their first jobs, taking steps toward independent entrepreneurship, and beginning to form families of their own." They found, however, that "[a] sizable segment – a minority found mostly among the children of Mexican, Haitian, and West Indian immigrants – is being left behind. Young adults caught in a cycle of menial jobs, low incomes, early childbearing, and frequent confrontations with law enforcement face immense obstacles for the future, reinforcing the same racial and ethnic stereotypes that helped contribute to their situation in the first place" (Portes and Rumbaut 2006). Educational outcomes may differ depending on the status of the parents. One study in Los Angeles found that the "adult offspring of ... fathers [who] had legalized or naturalized displayed stronger English language proficiency, higher levels of education, better jobs, and higher earnings than the offspring of those whose fathers remained unauthorized migrants or returned to Mexico" (Bean et al. 2006).

Acquisition of English is crucial to the future success of immigrants and their children. Although many immigrants are able to find jobs without knowing English, upward mobility in the U.S. labor force is dependent on the ability to speak, read, write, and understand English. Most children of immigrants quickly become conversant in English. Studies of English-language acquisition among immigrants and their children tend to confirm the strong pull of the language. In one of the most comprehensive reports on the impact of immigration on the United States, the National Research Council of the National Academies of Sciences concluded: "over time and with extended exposure to the new language, immigrants who have arrived without English skills tend to acquire them" (Smith and Edmonston 1997). The report further found: "with rare exceptions, native-born persons have competence in English. Many children of immigrants have skills in two languages – English and the language of their parents' country of origin. And although some children of immigrants face special challenges in school because of the bilingual nature of their environment, English language proficiency is almost universal" (Smith and Edmonston 1997).

In fact, loss of native languages among second-generation children of immigrants (as well as among immigrants who came to the United States at a young age) continues to be more common than failure to learn English. The children of today's immigrants may be losing native languages more quickly than their predecessors. According to the ERIC Clearinghouse on Urban Education, "There is a trend towards monolingual English speaking among the children of immigrants. Previously it took three generations for a family to lose its native tongue" (Schwartz 1996).

The federal government plays an important role in ensuring that immigrant children have access to appropriate language training. Title VI of the Civil Rights Act of 1964 bans discrimination based on the ground of race, color, or national origin, in "any program or activity receiving federal financial assistance." Title VII of the Elementary and Secondary Education Act guaranteed the rights of children with limited English proficiency children to receive special assistance from public schools. Passed in 1968, the law did not specify a method of instruction, urging school systems to develop programs suitable for their districts. In 1974, drawing on the Civil Rights Act, the Supreme Court, in *Lau v. Nichols*, found a San Francisco program to be inadequate, holding that "there is no equality of treatment merely by providing students with the same facilities, textbooks, teachers, and curriculum; for students who do not understand English are effectively foreclosed from any meaningful education."

Following the Supreme Court decision, Congress amended the law to restrict the choices of local school districts. A range of programs was developed, including transitional bilingual education, with early exit to mainstream programs; maintenance bilingual education, with longer periods of native-language instruction; two-way bilingual programs in which native English speakers learn Spanish (or another language) and native Spanish (or other language) speakers learn English, sharing the same classroom; and intensive English as a Second Language programs. What was not permissible were the "sink or swim" programs that *Lau* found unconstitutional.

Most of the controversy has focused on bilingual education programs, particularly those that allow for lengthy transition periods. Many educators support such programs as the most effective way to teach subject matter along with English to Limited English Proficient (LEP) students. Others oppose it, arguing that bilingual programs retard English acquisition by focusing on native-language instruction. This argument certainly prevailed among California voters who supported Proposition 227, which required public schools to teach LEP students "overwhelmingly in English" through sheltered/structured English immersion (SEI) programs during a transition period and then transfer them to mainstream English-language classrooms.

After a thorough review of the literature on the effectiveness of different pedagogical models of instruction, the U.S. Commission on Immigration Reform (1997a) concluded "there is no strong evidence that one model works better than another or that one type of instruction is preferable." Programs work as well as they can depending on resources and on teacher availability and training as well as other factors. Involvement of parents in the education of their children was one of the most important factors in explaining the effectiveness of language instruction models (U.S. Commission on Immigration Reform 1997a). Many programs are not designed, however, to allow for the active participation of non-English-speaking parents in making decisions about their children's education. Regular evaluations of students' English competence and their ability to apply it to academic subjects are also important predictors of successful programs.

At its worst, the process of English language acquisition may leave the children of immigrants with low levels of literacy in both the native language and English. During field work in Miami, for example, I heard complaints from companies doing business in Latin America that the children of

Spanish-speaking immigrants were barely able to communicate in Spanish and their level of literacy in English left much to be desired. These business leaders advocated true bilingual education that would teach students to be fully literate in both languages.[7]

English-language acquisition for adults is equally important for their full economic, social, and civic participation. Knowledge of English and civics remains a prerequisite for naturalization and full participation in the political process. Lack of English impedes access to health care when patients find it difficult to speak directly with health care providers. Tensions between generations still mount when parents must rely on children to interpret for them.

Studies of English-language acquisition among immigrants tend to show that the major issue facing immigrants is not an unwillingness to learn English but inadequate English-language class capacity and availability. The Commission on Immigration Reform (1997b: 235) found that although "adult education enrollment has increased [since the 1991 Adult Literacy Act], the number who do not have access to basic skills programs, especially ESL [English as a Second Language] courses, also has grown. Public and private literacy programs currently serve only 15 percent of the 44 million adults in the U.S. with the lowest level of basic literacy skills." Of the 44 million, 11 million were immigrants.

Several barriers exist for immigrants who want to enroll in language training programs. Availability of programs is an immediate problem. Waiting lists exist in every city with high numbers of Limited English Proficient adults (U.S. Commission on Immigration Reform 1997b: 264). Financial resources are another challenge. Subsidized programs are hard to find and many immigrants cannot afford to spend large amounts of money on tuition. This is not to say that immigrants are unwilling to invest in English language classes; many programs with lengthy waiting lists charge tuition. Trained teachers are a further problem. The remarks made by an ESL teacher at a commission hearing capture the problems even for those who want to remain in the field: "But I won't miss working many unpaid hours necessary for being the teacher I wanted to be. I won't miss doing tedious paperwork and driving to locations other than where I teach to do my photo copying and getting my teacher resources. I won't miss working at night" (U.S. Commission on Immigration Reform 1997b: 232). Work conflicts, childcare responsibility and transportation barriers are also among the problems faced by immigrants seeking to learn English.

With almost 40 million foreign-born residents of the United States, addressing these problems is beyond the capacity of any one actor, even the federal government. As in the Americanization movement of the early twentieth

---

[7] Education appears to be the key to greater economic success for the individual, not bilingualism itself. Fry and Lowell found that bilingual skills "do not make a statistically significant contribution to weekly wages, once all workers' human capital characteristics are held constant. Thus, the market little values foreign language proficiency and creates no incentive to acquire or maintain it, doubtless contributing to the relatively rapid shift to monolingualism across generations" (Fry and Lowell 2003).

century, efforts in the early twenty-first century require tapping the resources of the public and private sectors at national, state and local levels. Integration takes place in families, religious institutions, schools, ethnic associations and businesses. All of these groups have a role to play in providing opportunities for immigrants to learn English, increase their skills and become conversant in American history and civic values.

Conclusion

For all its history, the United States has been a nation of immigrants. It continues to be the largest country of immigration in the world. Immigration has built the nation and the country, as a society, has benefited from the contributions that immigrants have made. The country has not had a uniform view of immigration, however. From its very beginnings, immigration has served multiple interests – some good, some bad. Immigrants have sometimes been exploited and the target of discrimination. Some have been imprisoned and expelled because of their religion and ideology. However, millions of immigrants have had the opportunity to build better lives for themselves and their children. To understand the role of immigration in American history, one must acknowledge these multiple forms of immigration and the impact they have had on the immigrants and on American society.

Immigration brings change and, with change, comes apprehension. Such critics of immigration as Samuel Huntington fear that today's immigration is changing the American identity. He is probably right. America will not be the same country in the twenty-first century that it was in the past. Huntington's view of American identity is rather skewed, however. He describes "the American dream created by an Anglo-Protestant society" (Huntington 2005: 256). That may have been the dream in eighteenth-century America, but even then it ignored the aspirations of African slaves and Native Americans who were also part of American society. It certainly ignores the American dream of the Catholic and Jewish immigrants of the nineteenth and twentieth centuries.

The true power of the American dream is that it is inclusive of newcomers. At its best, when the Pennsylvania model is allowed to work, both immigrants and citizens are transformed into new Americans. French immigrant Hector St. Jean de Crevecoeur (1986: 38), writing about America in 1781, prophesied the transformation: "*He* is an American, who leaving behind him all his ancient prejudices and manners, receives new ones from the new mode of life he has embraced, the new government he obeys, and the new rank he holds. He becomes an American by being received in the broad lap of our great *Alma Mater*. Here individuals of all nations are melted into a new race of men, whose labours and posterity will one day cause great changes in the world."

References

Adams, Willi Paul. 1999. "German Translations of the American Declaration of Independence." *The Journal of American History* 85, 4: 1325–49.

American Immigration Lawyers Association. 2005. *The Border Protection, Antiterrorism, and Illegal Immigration Control Act of 2005 (H.R. 4437), as Amended and Passed by the House on 12/16/05, Section-by-Section Analysis*, 5.

An Act Concerning Aliens. 1798. Available at: http://www.constitution.org/rf/alien_1798.html

An Act Respecting Alien Enemies. 1798. Available at: http://avalon.law.yale.edu/18th_century/alien.asp

Anbinder, Tyler. 2002. "From Famine to Five Points: Lord Lansdowne's Irish Tenants Encounter North America's Most Notorious Slum." *The American Historical Review* 107, 2: 351–87.

Anderson, Virginia DeJohn. 1985. "Migrants and Motives: Religion and the Settlement of New England, 1630–1640." *The New England Quarterly* 58, 3: 339–83.

———. 1993. *New England's Generation*. Cambridge University Press.

Andersson, Theodore. 1971. "Bilingual Education: The American Experience." *The Modern Language Journal* 55, 7: 427–40.

Andrews, Charles M. 1964. *The Colonial Period of American History: The Settlements*, 4 Volumes. Yale University Press.

Aptheker, Herbert. 1940. "The Quakers and Negro Slavery." *The Journal of Negro History* 25, 3:331–62.

Arnade, Charles W. 1960. "The Failure of Spanish Florida." *The Americas* 16, 3: 271–81.

Atwood, Rodney. 2002. *The Hessians*. Cambridge University Press.

Aytes, Mike. 2009. Written Testimony of Mike Aytes, Acting Deputy Director, U.S. Citizenship and Immigration Services, for a Hearing on "Interior Enforcement Of Immigration Laws: Eliminating Employer Demand for Illegal Immigrants as Part of Comprehensive Immigration Reform" Before the Senate Committee on the Judiciary Subcommittee on Immigration, Refugee and Border Security, July 21, 2009.

Baines, Dudley. 1994. "European Emigration, 1815–1930: Looking at the Emigration Decision Again." *The Economic History Review*, New Series 47, 3: 525–44.

Balch, Emily Greene. 1914. "Housework, English and Immigrants" *The Journal of Home Economics* 6, 5: 447–49.

Bannon, John Francis. 1979. "The Mission as a Frontier Institution: Sixty Years of Interest and Research." *The Western Historical Quarterly* 10, 3: 303–22.

Barrett, James R. 1992. "Americanization from the Bottom Up: Immigration and the Remaking of the Working Class in the United States, 1880–1930." *The Journal of American History* 79, 3: 996–1020.

Baseler, Marilyn C. 1998. *"Asylum for Mankind": America, 1607–1800*. Cornell University Press.

Bean, Frank D., Susan K. Brown, Mark Leach, Jim Bachmeier, Leo R. Chávez, Louis DeSipio, Rubén G. Rumbaut and Jennifer Lee. 2006. How Pathways to Legal Status and Citizenship Relate to Economic Attainment Among the Children of Mexican Immigrants. Pew Hispanic Center.

Becker, Laura L. 1982. "Diversity and Its Significance in an Eighteenth Century Pennsylvania Town," in Michael Zuckerman ed. *Friends and Neighbors: Group Life in America's First Plural Society*. Temple University Press.

Bekken, Jon. 2000. "Negotiating Class and Ethnicity: The Polish-Language Press in Chicago." *Polish American Studies* 57, 2: 5–29.

Benedict, Lawrence. 1930a. "Mexican Influx Curbed Heavily." *Los Angeles Times*, February 13, 1930, p. 4.

Benedict, Lawrence. 1930b. "Restriction Scheme Hit." *Los Angeles Times*, Jan 25, 1930, p. 1.

Bernhard, Virginia. 1992. "Men, Women and Children" at Jamestown: Population and Gender in Early Virginia, 1607–1610," *The Journal of Southern History*, 58, 4: 599–618.

Bethell, Leslie. 1990. *The Cambridge History of Latin America*. Cambridge University Press.

Beyer, Gregg. 1992. "Establishing the United States Asylum Officer Corps." *International Journal of Refugee Law* 4, 4: 455–86.

Blackmun, Harry. 1994. "The Haitian Refoulement Case: Dissenting Opinion." *International Journal of Refugee Law* 6, 1: 71–84.

Bon Tempo, Carl J. 2008. *Americans at the Gate: the United States and Refugees during the Cold War*. Princeton University Press.

Boyd, Monica. 1974. "The Changing Nature of Central and Southeast Asian Immigration to the United States: 1961–1972." *International Migration Review* 8, 4: 507–19.

Bozeman, Theodore Dwight. 1988. *"To Live Ancient Lives": The Primitivist Dimension in Puritanism*. University of North Carolina Press.

Breen, Timothy H. and Stephen Foster. 1973a. "Moving to the New World: The Character of Early Massachusetts Immigration." *William and Mary Quarterly*. Third Series 30, 2: 190–222.

———. 1973b. "The Puritans' Greatest Achievement: A Study of Social Cohesion in Seventeenth-Century Massachusetts." *The Journal of American History* 60, 1: 5–22.

Breitman, Richard and Alan M. Kraut. 1987. *American Refugee Policy and European Jewry, 1933–1945*. Indiana University Press.

Brewer, Jan. 2010. Statement by Governor Jan Brewer on signing S.B. 1070, available at http://azgovernor.gov/dms/upload/PR_042310_StatementByGovernorOnSB1070.pdf

Brown, David C. 1994. "The Keys of the Kingdom: Excommunication in Colonial Massachusetts." *The New England Quarterly* 67, 4: 531–66.

Brown, Martin and Peter Philips. 1986. "Competition, Racism, and Hiring Practices among California Manufacturers, 1860–1882." *Industrial and Labor Relations Review* 40, 1: 61–74.

Brownlow, William Gannaway. 1856. Americanism contrasted with foreignism, Romanism, and bogus democracy, in the light of reason, history, and Scripture; in which certain demagogues in Tennessee, and elsewhere, are shown up in their true colors, at http://www.archive.org/details/americanismcontroobrow

Bruce, Philip A. 1896. *Economic History of Virginia in the Seventeenth Century: An Inquiry into the Material Condition of the People, Based on Original and Contemporaneous Records.* Macmillan.

Butler, James Davie. 1896. "British Convicts Shipped to American Colonies." *American Historical Review* 2: October: 12–33.

Calavita, Kitty. 1984. *U.S. Immigration Law and the Control of Labor: 1820–1924.* Academic Press, Inc.

Calavita, Kitty. 1992. *Inside the State: the Bracero Program, Immigration and the I.N.S.* Routledge.

Camarillo, Albert. 1979. *Chicanos in a Changing Society: From Mexican Pueblos to American Barrios in Santa Barbara and Southern California, 1848–1930.* Harvard University Press.

Campbell, Ballard. 2002. "Comparative Perspectives on the Gilded Age and Progressive Era" *The Journal of the Gilded Age and Progressive Era* 1, 2: 154–78.

Campbell, Mildred. 1959. "Social Origins of Some Early Americans" in Smith, James M. *17th Century America: Essays in Colonial History.* University of North Carolina Press: 63–89.

Cannato, Vincent J. 2009. *American Passage: The History of Ellis Island.* Harper Collins Publishers.

Carpenter, A. H. 1904. "Naturalization in England and the American Colonies." *American Historical Review* 9: 288–303.

Carter, Edward C. II. 1989. "A 'Wild Irishman' under Every Federalist's Bed: Naturalization in Philadelphia, 1789–1806." *Proceedings of the American Philosophical Society* 133, 2: 178–89.

Castle, Timothy N. 1993. *At War in the Shadow of Vietnam: U.S. Military Aid to The Royal Lao Government, 1955–1975.* Columbia University Press.

Charter for the Province of Pennsylvania (1681) http://avalon.law.yale.edu/17th_century/pa01.asp

Charter of Massachusetts Bay (1629) available at http://avalon.law.yale.edu/17th_century/mass03.asp

Charter of Privileges Granted by William Penn, esq. to the Inhabitants of Pennsylvania and Territories, October 28, 1701 available at http://avalon.law.yale.edu/18th_century/pa07.asp

Charter or Fundamental Laws of West New Jersey (1676) available at http://avalon.law.yale.edu/17th_century/nj05.asp

Chen, Yong. 1997. "The Internal Origins of Chinese Emigration to California Reconsidered." *The Western Historical Quarterly* 28, 4: 521–46.

Clark, Peter. "Migration in England during the late seventeenth and early eighteenth centuries in Peter Clark and David Souden. *Migration and Society in Early Modern England.* Barnes and Noble Books: 213–52.

Clark, Peter and David Souden. 1988. *Migration and Society in Early Modern England.* Barnes and Noble Books.

CNN. 2004. "Democrats: Bush Immigration Plan Not Enough," CNN News, January 7, 2004.

Cohn, Raymond L. 2000. "Nativism and the End of the Mass Migration of the 1840s and 1850s." *The Journal of Economic History* 60, 2: 361–83.

Collinson, Peter and Alan W. Armstrong. 2002 *"Forget not mee & my garden –": Selected Letters 1725–1768 of Peter Collinson.* American Philosophical Society.

Commission for the Study of International Migration and Cooperative Economic Development. 1990. *Unauthorized Migration: An Economic Development Response.* Government Printing Office.

Commonwealth of Massachusetts. 1799. Resolution. http://www.constitution.org/rf/vr_04.html

Congressional Record. 1906. 59th Congress, 1st Session, v. 60.

Congressional Record. 1996. 104th Congress, 2nd Session, v. 142.

Congressional Research Service. 1980. "Temporary Worker Programs: Background and Issues: A Report Prepared at the Request of Senator Edward M. Kennedy, Chairman, Committee on the Judiciary, United States Senate, for the use of the Select Commission on Immigration and Refugee Policy." Government Printing Office. Available at http://www.uflib.ufl.edu/ufdc/?m=hdFC&i=146624

Cooper, Dereck W. 1985. "Migration from Jamaica in the 1970s: Political Protest or Economic Pull?" *International Migration Review* 19, 4: 728–45.

Coupeau, Steeve. 2008. *The History of Haiti.* Greenwood Publishing Group.

Cressy, David. 1987. *Coming Over: Migration and Communication Between England and New England in the Seventeenth Century.* Cambridge University Press.

Crouse, Nellis M. 1932. "Causes of the Great Migration 1630–1640." *The New England Quarterly* 5, 1: 3–36.

Daniels, Roger. 2004. *Guarding the Golden Gate: American Immigration Policy and Immigrants since 1882.* Hill and Wang.

De Crevecoeur, J. Hector St. John. 1986. *Letters from an American Farmer and Sketches of Eighteenth-Century America.* Penguin Classics.

De Jong, Gordon F., Brenda Davis Root and Ricardo G. Abad. 1986. "Family Reunification and Philippine Migration to the United States: The Immigrants' Perspective." *International Migration Review* 20, 3: 598–611.

De Tocqueville, Alexis. 2000. *Democracy in America.* Edited and translated by Harvey C. Mansfield and Delba Winthrop. University of Chicago Press.

Diner, Hasia R. 1983. *Erin's Daughters in America: Irish Immigrant Women in the Nineteenth Century.* Johns Hopkins University Press.

Diner, Hasia R. 1994. *The Jewish People in America, volume II, A Time for Gathering: The Second Migration.* Johns Hopkins University Press.

Drake, James. 1997. "Restraining Atrocity: The Conduct of King Philip's War." *The New England Quarterly* 70, 1: 33–56.

Dublin, Thomas and Walter Licht. 2005. *The Face of Decline: the Pennsylvania Anthracite Region in the Twentieth Century.* Cornell University Press.

Dunn, Richard S. 1983. "William Penn and the Selling of Pennsylvania, 1681–1685." *Proceedings of the American Philosophical Society* 127, 5: 322–29.

Dysart, Jane. 1976. "Mexican Women in San Antonio, 1830–1860: The Assimilation Process." *Western Historical Quarterly* 7, 4: 365–75.

Easterlin, Richard A. 1961. "Influences in European Overseas Emigration before World War I." *Economic Development and Cultural Change* 9, 3, Essays in the Quantitative

Study of Economic Growth, Presented to Simon Kuznets on the Occasion of His Sixtieth Birthday, April 30, 1961, by His Students and Friends: 331–51.

Ekirch, A. Roger. 1985. "The Transportation of Scottish Criminals to America during the Eighteenth Century." *Journal of British Studies* 24, 3: 366–74.

Eltis, David. 1983. "Free and Coerced Transatlantic Migrations: Some Comparisons." *American Historical Review* 88, 2: 251–80.

Engstrom, David Wells. 1997. *Presidential Decision Making Adrift: The Carter Administration and the Mariel Boatlift*. Rowman & Littlefield.

Escobar Latapí, Agustín and Susan Forbes Martin. 2008. *Mexico–U.S. Migration Management: a Binational Approach*. Lexington Books.

Farrand. Max, ed. 1911. *The Records of the Federal Convention of 1789*, Volume II. Yale University Press.

Feer, Robert A. 1952. "Official Use of the German Language in Pennsylvania." *Pennsylvania Magazine of History and Biography* 76, 4: 394–405.

First Chart of Virginia (1606) Available at http://avalon.law.yale.edu/17th_century/va01.asp

Fischer, David H. (1991). *Albion's Seed: Four British Folkways in America*. Harvard University Press.

Fish, Catherine L. and Michael J. Wishnie. 2005. "Hoffman Plastic Compounds, Inc. v. NLRB: The Rules of the Workplace for Undocumented Immigrants." in David A. Martin and Peter H. Schuck. *Immigration Stories*. Foundation Press.

Fogleman, Aaron. 1992. "Migrations to the Thirteen British North American Colonies, 1700–1775: New Estimates." *Journal of Interdisciplinary History* 22, 4: 691–709.

Forbes [Martin], Susan. 1982. "Quaker Tribalism" in Michael Zuckerman, ed. *Friends and Neighbors: Group Life in America's First Plural Society*. Temple University Press.

Forbes [Martin], Susan. 1983. The Geographic Distribution of Indochinese Refugees. Refugee Policy Group.

Forbes [Martin], Susan. 1984. Residency Patterns and Secondary Migration of Refugees: A State of the Information Paper. Refugee Policy Group.

Forbes [Martin], Susan. 1985. Adaptation and Integration of Recent Refugees to the United States. Refugee Policy Group.

Forbes [Martin], Susan and Peter Lemos. 1981. "A History of American Language Policy" in Select Commission on Immigration and Refugee Policy. *Appendix A of the Staff Report, Supplement to the Final Report and Recommendations of the Select Commission on Immigration and Refugee Policy*: 9–194.

Forbes [Martin], Susan and Patricia Fagen. 1984. *Unaccompanied Refugee Children: The Evolution of U .S. Policies – 1939 to 1984*. Refugee Policy Group Available at http://repository.forcedmigration.org/show_metadata.jsp?pid=fmo:151

Franklin, Benjamin and Ralph Louis Ketcham. 2003. *The Political Thought of Benjamin Franklin*. Hackett Publishers.

Franklin, Benjamin. 1755. *Observations Concerning the Increase of Mankind, Peopling of Countries, etc.* http://bc.barnard.columbia.edu/~lgordis/earlyAC/documents/observations.html

Franklin, Frank George. 1906. "*The Legislative History of Naturalization in the United States from the Revolutionary War to 1861.*" Dissertation submitted to the History Department, University of Chicago.

Friedman, Max Paul. 2007. "Beyond "Voting with their Feet": Toward a Conceptual History of "America" in European Migrant Sending Communities, 1860s to 1914." *Journal of Social History* 40, 3: 557–75)

Frothingham, Arthur L. 1919. Handbook of War Facts and Peace Problems Available at http://net.lib.byu.edu/~rdh7/wwi/comment/WarFacts/wfacts5.htm

Fry, Richard and B. Lindsay Lowell. 2003. "The Value of Bilingualism in the U.S. Labor Market." *Industrial and Labor Relations Review* 57, 1: 128–40.

Fuchs, Lawrence H. "Some Political Aspects of Immigration." *Law and Contemporary Problems* 21, 2: 270–83.

Fuchs, Lawrence H. 1983. "Immigration Reform in 1911 and 1981: The Role of Select Commissions." *Journal of American Ethnic History* 3, 1: 58–89.

Fuchs, Lawrence H. 1990. *The American Kaleidoscope: Race, Ethnicity, and the Civic Culture.* Wesleyan University Press.

Galenson, David W. 1978. "British Servants and the Colonial Indenture System in the Eighteenth Century." *Journal of Southern History* 44, 1: 41–66.

Galenson, David W. 1984. "The Rise and Fall of Indentured Servitude in the Americas: An Economic Analysis." *The Journal of Economic History* 44, 1: 1–26.

Gallagher, Dennis, Susan Forbes [Martin], and Patricia Fagen. 1985. Of Special Humanitarian Concern: U.S. Refugee Admissions Since Passage of the Refugee Act. Refugee Policy Group.

Gallagher, Dennis, Susan Forbes Martin, and Patricia Weiss Fagen. 1989. "Temporary Safe Haven: The Need for North American-European Responses" in Gilburt Loescher and Laila Monahan, eds., *Refugees and International Relations.* Oxford University Press.

Games, Alison. 1999. *Migration and the Origins of the English Atlantic World.* Harvard University Press.

Gamio, Manuel. 1969a. *Mexican Immigration to the United States.* Arno Press and The New York Times.

Gamio, Manuel. 1969b. *The Mexican Immigrant: His Life-Story.* The University of Chicago Press.

Gamm, Gerald and Robert D. Putnam. 1999. "The Growth of Voluntary Associations in American, 1840-1940." *Journal of Interdisciplinary History* 29, 4: 511–57.

Gartner, Lloyd P. 1986. "Jewish Migrants En Route from Europe to North America: Traditions and Realities." *Jewish History* 1, 2: 49–66.

Gemery, Henry A. 1989. "Disarray in the Historical Record: Estimates of Immigration to the United States, 1700–1860." Symposium on the Demographic History of the Philadelphia Region, 1600–1860 in Proceedings of the American Philosophical *Society* 133, 2: 123–27.

Georgetown University Law Center Human Rights Institute. 2006. Unintended Consequences: Refugee Victims of the War on Terror Available at http://isim.george town.edu/Publications/AndyPubs/Unintended%20Consequences%20Refugee% 20Victims%20of%20the%20War%20on%20Terror.pdf

Guerin-Gonzales, Camille. 1994. *Mexican Workers and American Dreams: Immigration, Repatriation, and. California Farm Labor, 1900–1939.* Rutgers University Press.

Gimpel, James G. and James R. Edwards. 1999. *The Congressional Politics of Immigration Reform.* Allyn and Bacon.

Global Security.com. ND. El Salvador Civil War. Available at http://www.global security.org/military/world/war/elsalvador2.html

Gold, Steven J. 1999. "From "The Jazz Singer" to "What a Country!" a Comparison of Jewish Migration to the United States, 1880–1930 and 1965–1998." Journal of American Ethnic History 18,3, The Classical and Contemporary Mass Migration Periods: Similarities and Differences: 114–41.

Goodfriend, Joyce D. 1992. *Before the Melting Pot: Society and Culture in Colonial New York City, 1664–1730.* Princeton University Press.

Gordon, Michael R. 1994. "In Shift, U.S. Will No Longer Admit Haitians at Sea." *N.Y. Times,* July 6, 1994, at A1, A4.

Gottfried, Marion H. 1936. "The First Depression in Massachusetts." *The New England Quarterly* 9, 4: 655–78.

Gould, Roger V. 1996. "Patron-Client Ties, State Centralization, and the Whiskey Rebellion." *The American Journal of Sociology* 102, 2: 400–29.

Gozdziak, Elzbieta and Susan Martin. 2005. *Beyond the Gateway: Immigrants in a Changing America.* Lexington Books.

Gozdziak, Elzbieta and Micah Bump. 2008. *New Immigrants, Changing Communities: Best Practices for a Better America.* Lexington Books.

Grabbe, Hans-Jürgen. 1989. "European Immigration to the United States in the Early National Period, 1783–1820." *Proceedings of the American Philosophical Society* 133, 2: 190–214.

Grasmuck, Sherri. 1982. "Migration within the Periphery: Haitian Labor in the Dominican Sugar and Coffee Industries." *International Migration Review* 16, 2: 365–77.

Griffen, Clyde. 1972. "Occupational Mobility in Nineteenth-Century America: Problems and Possibilities." *Journal of Social History* 5, 3: 310–30.

Grove, Wayne A. 1996. "The Mexican Farm Labor Program, 1942–1964" *Agricultural History* 70, 2: 302–20.

Grubb, Farley. 2000. "The Transatlantic Market for British Convict Labor," *Journal of Economic History* 60, 1: 94–122.

Gutiérrez, David Gregory. 2004. *The Columbia history of Latinos in the United States since 1960.* Columbia University Press.

Haberlein, Mark. 1993. "German Migrants in Colonial Pennsylvania: Resources, Opportunities, and Experience." *The William and Mary Quarterly,* Third Series 50, 3: 555–74.

Haines, David W. and Karen Elaine Rosenblum. 1999. *Illegal Immigration in America: a Reference Handbook.* Greenwood Publishing Group.

Hamilton, Alexander. 1827. Report on the Subject of Manufactures. http:\\books .google.com,books?id=3srvO_cYTCsC&dq=disturbed±state±of±Europe,± inclining±its±citizens±to±emigration&client=firefox-a&source=gbs_navlinks_s

Hamre, James S. 1981. "Norwegian Immigrants Respond to the Common School: A Case Study of American Values and the Lutheran Tradition." *Church History* 50, 3: 302–15.

Handlin, Oscar. 1951. *The Uprooted: The Epic Story of the Great Migrations That Made the American People.* Grosset & Dunlap.

Harding, Warren G. 1921. Inauguration Address, 4 March 1921 Available at http://www.firstworldwar.com/source/harding1921inauguration.html

Hatton, Timothy and Jeffrey Williamson.1998. *The Age of Mass Migration: Causes and Economic Impact.* Oxford University Press.

Hertzberg, Arthur. 1998. *The Jews in America: Four Centuries of an Uneasy Encounter: A History.* Columbia University Press.

Higham, John. 1955. *Strangers in the Land: Patterns of American Nativism, 1860–1925.* Rutgers University Press.

Hill, Gladwin. 1953. "'Wetback' Influx near the Record." *New York Times,* Nov 22, 1953, p. 65.

Hirata, Lucie Cheng. 1979. "Free, Indentured, Enslaved: Chinese Prostitutes in Nineteenth-Century America." *Signs* 5, 1: 3–29.

Hirschman, Charles. 2004. "The Role of Religion in the Origins and Adaptation of Immigrant Groups in the United States." *International Migration Review* 38, 1206–33.

Hofstra, Warren R. 1998. "'The Extention of His Majesties Dominions': The Virginia Backcountry and the Reconfiguration of Imperial Frontiers" *The Journal of American History* 84, 4: 1281–1312.

Horn, J.P. "Moving on in the New World: migration and out-migration in the seventeenth-century Chesapeake." in Peter Clark and David Souden. *Migration and Society in Early Modern England*. Barnes and Noble Books: 172–212.

Hoyt, Edward A. 1952. "Naturalization under the American Colonies: Signs of a New Community." *Political Science Quarterly* 67, 2: 248–66.

Huntington, Samuel P. 2005. *Who are we? The Challenges to America's National Identity*. Simon and Schuster.

Immigration Commission. 1911a. *Reports of the Immigration Commission*. Volume 1. Government Printing Office.

Immigration Commission. 1911b. *Emigration Conditions in Europe. Reports of the Immigration Commission*. Volume 4. Government Printing Office.

Immigration Restriction League. n.d. Constitution Available at http://pds.lib.harvard .edu/pds/view/5233215?action=jp2zoomin&imagesize=1200&jp2x=1&jp2y=&
jp2Res=0.5&rotation=0&n=1&op=j&bbx1=0&bby1=0&bbx2=82&bby2=130&
zoomin.x=8&zoomin.y=9)

Jachimowitz, Maia and Ramah McKay. 2003. "'Special Registration'" Program. Migration Policy Institute Available at http://migrationinformation.org/USfocus/display .cfm?ID=116

Jacoby, Susan. 2008. *The Age of American Unreason*. Pantheon Books.

Jefferson, Thomas. 1993. Notes on the State of Virginia http://etext.virginia.edu, etcbin,toccer-new2?id=JefVirg.sgm&images=images,modeng&data=,texts,english, modeng,parsed&tag=public&part=teiHeader

Jennings, Francis. "Goals and Functions of Puritan Missions to the Indians." *Ethnohistory* 18, 3: 197–212.

Johnson, James H. 1990. "The Context of Migration: The Example of Ireland in the Nineteenth Century. *Transactions of the Institute of British Geographers*, New Series 15, 3: 259–76.

Johnson, Lyndon Baines. 1965. *"Remarks at the Signing of the Immigration Bill*, Liberty Island, New York, October 3, 1965 Available at http://www.lbjlib.utexas .edu,Johnson,archives.hom,speeches.hom,651003.asp

Jones, Maldwyn. 1960. *American Immigration*. University of Chicago Press.

Jordan, Barbara. 1994. "Testimony of Barbara Jordan, Chair, U.S. Commission on Immigration Reform Before the U.S. House of Representatives Committee on Ways and Means, Subcommittee on Human Resources, August 9, 1994.

Jordan, Barbara. 1995a. "The Americanization Ideal." *New York Times*, September 11.

Jordan, Barbara. 1995b. Testimony of Barbara Jordan, Chair, U.S. Commission on Immigration Reform Before a Joint U.S. House of Representatives Committee on the Judiciary Subcommittee on Immigration and Claims and U.S. Senate Committee on the Judiciary Subcommittee on Immigration, June 28, 1995.

Joselit, Jenna. 1981. "The Perceptions and Realities of Immigrant Health Conditions: 1840–1920" in Select Commission on Immigration and Refugee Policy. Appendix A of the Staff Report, Supplement to the Final Report and Recommendations of the Select Commission on Immigration and Refugee Policy: 195–286.

Keeling, Drew. 2005. "The Business of Transatlantic Migration between Europe and the USA, 1900–1914." Dissertation,University of California, Berkeley.

Kennedy, Edward M. 1966. "The Immigration Act of 1965." *Annals of the American Academy of Political and Social Science* **367**: 137–49.

Kennedy, Edward M. 1981. "Refugee Act of 1980." *International Migration Review*, **15**, 1/2: 141–56.

Kennedy, John F. 1964. *A Nation of Immigrants*. London, Hamish Hamilton.

Kercher, Bruce. 2003. "Perish or Prosper: The Law and Convict Transportation in the British Empire, 1700–1850." *Law and History Review* **21**, 3: 527–84.

Kessell, John L. 2003. *Spain in the Southwest*. University of Oklahoma Press.

Kessner, Thomas. 1981. "History of Repatriation" in Select Commission on Immigration and Refugee Policy. *Appendix A of the Staff Report, Supplement to the Final Report and Recommendations of the Select Commission on Immigration and Refugee Policy*: 287–388.

King, Desmond. *The Liberty of Strangers: Making the American Nation*. Oxford University Press, 2005.

Klein, Herbert S. 2004. *A Population History of the United States*. Cambridge University Press.

Klepp, Susan E. 1989. "Demography in Early Philadelphia, 1690–1860." *Proceedings of the American Philosophical Societ* **133**, 2: 85–111.

Kraut, Alan M., Richard Breitman, and Thomas W. Imhoof. 1984. "The State Department, the Labor Department, and German Jewish Immigration, 1930–1940." *Journal of American Ethnic History* **3**, 2: 5–38.

Krutz, Gordon V. 1971. "Chinese Labor, Economic Development and Social Reaction." *Ethnohistory* **18**, 4: 321–33.

Laurie, Bruce, Theodore Hershberg, and George Alter. 1975. "Immigrants and Industry: The Philadelphia Experience, 1850–1880." *Journal of Social History* **9**, 2: 219–48.

Leonard, Thomas (Tim). 2006. "American Progressivism and the Rise of the Economist as Expert." Social Science Research Network Available at http://papers.ssrn.com/sol3/papers.cfm?abstract_id=926635

Levine, Bruce. 2001. "Conservatism, Nativism, and Slavery: Thomas R. Whitney and the Origins of the Know-Nothing Party." *The Journal of American History* **88**, 2: 455–88.

Lissak, Rivka. 1983. "Myth and Reality: The Pattern of Relationship between the Hull House Circle and the 'New Immigrants' on Chicago's West Side, 1890–1919. *Journal of American Ethnic History* **2**, 2: 21–50.

Liu, John M. 1992. "The Contours of Asian Professional, Technical and Kindred Work Immigration, 1965–1988." *Sociological Perspectives* **35**, 4: 673–704.

Locke, John. 1979. An Essay Concerning Human Understanding, Book III. Oxford University Press.

Lodge, Henry Cabot. 1919. Speech on the League of Nations, 12 August 1919. Available at http://www.firstworldwar.com/source/lodge_leagueofnations.htm

Loescher, Gilburt. 1993. *Beyond Charity: International Cooperation and the Global Refugee Crisis*. Oxford University Press.

Loescher, Gilburt and John Scanlan. 1984. "Human Rights, U.S. Foreign Policy, and Haitian Refugees." *Journal of Interamerican Studies and World Affairs* **26**, 3: 313–56.

Loescher, Gilburt and John Scanlan. 1986. *Calculated Kindness: Refugees and America's Half-Open Door, 1945 to the Present*. Free Press and Collier Macmillan.

Los Angeles Times. 1928. "It Must Not Pass." *Los Angeles Times*, Jan 22, 1928: J4.

Los Angeles Times. 1929a. "Fewer Mexicans Cross Line," *Los Angeles Times*, Jan. 11, 1929: 1.

Los Angeles Times. 1929b. "Mexican Influx Curbed by Half." *Los Angeles Times*, June 18, 1929: 8.

Los Angeles Times. 1930. "Mexico Plans New Reforms." *Los Angeles Times*, January 11, 1930: 6.

Lowell, B. Lindsay. 1987. *Scandinavian Exodus.* Westview Press.

Lowell, B. Lindsay, Susan Martin and Micah Bump. 2008. Worksite Solutions to Unauthorized Migration. Institute for the Study of International Migration, Georgetown University Available at http://isim.georgetown.edu/Publications/SRFMaterials/WorksiteSolutions.pdf

Lowenherz, Robert J. 1959. "Roger Williams and the Great Quaker Debate." *American Quarterly* 11, 2, Part 1: 157–65.

Maingot, Anthony P. 1987. "Haiti: Problems of a Transition to Democracy in an Authoritarian Soft State." *Journal of Interamerican Studies and World Affairs* 28, 4: 75–102.

Manchester Guardian. 1936. Article, May 23, 1936, p. 18.

Markel, Howard and Alexandra Minna Stern. 2002. "The Foreigness of Germs: The Persistent Association of Immigrants and Disease in American Society." *The Milbank Quarterly* 80, 4: 757–88.

Marrus, Michael Robert. 2002. *The unwanted: European refugees from the First World War through the Cold War.* Temple University Press.

Martin, Philip. 2001. "Immigrant Workers in Rural and Agricultural Areas." Prepared for conference on Host Societies and the Reception of Immigrants: Institutions, Markets, and Policies, May 10–12, 2001 Available at http://www.wcfia.harvard.edu/sites/default/files/Martinpaperforposting.pdf

Martin, Philip. 2006. Managing Labor Migration: Temporary Worker Programmes for the 21ST Century, paper presented at International Symposium on International Migration and Development, Turin, Italy, 28–30 June 2006. Available at http://www.un.org/esa/population/migration/turin/Symposium_Turin_files/P07_Martin.pdf

Martin, Susan. 2002. "The Attack On Social Rights: US Citizenship Devalued," in Patrick Weil and Randall Hansen, eds. *Dual Nationality, Social Rights and Federal Citizenship in the US and Europe: the Reinvention of Citizenship.* Berghahn Press.

Martin, Susan. 2003. "The Politics of US Immigration Reform" in Sarah Spencer, ed., *The Politics of Migration: Managing Opportunity, Conflict and Change.* Political Quarterly.

Martin, Susan. 2005. "Language and Immigration," in Joanne van Selm and Elspeth Guild, eds. *International Migration and Security: Culture and Identity, Opportunities and Challenges.* Routledge Press.

Martin, Susan, Andrew Schoenholtz and Deborah Waller Meyers. 1998. "Temporary Protection: Towards a New Regional and Domestic Framework." *Georgetown Immigration Law Journal* 12, 4: 543–87.

Martin, Susan, B. Lindsay Lowell and Philip Martin. 2002. "U.S. Immigration Policy: Admission of High Skilled Workers." *Georgetown Immigration Law Journal* 16, 3.

Martin, Susan and B. Lindsay Lowell. 2005. "Competing for Skills: US Immigration Policy Since 1990," *Law and Business Review of the Americas* 11, 3–4.

Martin, Susan and Philip Martin. 2004. "International Migration and Terrorism: Prevention, Prosecution and Protection," *Georgetown Immigration Law Journal*, 18, 2: 329–44.

Mason, Matthew E. 2000. "Slavery Overshadowed: Congress Debates Prohibiting the Atlantic Slave Trade to the United States, 1806–1807." *Journal of the Early Republic.* 20, 1: 59–81.

Massey, Douglas et al. (1993) "Theories of international migration: A review and appraisal," *Population and Development Review* 3: 431–65.

Mayflower Compact (1620) available at http://www.yale.edu/lawweb/avalon/states/mass01.htm

Mei, June. 1979. Socioeconomic Origins of Emigration: Guangdong to California, 1850–1882. *Modern China* 5, 4: 463–501.

Melville, Herman. 1983. Redburn: His First Journey. Library of America.

Menard, Russell R. 2001. *Migrants, Servants and Slaves*. Ashgate.

Metzker, Isaac. 1971. *A Bintel Brief*. Doubleday.

Migration News. 1994. "SOS Dominates California Campaign." *Migration News* 0, 4 Available at http://migration.ucdavis.edu/mn/comments.php?id=464_0_2_0_C/

Miller, Perry and Thomas Herbert Johnson. 1963. *The Puritans*. Harper and Row.

Mitchell, Christopher. 2004. *Western Hemisphere Immigration and the United States Foreign Policy*. Pennsylvania State Press.

Morgan, Edmund S. 1975. *American Slavery, American Freedom: The Ordeal of Colonial Virginia*. Norton Press.

Morris, Richard B. 1950. "The Course of Peonage in a Slave State." *Political Science Quarterly* 65, 2: 238–63.

Morse, Samuel Finley Breese. 1835. Imminent dangers to the free institutions of the United States through foreign immigration, and the present state of the naturalization laws. http://pds.lib.harvard.edu/pds/view/4392276

Motomura, Hiroshi. 2006. Americans in Waiting: The Lost Story of Immigration and Citizenship in the United States. Oxford University Press.

Munger, Donna B. 1993. *Pennsylvania Land Records: A History and Guide for Research*. Scholarly Resources Inc.

Murdoch, Alexander. 2004. *British Emigration: 1603–1914*. Palgrave MacMillan.

Murray, Robert K. 2009. *Red Scare: A Study In National Hysteria, 1919–1920*. University of Minnesota Press.

National Commission on Terrorist Attacks Upon the United States. 2004. The 9/11 Commission Report. Available at http://govinfo.library.unt.edu/911/report/index.html

National Council of State Legislatures, Immigrant Policy Project. 2009. "State Laws Related to Immigrants and Immigration in 2008." Available at http://www.ncsl.org/Portals/1/documents/immig/StateImmigReportFinal2008.pdf

Naturalization Act. 1790. Available at: http://rs6.loc.gov,cgi-bin,ampage?collId=llsl&fileName=001,llsl001.db&recNum=226

Naturalization Act. 1795. Available at: http://memory.loc.gov/cgi-bin/ampage?collId=llsl&fileName=001/llsl001.db&recNum=537

Naylor, James. 1653. *A Discovery of the Wisdom which is from Beneath, And The Wisdom which is from Above* http://www.strecorsoc.org/jnayler/wisdom.html

Neuman, Gerald L. 1993. "The Lost Century of American Immigration Law (1776–1875)." *Columbia Law Review* 93, 8: 1833–1901.

New Castle. 1935. *Records of the Court of New Castle on Delaware, Vol. II, 1681–1699*, Tribune Publishing, p. 37. http://homepages.rootsweb.ancestry.com/~stiddem/photos/wmpenn.html

New York Times. 1954a. "U.S. Spreads Net for 'Wetbacks.'" *New York Times*, June 13, 1954, p. 24.

New York Times. 1954b. "'Wetbacks' Have to Pay," *New York Times*, July 19, 1954, p. 21.

New York Times. 1954c. "'Wetback' Controls Spur Labor Demand," *New York Times*, July 15, 1954, p. 12.

New York Times. 2004. "Powell, in Mexico, Pledges Migrant Reform," *New York Times*, November 10, 2004. Available at http://www.nytimes.com/2004/11/10/international/americas/10mexico.html

Ngai, Mae M. 2004. *Impossible Subjects: Illegal Aliens and the Making of Modern America*. Princeton University Press.

Nicholson, Bradley J. 1994. "Legal Borrowing and the Origins of Slave Law in the British Colonies" *The American Journal of Legal History* 38, 1: 38–54.

North, David and Marion Houston. 1976. "A Summary of Recent Data on and Some of the Public Policy Implications of Illegal Immigration." National Council on Employment Policy: 36–51.

Office of the Inspector General, US Department of Justice. 2003. The September 11 Detainees: A Review of the Treatment of Aliens Held on Immigration Charges in Connection with the Investigation of the September 11 Attacks. Available at http://www.usdoj.gov/oig/special/0306/index.html

Olivas, Michael A. 2005. "Plyler v. Doe, the Education of Undocumented Children, and the Polity" in David A. Martin and Peter H. Schuck. Immigration Stories. Foundation Press.

O'Rourke, Kevin H. and Jeffrey G. Williamson. 2001. Globalization and History: The Evolution of a Nineteenth-Century Atlantic Economy. MIT Press.

Paine, Thomas and Edward Larkin. 2004. Common Sense. Broadview Press.

Passel, Jeffrey S. and D'Vera Cohn. 2008. "Trends in Unauthorized Immigration: Undocumented Inflow Now Trails Legal Inflow." *Pew Hispanic Center*. Available at http://pewhispanic.org/reports/report.php?ReportID=94

Passel, Jeffrey S. and D'Vera Cohn. 2009. "Mexican Immigrants: How Many Come? How Many Leave?" *Pew Hispanic Center*. Available at http://pewhispanic.org/files/reports/112.pdf

Penn, William. 1682. Frame of Government of Pennsylvania, May 5, 1682 http://avalon.law.yale.edu/17th_century/pa04.asp

Penn, William. 1683. Frame of Government of Pennsylvania, February 2, 1683 http://avalon.law.yale.edu/17th_century/pa05.asp

Penn, William. 1807. /books?id=hVQrAAAAYAAJ&dq=William±Penn±acquain No Cross, No Crown. http://books.google.comted±with±God±as±a±spirit,± consider±him,±and±worship±him±as±such&source=gbs_navlinks_s

Pestana, Carla Gardina. 1993. "The Quaker Executions as Myth and History." *The Journal of American History* 80, 2: 441–69.

Pestana, Carla Gardina. 1983. "The City upon a Hill under Siege: The Puritan Perception of the Quaker Threat to Massachusetts Bay, 1656–1661." *The New England Quarterly* 56, 3: 323–53.

Pezzullo, Ralph. 2006. *Plunging into Haiti: Clinton, Aristide, and the Defeat of Diplomacy*. University Press of Mississippi.

Pierenkemper, Toni and Richard H. Tilly. 2004. The German Economy During the Nineteenth Century. *Berghahn Books*.

Poitras, Guy. 1981. "The U.S. Experience of Return Migrants from Costa Rica and El Salvador." in Select Commission on Immigration and Refugee Policy. *Appendix E of the Staff Report, Supplement to the Final Report and Recommendations of the Select Commission on Immigration and Refugee Policy.*

President's Commission on Migratory Labor. 2007. "The Bracero Program." Reprinted in Al Smith. *American Cultures: Readings in Social and Cultural History.*

Pulsipher, Jenny Hale. 2001. "'Our Sages are Sageles': A Letter on Massachusetts Indian Policy after King Philip's War." *The William and Mary Quarterly*, Third Series 58, 2: 431–48.

Puttkammer, E. W. (1953). "Review, *Whom Shall We Welcome: Report of the President's Commisssion on Immigration and Naturalization.* The Social Service Review 27, 2: 243–44.

Ranlet, Philip. 1988. "Another Look at the Causes of King Philip's War." *The New England Quarterly* 61, 1: 79–100.

Reimers, David M. 1981. "Post-World War II Immigration to the United States: America's Latest Newcomers." *Annals of the American Academy of Political and Social Science* 454: 1–12.

Reimers, David M. 1992. *Still the Golden Door: The Third World Comes to America.* Columbia University Press.

Remennick, Larissa I. 2007. *Russian Jews on Three Continents.* Transaction Publishers.

Rumbaut, Rubén G. 1994. "Origins and Destinies: Immigration to the United States since World War II." *Sociological Forum* 9, 4: 583–621.

Rumbaut, Rubén G. and Alejandro Portes. 2006. "The Second Generation in Early Adulthood: New Findings from the Children of Immigrants Longitudinal Study." *Migration Information Source.* Available at http://www.migrationinformation .org/Feature/print.cfm?ID=445

Salisbury, Neal. 1996. "The Indians' Old World: Native Americans and the Coming of Europeans," *The William and Mary Quarterly*, 3rd Ser. 53, 3: 435–58.

Sandos, James A. and Harry E. Cross. 1983. "National Development and International Labour Migration: Mexico 1940–1965." *Journal of Contemporary History* 18, 1: 43–60.

Schlossman, Steven L. 1983. "Is There an American Tradition of Bilingual Education? German in the Public Elementary Schools, 1840–1919." *American Journal of Education* 91, 2: 139–86.

Schmidt, Regin. 2000. *Red Scare: FBI and the Origins of Anticommunism in the United States, 1919–1943.* Museum Tusculanum Press.

Schoenholtz, Andrew I and Jennifer Hojaiban. 2008 "International Migration and Anti-Terrorism Laws and Policies" *Transatlantic Perspectives on Migration Policy Brief #4.* Available at http://isim.georgetown.edu/Publications/GMF% 20Materials/AntiTerrorismLaws.pdf

Schuck, Peter. 1998. *Citizens, Strangers, and In-Betweens.* Westview Press.

Schwartz, Wendy. 1996. Immigrants and Their Educational Attainment: Some Facts and Findings, Number 116, November 1996, EDO-UD-96-4, ISSN 0889-8049.

Scruggs, Otey M. "The United States, Mexico, and the Wetbacks, 1942–1947." *The Pacific Historical Review* 30, 2: 149–64.

Second Charter of Virginia (1609) available at http://avalon.law.yale.edu/17th_century/va02.asp

Seigal, Jacob S., Jeffrey Passel and J. Gregory Robinson. 1980. "Preliminary Review of Existing Studies of the Number of Illegal Residents in the United States." Paper prepared as a working document for the use of the Select Commission on Immigration and Refugee Policy.

Select Commission on Immigration and Refugee Policy. 1981a. U.S. Immigration Policy and the National Interest. Government Printing Office.

Select Commission on Immigration and Refugee Policy. 1981b. U.S. Immigration Policy and the National Interest: Staff Report. Government Printing Office.

Select Commission on Immigration and Refugee Policy. 1981c. U.S. Immigration Policy and the National Interest: Staff Report. Appendix H. Government Printing Office.

Sen, Amartya Kumar. 1982. Poverty and Famines: An Essay on Entitlement and Deprivation. Oxford University Press.

Shalhope, Robert E. 2004. *The Roots of Democracy*. Rowman and Littlefield.

Shapiro, Steven R. 1987. "Ideological Exclusions: Closing the Border to Political Dissidents." *Harvard Law Review* 100, 4: 930–45.

Singer, Audrey, Susan W. Hardwick and Caroline Brettell, eds. 2008. Twenty-First Century Gateways: Immigrant Incorporation in Suburban America. Brookings Institution Press.

Slaughter, Thomas Paul. 1988. The Whiskey Rebellion: Frontier Epilogue to the American Revolution. Oxford University Press.

Smith, James and Barry Edmonston. 1997. *The New Americans: Economic, Demographic and Fiscal Effects of Immigration*. National Academy of Sciences Press.

Smith, James Morton. 1954a. "Alexander Hamilton, the Alien Law, and Seditious Libels." *The Review of Politics* 16, 3: 305–33.

Smith, James Morton. 1954b. "Background for Repression: America's Half-War with France and the Internal Security Legislation of 1798." *The Huntington Library Quarterly* 18, 1: 37–58.

Smith, James Morton. 1954c. "The Enforcement of the Alien Friends Act of 1798." *The Mississippi Valley Historical Review* 41, 1: 85–104.

Soderlund, Jean R. 1987. "Women's Authority in Pennsylvania and New Jersey Quaker Meetings, 1680–1760." *The William and Mary Quarterly*, Third Series 44, 4: 722–49.

Soderlund, Jean R. 1989. "Black Importation and Migration into Southeastern Pennsylvania, 1682–1810." *Proceedings of the American Philosophical Society* 133, 2: 144–53.

Souden, David. 1988. "'Rogues, whores and vagabonds'? Indentured servant emigration to North America and the case of mid seventeenth century Bristol" in Peter Clark and David Souden. *Migration and Society in Early Modern England*. Barnes and Noble Books: 150–71.

Sridharan, Swetha. 2008. "Material Support to Terrorism – Consequences for Refugees and Asylum Seekers in the United States" *Migration Policy Institute* Available at http://www.migrationinformation.org/Feature/display.cfm?id=671

Stahle, David W., Malcolm K. Cleaveland, Dennis B. Blanton, Matthew D. Therrell, David A. Gay. 1998. "The Lost Colony and Jamestown Droughts." *Science*, New Series 280, 5363: 564–67.

Stana, Richard. 2008. Employment Verification: Challenges Exist in Implementing a Mandatory Electronic Employment Verification System, Statement for the Record. *Government Accountability Office*. Available at http://www.gao.gov/new.items/do8895t.pdf

Stark, Rodney and Roger Finke. 1988. "American Religion in 1776: A Statistical Portrait." *Sociological Analysis* 49, 1: 39–51.

Steele, Ian Kenneth. 1986. *The English Atlantic, 1675–1740: An Exploration of Communication and Community*. Oxford University Press.

Stein, Barry. 1979. "The Geneva Conferences and the Indochinese Refugee Crisis." *International Migration* Review 13, 4: 716–23.

Steinbeck, John. 1939. *Grapes of Wrath*. The Library of America.

Steinberg, Alan. 1981. "History of Immigration and Crime" in Select Commission on Immigration and Refugee Policy. *Appendix A of the Staff Report, Supplement to the Final Report and Recommendations of the Select Commission on Immigration and Refugee Policy*: 463–630.

Stevens, Gillian. 1999. "A Century of U.S. Censuses and the Language Characteristics of Immigrants." *Demography* 36, 3: 387–97.

Stephenson, George M. 1926. "The Background of the Beginnings of Swedish Immigration, 1850–1875." *The American Historical Review* 31, 4: 708–23.

Stepick, Alex. 1987. "Haitian Exodus," in Barry B. Levine, ed. *The Caribbean Exodus*. Greenwood Publishing Group.

Sturtevant, William C. 1962. "Spanish-Indian Relations in Southeastern North America." *Ethnohistory* 9, 1: 41–94.

Sweeney, John J. 2004. "Statement by AFL-CIO President John J. Sweeney on President Bush's Principles for Immigration Reform," *American Federation of Labor-Congress of Industrial Organizations*, January 8, 2004, Available at www.afl-cio.org/mediacenter/prsptm/pro1082004.cfm

Swain, Carol M. 2008. *Debating Immigration*. Cambridge University Press.

Swierenga, Robert P. 1989. "The Settlement of the Old Northwest: Ethnic Pluralism in a Featureless Plain." *Journal of the Early Republic* 9, 1: 73–105.

Third Charter of Virginia (1611). Available at http://avalon.law.yale.edu/17th_century/va03.asp

Tichenor, Daniel J. 2002. *Dividing Lines: The Politics of Immigration Control in America*. Princeton University Press.

Tolles, Frederick B. 1963. "Nonviolent Contact: The Quakers and the Indians." *Proceedings of the American Philosophical Society* 107, 2: 93–101.

Totten, Robbie. 2008. "National Security and U.S. Immigration Policy, 1776–1790." *Journal of Interdisciplinary History*, 39, 1: 37–64.

Trachtenberg, Alan. 1982. *The Incorporation of America: Culture and Society in the Gilded Age*. Hill and Wang.

Treaty of Guadalupe Hidalgo. 1848. Available at http://www.ourdocuments.gov/doc.php?flash=false&doc=26&page=transcript

Treaty of Paris. 1783. Available at: http://www.ourdocuments.gov/doc.php?flash=false&doc=6&page=transcript

Treaty of Versailles, Covenant of the League of Nations. 1919. Available at http://net.lib.byu.edu/~rdh7/wwi/versa/versa1.html

Truett, Samuel. 2006. *Fugitive Landscapes: The Forgotten History of the U.S.-Mexico Borderlands*. Yale University Press.

Truman, Harry S. 1945. Statement and Directive by the President on Immigration to the United States of Certain Displaced Persons and Refugees in Europe. December 22, 1945 Available at http://www.presidency.ucsb.edu/ws/index.php?pid=12253

Truman, Harry S. 1950. Executive Order 10129 – Establishing the President's Commission on Migratory Labor, June 3, 1950 Available at http://www.presidency.ucsb.edu/ws/index.php?pid=78306

Turner, Frederick Jackson. 1920. The Frontier in American History. Henry Holt and Company.

U.N. High Commissioner for Refugees. 2000. *The State of the World's Refugees 2000: Fifty Years of Humanitarian Action*. Available at http://www.unhcr.org/4a4c754a9 .html

U.N. High Commissioner for Refugees. 1994. "The Haitian Interdiction Case 1993 Brief Amicus Curiae. *International Journal of Refugee Law* 6, 1: 85–102.

United Press. 1954. "U.S. to Hire 90,000 Mexicans for Farms." *Washington Post and Times Herald*, July 16, 1954, p. 17.

U.S. Bureau of Labor Statistics. ND. Employment status of the civilian non-institutional population, 1940 to date. Available at http://www.bls.gov/cps/cpsaat1.pdf)

U.S. Commission on Immigration Reform. 1994. *U. S. Immigration Policy: Restoring Credibility*. Government Printing Office.

U.S. Commission on Immigration Reform. 1995. *Legal Immigration: Setting Priorities*. Government Printing Office.

U.S. Commission on Immigration Reform. 1996. *U.S. Refugee Policy: Taking Leadership*. Government Printing Office.

U.S. Commission on Immigration Reform. 1997a. *Becoming an American: U.S. Immigration and Immigrant Policy*. Government Printing Office.

U.S. Commission on Immigration Reform. 1997b. "Americanization and Integration of Immigrants," Appendix to *Becoming an American: Immigration and Immigrant Policy*. Available at National Archives.

U.S. Committee for Refugees. 1995. *World Refugee Survey 1995*. U.S. Committee for Refugees.

U.S. Committee for Refugees. 1996. *World Refugee Survey 1996*. U.S. Committee for Refugees.

U.S. Congress, House Committee on Foreign Affairs. 1856. Foreign criminals and paupers: report to accompany Bill H. R. 124, August 16, 1856 at http://www.archive .org/details/foreigncriminalsoounit

U.S. Congress, House Subcommittee on Subcommittee on International Law, Immigration, and Refugees of the Committee on The Judiciary. 1994. Hearing on H.R 3663, H.R 4114, and H.R. 4264.

U.S. Congress, Senate Joint Special Committee to Investigate Chinese Immigration. 1877. Report Available at http://cprr.org/Museum/Chinese_Immigration.html

U.S. Congress, House Committee on Immigration and Naturalization. 1919. Percentage plans for restriction of immigration: hearings before the Committee on Immigration and Naturalization, House of Representatives, Sixty-sixth Congress, first session, June 12, 13, 14, 18, 19 and 20, and September 25, 1919. Government Printing Office.

U.S. Congress, Senate Committee on Immigration. 1921. Emergency immigration legislation: hearings before the Senate Committee on Immigration, United States Senate, sixty-sixth Congress, third session, on H.R. 14461: a bill to provide for the protection of the citizens of the United States by the temporary suspension of immigration, and for other purposes. Government Printing Office.

U.S. Congress, Senate Committee on the Judiciary. 1950. Report of the Committee on the Judiciary Pursuant to S. Res. 137, A Resolution to Make an Investigation of the Immigration System, April 20, 1950.

U.S. Customs and Border Protection, Department of Homeland Security. 2003. Border Patrol History. Available at http://www.cbp.gov/xp/cgov/border_security/ border_patrol/border_patrol_ohs/history.xml

U.S. Department of Homeland Security. 2004. "Budget in Brief – Fiscal Year 2005," February 2, 2004.

U.S. Department of State, Bureau of Population, Refugees and Migration. 1994. *Daily Interdiction of Haitian Boat People by U.S. Coast Guard and U.S. Navy, 6/15/94–10/6/94.*

U.S. Holocaust Museum. ND. Voyage of the St. Louis. Available at http://www.ushmm.org/wlc/article.php?ModuleId=10005267

U.S. Public Health Service. ND. "Pandemics and Pandemic Threats since 1900." Available at http://www.pandemicflu.gov/general/historicaloverview.html

Valdes, Dennis Nodin. 1988. "Revolutionary Nationalism and Repatriation during the Great Depression." *Mexican Studies/Estudios Mexicanos* 4, 1: 1–23.

Vargas, Zaragosa. 1991. "Armies in the Fields and Factories: The Mexican Working Classes in the Midwest in the 1920s." *Mexican Studies/Estudios Mexicanos* 7, 1: 47–71.

Vaughan, Alden T. 1978. "'Expulsion of the Salvages': English Policy and the Virginia Massacre of 1622." *The William and Mary Quarterly*, 3rd Ser. 35, 1: 57–84.

Vecchio, Diane C. 1989. "Italian Women in Industry: The Shoeworkers of Endicott, New York, 1914–1935." *Journal of American Ethnic History* 8, 2: 60–86.

Vecoli, Rudolph J. 1969. "Prelates and Peasants: Italian Immigrants and the Catholic Church." *Journal of Social History* 2, 3: 217–68.

Virginia. 1798. Resolution. Available at http://www.constitution.org/cons/virg1798.html

Virginia. 1799. Report of House of Delegates. Available at http://www.constitution.org/rf/vr_1799.html

Vought, Hans. 1994. "Division and Reunion: Woodrow Wilson, Immigration, and the Myth of American Unity." *Journal of American Ethnic History* 13, 3: 24–50.

Wallace, Anthony F. C. 1956. "New Religions among the Delaware Indians, 1600–1900." *Southwestern Journal of Anthropology* 12, 1: 1–21.

Ward, David. 1968. "The Emergence of Central Immigrant Ghettoes in American Cities: 1840–1920." *Annals of the Association of American Geographers* 58, 2: 343–59.

Wasem, Ruth Ellen and Geoffrey K. Collver. 2001. "RL30852: Immigration of Agricultural Guest Workers: Policy, Trends, and Legislative Issues." *Congressional Research Service.*

Washburn, Wilcomb E. 1959 "The Moral and Legal Justifications for Dispossessing the Indians" in James M. Smith. *17th Century America: Essays in Colonial History.* University of North Carolina Press: 15–32.

Weaver, Glenn. 1957. "Benjamin Franklin and the Pennsylvania Germans." *The William and Mary Quarterly*, Third Series 14, 4: 536–59.

Weber, David J. 1982. The Mexican Frontier, 1821–1846. University of New Mexico Press.

Webster, Noah. 1789. *Dissertation on the English Language.* Isaiah Thomas and Company.

Wells, Robert V. 1992. "The Population of England's Colonies in America: Old English or New Americans?" *Population Studies* 46, 1: 85–102.

White House Press Office. 2004. "President Bush Proposes New Temporary Worker Program," January 7, 2004. Available at www.whitehouse.gov/news/releases/2004/01/20040107-3.html

Whyte, Ian D. 2000. *Migration and Society in Britain: 1550–1830.* St. Martin's Press.

Williams, Johnny. 2003. Statement of Johnny Williams, Executive Associate Commissioner for Field Operations, U.S. Immigration and Naturalization Service

before the Senate Committee on Finance regarding Combating Terrorism: Protecting the United States (January 30, 2003). Available at http://www.immigration
.gov/graphics/aboutus/congress/testimonies/2003/Williams.pdf

Williams, Roger and James Calvin Davis. 2008. *On Religious Liberty: Selections from the works of Roger Williams.* Harvard University Press.

Winthrop, John. 1630. A Modell of Christian Charity. *Hanover Historical Texts Project.* http://history.hanover.edu/texts/winthmod.html

Wilson, Woodrow. 1902. History of the American People. Volume 5. Harper and Brothers.

Wilson, Woodrow. 1914. *Message to Congress,* 63rd Cong., 2d Sess., Senate Doc. No. 566:3–4. Available at http://wwi.lib.byu.edu/index.php/President_Wilson%27s_Declaration_of_Neutrality

Wilson, Woodrow. 1917a. Veto Message on HR 10384.

Wilson, Woodrow. 1917b. *War Messages,* 65th Cong., 1st Sess. Senate Doc. No. 5, Serial No. 7264, Washington, D.C. Available at http://wwi.lib.byu.edu/index
.php/Wilson%27s_War_Message_to_Congress

Wilson, Woodrow. 1919. President Woodrow Wilson's Address in Favour of the League of Nations, 25 September 1919 Available at http://www.firstworldwar
.com/source/wilsonspeech_league.html

Wokeck, Marianne S. 1989. "German and Irish Immigration to Colonial Philadelphia." *Proceedings of the American Philosophical Society* 133, 2: 128–43.

Wokeck, Marianne S. 1999. *Trade in Strangers: The Beginnings of Mass Migration to North America.* Pennsylvania State University Press.

Woolman, John. 1994. Journal of John Woolman. University of Virginia Library http://etext.lib.virginia.edu/toc/modeng/public/WooJour.html

World Net Daily. 2004. "Bush Plan Allows Illegals to Stay," *World Net Daily,* January 7, 2004. Available at www.worldnetdaily.com/news/article.asp?ARTICLE_
ID=36496

Yeager, Timothy J. 1995. "Encomienda or Slavery? The Spanish Crown's Choice of Labor Organization in Sixteenth-Century Spanish America." *The Journal of Economic History* 55, 4: 842–59.

Yans-McLaughlin, Virginia. 1982. *Family and Community: Italian Immigrants in Buffalo: 1880–1930.* University of Illinois Press.

Zeidel, Robert F. 2004. *Immigrants, Progressives, and Exclusion Politics: The Dillingham Commission, 1900–1927.* Northern Illinois University Press.

Zolberg, Aristide R., Astri Suhrke and Sergio Aguayo. 1989. *Escape From Violence: Conflict and the Refugee Crisis in the Developing World.* Oxford University Press, 1989.

Zolberg, Aristide R. 2006. *A Nation by Design: Immigration Policy in the Fashioning of America.* Harvard University Press.

Zucker, Norman L. and Naomi Flink Zucker. 1987. *The Guarded Gate: The Reality of American Refugee Policy.* Harcourt Brace Jovanovich.

Zucker, Norman L. and Naomi Flink Zucker. 1996. *Desperate Crossings: Seeking Refuge in America.* M.E. Sharpe, Inc.

Zubrzycki, Jerzy. 1958. "The Role of the Foreign-Language Press in Migrant Integration." *Population Studies* 12, 1: 73–82.

Index